The German Rifle

Gewehr 98, with Lange-Visier for S-Patrone: 1905-15.

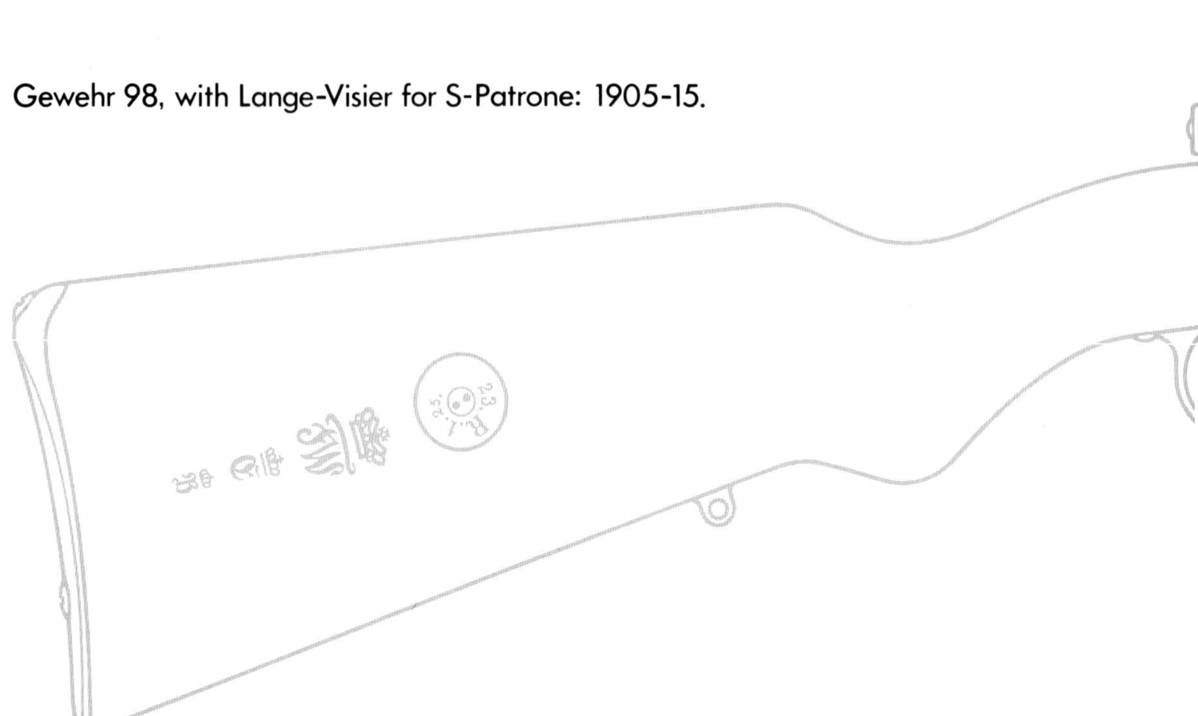

The German Rifle

A comprehensive illustrated history of the standard bolt-action designs, 1871-1945

John Walter

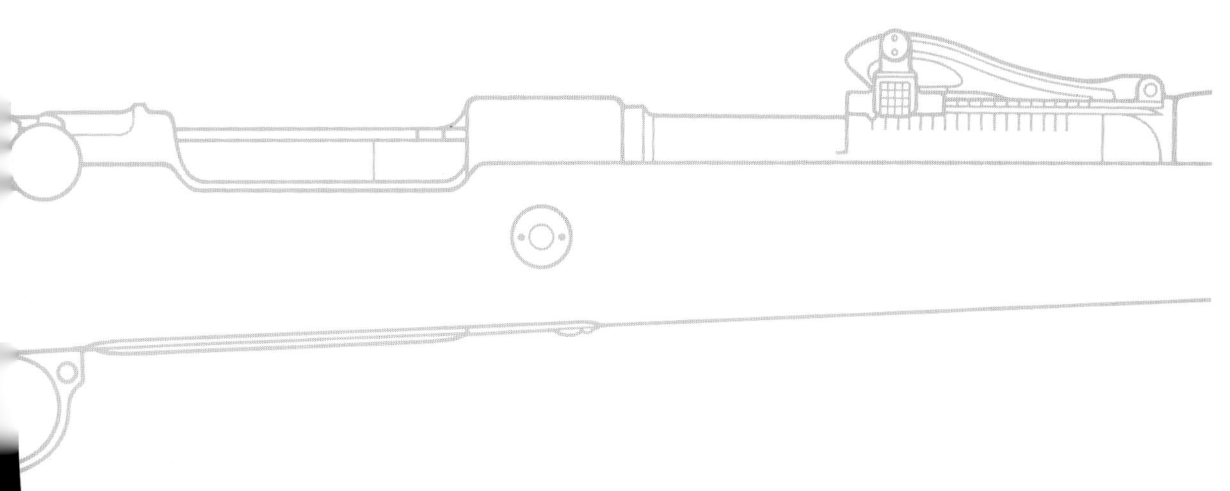

Arms and Armour Press: London-Melbourne.
Fortress Publications Inc.: Ontario.

Published in Great Britain by
Arms and Armour Press
Lionel Leventhal Limited
2—6 Hampstead High Street
London NW3 1QQ

ISBN 0 85368 312 3

Published in North America by
Fortress Publications Inc.
PO Box 241
Stoney Creek
Ontario L8G 3X9

ISBN 0 96904 868 8

British Library Cataloguing in Publication Data:
Walter, John
The German rifle.
1. Rifles—History.
2. Germany. Heer—Firearms—History.
I. Title
623.4'425 UD390
ISBN 0—85368—312—3

Edited by Tessa Rose.
Typeset by Trade Linotype, Birmingham, England.
Printed and bound by William Clowes & Sons Limited, Beccles.

Contents

Part one

Part two

Part three

Acknowledgements

The compilation of this book has been made infinitely easier and vastly more enjoyable by the co-operation, assistance and friendship of many people.

My special thanks must go to Manfred John—translator of my books into German—who perused the sections devoted to the Dreyse needle rifles, offered many vital amendments and corrections, and supplied material from which some of the line drawings were prepared. Major a.D. Hans-Rudolf von Stein has supplied invaluable information over a period spanning almost a decade, and kindly revised Appendix 3 when it was in draft form; he, too, eliminated errors that may otherwise have appeared in print. Reinhard Kornmayer also made an important contribution to the Appendices.

De Witt Bailey willingly shared his knowledge of German weaponry during several informal discussions, drawing attention to subtle nuances of Dreyse design (in particular) that may otherwise have escaped my notice; Herb Woodend of the Pattern Room, RSAF Enfield Lock, read the chapters dealing with the metallic-cartridge firing weapons, and uncomplainingly lent his time as I sketched some of the rifles in his care; and David Penn of the Imperial War Museum supplied some extremely useful listings of the guns in the museum's collection.

I greatly value the assistance of Bill Stonley, who let me draw on his considerable knowledge of DWM's and Mauser's production history. Frank de Haas, author of *Bolt Action Rifles* (which contains excellent assessments of the actions of the Mauser rifles), kindly supplied many photographs, as did Ian Hogg and Gordon Conway.

Anthony Carter, Fred Stephens, Joe Schroeder, Dr Rolf Gminder and Mauser-Jagdwaffen GmbH, the patent offices in Britain and Germany, Wallis & Wallis, Weller & Dufty, Fabrique Nationale, Mr J. Bucknell of the QAD(W) at RSAF Enfield Lock, and many other individuals, bureaux, libraries and government departments have all made contributions to the project. And Bert Ford and the staff of Service 24 Ltd, Brighton, deserve my continued thanks for diligently processing my drawings, despite the unprofessional methods by which I have supplied some of them.

Finally, I should like to record my appreciation of the work undertaken by Miss Vanessa Woods, who cheerfully ensured that my enthusiasm was curbed sufficiently to keep the manuscript within the proscribed word-length limit; and to Miss Teresa Rose, who edited her way through my jargon to make the final manuscript at least comprehensible.

However, despite all the assistance I have sought—and all the sources I have so freely quoted—I cannot seek to disown the errors that may yet be discovered, nor the opinions ventured: the responsibility for them remains mine alone.

John Walter, Brighton, 1978.

Introduction

The conclusion of the Franco-Prussian War—the peace treaty was signed in Frankfurt on 10 May 1871—found the German states united in a single empire, the Deutsches Reich. One of the articles of the agreement dating from 18 January 1871 had amalgamated all the armies in a single numbered sequence, with the exception of Bavaria, which had been allowed to retain some vestiges of independence[1].

1. This had resulted from an agreement between the kings of the two major states—Prussia and Bavaria—on 23 November 1870.

It was clear that some kind of standardization of weapons was urgently required, since the armies of Prussia, Saxony and Württemberg were carrying Dreyse needle-guns while the Bavarians had the infinitely superior M/69 Werder block-action breech-loader. The matter was further complicated by the appearance of a motley collection of percussion-ignition muzzle-loaders and rudimentary breech-loaders in the hands of the ancillary and reserve units in each state.

The Franco-Prussian War had been largely fought with the Dreyse Zündnadelgewehre, which was adopted by the Prussian Army in December 1840 and was first used in action eight years later. Although it can be justifiably argued that the Dreyse had helped the Prussians destroy the Austrians in the Seven Weeks' War of 1866—as the casualty figures from Königgrätz and elsewhere testify[2]—the same cannot be said of 1870-71. Even the Prussian authorities were well aware of the ballistic superiority of the French Mle 1866 (Chassepot) needle-fire infantry rifle, and had been experimenting with the Beck bolt improvements since 1868-69. Beck rifles were finally adopted on 10 March 1870, several months before the hostilities commenced, but only three Prussian units carried them during the fighting: 4.Garde-Regiment zu Fuss, and Infanterie-Regimenter Nr. 71 and Nr. 94.

2. At Königgrätz, the Austrians lost 23,598 men killed or wounded; the Prussian figures totalled 8,894. Even at Trautenau (an Austrian victory) the figures were 3,611 and 1,252. Generally, the Prussian casualties were about 33 per cent of their opponents.

Despite many claims to the contrary, the Prussians did not win the Franco-Prussian War because they had Dreyse rifles. On the few occasions when well-led French troops met Prussian units deprived of their efficient artillery, the results were always the same: the French gave as good as they got, and sometimes cut the Prussians to pieces. There are several well-documented instances of the latter; at St. Privat/Gravelotte, for example, the French casualties amounted to 12,273 compared with the Prussians' 20,163. The Prussian Gardekorps alone lost nearly eight thousand men—almost a quarter of its strength—at St. Privat. Although the casualty figures greatly favoured the Prussians[3], there is no doubt that much of their superiority was due to the efficient handling of field artillery. As far as the infantry rifles were concerned, the Chassepot ruled the field.

3. The German armies lost 174,456 men; the French, 262,871 plus 19,000 who died in German captivity.

By the end of the war, the Germans had captured huge quantities of Mle 1866 needle-rifles, as well as many Tabatière breech-loaders and other obsolete weapons. The total numbers acquired in this way comfortably exceeded a million, 665,327 of which were Chassepots. There were 540,000 such guns in Prussia and, apparently, 44,000 more in Bavaria, although different sources give differing figures. Many of the guns had been used during the war by German cavalry and artillerymen, since the issue Dreyse needle-carbines were in short supply. They had, in any case, only been issued to the dragoons and the hussars.

The Prussian authorities ultimately converted many of the ex-French guns for the 11mm Reichspatrone, or M 1871, a metal-case cartridge that had been adopted in December 1871 for the then experimental Mauser rifle. However, the cartridge-rifles did not enter service until the middle of 1875, which meant that the obsolescent Dreyse—converted for Beck's bolt head—remained the front line firearm for four years after the Franco-Prussian War. Meanwhile, efficient breech-loaders were being issued elsewhere in Europe; Switzerland had adopted the Vetterli bolt-action magazine rifle as early as 1868.

The Mauser proved to be very successful, but its success was undoubtedly helped by the failure of the Bavarians to adapt the M/69 Werder block-action rifle to the powerful Reichspatrone; the Bavarian Army, which had previously defended the Werder against all its detractors, conceded defeat and adopted the Mauser in August 1877. A Mauser

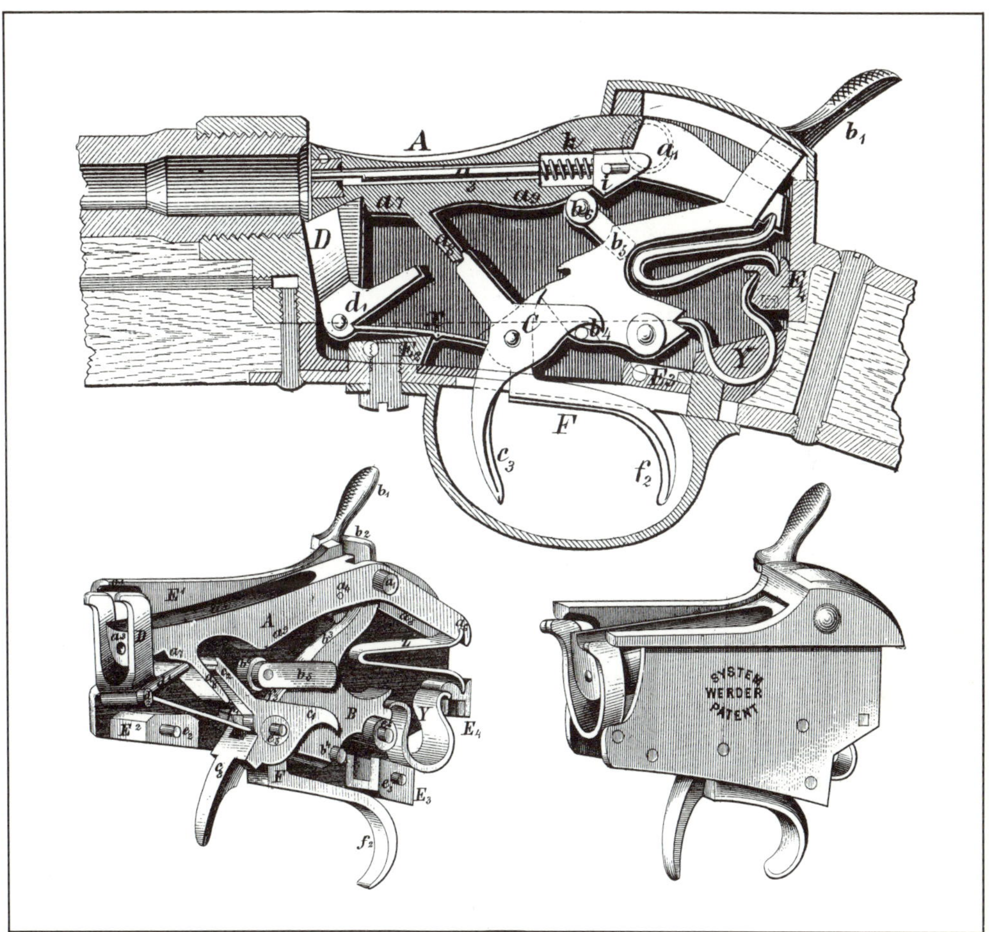

Right: the dropping-block action of the Bavarian M/69 'Werder' rifle, an important competitor of the Mauser bolt-action type in the early 1870s.

Jägerbüchse and a cavalry carbine were adopted in 1876, but it was clear by 1880 that a magazine firearm was needed if the German Army was to remain in the forefront of contemporary small arms design; considerable advances were being made in Austria and elsewhere through the efforts of inventors such as Früwirth, Kropatschek and Vetterli. The result of Mauser's experimentation, which established him as Germany's premier firearms designer, once and for all, was the Infanterie-Gewehr M 71/84. It was issued in 1886 and had a tubular under-barrel magazine of relatively conventional pattern. But no sooner had the first rifles been distributed to the two Prussian army corps, XV. and XVI., guarding the borders in Elsass-Lothringen, than the French introduced the Mle 1886 Lebel rifle. Small arms technology was revolutionized overnight, not on account of the rifle, which was scarcely more efficient than the Gewehr 71/84, but because of the successful development of a smokeless propellant for its cartridge. The Germans were caught unawares, and were forced to design, develop and introduce the Gewehr 88 in a very short time indeed. The gun was adopted in November 1888 and the first issues were made in the spring of 1889—once again, to the army corps in Elsass-Lothringen.

The first German small-bore rifle was a hastily conceived amalgam of Mauser, Mannlicher, Mieg and other features; and while it was undoubtedly a better weapon than the Lebel, it had the misfortune to goad Mauser into developing something better. This he achieved in an embarrassingly short time—so far as the Germans were concerned—and his perfected rifles sold in vast numbers in the period 1890-1914.

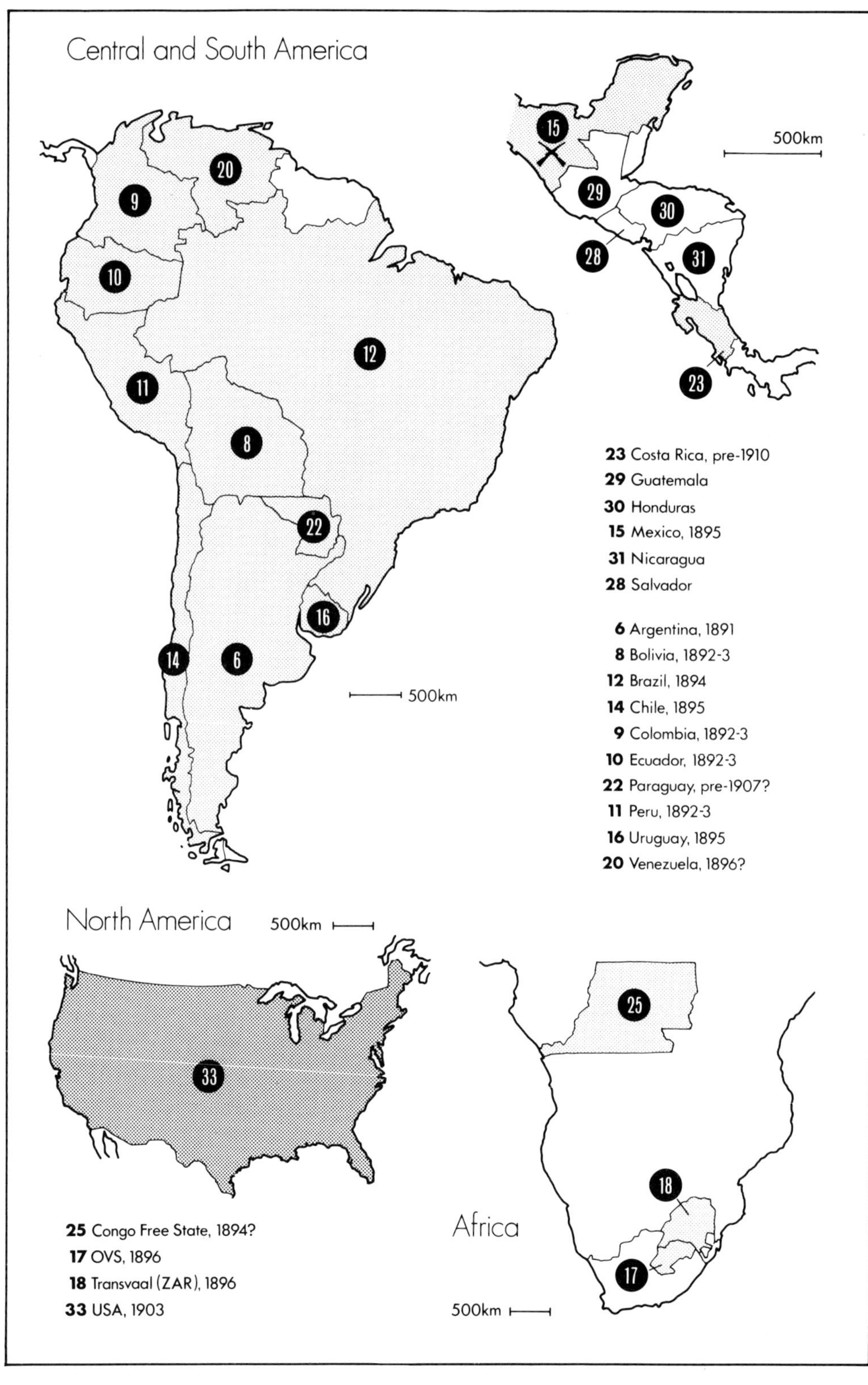
Central and South America
500km
15
29
30
28
31
23
20
9
10
12
11
8
22
16
14
6
500km
23 Costa Rica, pre-1910
29 Guatemala
30 Honduras
15 Mexico, 1895
31 Nicaragua
28 Salvador
6 Argentina, 1891
8 Bolivia, 1892-3
12 Brazil, 1894
14 Chile, 1895
9 Colombia, 1892-3
10 Ecuador, 1892-3
22 Paraguay, pre-1907?
11 Peru, 1892-3
16 Uruguay, 1895
20 Venezuela, 1896?
North America
500km
33
25
18
17
Africa
25 Congo Free State, 1894?
17 OVS, 1896
18 Transvaal (ZAR), 1896
33 USA, 1903
500km

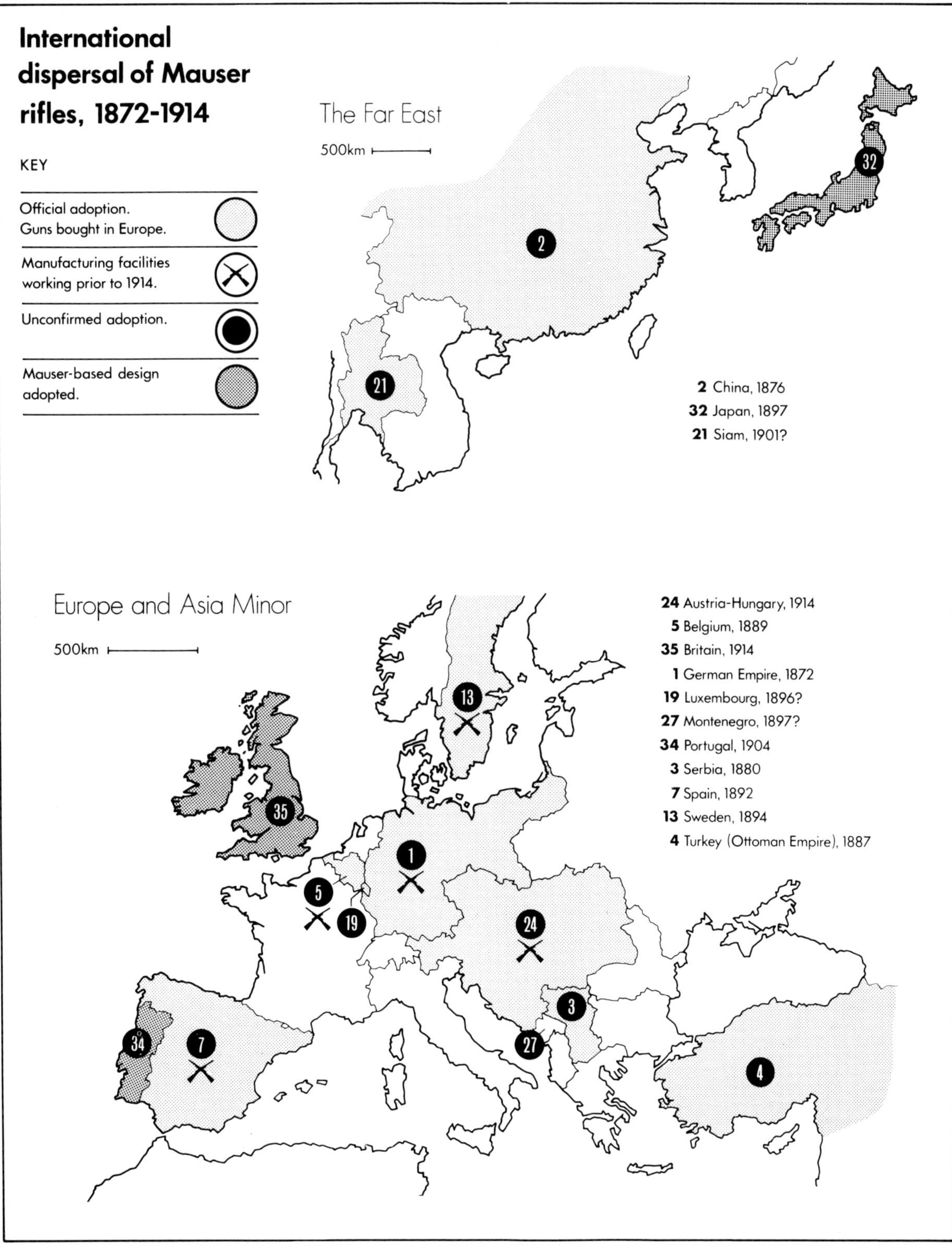
International dispersal of Mauser rifles, 1872-1914
KEY
Official adoption. Guns bought in Europe.
Manufacturing facilities working prior to 1914.
Unconfirmed adoption.
Mauser-based design adopted.
The Far East
500km
2 China, 1876
32 Japan, 1897
21 Siam, 1901?
Europe and Asia Minor
500km
24 Austria-Hungary, 1914
5 Belgium, 1889
35 Britain, 1914
1 German Empire, 1872
19 Luxembourg, 1896?
27 Montenegro, 1897?
34 Portugal, 1904
3 Serbia, 1880
7 Spain, 1892
13 Sweden, 1894
4 Turkey (Ottoman Empire), 1887

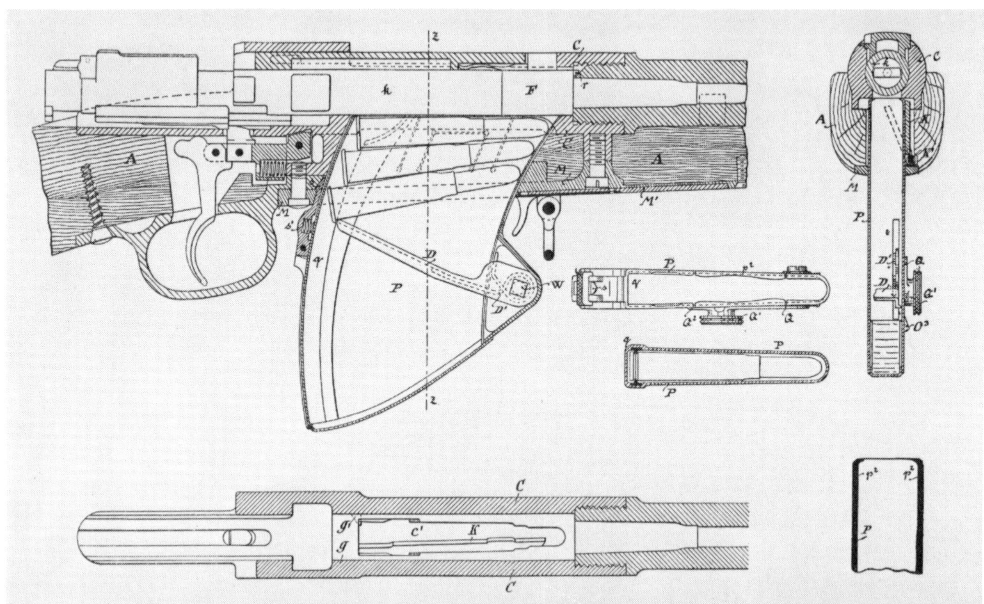

Right: some of the drawings accompanying the printed specification of DRP 45,561.

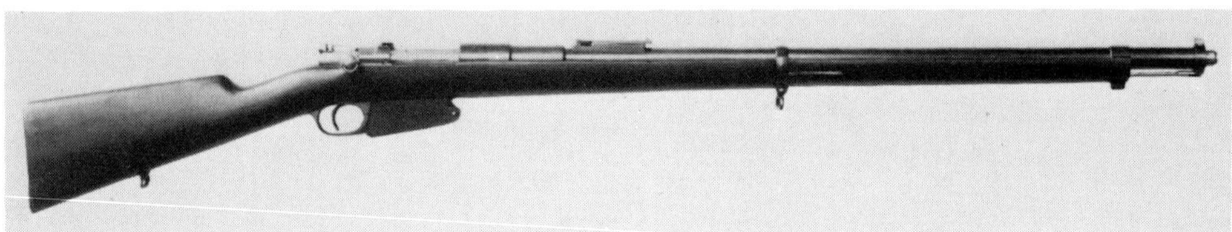

Right: the Belgian Mle 1889 was the first of the perfected Mauser small-bore rifles. Courtesy of Fabrique Nationale.

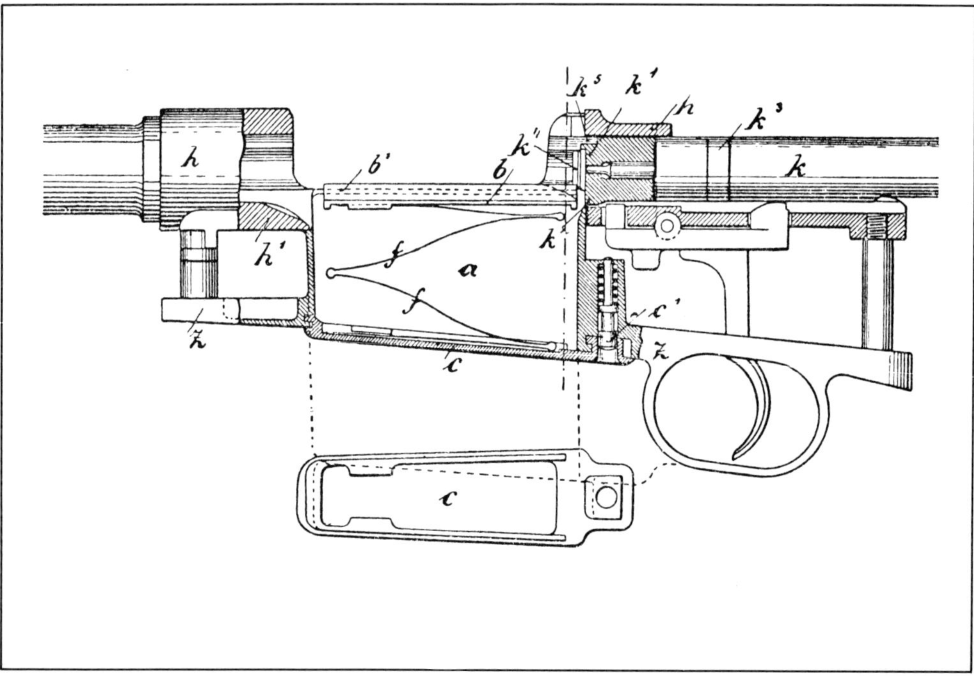

Right: the Mo 1893 Spanish rifle was the first to use the distinctive staggered-column box magazine, carried within the stock. From DRP 74,162.

The final nail in the Gewehr 88's coffin was the development of the 'Spanish' or 1893-model Mauser, with its internal staggered-row box magazine and unerring accuracy. These guns were to prove excellent in the Spanish-American War, the Boer War—from which came the British superstition that it is unlucky to light three cigarettes from a single match[4]—and countless South American revolutions. After a series of trials in the mid-1890s, the Gewehr-Prüfungs-Kommission (Rifle Testing Commission) recommended the adoption of the Gewehr 98 (5 April 1898, issued 1899-1900 and later) which, together with the Karabiner 98 AZ short rifle of 1908, armed the German troops in August 1914.

4. The Boer, it was said, saw the first, aimed at the second—and fired at the third.

Even the German small arms industry, which had been happily supplying the German armies and countless export orders, could not cope with the enormous demands made by the fast-growing wartime armies. As a result, the surviving 1871, 71/84 and 88-model rifles were brought out of store, refurbished, and issued to the Reserve, the Landwehr (Territorial Reserve) and the Landsturm (Home Guard). Some even appeared in front line service (Gewehre 88/05, 88/14). Additionally, there were large quantities of 'Beutegewehre' (captured weapons) purchased from dealers such as A. L. Frank or taken from the British, the French, the Russians and others. One contemporary source[5] lists them as:

5. *Kurze Beschreibung der an Ersatztruppen und Rekrutendepots verausgabten fremländischen Gewehre,* 1915.

AUSTRIA-HUNGARY
M 1895 (Mannlicher) rifle and short rifle
BELGIUM
Mle 1889 (Mauser) rifle
BRITAIN
SMLE Mks 1 and 3
CANADA
Ross Rifle Mk 3 (M 1910)
FRANCE
Mle 1866 (Chassepot) rifle and carbine
Mle 1874 (Gras) rifle, musketoon and carbine
Mle 1878 (Kropatschek) rifle
Mle 1886/93 (Lebel) rifle
Mle 1890 (Berthier) carbine
Mle 1892 (Berthier) carbine

ITALY
Mo 1870/87 (Vetterli-Vitali) rifle and carbine
Mo 1891 (Mannlicher-Carcano) rifle
NETHERLANDS
M 1873 (Beaumont) rifle
M 1895 (Mannlicher) rifle
RUSSIA
Obr. 1871g (Berdan II) rifle
Obr. 1891g (Mosin-Nagant) rifle
Obr. 1910g (Mosin-Nagant) carbine

The Russian rifles were the most numerous; many, converted for the standard German rifle cartridge (8mm), equipped front line infantry units during the early part of the First World War.

Few significant innovations occurred in the 1914-18 period, for although the introduction of the Bergmann Maschinenpistole 18 ultimately called the tactical role of the infantry rifle into question, there were too few of them to make any notable impact before the 1918 Armistice. The Gewehr-Prüfungs-Kommission contented itself with developing snipers' rifles, detachable box magazines, night sights and bolt covers for the Gewehr 98 and the Karabiner 98 AZ, but achieved few lasting results. Complaints that the rifles were too long for trench combat—experienced men, nicknamed 'Frontschweine', preferred items such as grenades and sharpened trench-spades—and that there was no adequate hold-open device to warn the firer that he had an empty magazine were largely ignored, although desultory experimentation was undertaken. This led to the so-called Gewehr 98/17 and the Mauser-Gewehr 18, but few were introduced before the war ended.

Right: sailors of 1.Matrosen-Division pose with their rifles—modified ex-Russian Mosin-Nagants. From a photograph taken in 1918. Courtesy of Greg Engelman.

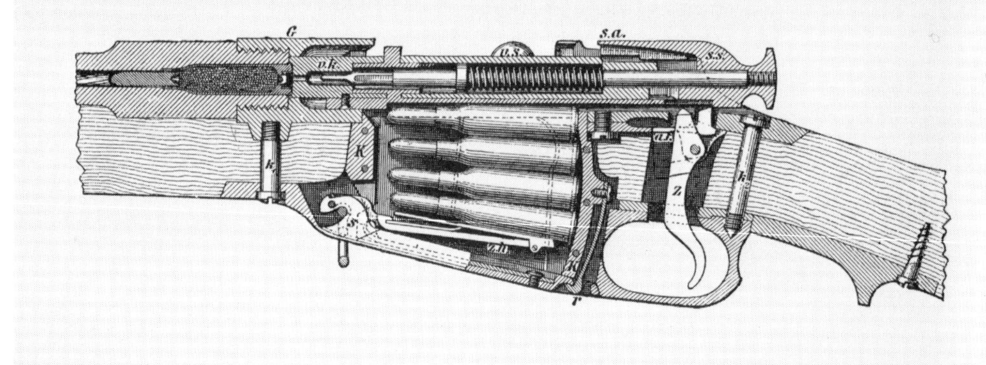

Right: the action of the Mosin-Nagant, which owed something to the French Lebel. Note the complicated design of the bolt, and the distinctive magazine unit.

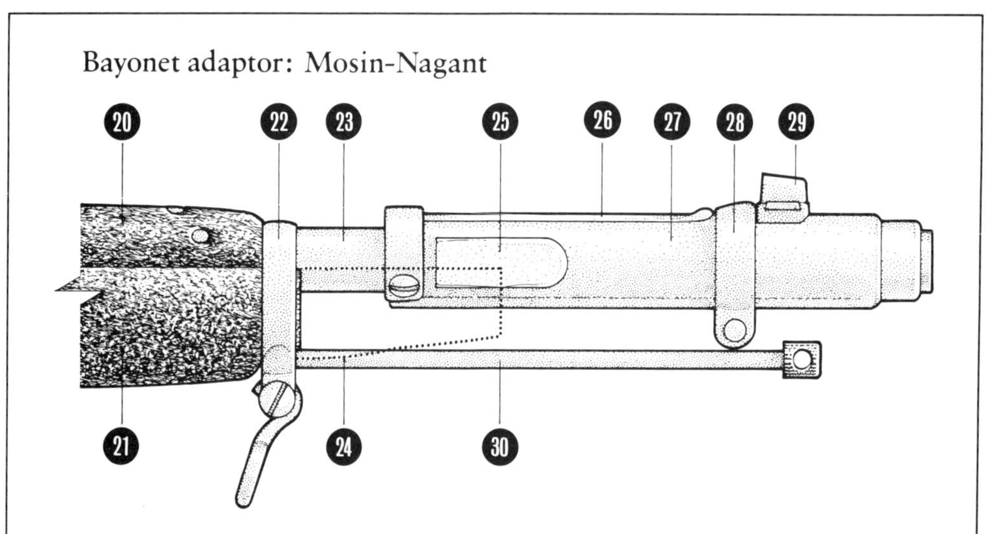

Right: one of the bayonet adaptors fitted to the captured Russian rifles, so that standard German bayonets could be used.

The Armistice put an end to the development of the German bolt-action rifle, partly because the Allies were supervising disarmament but principally because little further improvement was possible. Automatic weapons were understandably accorded priority when clandestine research and development programmes began in the late 1920s.

The principal infantry rifle of the Wehrmacht (Armed Forces), the Karabiner 98k (adopted in 1934), was nothing more than a shortened Gewehr 98; the advances in technology in the 1933-45 era were to benefit automatic rather than manually-operated rifles and carbines. However, vast numbers of bolt-action guns were captured before and during the Second World War—Mausers from Belgium, Czechoslovakia, Poland, Estonia, Greece, Latvia, Lithuania and Yugoslavia; Mosin-Nagants from Russia, Krag-Jørgensens from Denmark and Norway, and Mannlichers from Austria.

The Heereswaffenamt (Army Weapons Office) even continued production of Mauser rifles in the factories of Fabrique Nationale (Belgium), Československá Zbrojovka (Czechoslovakia) and Steyr-Daimler-Puch (Austria), and ordered a modified Mauser-magazined Mannlicher from Hungary. That this was necessary at all is mute testimony to the bickering between designers, manufacturers, government departments and the armed forces themselves: had the efforts been satisfactorily coordinated, and not dependent on too much jealousy and antagonism, a semi-automatic rifle should have been in service by 1940—not 1943.

Overall direction in the German war effort was sadly lacking, despite the efforts of Speer and the armaments ministry: the damage had been done a long time previously, but that was a common enough story.

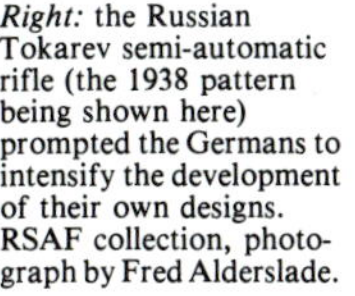

Right: the Russian Tokarev semi-automatic rifle (the 1938 pattern being shown here) prompted the Germans to intensify the development of their own designs. RSAF collection, photograph by Fred Alderslade.

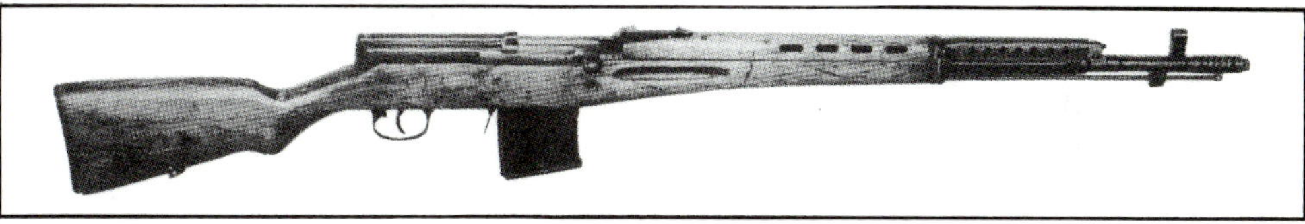

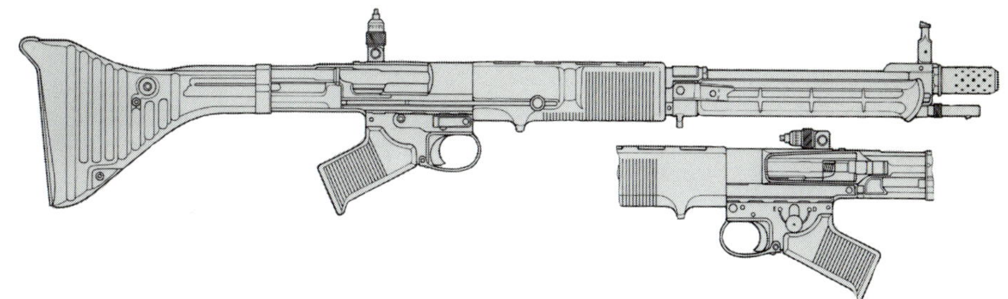

Right: the FG 42 parachutists' rifle, one of the highly advanced light automatic weapons produced by the German smallarms industry during the Second World War.

Right: the MKb 42H, prototype of the first 'assault rifle'—the MP 43. RSAF collection, photograph by Fred Alderslade.

Coverage

The directory that follows contains details of all the Dreyse bolt-action needle-rifles, short rifles and carbines officially adopted by the Prussian Army between 1840 and 1870, since virtually all of them served in one form or another until the mid-1870s. The service firearms developed by the Gewehr-Prüfungs-Kommission, Mauser and others in the period 1870-1945 are also covered in depth. There is a section devoted to the small-calibre Kleinkaliber-Wehrsportsgewehr (KKW), many of which were used as military trainers during the Third Reich; and another on the Hungarian Gewehr 98/40, which was a modified Mannlicher rather than a Mauser.

A number of obscure weapons have been omitted on the grounds that they were discarded immediately after the Franco-Prussian War had ended, and that, despite intruding into the period under review, they had no lasting significance in the development of German rifle technology.

1. Gustav Lehmann *Die Mobilmachung von 1870/71,* Anlage 8, p. 235.

They include the Defensions-Zündnadelwaffen, and Dreyse conversions of a motley collection of minor states' muskets and some old Prussian Jäger rifles. Lehmann[1] lists these as:

Quantity on hand, 15 July 1870

Füsilier-Gewehr H/M	832
Zündnadelgewehr H/M	5,297
Defensions-Zündnadelgewehr Ö/M	35,599
Defensions-Zündnadelbüchse Ö/M	1,958
Defensions-Zündnadelgewehr B/M	950
Defensions-Zündnadelgewehr Br/M	3,397
Defensions-Zündnadelgewehr Na/M	4,547
Defensions-Zündnadelbüchse u/M	8,662
	61,242
Kavallerie-Karabiner u/M[2]	17,358
	78,600

2. Not a Dreyse, but percussion-ignition.

The H/M guns belonged to the army of the grand duchy of Hessen ('Hessisches Muster', Hessian pattern); similarly, B/M guns came from Baden, Br/M guns from Brunswick, Na/M guns from Nassau and Ö/M guns from Austria. The last were converted from Lorenz rifle-muskets captured during the short Austro-Prussian War of 1866[3].

The Defensions-Zündnadelbüchse u/M was converted from the old Prussian Jägerbüchse M 35/48. This had begun life as the flintlock Neuer Corpsbüchse in 1810, had been changed to the percussion system during the mid-1830s, and then converted for a Thouvenin-type pillar breech in the late 1840s. Apparently, the guns were adopted in 1868[4], and could be recognized by the distinctive bayonet bar on the right side of the muzzle. The Ö/M and u/M guns, at least, made use of the short Dreyse carbine action, with the same bad features as those of the Zündnadelkarabiner M 1857 (qv). The weapons were altered in Suhl (Ö/M) or Sömmerda (u/M). Most of them remained in store or on garrison duties during the Franco-Prussian War.

3. Ludwig Baer, *Die leichten Waffen der deutschen Armeen, 1841-1945,* p. 25, gives the introduction date of the Defensions-Zündnadelgewehr O/M as 14 December 1870, but this seems too late.

4. Ludwig Baer, *Die leichten Waffen der deutschen Armeen, 1841-1945,* p. 26.

Other omissions include a small Saxon Dreyse-type cavalry carbine called the Reiterkarabiner M 1863[5], two Dreyse-system infantry rifles issued in Württemberg (M 1867, M 1868), and a number of muzzle-loading percussion-ignition rifle-muskets and Jägerbüchsen. Baden's Terry-pattern breech-loading Jäger rifle, which by stretching the imagination a little could be described as bolt-action, has also been ignored; and so too are the Bavarian Lindner conversions of the M/58 rifle-muskets, which had been superseded by the Werder rifle by 1872.

5. Which had been converted from an old flintlock weapon dating from 1829, by way of the percussion system.

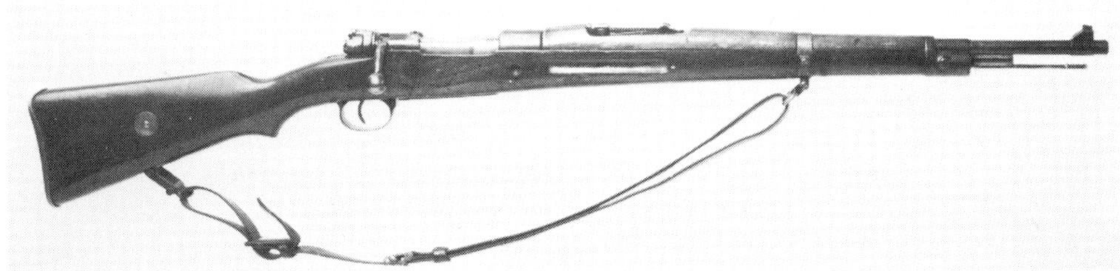

Right: the so-called 'Modell 29', an Austrian-made rifle used in small numbers by the Luftwaffe and others. The relationship between this and the so-called 'Gewehr 29/40' has not been established. RSAF collection, photograph by Ian Hogg.

The only twentieth century weapons to have been omitted are the Gewehr 29/40 (ö) (Österreichisch, Austrian), issued to the Luftwaffe but of uncertain official status, and the Mauser-system anti-tank rifle (T-Gewehr) of the First World War. The latter will be covered elsewhere, alongside the block-action anti-tank weapons of the Third Reich era.

No captured weapons ('Beutegewehre') have been included, because to do so with any accuracy would double the size of the book, but some are listed in the Introduction. An exception has been made for the French Mle 66 (Chassepot) needle-rifle, described in Appendix 1, since huge numbers were captured during the Franco-Prussian War and provided the basis for the Saxon M 1873 and Prussian M 1871 carbines (qv).

Exceptions must inevitably be made to every rule, and the unsuccessful Prussian Zündnadelbüchse M 1849 has been included on the grounds that its development had considerable relevance to the history of the Zündnadelkarabiner M 1857 and the Defensionsgewehre. But fewer than three thousand M 1849 rifles remained serviceable by 1870, and even they were in store. A few experimental firearms have been covered for one of two reasons: either that they were derived from standard service weapons, or were made in quantities running into the thousands. There were, for example, 2,185 rifles of the experimental '1896' patterns.

Right: the muzzle of the Defensions-Zündnadelbüchse u/M, formerly the percussion-ignition Jägerbüchse Modell 1835/48. Key: 1, barrel; 2, bayonet bar; 3, notched tip of bar (into which the bayonet locked); 4, front sight; 5, nosecap; 6, ramrod; 7, stock; 8, sling swivel; and 9, rod pipe.

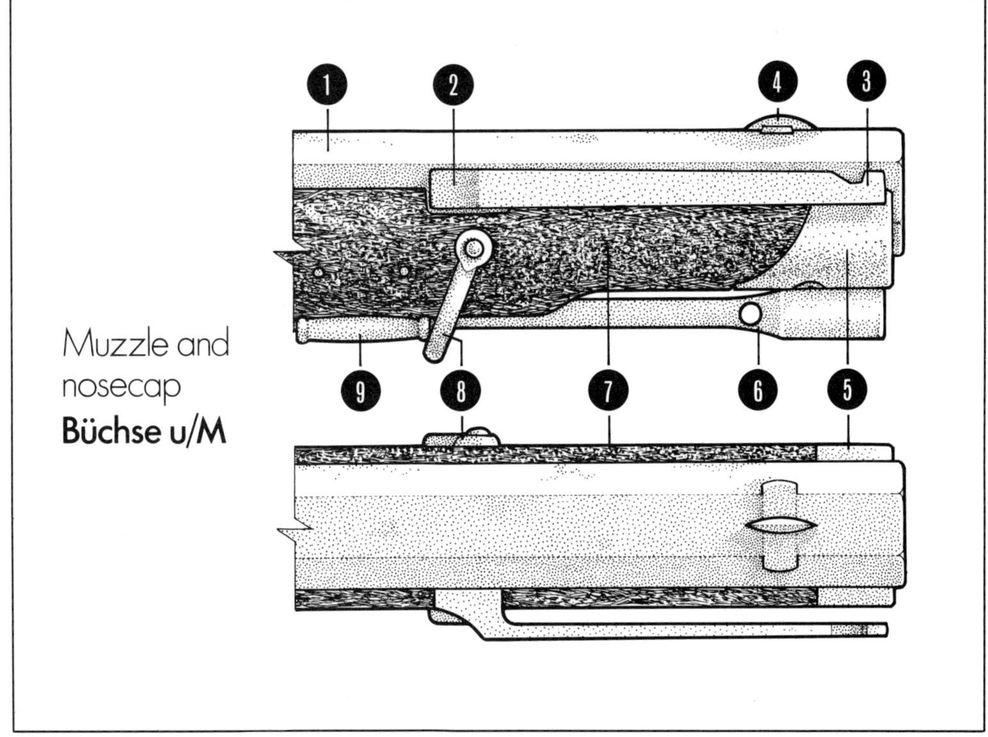

Sources

Many of the printed sources consulted are listed in the footnotes, but particularly worthy of mention are Hans-Dieter Götz's *Die deutschen Militärgewehre und Maschinenpistolen, 1871-1945* (Motor-Buch Verlag, Stuttgart, 1973), particularly for its pre-1918 coverage; Ludwig's Baer's *Die leichten Waffen der deutschen Armeen, 1841-1945* (Journal-Verlag Schwend, Schwäbisch Hall, 1976), although it is rather too much of a brief catalogue; R. H. Korn's *Mauser Gewehre und Mauser* Patente (Ecksteins Bibliographischem-Verlag, 1908, and Akademische Druck- und Verlagsanstalt, 1971) for details of pre-1908 Mauser rifle patents; W. Von Menges' *Die Bewaffnung der Preussischen Fusstruppen* (1913, reprinted by Jurgen Olmes, Krefeld, 1969), which remains the only readily available history of the Dreyse needle-rifles; and Werner Eckardt & Otto Morawietz' *Die Handwaffen des brandenburgisch-preussisch-deutschen Heeres, 1600-1945* (Verlag Helmut Gerhard Schulz, Hamburg, 1957 and 1973), which contains a lot of useful information, but is very badly illustrated. All references to 'TGB' are keyed to *The German Bayonet* by John Walter (Arms and Armour Press, London, 1976).

Datastrip legend

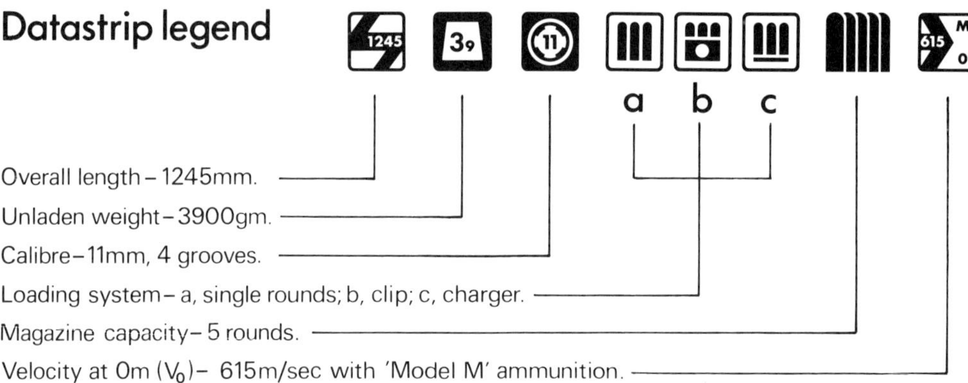

The German Rifle

Part one

The Dreyse needle-fire weapons

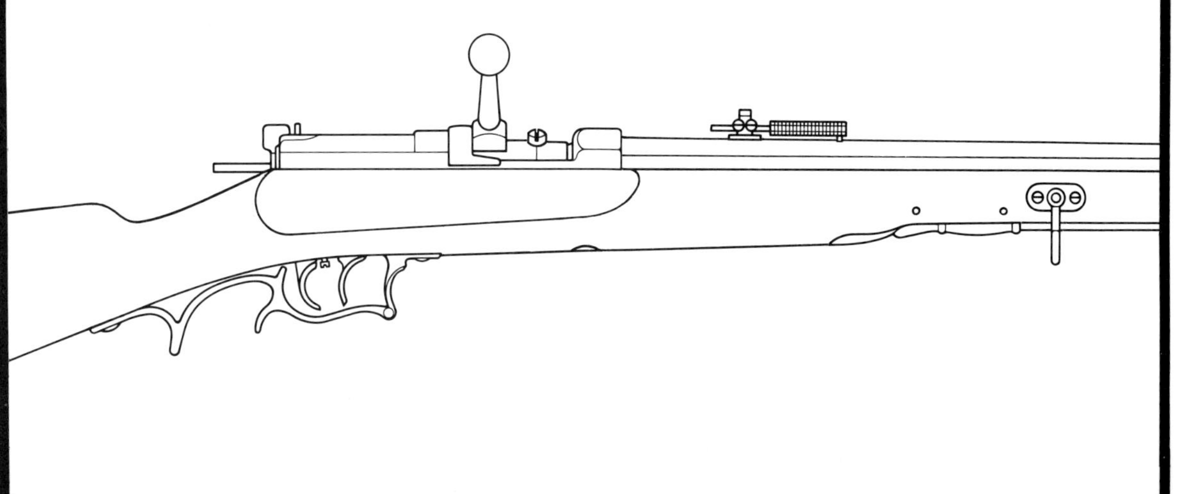

Zündnadelgewehr Modell 1841 Infantry rifle

The development of the Zündnadelgewehr, in which a long needle-like firing pin was used to detonate the fulminate contained within a combustible paper cartridge, occurred in the early 1820s. The idea supposedly came to Dreyse when the mercuric fulminate he was scraping from a percussion cap with a needle suddenly ignited. Despite the questionable validity of this rather colourful story, he was subsequently granted a patent in 1827 to protect the development and exploitation of his discovery for eight years. Small numbers of muzzle-loading sporting guns were made using a rudimentary form of needle ignition, in which a long spring-loaded needle assembly, in the rear of the breech, was cocked by a lever on the rear right side of the barrel[1]. The first Dreyse gun embodying the experimental action was submitted to the Kriegsministerium (War Ministry) in 1827, but offered little advantage over the conventional muzzle-loading muskets.

1. One example is depicted in the illustrations section of Jaroslav Lugs, *Handfeuerwaffen*, Band I, p. 90.

The contemporary Prussian ordnance authorities were as conservative as their colleagues elsewhere and rejected the Dreyse. Undismayed, the inventor outmanoeuvred them by presenting a sporting carbine to Crown Prince Wilhelm, who was something of a connoisseur of firearms and firearms design. Although the gun was still a muzzle-loader, its recipient was sufficiently astute to see its development potential—and the certainty of ignition compared with the regular percussion system[2]. Dreyse's chances of persuading the Kriegsministerium (War Ministry) to undertake further trials were greatly enhanced by royal patronage, and detailed experimentation was carried out between 1832 and 1836. Each submission was an improvement on its predecessor, and it seems that the gun submitted in 1833 was the first breech-loader.

2. A percussion-ignition musket, under service conditions, could be expected to misfire several times in a hundred rounds, although much better figures were obtained from trials.

Its mechanism consisted of a simple sliding bolt, the projecting handle of which turned down into a locking recess in the receiver. There may be some doubt that Dreyse was responsible for its design—it is possible that the method was mentioned to rather than by Dreyse—but this is pertinent only to his reputation as a designer and has no bearing on the history of the Dreyse rifles.

Experiments with the breech-loaders convinced the Prussians that they had enormous potential, and field-trials were planned for 1836. A commission was formed to supervise these trials, from which the rifles emerged with great credit, and small quantities of mass produced[3] Zündnadelgewehre were ordered from their inventor. As a result, 155 rifles were delivered to the Prussian Army in 1839 and issued for the Great Trials ('grosseren Versuche'); it is assumed that they were made in Dreyse's workshop in Sömmerda, and that an earlier locksmithing partnership with Kaufmann Collenbusche had been dissolved[4]. Whether the latter died or simply wished to pursue less warlike trades has yet to be established. The trial rifles were intended to fire an 'Einheitspatrone', a self-contained cartridge similar to the experimental ammunition developed in the late 1820s. The round lead ball ('Rundkugel'), lubricated with tallow, was inserted in a special papier-mâché sabot. The diameter of the ball was 15.2mm and the powder charge weighed 4.3gm; a priming pellet of mercuric fulminate lay in the base of the sabot immediately behind the bullet, and the external surface of the cartridge case was coated with tallow waterproofing.

3. They were, of course, almost completely hand-made, but to a consistent design; the previous guns had been largely one of a kind.

4. They had traded as Dreyse & Collenbusche since c.1820.

The tests were extremely successful and the needle-gun was adopted by a royal decree of 4 December 1840. Dreyse himself was given orders to supply the Prussian Army with its first sixty thousand rifles, and seems to have remained the only contractor until the government arsenal in Spandau was established in the mid-1850s[5]. The resulting Leichte Percussions-Gewehr M 1841 was renamed the Infanterie-Gewehr M 1841 in 1855, when the M 1839/55 (Minié) rifle-musket was introduced and the novelty of the Dreyse system had declined to a point where it was no longer considered a state secret. It seems to have taken Dreyse a long time to achieve volume production, but the first guns were delivered in late 1842.

5. The factory, founded in Potsdam in 1722, was moved to Spandau in 1855.

The M 1841 needle-rifle holds the distinction of being the first breech-loader to be adopted for general service—though others had been used elsewhere for specialized tasks—and was held in great awe by the Prussian authorities. One immediate result of its clandestine development and introduction was that Dreyse's name, although revered by the Prussians, did not become a household name until shortly before his death in 1867. However, the Gewehr-Prüfungs-Kommission and many other Prussian military authorities were well aware of the potential in the Dreyse needle-rifle[6].

6. Werner Eckardt and Otto Morawietz, *Die Handwaffen des brandenburgisch-preussisch-deutschen Heeres, 1600-1945,* p. 116

7. C. H. Roads, *The British Soldier's Firearm, 1850-1864,* p. 29.

The Dreyse system was not destined to stay a total secret for long: indeed, one needle-gun was sent for trials in Britain in 1849[7]. Examples had also seen service in Baden, Dresden and Schleswig-Holstein in 1849. By 1850, issues of the new needle-rifles had been made to all the fusilier battalions of the Gardekorps and II., III. and IV.Armeekorps; to the grenadier battalions of 1. and 2.Garde-Regiment zu Fuss; to all of the Garde-Reserve-Regimenter; and to all of the infantry fusilier battalions, attached to the first thirty-two infantry regiments (1-32). However, this meant—especially in the Garde and Armeekorps—that dissimilar weapons firing different cartridges were often being used in the same units, and inevitably complicated logistics.

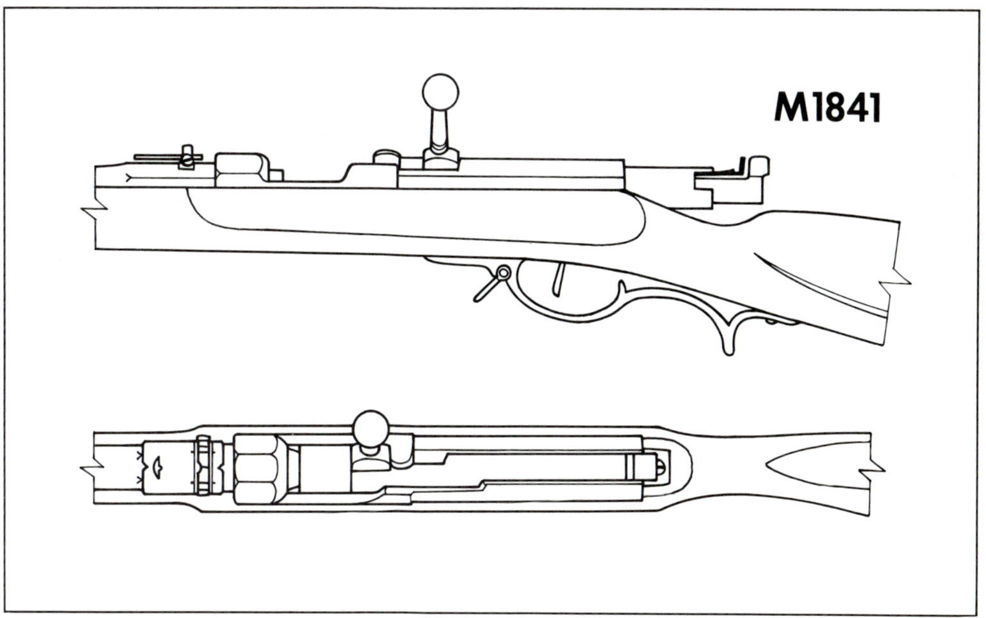

The mechanism of the M 1841 infantry rifles, which remained in service for virtually the entire life of the Dreyse system (1840-c.1875/6), provided the basis for all the later models except the Zündnadelbüchse M 1849, the carbines of 1855 and 1857, and most of the Defensions-Zündnadelwaffen. It was a rudimentary bolt-action system in which locking was provided by the abutment of the bolt handle base on the receiver bridge; not the strongest of methods, but adequate for the low power generated by the combustible cartridges. The guns originally fired a 'Patrone mit Rundkugel' (cartridges loaded with a lead ball) but an improved design, the Patrone M 1847, led to a wholesale revision of the sights for an oviform projectile. This was made before the guns entered service.

8. The most important of these was the M 1839 smoothbore musket. Von Menges, *Die Bewaffnung der Preussischen Fusstruppen,* Anlage 2, gives details of the units carrying them in the campaigns of 1848-49.

The campaigns undertaken in 1849 demonstrated that the Dreyse was considerably superior to the older muzzle-loaders, many of which had also served in Schleswig-Holstein and Baden[8]. However, it was found that the gas seal between the barrel extension and the bolt required careful machining to be effective, and that there was often appreciable gas leakage from guns that had not been well-made or had seen an undue amount of service.

9. Smith & Smith, *Small Arms of the World*, tenth edition, p. 44, record that of 37,574 muskets salvaged from the battle field, 6,000 had one load in the barrel, 12,000 had two, 6,000 had from three to ten loads . . . and one gun had no less than 23!

There was one feature of the needle-rifles that should not have been ignored by so many military authorities: they were genuine *breech-loaders*. Although the British, the Swiss, the Austrians, the Americans and others had all tested the Dreyse, all had discarded it on the grounds that it was insufficiently robust for service use and that it leaked gas into the bargain. But a breech-loader could be loaded—with equal facility—while lying prone, behind minimal cover, on horseback or on the move; it could also be fired faster than a rifle-musket, and could even be unloaded with relative ease. The experience at the Battle of Gettysburg during the American Civil War[9], where many multiply-loaded rifle-muskets were recovered from the battlefield, indicated a need for foolproof loading.

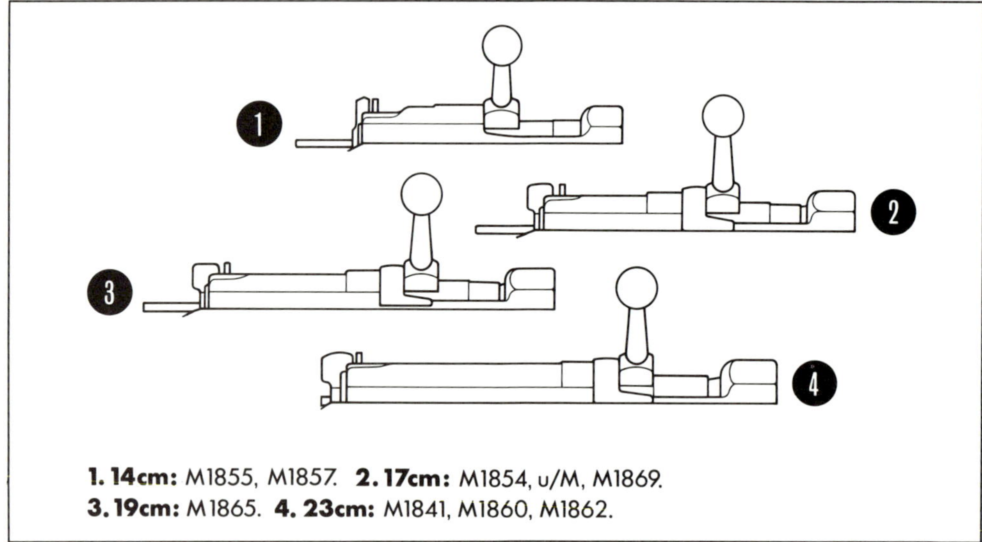

1. 14cm: M1855, M1857. **2. 17cm:** M1854, u/M, M1869. **3. 19cm:** M1865. **4. 23cm:** M1841, M1860, M1862.

But the contemporary European obsession with linear tactics, used to undeniably great effect in the battles of the early nineteenth century, influenced too many important people. Of course, many of the high ranking ordnance personnel of the 1850s had seen action decades before in the Napoleonic Wars; the Duke of Wellington, for one, was fond of quoting Napoleon's opinion that the massed fire of the British troops at Waterloo was the most devastating thing imaginable. When it is recalled that the trials of the Dreyse in Britain were undertaken in 1850-51, when Wellington was still alive, it is scarcely surprising that the design was rejected. Rifle-muskets firing Minié-type bullets were often capable of much better accuracy at much longer ranges than the needle-guns, but they were still muzzle-loaders and their advent brought few noticeable changes in mid-nineteenth century tactics.

10. Busk was a well-respected British authority on firearms, and the author of many books and pamphlets. The best known is *The Rifle and How to Use It* (published in 1860).

In conclusion, it has to be noted that there were many differing opinions among the contemporary small arms experts. Hans Busk[10] recorded that the Dreyse was "not adapted to general military purposes"; but another writer, who remains anonymous, stated that "The only point to be determined in practice is, whether they [Dreyse needle rifles] fulfil their theoretical indications. . . . In England the authorities say, that if made, they would not answer. In Prussia, being made and employed, they are found to answer . . .". The Austro-Prussian or Seven Weeks' War of 1866 showed the second quote to be the more perceptive, and that a breech-loader—even the Dreyse, which was not the most efficient—was infinitely preferable to even the best rifle-musket. It took twenty-five years and a catastrophic war to convince most people of something that should have been evident at the outset.

Production history

The M 1841 rifle was made, apparently exclusively, by Dreyse's workshops in Sömmerda. It has been stated that some were made by the Prussian government arsenal in Spandau, which was not established until 1855, but none has yet been examined. Sixty thousand Zündnadelgewehre were ordered from Dreyse in early 1841, the first being delivered at the end of the following year. Total production is believed to have exceeded half a million in the period 1841-65, when production was suspended in favour of the improved M 1862 infantry rifle (qv). There were 448,510 M 1841 rifles on the Prussian inventory at general mobilization in July 1870; many were serving with the Landwehr and the Reserve, but a surprising number were carried by line infantrymen during the ensuing Franco-Prussian War. Despite the introduction of the M 1862, all of the infantry regiments numbered above 33 were still armed with the older guns. They were subsequently relegated to the Landwehr after being declared obsolete in the army on 15 August 1872[11].

11. This date, however, has not been confirmed; it may, perhaps, refer to the day on which the infantry rifles were transferred to other units.

Markings

Apart from some very early guns, most Dreyse rifles bore the mark of the manufacturer—usually a script *Soemmerda ND*—on the left rear side of the receiver. This often appeared in close proximity to a date such as 1848, the year of production; guns bearing double dates (1842-1849) indicate that issue was undertaken several years after manufacture, the rifles having been stored in the interim. It has been suggested that the second date represented a major modification, such as the fitting of new sights, but this is now discredited. Unlike many of their successors, the M 1841 needle-rifles do not display designation stamps on the receiver side.

The serial number lies on the left side of the receiver alongside the chamber, and on the left side of the barrel at the breech. Both are accompanied by small displayed eagle proof marks ('Beschussadler neuer Art', new pattern proof eagle). The full serial number is repeated on the base of the bolt handle, while the last two digits appear on most of the removable parts and screws.

Small crowned gothic letters—inspectors' markings—may be found on many parts, including a whole string along the right side of the barrel at the breech. One was added at each separate proof and view stage. The monarch's cypher, consisting of a crown over FW, can often be found on the right side of the butt, occasionally with a date and two large crowned gothic-letter inspectors' marks. There may also be a 10mm roman letter on the left side of the butt, applied after 28 August 1852 in accordance with the code:

A.: 'Ausschuss': unserviceable owing to a shot-out barrel.

D.: 'Defensionsgewehr': relegated to garrison use.

E.: 'Exerzierwaffen': suitable only for training purposes.

L.B.: 'Landesbewaffnung': relegated to the Landsturm.

Guns made after about 1862 may be found with long ('L.A.') or short ('K.A.') butts.

Mechanical description and variations

Dreyse Zündnadelgewehre are rudimentary bolt-action designs in which locking is effected by the abutment of the base of the bolt handle block on the reinforced shoulders of the receiver bridge. The operation is relatively simple: starting with the mechanism in a 'fired' state, the thumb-piece attached to the inner portion of the bolt and the leaf spring—which prevents the firer opening the breech unless it is cocked first—is retracted, a movement which withdraws the needle through its protective housing. The bolt is rotated and drawn to the rear to expose the chamber, and a cartridge is then placed in the feedway and pushed forward with the finger until it rests against the step at the juncture of the chamber and barrel. The bolt is pushed forwards and turned clockwise (viewed from the rear) through about 25° to lock, compressing the spiral spring while the needle sleeve is retained by the sear bar attached to the trigger mechanism. The rear of the needle provides a visible and tactile cocking indicator, since it protrudes from the back of the bolt unit. The trigger is then pressed, against the resistance offered by its spring, to disengage the sear from the needle sleeve and allow the spring to propel the needle through the needle housing, through the base of the cartridge and into the primer inserted in the papier-mâché sabot. A gas seal is provided—in theory, if not always in practice—by the coned face of the bolt meshing with the barrel extension, which was common to all Dreyse weapons except the 'short rifle' of 1849, the carbines of 1855 and 1857 and the Defensions-Zündnadelwaffen. These had an obturation system consisting of a seat cut in the breech face for the bolt-tip. An expansion chamber, usually referred to as the 'Luftkammer' (air chamber), was cut inside the bolt face to collect fouling débris and, so it was believed, improve combustion.

The special paper-clad cartridge contained a lead ball, inserted in a papier-mâché sabot holding a small pellet of mercuric fulminate in its base. It was the forerunner of the subsequent Patronen M 1847 and M 1855 which, however, used oviform (egg-shaped) rather than spherical projectiles.

Many writers have questioned the wisdom of Dreyse's decision to place the fulminate igniter ahead of the main charge, through which the needle had to pass. The needle, therefore, was exposed to the combustion of the charge and corroded very quickly; so quickly that the soldiers were issued with spare needles. However, there may be two mitigating circumstances to explain Dreyse's actions. Firstly, it was difficult to devise a rigid paper-based self-contained cartridge, since the paper body was basically weak and susceptible to damage in storage or transit. It could easily be damaged in such a way that the primer, if placed in the base of the paper case, could be moved out of the path of the striker needle; consequently, the gun would fail to fire, and premature ignition could occur if it were struck during handling. By recessing the primer in the sabot, where it was cushioned from blows by the sabot material and the propellant, a safety factor was included; additionally, the primer was infallibly presented in front of the needle.

Secondly, the burning pattern of a main charge is not a true detonation: all of it, in other words, does not change from solid to gas immediately, but instead over a small period of time (measurable in micro-seconds) as a progressive burning occurs. All cartridges designed since Dreyse have initiated the combustion process from the rear, which means that the gaseous products have to displace the unconsumed propellant in front of them to act on the projectile base. Dreyse may have considered that it was more efficient to begin the process at the front, liberating the gases to work directly on the bullet through the intermediate sabot. But this argument, even if accurate, is somewhat academic and in practical terms the improvement would be very slight. The penalty of needle erosion in the Dreyse was a severe price to pay.

Right: a comparison between the M 1847 and M 1855 combustible cartridges.

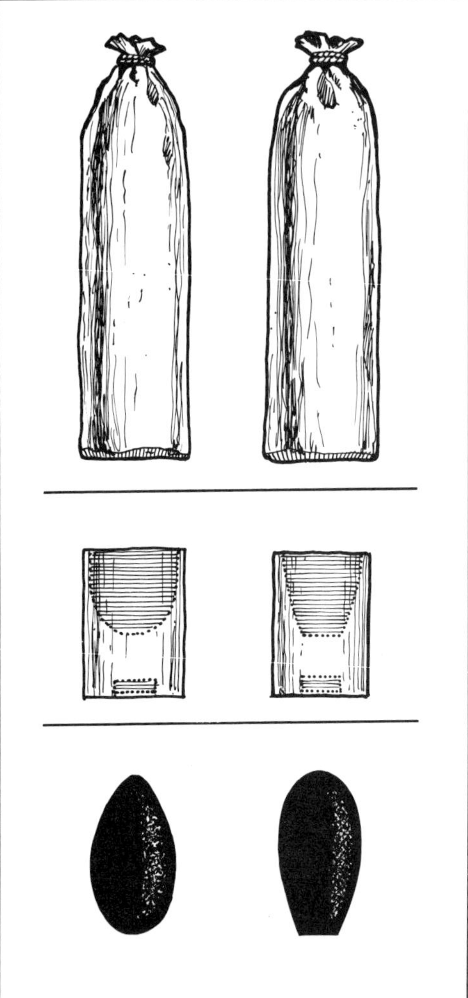

It is widely believed that the worst fault of the needle-guns lay in the leakage of propellant gas at the joint of the bolt and chamber. This, it is said, became more serious as the weapons aged and erosion gradually enlarged the gaps through which the leaks occurred. Many Prussians are said to have fired their rifles from the hip in an attempt to avoid back-blast from worn Dreyse breeches. William McElwee[12] states that "In spite of its great reputation and staggering successes, the Dreyse rifle was seriously open to both the latter criticisms [wear in the relatively delicate mechanism and poor breech sealing]. The needle from which it took its name had to pierce the whole length of the cardboard cartridge to reach the detonating charge and was of necessity long and easily bent, or even broken. This was not . . . a frequent enough occurrence to outweigh its overwhelming advantages. The shortcomings of its breech mechanism were far more important. After the first half-dozen rounds the imperfect closure of the bolthead allowed not only the escape of gases, but of fragments of burning powder which frequently inflicted painful burns on the faces of the firers, and sometimes even blinded them. In the face of this risk even the best trained infantryman . . . could not be brought to hold his cheek close against the butt of his rifle to take careful aim. He flinched away from the discharge; and by the end of the war of 1870 most of them preferred to fire the weapon from the hip . . ."

Unfortunately, this passage perpetuates a myth; there is very little gas leakage from a properly closed Dreyse breech, because of the conical seat between the bolt face and the barrel extension, and the slight camming action of the bolt handle block on the reinforced receiver bridge, which ensured that much of the wear was taken up. Gas probably did leak from some guns in which the standards of manufacture were inferior; but it did so, because of the bolt/barrel extension seating, upwards and forwards rather than back into the firer's face. Gas could also run back inside the bolt body, but could not easily escape through the needle housing. A modern trial with an M 1841 Zündnadelgewehr[13], the oldest and poorest-made pattern, has proved that gas leaks have hardly any significance and no stories of blast problems could be found in any contemporary history or memoirs[14]. The Prussian troops loaded their rifles from the hip, as the cartridge pouch was on the soldier's belt; there may also have been occasions when the troops actually fired from the hip, in circumstances of desperation, since the quickest fire-rate was achieved by having the single-shot rifles as close as possible to the ammunition supply. However, none of the Prussian manuals confirm that this was an official practice.

It is also widely believed that the French Mle 66 (Chassepot) needle-rifle was more gas-tight than the Dreyse; this, too, is a fallacy. Antoine Chassepot, for some inexplicable reason, placed an india-rubber washer in the front part of his rifle's bolt, hoping that this would achieve a proper breech seal. For a few rounds, it did: but placing the rubber so close to a source of considerable heat caused it to become hard

12. William McElwee, *The Art of War: Waterloo to Mons*, p. 121.

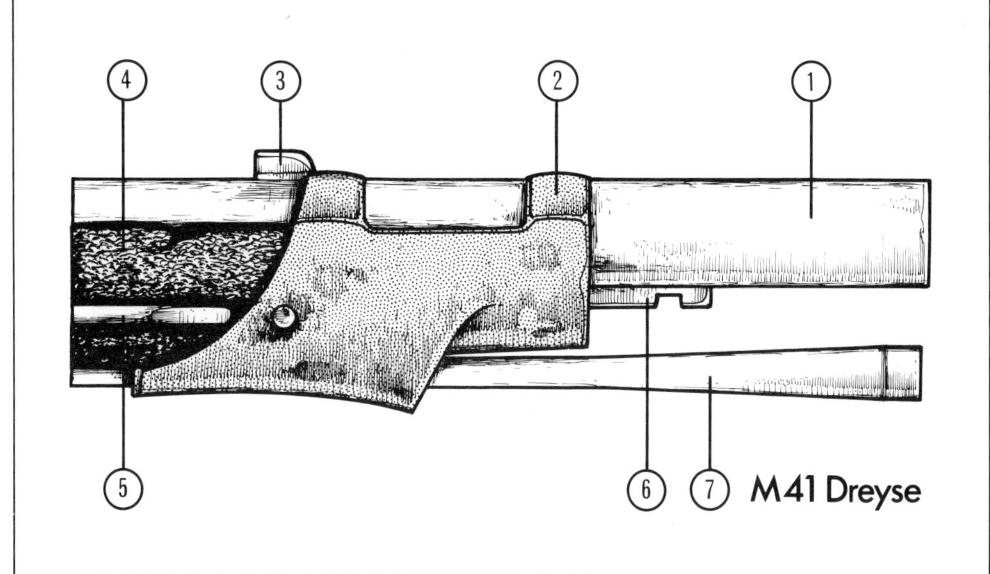

Right: the muzzle and nosecap of the M 1841 infantry rifle. Key: 1, barrel; 2, nosecap; 3 front sight; 4, stock; 5, nosecap spring; 6, bayonet retainer; and 7, ramrod.

and brittle until, after a few rounds, it disintegrated. The gas blast from the breeches of the Mle 66 rifles as their washers deteriorated was frightful. Even a worn Dreyse, because of its entirely metallic parts, gave much less trouble. Though the ballistic superiority and better accuracy of the Mle 66 cannot be denied, the Dreyse remained a better military weapon in at least one respect, since it could not be easily rendered unserviceable.

No basic variations of the M 1841 have yet been identified, but it seems likely that a few experimental rifles were fitted with rod bayonets before the introduction of the M 1854 Pikenbüchse (qv) and there may also have been some forerunners of the M 1849 Jägerbüchse. The original curled-over finger-rest terminal on the trigger guard was replaced by a simplified form shortly after production had begun, and the sights were revised in the mid-1850s after the introduction of the Patrone M 1855. The old sights graduated for the Patrone M 1847 had only two leaves; the new ones had three.

13. Undertaken and reported by De Witt Bailey.

14. According to Hans-Rudolf von Stein and others, but records may yet be found.

Appearance, distinctive features and data

The M 1841 is a long and very clumsy bolt-action rifle-musket, its size being typical of its period. It can easily be distinguished by the long bolt mechanism, which is much too long for so short a cartridge, and by the fact that the bolt handle does not lock down horizontally in front of the receiver reinforcement or bridge. The receiver is split longitudinally to allow the bolt handle to slide rearwards after it has been turned anti-clockwise (viewed from the rear) to unlock. The barrel is cylindrical, apart from an octagonal section in front of the receiver which carries the back sight mounting. There are three spring-retained brass barrel bands, the foremost of which acts as the nose-cap while the middle one carries the front sling swivel. The second swivel is attached to the front of the cast brass trigger guard, whose long rearward-extending finger-rest terminates in a small curled-over (old) or straight (new) spur. The one-piece walnut stock has prominent 'flats' alongside the action, like all Dreyse weapons, and there is a rudimentary cheek-piece on the left side of the butt.

DATA

Calibre: 15.43 ± 0.13mm.
Rifling: concentric, 4 grooves 0.78mm deep and 6mm wide; 1 turn in 732mm, right hand (pitch of 3° 47').
Magazine capacity: none—single-shot only.
Loading system: manual insertion of cartridge in chamber.
Length overall: 1,425mm.
Barrel length: 907mm.
Weight: about 4,975gm without sling.
Sights: (Visier M 1847) a combined block and two-leaf sight with a standing 'battle sight' for 300 paces, a small leaf for 400 and a large leaf for 500 and 600 paces. (Visier M 1855) A combined block and three-leaf pattern, with a standing 'battle sight' for 300 paces, a small leaf for 400, an intermediate leaf for 500, and a large leaf for 600 and 700 paces.
Performance: see cartridge data (Appendix 2).

Accessories

BAYONET

The Zündnadelgewehr M 1841 was issued with the M 1841 socket bayonet, which had a locking ring around the base of its socket body and a triangular-section blade.

OTHERS

A sling, a clearing rod, a muzzle stopper, a rainproof cover for the bolt mechanism, a wooden cylinder, two spare needles, and a cleaning kit for the expansion chamber in the front of the bolt. Corporals ('Unteroffiziere') carried spare mainsprings.

Zündnadelbüchse Modell 1849

The identification of this particular Dreyse rifle, a short-lived pattern intended for the riflemen, has been the subject of debate. Several M 1849 designs have been tentatively identified, but it is clear that all but one must be wrong; indeed, all may be wrong. Von Menges[1] says that the M 1849 had its "Barrel browned, octagonal to the sight, then conical to the muzzle. The lock is shortened ['komprimiert'] . . . The receiver has been similarly shortened, 15cm instead of 25.3cm for the Mod. 41". Assuming that von Menges was correct, this information pinpoints the action length of the Zündnadelbüchse M 1849. He goes on to describe how the barrel was retained in the stock by a combination of a lateral key and several screws (not barrel bands), and that the back sight was originally a much too complicated pattern with sight leaves for 300, 500, 400/600 and 700/800/900 paces. This provided the firer with such a confusing set of options that it was replaced by a slightly simplified pattern with leaves for 300, 400, 500 and 600/700 paces.

The most important feature concerned a basic change in the obturation system, adopted with the laudable intention of shortening the action; that of the M 1841 infantry rifle was really much too long for a combustible cartridge as short as Dreyse's. Von Menges says of the 1849-type action that "The chamber mouth does not slide over the barrel extension, but has a plug-type extension . . . that fits in a recess cut in the chamber. Escaping powder gases could consequently place the firers in more peril . . .".

This breech sealing system proved inferior to the regular Dreyse coned pattern and—though perpetuated on the 1855 and 1857 carbines, where a short action was essential—was discarded from all subsequent longarms. The 'coned' breech system remained in vogue until the appearance of the Beck Transformation (qv) in the late 1860s.

The Zündnadelbüchse M 1849 was adopted by an AKO (Allerhöchtsse-Kabinetts-Ordre, Imperial Cabinet Decree) of 11 December 1851, presumably after extensive experimentation with modified rifles had been made. It obtained a very limited distribution to the Garde-Jäger and Garde-Schützen, despite being unsuccessfully considered as an infantry weapon. The small numbers that remained in service in the mid-1850s were speedily replaced by the Zündnadelbüchse M 1854[2]. The M 1849 Dreyse does not seem to have been used in any field campaigns, although several thousand remained on the army inventory in 1870.

1. W. von Menges, *Die Bewaffnung der Preussischen Fusstruppen*, p. 42.

2. Adopted in March 1855.

Production history

It is believed that the small quantities of Zündnadelbüchsen M 1849 were made exclusively in the Dreyse factory in Sömmerda, and that the total did not exceed four thousand guns. By July 1870, 2,973 remained on the inventory, but they were discarded immediately after the end of the Franco-Prussian War.

Markings

Von Menges records that examples of the M 1849 were marked *Soemmerda ND*, in script on the left rear of the receiver, above the dates '1850' or '1851'. However, no actual rifle has been examined and the specimen pictured by Baer[3]—this may be a special presentation gun as it also bears 'N. v D.' over the chamber—has a longer inscription on the left side of the receiver running almost from the bolt handle to the back of the action.

The other marks (proof eagles, inspectors' stampings, the serial and parts numbers) presumably paralleled those of the M 1841 infantry rifle (qv), since they represented the standard military method. It is not known whether unit designations were marked on the Zündnadelbüchsen M 1849.

Mechanical description and variations

The breech mechanism of the M 1849 greatly resembles that of the M 1841 infantry rifle (qv), apart from the means of sealing the breech against the escape of propellant gases. The original Dreyse had a coned barrel extension that slid into the hollowed bolt face, and the slight camming action of the bolt handle base against the receiver bridge ensured that the two components meshed as well as they could to provide a passable gas seal—even allowing for the fact that contemporary manufacturing tolerances were not as small as they could have been, judged by modern standards. The M 1849, and the two later carbines[4], had a circumferential ring milled out of the chamber lip, into which the bolt head was forced. This system proved to be much the poorer, since gas could escape backwards from the breech as shown in the diagrams. The coned barrel extension and hollowed bolt face tended to direct the leaks, such as they were, forwards and upwards where they did little damage.

Appearance, distinctive features and data

The M 1849 is a typical Dreyse bolt-action rifle, with a short action (15cm long) and a bolt handle that locks diagonally rather than horizontally. The

3. Ludwig Baer, *Die leichten Waffen der deutschen Armeen 1841-1945*, p. 10.

4. As well as the majority of the so-called 'Defensions-Zündnadelwaffen'.

receiver is split longitudinally to allow the bolt handle to slide backwards after it has been turned anti-clockwise to unlock. The barrel is a slightly conical cylinder, apart from a short octagonal portion in front of the receiver which carries the back sight. Unlike the M 1841, the M 1849 discards barrel bands in favour of one transverse key and an assortment of screws running upwards from the underside of the one-piece walnut stock. There is a brass nose-cap, and the T-lug for the bayonet is brazed to the right side of the muzzle. The front sling swivel is attached by a lateral screw running through the fore-end and the back swivel is anchored on the underside of the butt. The cast brass trigger-guard bow has a long rearward extension, which serves as a finger-rest, and there are prominent 'flats' on the stock alongside the bolt mechanism—so characteristic of Prussian Dreyse rifles and carbines. The butt has a cheek-piece on the left side and the butt plate is made of iron.

No variations of the Zündnadelbüchse M 1849 have yet been identified, but some may exist as the gap between the year-designation and the official adoption papers (December 1851) suggests prolonged gestation.

*Taken from von Menges' figures in *Die Bewaffnung der Preussischen Fuss-truppen*; no example of the M 1849 has yet been available for examination.

DATA
Calibre: 15.43 ± 0.13mm.
Rifling: concentric, 4 grooves 0.78mm deep and 6mm wide; 1 turn in 732mm (pitch of 3° 47').
Magazine: none—single-shot only.
Loading system: manual insertion of cartridge in chamber.
Length overall: 1,250mm approximately.*
Barrel length: 790mm approximately.*
Weight: 4,585gm approximately*, without sling.
Sights: (front) unprotected barleycorn; (back) (*original*) a combined block and leaf sight, with a standing 'battle sight' for 225 paces, and leaves for 300, 500, 400/600 and 700/800/900 paces; (*second pattern*) a combined block and leaf sight, with a standing 'battle sight' for 225 paces, and leaves for 300, 400, 500 and 600/700 paces.
Performance: see cartridge data (Appendix 2).

Accessories

BAYONET
The Zündnadelbüchse M 1849 was issued with the so-called Garde-Hirschfänger M 1849, which had a cast brass hilt, a wrought iron crossguard with a muzzle ring, and a 54cm blade.

OTHERS
The same as the M 1841 infantry rifle (qv).

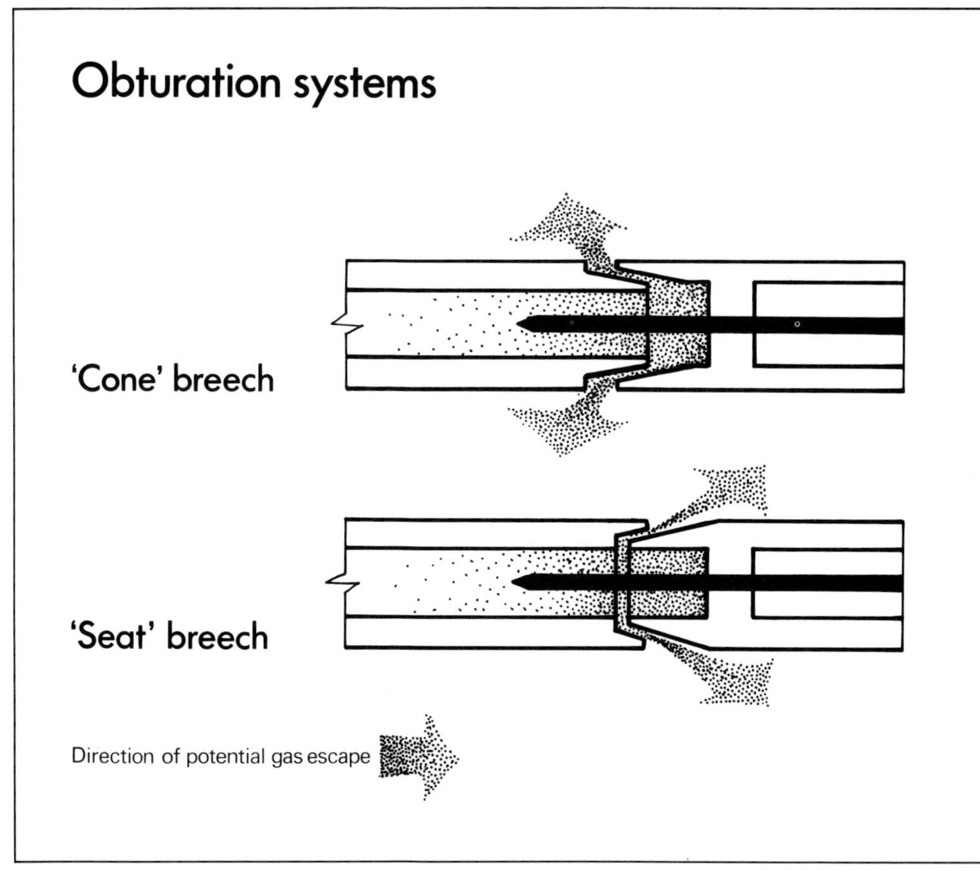

Zündnadelbüchse Modell 1854 Pikenbüchse

After the relatively unsuccessful experiments with the Zündnadelbüchse M 1849 (qv) had been concluded, the Prussians introduced a revised Dreyse needle-rifle for the élite Jäger-Bataillone. The M 1854 was adopted by an AKO of 22 March 1855 and remained in the hands of the riflemen, despite the introduction of better rifles to the fusiliers in 1860 and the infantry in 1862, until supplies of the perfected Zündnadelbüchse M 1865 became available in 1866-68[1]. It is generally believed that some of the surviving M 1854 rifles were re-issued to the navy[2], while the remainder were converted to u/M pioneer rifles.

1. Jäger-Bataillone Nr.5 and Nr.6 had been re-armed experimentally in 1865.

2. There is a plausible alternative theory that the M 1854 was adopted by the navy as early as 1855. Few rifles with naval marks have also had army types. Each theory has its champions, but neither has been proved.

The most obvious feature of the M 1854, apart from its short (17cm) action, lay in the special rod bayonet carried under the barrel and locked in position by a spring-catch in the specially adapted nose-cap. The bayonet/nose-cap assembly seriously altered the balance of the rifles owing to its weight, and the fitment was never regarded as especially successful.

An attempt was made to revise the sights, as befitting the Jäger units' function. The sight leaves were widened to make them easier to operate, although it is hard to understand why the Prussians persisted with a multi-leaf pattern rather than adopt a tangent-leaf sight when the latter was undeniably easier to use. The sighting distance was increased to 800 paces, or about 605 metres, at which the Dreyse rifles were not particularly accurate.

Examples of the Zündnadelbüchsen M 1854 were carried by the Jäger-Bataillone Nr. 3 and Nr. 7 during the short war with Denmark in 1864, and the Garde-Jäger, the Garde-Schützen, and Jäger-Bataillone—1-4 and 7-9—during the Austro-Prussian War of 1866. However, all the guns had been discarded by the outbreak of the Franco-Prussian War, apart from those serving the navy and the others that had been converted to u/M pioneer rifles in 1866-67. The naval rifles, supplemented by some Zündnadelbüchsen M 1865 after 1874-75, were issued until they were replaced by Mausers in the late 1870s. Naval M 1854 rifles had their barrels brightly polished in preference to the browned army-issue finish. The polish was intended to counteract the corrosive properties of seawater and airborne salt, as the Polish showed rusting much more quickly than the browning; thus, corrective action could be taken more promptly. Most of the rifles with brightly polished barrels also have distinctive naval unit marks (see Markings).

Production history

Zündnadelbüchsen M 1854 seem to have been made exclusively by the Prussian government arsenals—notably the establishment in Spandau—although there have been unconfirmed reports of Dreyse-made items elsewhere. The production quantity remains uncertain, but may have exceeded 30,000.

3. The 1st sailors division, rifle number 924. The letters W.D., a Werft or dockyard, division, may also be found.

Markings

The marks applied to the Zündnadelbüchsen M 1854 are very much like those on the other earlier guns; some are said to have been made by Dreyse in Sömmerda (and would have been marked *Soemmerda ND* on the rear left side of the receiver), but most of those examined were the work of the Prussian government arsenal in Spandau. They bear a spread eagle on the upper left rear side of the receiver above 'SPANDAU' and 'MOD. 54', the designation being in fraktur (gothic script). The proof eagles, or Beschussadler neuer Art, may be found on the left side of the barrel and the receiver, while small crowned-letter inspectors' marks may be found on most of the removable parts. The full serial number, '1434' for example, is located on the left side of the receiver alongside the chamber, on the left side of the barrel at the breech and on the base of the bolt handle. The last two or three digits of the number are repeated on most of the major components, and even on the screws and bolts.

The unit markings on the original guns would indicate a Jäger battalion—'2.J.3.35.', for instance, being Jäger-Bataillon Nr.2—but many guns have naval marks on the butt plate and receiver. Rifle 1434, made at Spandau, has two sets: 'K.M.35.' on the butt plate, with '35' on top of the receiver above the chamber, and '1.M.D.924.' on the left side of the receiver alongside the breech as shown. The first mark was applied by the Königliche Marine (Royal Navy), the second by 1.Matrösen-Division[3].

Mechanical description and variations

The M 1854 Dreyse, rather than perpetuate the inefficient seat-type obturation system of the unsuccessful M 1849 (qv), returned to the cone pattern used by the M 1841 infantry rifle and all the other guns other than the two carbines of 1855 and 1857. There is no doubt that the cone pattern, despite its excessive length, gave a much better gas seal. However, a concerted effort was made to shorten the action of the M 1854, until the result measured only

17cm overall, compared with 25.3cm. The other mechanical details paralleled those of the M 1841, to which reference should be made. The special nose-cap housing the rod bayonet, which had no bearing on the actual functioning of the gun, is considered in the paragraph on Appearance, distinctive features and data. No variations are known.

Appearance, distinctive features and data

The M 1854 is a typical Dreyse bolt-action rifle, with a longitudinally split receiver and a diagonally locking bolt handle. The short action measures 17cm but, unlike those of the M 1849, the carbines and the various Defensions-Gewehre, has a prominent reinforce where the bolt-handle base abuts the receiver. The barrel is virtually cylindrical for its entire length, apart from a short octagonal portion at the breech that acts as a base for the multi-leaf back sight, and is retained by three brass fixtures—two barrel bands and a special nose-cap. The bands are retained by leaf springs, while the nose-cap is adapted to receive the spring-loaded locking catch for the rod bayonet—the only one of its type ever to be issued to the Prussian Army—running in a channel in the underside of the fore-end, where a cleaning rod would normally be found. The bayonet and its retaining mechanism were clumsy, too heavy, and affected the rifle's balance so adversely that they were removed when many guns were converted into u/M pioneer rifles in the late 1860s.

One sling swivel is attached to the intermediate barrel band while the other is anchored on the underside of the butt, just behind the long finger-rest extension on the cast brass trigger-guard bow.

DATA

Calibre: 15.43 ± 0.13mm.
Rifling: concentric, 4 grooves 0.78mm deep and 6mm wide; 1 turn in 732mm (pitch of 3° 47').
Magazine: none—single-shot only.
Loading system: manual insertion of cartridge in chamber.
Length overall: 1,245mm (bayonet retracted).
Barrel length: 785mm.
Weight: about 4,580gm without sling.
Sights: (front) unprotected barleycorn; (back) a combined block and leaf sight, with a standing 'battle sight' for 300 paces and four leaves for 400, 500, 600 and 700/800 paces.
Performance: see cartridge data (Appendix 2).

Accessories

BAYONET

This took the form of a triangular-section rod, sliding in a channel underneath the fore-end of the stock and locked in the extended or retracted position by a spring-catch under the muzzle. The bayonet proved to be weak and awkward, and was not widely liked. The length of the rifle and extended bayonet was about 1,665mm. The brass-hilted Hirschfänger 57, a sidearm, was issued to compensate for the lack of a sword bayonet.

OTHERS

A sling, a combined muzzle protector and sight guard, a cover for the back sight, two spare needles and cleaning equipment for the bolt expansion chamber.

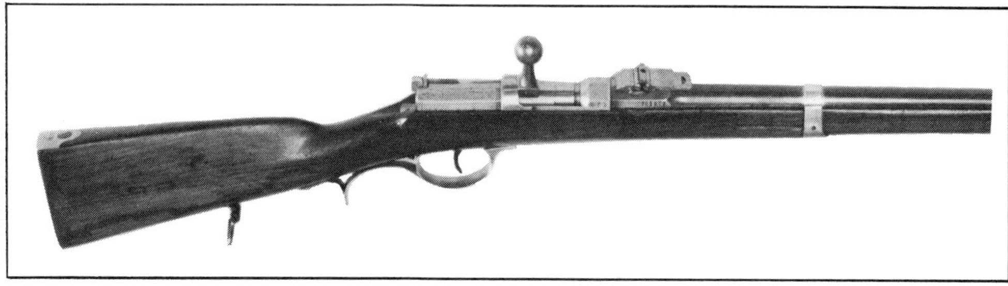

Right: the butt and breech of the M 1854 Pikenbüchse. This gun, number 1454, was made by the Prussian government factory at Spandau and bears naval markings. RSAF collection, photograph by Fred Alderslade.

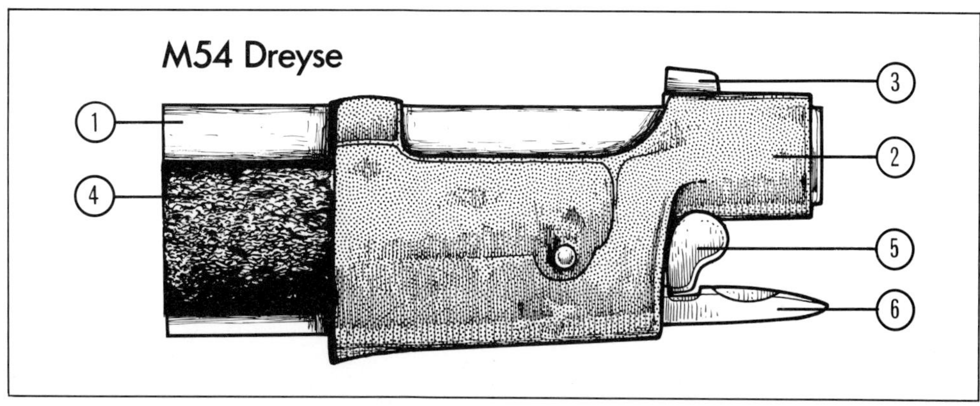

Right: the brass nosecap of the M 1854, showing its unique rod bayonet where the ramrod would normally lie. Key: 1, barrel; 2, nosecap; 3, front sight; 4, stock; 5, bayonet catch; and 6, bayonet.

Zündnadelkarabiner 1855-7

By the mid-1850s, with the Dreyse needle-rifles in service in quantity, the Prussian military authorities turned their attention to the firearms of the cavalry, who were carrying a motley collection of muzzle-loading percussion carbines and pistols. Only dragoon and hussar units were considered suitable recipients of Dreyse needle-carbines, since they were often used for reconnaissance and picket duties and had need of firearms for more than purely personal defence. The Ulanen (lancers) and cuirassiers (heavy cavalry) were intended as genuine cavalrymen, fighting on the battlefield with sword and lance, and were consequently only issued with pistols[1].

1. During the Franco-Prussian War, it was predictably found that all cavalry had uses for carbines. So the Ulanen and cuirassiers were armed with French Mle 66 Chassepot rifles, many of which were later converted to carbine length and adapted for metallic case ammunition.

In May 1855, 25 men in each dragoon and hussar regiment were given needle-carbines. The protracted experiments proved to be successful and, by an AKO of 3 February 1859, the perfected Zündnadel-Karabiner M 1857 was introduced. Apart from the substitution of a steel barrel for the original wrought iron pattern of the limited-issue M 1855, the 1857 carbine was identical with its predecessor—for this reason they are being treated together rather than separately. The M 1857 carbines were issued to all ranks of the dragoon and hussar regiments, which numbered six and thirteen respectively after the army reforms of 1860[2], apart from the NCOs and the trumpeters (all of whom retained the M 1850 percussion pistols).

2. These comprised two guard and four line dragoon regiments, and one 'Leib-Garde' (Life Guard) and twelve line hussar regiments.

Owing to a major revision to the seating between the barrel extension and the bolt face (the layout of which was reversed, see Mechanical description), the needle-carbines seem to have suffered more from gas leakage problems than the standard Dreyse rifles and Büchsen. However, they remained in service until the introduction of converted Chassepot and new M 1871 (Mauser) cavalry carbines in 1875-76. Five hundred M 1857 carbines and 150,000 rounds of combustible ammunition had been supplied to the Bavarian Army at the outbreak of the Franco-Prussian War, but this was scarcely enough to cause a shortage. They were issued to the Bavarian Chevaulegers (light cavalry) on the scale of 80-90 to each regiment. Most of the Prussian carbines were withdrawn from the cavalry between 1872 and 1876, although many were given rifle-type slings and sling swivels in place of the large cavalry saddle ring and issued to stretcher bearers. In addition, small numbers of new carbines are believed to have been made with sling swivels, no cheek pieces on their butts and other minor revisions.

Right: the M 1857 cavalry carbine.

Production history

The M 1855 and M 1857 carbines seem to have been made exclusively by Dreyse's factory in Sömmerda and the Prussian government unit in Herzberg. There were 54,172 on the army inventory in July 1870—when mobilization for the Franco-Prussian War occurred—and since 26,663 were made during the war, the total production, allowing for attrition over eleven years, may have exceeded ninety thousand.

Markings

The M57 guns are generally marked *Soemmerda ND*, in flowing script, on the rear left side of the receiver above the designation 'MOD:57' in fraktur (gothic script). The date of manufacture, '1861' on carbine 863, appears, upside down, on the right side of the receiver behind the bolt handle abutment shoulder.

Proof eagles ('Beschussadler neuer Art') are to be found on the octagonal part of the receiver alongside the chamber and on the octagonal breech section of the barrel. The monarch's cypher, a crown over FW, may also be found on the left side of the barrel. The serial number, '863', appears in full on the left side of the receiver alongside the chamber, towards the front of the octagonal section of the barrel (on the left side), on the base of the bolt handle and on the left side of the cocking piece head. The last two, or three digits are usually repeated on each removable part and screw.

Small inspectors' marks, in the form of crowned

gothic letters, may be encountered on most of the parts, including several, in close proximity, along the right side of the barrel and receiver by the breech. The barrel, in particular, was subjected to several inspections and proof tests before being approved.

The steel barrels of the Karabiner M 1857 were marked 'STAHL' laterally across the top 'flat' of the barrel octagon immediately in front of the joint with the receiver; wrought iron M 1855 barrels were unmarked.

Mechanical description and variations

The Dreyse carbines, while mechanically very similar to the original M 1841 infantry rifle (qv), made use of an ultra-short action befitting their small size. Although the mechanism looked like an M 1841 in miniature, it lacked the reinforced bridge on which the bolt handle usually abutted and was instead a plain-surfaced cylinder[3]. The other major change concerned the design of the seating between the barrel extension and the bolt face. On all Dreyse needle-guns, apart from the Zündnadelbüchse M 1849 (qv) and the carbines, the hollowed bolt face slid over the coned barrel extension; but, for some inexplicable reason (size and space considerations?) the carbines reversed the component design so that the bolt face entered a milled-out circumferential recess in the chamber mouth. This did permit a shorter action, it is true, but had the disadvantage of allowing whatever gas leakage there was to escape backwards into the firer's face. A normal Dreyse action tended to deflect it forwards and upwards.

3. As such, it resembled the action of the Defensions-Gewehre, converted during the Franco-Prussian War.

The carbines and the rifles are otherwise identical, and no mechanical variations of the former have yet been identified.

Appearance, distinctive features and data

The M 1857 is a short carbine with a commensurately short receiver measuring a mere 13cm. Its browned[4] cylindrical barrel has a short octagonal section at the breech which carries the simple back sight. The barrel is retained in the stock by the special iron nose-cap, whose uppermost edges are continued upwards sufficiently far to protect the front sight. There are no barrel bands, keys or pins around or through the fore-end.

4. This finish, however, may have been applied after 1871.

The one-piece walnut stock has a brass butt plate and prominent 'flats' alongside the receiver. The plain brass trigger guard lacks the rearward finger-rest extension characteristic of most other Dreyse firearms, owing to the position of the large saddle ring retained by a smaller ring anchored in the underside of the butt. This ring, however, was replaced on carbines converted after 1872 for the stretcher bearers; on these, conventional rifle-type sling swivels were attached to the underside of the butt and fore-end.

A large stud for a lanyard lies on the small forward extension of the trigger guard bow.

DATA

Calibre: 15.43mm.
Rifling: concentric, 4 grooves 0.78mm deep and 6mm wide; 1 turn in 732mm, right hand (pitch of 3° 47').
Magazine: none—single-shot only.
Loading system: manual insertion of cartridge in chamber.
Length overall: about 805mm.
Barrel length: 382mm.
Weight: about 2,875gm without sling.
Sights: (front) protected barleycorn; (back) a small two-position pattern with a standing 'battle sight' for 200 paces and a small leaf for 300.
Performance: see cartridge data (Appendix 2).

Accessories

BAYONET
None.

OTHERS
A muzzle stopper, a cover for the back sight, two spare needles, and a wooden cylinder. Corporals ('Unteroffiziere') were issued with spare mainsprings.

Zündnadelgewehr Modell 1860 Fusilier rifle

The 1860-pattern Dreyse Zündnadelgewehr was a modified derivative of the guns of 1841, 1849 and 1854. Adopted on 4 August 1860, it was intended for the eight newly-created élite fusilier regiments, which had been formed from personnel of the Reserve infantry regiments and given the numbers 33 to 40 . The rifles first saw action during the 1864 War with Denmark, in the hands of Brandenburgisches Füsilier-Regiment Nr. 35.

1. Continuing the sequence of the line infantry regiments.

The mechanical details of the M 1860 remained substantially those of the M 1841 (qv), but the action was strengthened and made to finer tolerances to reduce problems of gas leakage encountered on a small scale in the earlier guns. In this respect, the M 1860 was an improvement on its predecessors, but the problems were never entirely overcome. Considerable changes were made to the stock, as the old barrel bands were replaced by an attachment system relying on transverse barrel keys. The M 1860 was the first Dreyse to use a 'keyed' barrel apart from what has been tentatively identified as the M 1849 Jägerbüchse (qv). A distinctive brass-hilted sword bayonet, called the Füsilier-Seitengewehr M 1860, was substituted for the older socket patterns.

The M 1860 rifles served the fusilier regiments in the Austro-Prussian (Seven Weeks') War of 1866 and the Franco-Prussian War of 1870-71. In the former, they were carried by the Garde-Füsilier-Regiment and all eight regular fusilier units (33-40); in the latter, by the Garde-Füsilier-Regiment and eleven fusilier regiments (33-40, 73, 80 and 86), as well as by the Saxon Schützen-Regiment Nr. 108. More than a hundred thousand rifles were available on general mobilization for the Franco-Prussian War on 15 July 1870.

Large numbers of the fusilier rifles were subjected to the Beck Transformation (qv) which, although developed prior to 1870, was not undertaken until after the Franco-Prussian War—apart from a small quantity of M 1862 infantry rifles issued to three regiments. The modified M 1860 rifles with Beck's bolt head were passed to the Landwehr in the early 1870s, after the introduction of the Mauser rifle to the line infantry, and ended their days in Landsturm depots; most were discarded long before 1880.

Right: the butt and breech of an M 1860 fusilier rifle (with subsequent Beck modifications), number 2580, made by Dreyse's Sömmerda factory in 1861. RSAF collection, photograph by Fred Alderslade.

Production history

Most of the fusilier rifles were made in the Dreyse factory in Sömmerda between 1860/1 and 1868, when production seems to have ceased. The total quantity must have exceeded 110,000, as 101,865 remained on the army inventory in July 1870 when the Prussian armies were mobilized to meet the French.

Markings

The guns inevitably bear their marker's mark—*Soemmerda ND* in script—on the left rear side of the receiver, above the designation mark 'F.G.MOD.60' in fraktur (gothic script). A date ('1861' on gun 2580) is stamped on the right side of the receiver. Small displayed eagle proof marks ('Beschussadler neuer Art', or new pattern proof eagles, used after 1813) are struck into the left side of the barrel and the left side of the barrel ('B', 'C', 'I', 'F', 'I', 'I'). These The word 'STAHL' (steel) appears on the top 'flat' of the barrel octagon, which extends a short way in front of the receiver and carries the back sight mounting. Several crowned inspectors' letters appear alongside the chamber on the right side of the receiver ('F', 'D', 'W' on the rifle examined) and the right side of the barrel ('B', 'C', 'I'. 'F', 'I', 'I'). These represent the many stages of proof and view—especially in the case of the barrel, which was examined before and after being rifled and proved.

The serial number, 2580, appears on the left side of the barrel, the left side of the receiver, the base of the bolt handle and the left side of the cocking piece. The last two digits ('80') are repeated on most of the

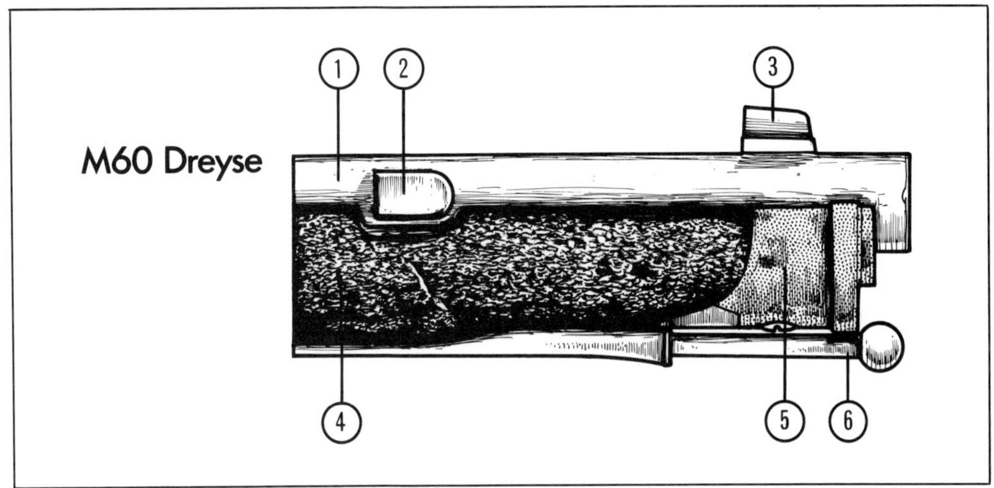

Right: the muzzle and nosecap of the M 1860. Key: 1, barrel; 2, bayonet lug; 3, front sight; 4, stock; 5, nosecap; and 6, ramrod.

minor parts and removable screws and bolts, since interchangeability was never guaranteed and rarely achieved. Most of these components also possess small crowned-letter inspectors' markings.

The crowned FW monarch's cypher, sometimes dated, is struck into the right side of the butt, with two large inspectors' letters. Eckardt & Morawietz[2] record that the butt should also be marked 'L.A.' or 'K.A.' (Langer or Kurzer Anschlag, long or short) depending on its length, as K.A. butts were about 1.95cm shorter, but this was apparently true only of fusilier rifles made or repaired after the introduction of the M 1862 infantry pattern; gun 2580, made in 1861, does not bear butt-length markings.

Unit stampings are usually to be found on the top surface of the butt plate; that on gun 2580 is '*G.H.*VIII.1.', which shows that the rifle was probably issued to the Handwerker-Abteilung (artificer detachment) of VIII.Armeekorps[3].

2. Werner Eckardt and Otto Morawietz, *Die Handwaffen der brandenburgisch-preussisch-deutschen Heeres, 1600-1945,* p. 134.

3. This is unlikely to have been the original unit, since the weapon is a *fusilier* rifle.

Mechanical description and variations

The M 1860 rifle operates in precisely the same way as the M 1841 (qv), which its construction—so far as its bolt unit is concerned—also greatly resembles. Some guns were subjected to the Beck Transformation in 1871-72 and were fitted with new bolt heads and back sights, but apart from these, and the two variations in stock length, no variants of the M 1860 have been reported.

Appearance, distinctive features and data

The M 1860 is a typical Dreyse breech-loader, with an overly long bolt mechanism, a bolt handle that locks at an upward angle of about 65° and a receiver split longitudinally for the movement of the bolt handle. Its stock design is most distinctive, however, as the barrel bands so characteristic of the older Zündnadelgewehre have been replaced by a transverse key through the stock above and slightly in front of the ramrod tailpipe. The furniture is cast from brass, including the ramrod pipes (fore and tail), the nose-cap, the trigger guard bow and the large washer through which the action retaining screw runs. A T-lug on the right side of the barrel permits the sword bayonet to be attached, its crossguard ring slipping around the muzzle to give extra support.

There are two large sling swivels, one anchored through the fore-stock mid-way between the nose-cap and the barrel retaining key (or wedge), and the other through the front portion of the trigger guard bow. The straight one-piece walnut stock, which lacks a cheek-piece, has distinctive 'flats' alongside the bolt unit—found on all German needle rifles—and a cast iron butt plate.

(Note: rifles altered in accordance with the Beck Transformation can be recognized by the prominent screw-head on the bolt unit, ahead of the operating handle. They also have a revised back sight of a wholly different design.)

DATA
Calibre: 15.43 ±0.13mm.
Rifling: concentric, 4 grooves 0.78mm deep and 6mm wide; 1 turn in 732mm, right hand (pitch of 3° 47').
Magazine capacity: none—single-shot only.
Loading system: manual insertion of a cartridge in the chamber.
Length overall: 1,300mm.
Barrel length: 785mm.
Weight: 4,725gm without sling.
Sights: (front) unprotected barleycorn; (back) a combination block and two-leaf pattern with a standing block 'battle sight' for 350 paces, a small leaf for 450 and a large leaf for 800 paces.
Performance: see cartridge data (Appendix 2).

Accessories

BAYONET
The M 1860 was issued with the distinctive brass-hilted Füsilier-Seitengewehr M 1860 (TGB, pp. 22-24), which had a 51cm straight swell-point blade.

OTHERS
Much the same as the Zündnadelbüchse M 1854 (qv).

Zündnadelgewehr Modell 1862 Infantry rifle

With the successful development and introduction of the 1860-pattern fusilier rifle, the Prussian Army was encouraged to develop an improved version of the M 1841 infantry rifle, made to finer tolerances and of better steels. The result was the Infanterie-Gewehr M 1862, widely known as the Zündnadelgewehr M 1862, which was adopted by an AKO of 28 July 1862. It was distinguished by its better finish, slightly smaller size and the absence of a cheek-piece on the butt; its sights were improved, although they remained of much the same pattern as those fitted to the perfected M 1841.

The new rifle was intended as a replacement for the M 1841, but production seems to have been slow (the factories may have been occupied with other projects[1]) and only a handful of infantry regiments had re-equipped by the beginning of the Austro-Prussian War in mid-1866. None of them took part in the fighting, according to von Menges[2] who records that all committed infantrymen carried the M 1841.

1. These included series production of the 1860-type fusilier rifle, as well as the development of new Jäger and pioneer weapons. A large-calibre Dreyse system wall-gun also appeared.

2. W. von Menges, *Die Bewaffnung der Preussischen Fusstruppen*, p. 74.

By the outbreak of the Franco-Prussian War, and general mobilization on 15 July 1870, there were about 435,000 M 1862 rifles on the army inventory, compared with nearly 450,000 of the older 1841 model. Consequently, only the Prussian guard infantrymen, the infantry regiments numbered between 1 and 32, and detachments from Baden, Hessen and Saxony were issued with the newer Dreyse needle-guns. The remaining infantry units, together with the bulk of the Landwehr, had the M 1841.

The M 1862 infantry rifle was the first of the needle-rifles to be submitted to the Beck Transformation (qv) in quantity, sufficient to arm three regiments during the Franco-Prussian War[3]. Many more guns were modified after peace had been concluded, but their service lives were short owing to the adoption of the Mauser bolt-action metallic cartridge breech-loader in 1872. Numerous M 1862 rifles were discarded by the infantry and subsequently re-issued to the foot artillery[4]; the remaining infantry rifles were all withdrawn by the mid-1870s.

3. 4.Garde-Regiment zu Fuss, and Infanterie-Regimenter 71 and 94.

4. By decrees of 21 December 1871 and 25 January 1872.

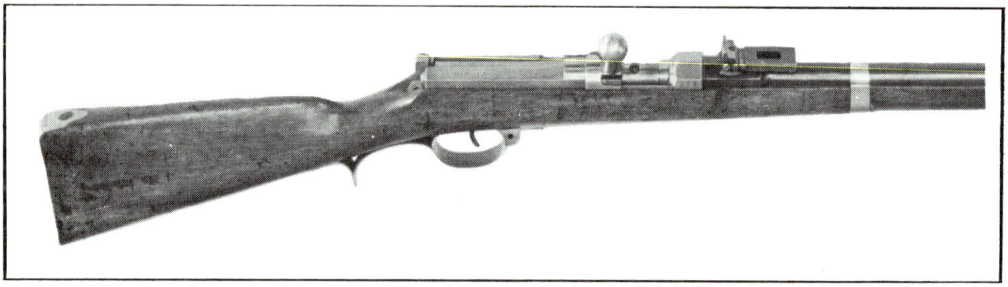

Right: the butt and breech of a Beck-transformed M 1862 infantry rifle, number 9356, made at Spandau in 1871 but not, apparently, issued until 1873. RSAF collection, photograph by Fred Alderslade.

Production history

M 1862 needle-rifles were made in large numbers in Dreyse's workshops in Sömmerda and the Prussian arsenals in Danzig and Spandau. By the Franco-Prussian War nearly half a million had been made, since 434,567 were on the inventory in July 1870[5]. Many were subsequently converted by the addition of Beck's bolt head, but most guns were passed to the Landwehr in the late 1870s and had been discarded by 1880.

5. In addition, 174,910 Dreyse-system infantry rifles (most of which are assumed to have been of the 1862 model rather than the obsolete M 1841) were made during the war period.

Markings

Rifles made by Dreyse usually bear his trademark—*Soemmerda ND* in script—on the left rear side of the receiver. The government-made examples, however, have an elaborate spread eagle stamped above 'SPANDAU' or 'DANZIG', which in turn lies above the designation 'Z.G.MOD.62' in fraktur (gothic script). Gun 9356, made in Spandau in 1871, has two dates ('1871-1873') on the right side of the receiver behind the reinforced bridge; the first is believed to be the date of manufacture, the latter, the date of issue. (Since the gun has been converted to the Beck system, the second date may be that of re-issue.)

The serial numbers may be found on the left side of the receiver alongside the chamber, on the left side of the barrel in front of the breech, on the left side of the cocking-piece head and on the base of the bolt handle. The last two or three digits, 56 or 356, are repeated on most of the removable parts and screws, while small crowned-letter inspectors' marks are also liberally scattered over the weapon: whole strings of them are visible on the right side of the barrel and the receiver alongside the breech. The monarch's cypher (a crown over FW) may be encountered on the right side of the butt, together with one or two large inspectors' marks. M62 rifles, like some M60, existed in two butt lengths—long and short—and the letters *L.A.* or *K.A.* may be found on the butt side as well.

Unit markings may be found on the top surface of

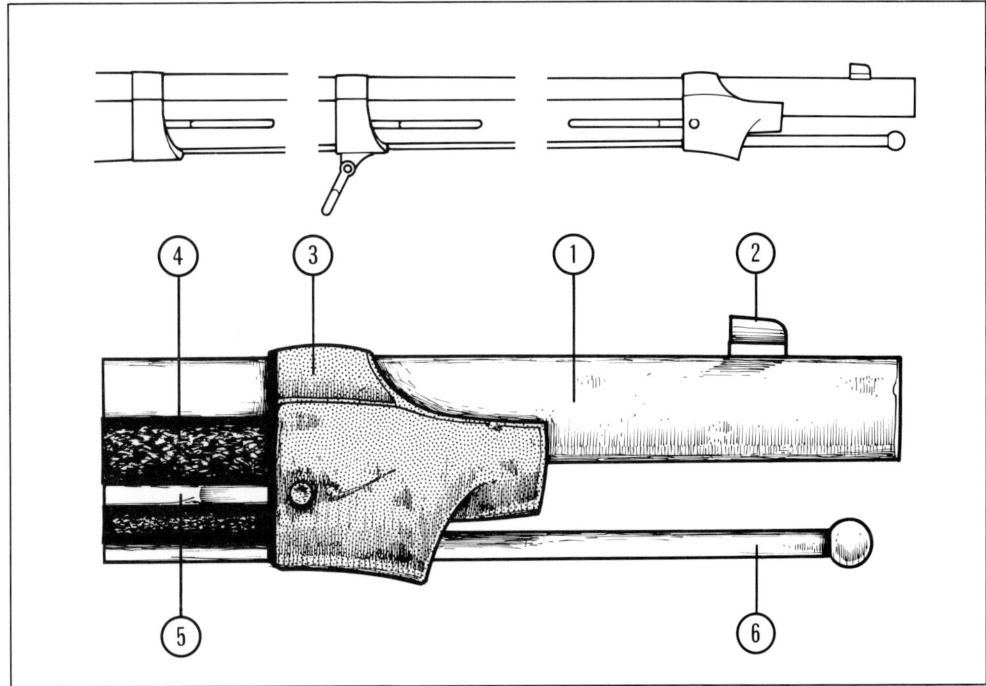

Right: the muzzle and nosecap of the M 1862 infantry rifle, together with some of the fittings. Key: 1, barrel; 2, front sight; 3, nosecap; 4, stock; 5, nosecap spring; and 6, ramrod.

the butt plate, although they are absent from rifle 9356. Large numbers of M 1862 rifles may be found with marks applied by the foot artillery, to whom many were re-issued in 1872-73. The key letters are usually A.F.

Mechanical description and variations

Despite rather better standards of manufacturer, to finer tolerances and of better materials, the M 1862 Dreyse needle-rifle operated in exactly the same way as the M 1841 (qv). Its construction also paralleled that of its predecessor. No variations have yet been noted, apart from the weapons altered by Beck's Transformation in 1869-73.

Appearance, distinctive features and data

The M 1862 greatly resembles the M 1841, being a long and clumsy bolt-action weapon with a very long mechanism—much too long for the relatively short Dreyse cartridge. However, it is slightly shorter, is better made, lacks the cheek-piece on the left side of the butt and has barrel bands of an improved design.

The browned barrel is cylindrical for the greater part of its length, the exception being the short octagonal section at the breech. This serves as a base for the combined block and leaf back sight. The three brass barrel fixtures, two spring-retained bands and the nose-cap, differ from those of the M 1841: the band springs run forwards rather than back, and the clumsy 1841-pattern nose-cap was replaced by a lightened design. A cleaning rod was still carried beneath the barrel. One sling swivel appears underneath the intermediate barrel band, while the other lies on the cast brass trigger guard. The one-piece walnut stock has prominent 'flats' alongside the bolt mechanism and a cast iron butt plate of conventional form.

DATA

Calibre: 15.43 ± 0.13mm.
Rifling: concentric, 4 grooves 0.78mm deep and 6mm wide; 1 turn in 732mm, right hand (pitch of 3° 47').
Magazine capacity: none—single-shot only.
Loading system: manual insertion of cartridge in chamber.
Length overall: 1,360mm (depending on butt length, 1,340mm with (K.A. type).
Barrel length: 841mm.
Weight: about 4,750gm without sling.
Sights: (front) unprotected barleycorn; (back) a combined block and two-leaf sight with a standing 'battle sight' for 350 paces, a small leaf for 450, and a large leaf for 600/700 paces.
Performance: see cartridge data (Appendix 2).

Accessories

BAYONET

The M 1862 infantry rifle was issued with the M 1862 socket bayonet, the last of its type to be introduced in the Prussian army (TGB, pp. 32-33). It had a conventional locking ring, a Z-slot and a triangular-section blade measuring 49.5cm. The bayonet, like the rifle barrel, was browned.

OTHERS

The same as those for the Zündnadelbüchse M 1854 (qv) and the Füsilier-Gewehr M 1860.

Zündnadelbüchse Modell 1865 Jägerbüchse

The introduction of the improved M 1860 fusilier and M 1862 infantry rifles caused the Prussian military authorities to develop a new weapon for the élite Jäger units (riflemen), who were making do with the obsolescent M 1854 Pikenbüchse and its crude rod bayonet. Issues of an experimental derivative of the fusilier rifle, which is sometimes called the 'Zündnadelbüchse M 1863', were made to Jäger-Bataillon Nr. 5 and Jäger-Bataillon Nr. 6 in 1865; and as a result of the successful trials, the perfected Zündnadelbüchse M 1865 was adopted for all the Jäger units on 16 March 1866. Only the two original 'trials battalions' had been issued with M 1865 rifles by the beginning of the Austro-Prussian War in June 1866, although all twelve, including one Saxon formation, had been re-equipped by 1870.

As M 1865 rifles were issued, supplies of the earlier M 1854 were converted to Zündnadel-Pioniergewehre u/M (qv) or given to the Prussian navy. The new Jäger rifles, which could be quickly recognized by their double-trigger mechanism, served until the issue of new Mauser rifles in 1875-76[1].

By 1868, the Prussians had realized that their Dreyse rifles were inferior to the new French Chassepot; this had become evident from campaigns undertaken by the French in northern Italy[2]. Experiments were undertaken to improve the Dreyse system (Dreyse himself having died in 1867), and resulted in the Beck Transformation (qv) being added to most needle-guns after the conclusion of the Franco-Prussian War. Very few examples of the M 1865 seem to have been converted before 1870, although most of the survivors were so treated in 1871-72. Their service life was short, however, since they were soon replaced by the Mausers and passed on to the Landwehr, where some were supposedly altered to use the French Mle 66 sabre bayonets captured during the war[3].

1. It has yet to be ascertained whether the Jäger received standard infantry rifles before the true Jägerbüchsen M 1871 were distributed early in 1876.

2. The commander of the French forces in Italy, Général de Failly, rather stupidly sent a telegraph message praising the new rifles, which were still more or less secret!

3. This became necessary as most of the M 1865 sword bayonets were bushed and retained for the Mausers. However, the use of the French bayonets has not been conclusively authenticated.

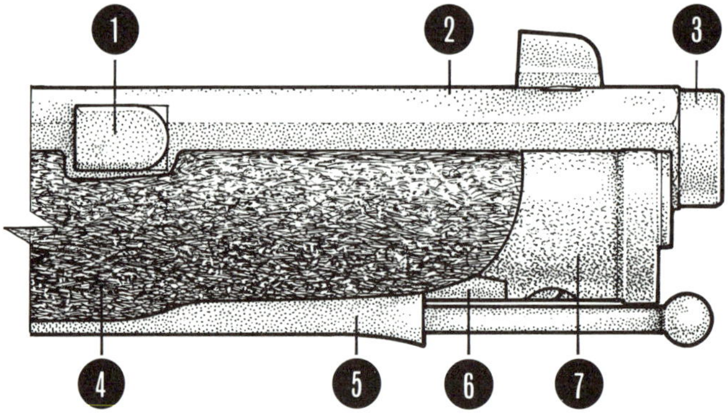

Muzzle and nosecap
Büchse M 1865

Right: the muzzle and nosecap of the M 1865 Jägerbüchse. Key: 1, bayonet lug; 2, barrel; 3, turned-down muzzle crown (for bayonet's muzzle ring); 4, stock; 5, ramrod; 6, nosecap extension (iron); and 7, nosecap (brass).

With its special trigger, the M 1865 was the zenith of Dreyse needle-gun design, especially when fitted with the Beck alterations. But its standard of design and construction were still notably inferior to the Chassepot. Even a cursory inspection of an example of the M 1865 gives the impression that it is much older than the French weapon, and that the French government arsenals were benefitting more from the Industrial Revolution than was Dreyse's provincial workshop. Although this may have been true of the pre-1870 German arms industry, it was soon to change.

Backsight and range settings **Büchse M 1865**

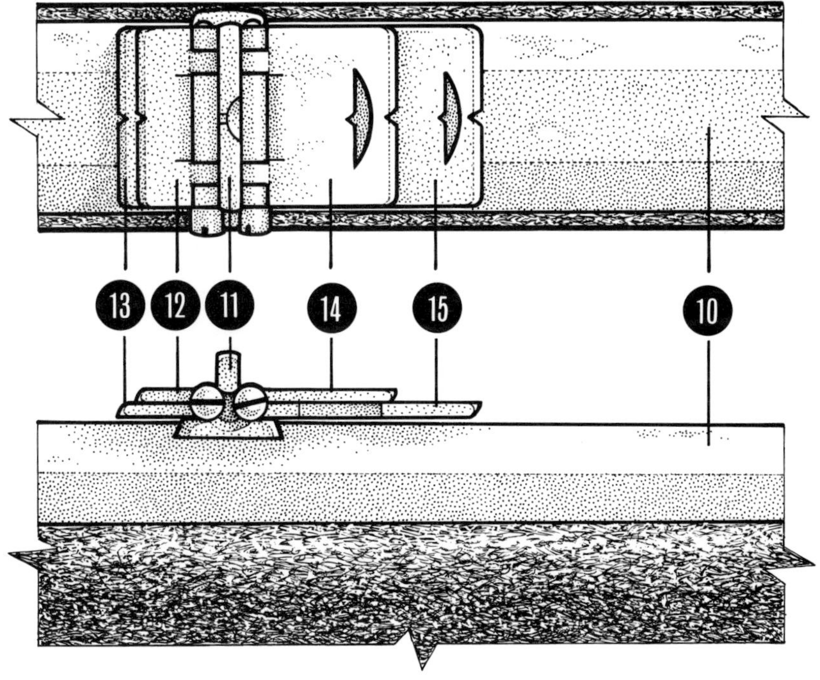

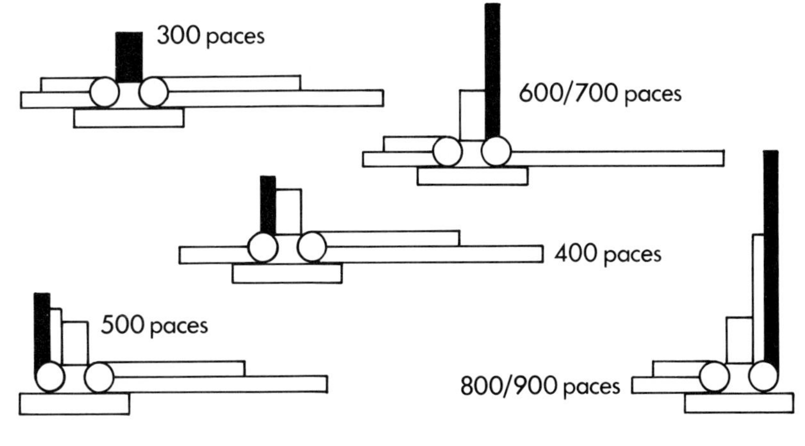

Right: the M 1865 backsight and its settings. Key: 10, barrel; 11, standing block for 300 paces; 12, leaf for 400 paces; 13, leaf for 500; 14 leaf for 600 and 700; 15, leaf for 800 and 900.

Production history

Most M 1865 rifles were made by Dreyse in Sömmerda and the Prussian government arsenal at Spandau between 1865/6 and 1872; 29,896 were on the Prussian Army inventory in July 1870. At least ten thousand of the survivors were converted by Beck's Transformation after the Franco-Prussian War had ended.

Markings

Made by Dreyse, the guns bear his maker's mark (*Soemmerda ND* in script) on the left rear of the receiver, directly above the designation 'ZB MOD.65' in fraktur (gothic script). Rifle 7660 is dated '1868-1869' on the right side of the receiver behind the reinforced bridge, showing that it was made in 1868 and issued a year later. There are proof eagles on the barrel and the receiver, and the serial number, '7660', is stamped into the left side of the barrel and receiver alongside the chamber, on the base of the bolt handle and on the left side of the cocking piece. The last two digits are repeated on many of the individual parts, while the usual collection of inspectors' crowned-letter marks are to be found on the right side of the barrel and receiver at the breech, and on each removable part or screw.

Most guns were issued to the Prussian Jäger-Bataillone and are consequently found with the crowned FW monarch's cypher on the right side of the butt, together with inspectors' letters. Rifle 7660, however, bears a Saxon unit marking and has no such impressions on the butt side. The top surface of the butt plate may display one or more unit marks, 7660's being stamped 'S.II.J.B.1.228.': the 228th rifle issued to the first company of Königlich Sächsisches Jäger-Bataillon Nr.2.

Mechanical description and variations

The M 1865 has a typical 'short' Dreyse bolt-action, much the same as that of the old M 1841 and sharing its basic operation (qv). The only major mechanical difference concerns the double or 'set' trigger, which gives a much lighter pull and, therefore, better accuracy. The M 1865 has two trigger levers protruding down into the trigger guard bow, one of which forms an intermediate sear release lever; and there are also two trigger springs, as well as a special arched lever fixed to the spring-bar that acts as the sear. The back trigger, which is the normal one, can be used to fire the gun with a heavy and somewhat creepy trigger-pull characteristic of military weapons; however, the front, or hair-trigger can be adjusted until the pull-weight is virtually nil. This gives much finer accuracy, since aim is not disturbed by the pressure required on the regular trigger.

Appearance, distinctive features and data

The M 1865 Jäger Dreyse cannot be confused with any other Prussian needle-rifle, as it has several very distinctive features. Its mechanism is quite standard, however; although the bolt unit is shorter than those of the M 1860 and M 1862, it shares the oblique-locking bolt handle and the longitudinally-split receiver. But the barrel is octagonal for its entire

Zündnadelbüchse M 1865

Büchse M 65

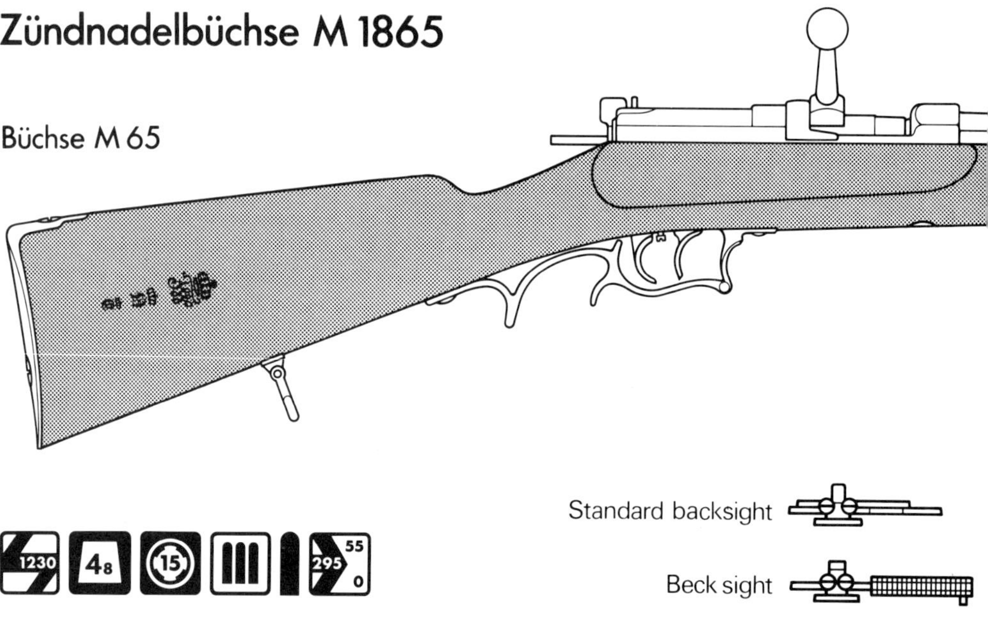

length—apart from a tiny cylindrical portion at the muzzle for the bayonet attachment ring—and is held to the stock by a transverse screw and a transverse key. The former lies immediately above and in front of the ramrod tailpipe, while the latter is placed above and behind the forepipe. The nose-cap is largely made of brass, though there is a small steel section at the rear.

The straight-grip one-piece walnut stock, plain and starkly proportioned, does not have a cheek-piece on the left side of the butt. The butt plate is made of cast iron. The cast ·brass trigger guard bow is a spectacularly ugly double-spurred finger-rest pattern influenced greatly by contemporary German sporting rifle design, and mercifully absent from the other Zündnadelgewehre. Nonetheless, it provides an excellent identification feature as it contains two trigger levers; the front lever is a 'set' trigger.

(Note: guns altered in accordance with the Beck Transformation can be recognized by the prominent screw-head on the bolt unit, ahead of the operating handle. They also have a revised back sight of wholly different design.)

DATA

Calibre: 15.43 ± 0.13mm.
Rifling: concentric, 4 grooves 0.78mm deep and 6mm wide; 1 turn in 732mm, right hand (pitch of 3° 47').
Magazine capacity: none—single-shot.
Loading system: manual insertion of a cartridge in the chamber.
Length overall: 1,230mm.
Barrel length: 768mm.
Weight: 4,375gm without sling.
Sights: (front) unprotected barleycorn; (back) a combination block and four-leaf pattern with a standing 'battle sight' for 300 paces, and leaves for 400, 500, 600/700 and 800/900 paces.
Performance: see cartridge data (Appendix 2).

Accessories

BAYONETS

The Zündnadelbüchse M 1865 was originally isssued with the Hirschfänger M 1865 (TGB, pp. 25-27), which had chequered leather grips, a steel pommel and crossguard, and a 50cm straight swell-point blade of very individualistic style. But many of these bayonets were retained for the Mauser rifles introduced in 1872-73, which meant that there was a shortage of bayonets when the M 1865 rifles were handed over to the Landwehr; the problem was solved by modifying supposedly ex-French Mle 66 (Chassepot) sabre bayonets (TGB, p. 43). The only alteration to the rifle comprised the cutting of a notch in the bayonet stud, since the French and German locking mechanisms differed slightly. However, this still lacks proper authentication and should be treated with caution.

OTHERS

The same as those issued with the Zündnadelbüchse M 1854 (qv), and the rifles of 1860 and 1862.

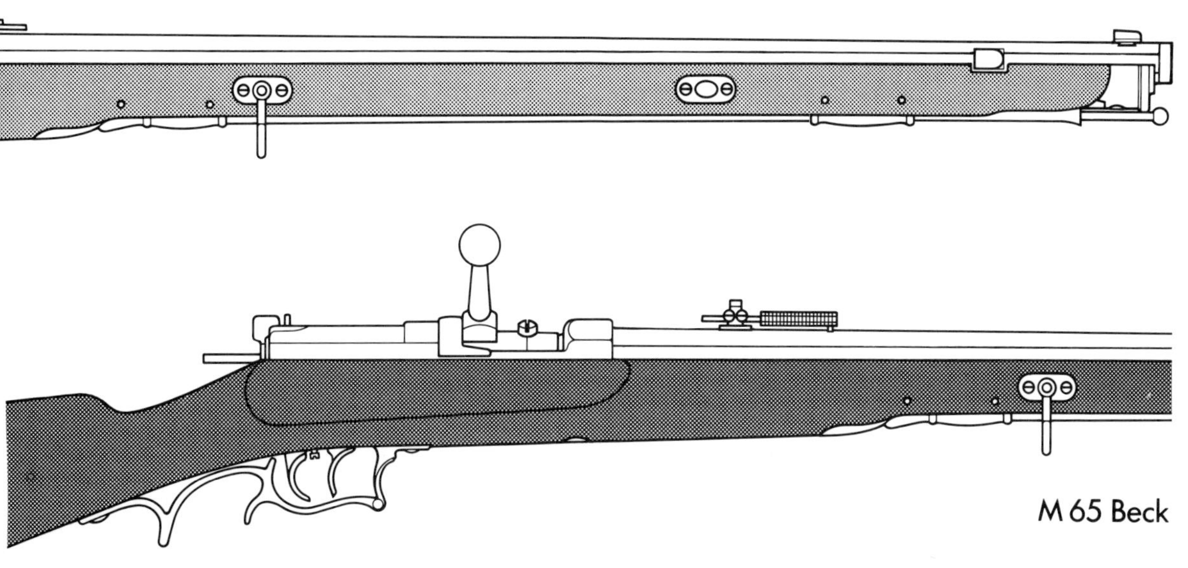

M 65 Beck

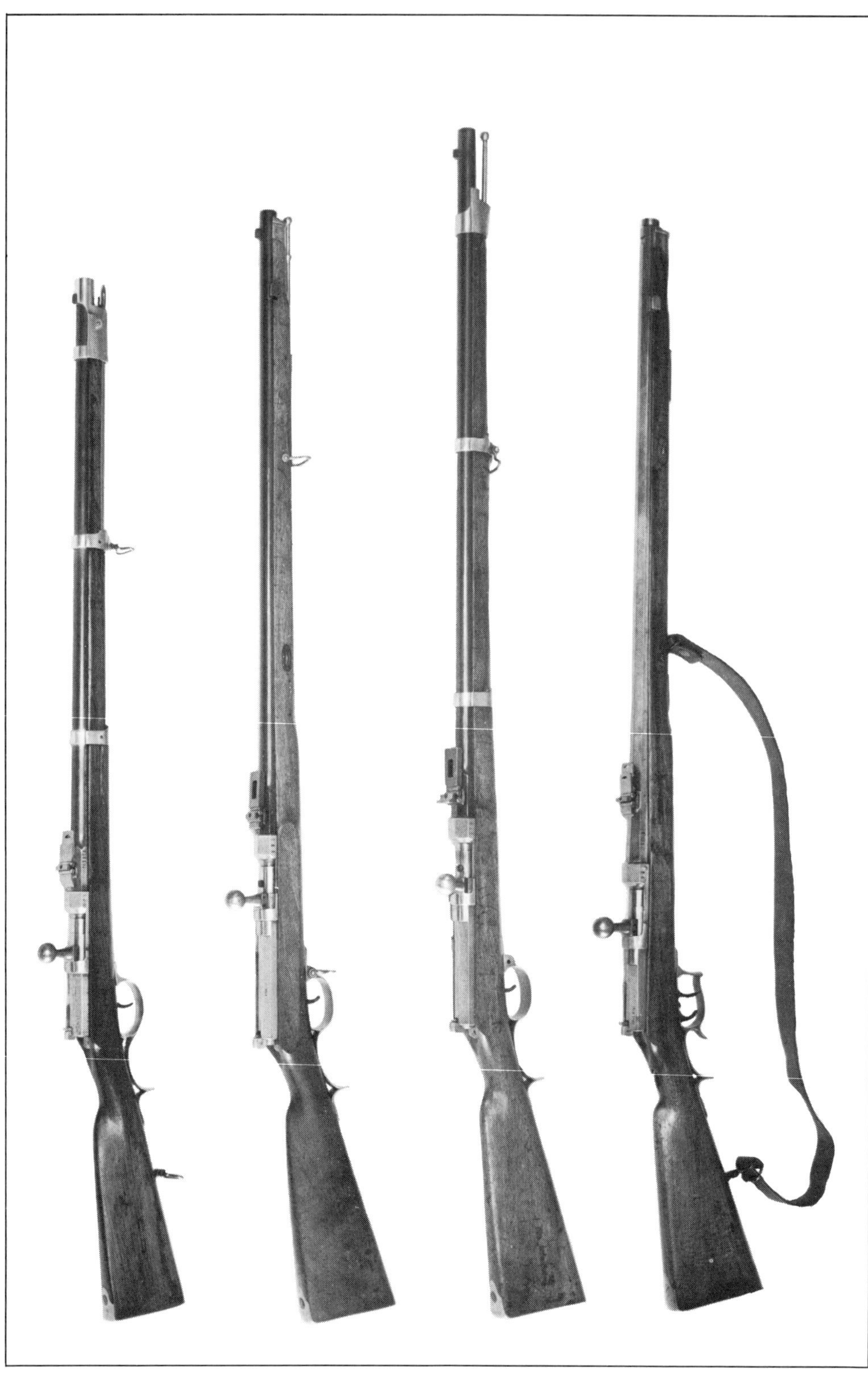

Right: four principal Dreyse-system weapons—(left to right) the M 1854 Pikenbüchse, the M 1860 fusilier rifle, the M 1862 infantry rifle and the M 1865 Jägerbüchse.

Zündnadelgewehr u/M Pioneer rifle

This weapon, which was adopted by an AKO of 16 November 1865, was converted from supplies of the obsolescent Zündnadelbüchse M 1854, of which several thousands had been discarded by Jäger-Bataillon Nr. 5 and Jäger-Bataillon Nr. 6 when they re-armed with the then-experimental Zündnadelbüchse M 1865 (qv). The discarded Jägerbüchsen were converted by removing the rod bayonet assembly, the barrel bands, 14cm of the barrel and the old back sight. The old stock was refurbished and fitted with a new brass nose-cap similar to that of the Füsilier-Gewehr M 1860 and the channel in the fore-end, which had previously housed the bayonet, was filled with a thin sliver of wood. In addition, a bayonet lug was brazed to the right side of the muzzle to take the heavy Pionierfaschinenmesser M 1865, which had been developed at the same time.

The results were issued to the pioneer battalions[1], first to supplement and then replace a converted muzzle-loader called the Gezogenes Pioniergewehr a/M[2]. The pioneers had no pressing need of Dreyse-system breech-loaders, but had nevertheless waited an inordinately long time: it had been twenty-five years since the introduction of the M 1841 infantry needle-rifle. The new u/M rifles, which were little more than carbine length, first saw action in the Austro-Prussian War of 1866 in the hands of the Garde-Pionier-Bataillon. They were officially known simply as 'Zündnadel-Pioniergewehre' until an Armee-Verordnungsblatt of 25 January 1869[3], when they were renamed 'umgeändertes Modell' (converted model) to distinguish them from the newly-made M 1869 pioneer weapon (qv). There were other features differentiating between the u/M and M 1869 pioneer rifles, and these differences are described later in the section.

1. Which had been formed from existing pioneer detachments in 1860.

2. This rifle had been an ex-French flintlock musket, a relic of the wars of 1813-15, which had been converted to percussion ignition in 1850 and rifled in 1857. It fired Minié expanding-ball ammunition.

3. The date on which the M 1869 was introduced.

Production history

Exactly how many M 1854 rifles were converted to Pioniergewehre u/M by the Prussian government workshops is not clear, but the total probably did not greatly exceed twelve thousand. It has proved extremely difficult to differentiate between stocks of the u/M and the later M 1869, but there were 12,449 u/M guns on hand in June 1870.

Markings

The Pioniergewehr u/M bears the marks applied when it was an unaltered Zündnadelbüchse M 1854 (qv), which, as the designation on the left rear of the receiver reads 'MOD. 54' in fraktur (gothic script), is something of a give away. The guns may also bear unit markings applied by the pioneer battalions, which inevitably include the letter 'P', in addition to those of the original Jäger formations, which always include 'J'.

Mechanical description and variations

The u/M makes use of a standard Dreyse action, with a cone-pattern obturation system rather than the unsuccessful seat type. The action (see M 1854) differs little from that of the later Pioniergewehr M 1869, although there are some notable detail differences in the design of the receiver immediately behind the bolt handle. The design of the reinforce on which the bolt-handle base abuts, and of the longitudinal slot in which the bolt handle moves, was modified. No variations are known.

Appearance, distinctive features and data

The u/M looks like virtually all the other Dreyse needle-guns so far as its bolt mechanism is concerned, but, apart from the two cavalry carbines, is the shortest of the entire series. It has a plain fore-end—the original barrel bands having been replaced by a transverse barrel retaining screw, which, running through special screw-anchored steel washers, also retains the sling swivel. A bayonet lug has been brazed to the right side of the muzzle and a new brass nose-cap has replaced the old M 1854 rod bayonet assembly. There is no cleaning rod, and the bayonet channel in the underside of the fore-end has been filled with a special wooden insert[4].

The second sling swivel lies on the underside of the butt, a short distance behind the rearward finger-rest extension of the cast brass trigger-guard bow. The one-piece walnut stock, unlike that of the M 1869, has a cheek-piece on the left side of the butt. A new simplified single-leaf back sight has replaced the original four-leaf M 1854 pattern: fitted to the octagonal section of the barrel just in front of the breech, its bed looks too wide for the gun.

The Pioniergewehr u/M is generally about 200gm lighter than the M 1869, which has a different stocking arrangement and is also provided with a cleaning rod.

4. Some altered guns, however, were re-stocked and have a solid fore-end.

DATA

Calibre: 15.43 ± 0.13mm.
Rifling: concentric, 4 grooves 0.78mm deep and 6mm wide; 1 turn in 732mm (pitch of 3° 47').
Magazine: none—single-shot only.
Loading system: manual insertion of cartridge in chamber.
Length overall: 1,100mm.
Barrel length: 675mm.
Weight: about 3,700gm without sling.
Sights: (front) unprotected barleycorn; (back) a combined block and leaf sight, with a standing 'battle sight' for 200 paces and a single leaf for 300.
Performance: see cartridge data (Appendix 2).

Accessories

BAYONET
The pioneer rifles, u/M or M 1869, were issued with the extremely unwieldy Pionierfaschinenmesser M 1869 (TGB, pp. 27-29), whose heavy saw-backed blade was 48.5cm long and 3.7cm broad.

OTHERS
A sling, a back sight cover, a special iron muzzle protector, a special 'piling hook', two spare needles and equipment for cleaning the bolt expansion chamber.

Far right: the distinctive nosecap of the u/M pioneer rifle.

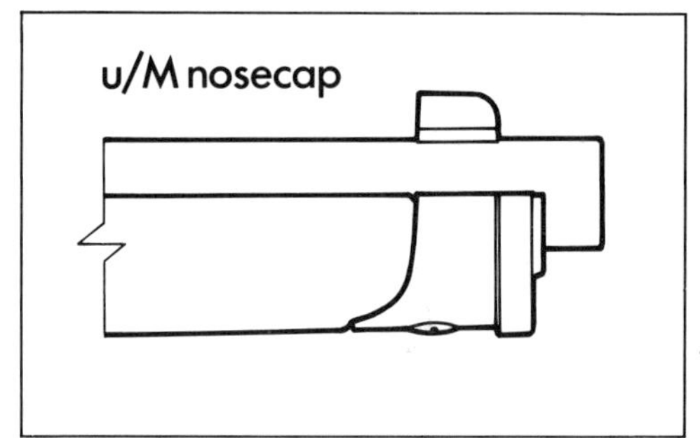

Dreyse rifles and carbines: an identification guide

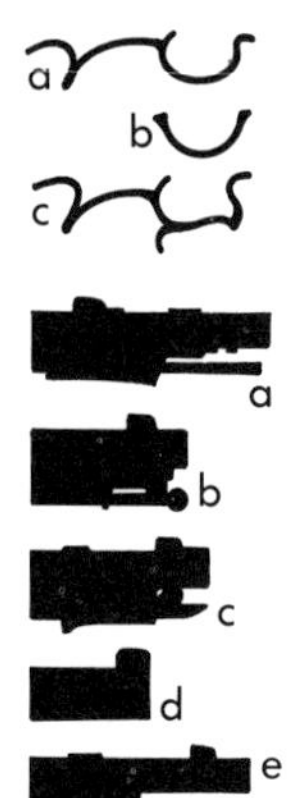

		M1841	M1849	M1854	M1855, M1857	M1860	M1862	M1865	u/M	M1869, M1869 Beck	M1860 Beck	M1862 Beck	M1865 Beck
ACTION LENGTH	cm	**23**	**15**	**17**	**14**	**23**	**23**	**19**	**17**	**17**	**23**	**23**	**19**
NOSECAP		a	b	c	d	b	e	b	b	b	b	e	b
TRIGGER GUARD		a	a	a	b	a	a	c	a	a	a	a	c
BARREL AND STOCK FIXTURES	bands	**2**		**2**			**2**					**2**	
	keys, transverse screws		**2**			**2**		**2**	**1**	**1**	**2**		**2**
SLING POINTS	butt edge		●	●	●			●	●	●			●
	trigger guard	●				●	●				●	●	
	barrel band	●		●			●					●	
	fore-end		●			●		●	●	●	●		●
SIGHT LEAVES		**2**	**4**	**4**	**1**	**2**	**2**	**4**	**1**	**1**	**2**	**2**	**2**
RAMROD		●	●			●	●	●		●	●	●	●
BAYONET	socket	●					●					●	
	rod			●									
	sword		●			●		●	●	●	●		●
	none				●								

Zündnadelgewehr Modell 1869 Pioneer rifle

In most respects, this gun, introduced on 25 January 1869 was little more than a version of the Zündnadel-Pioniergewehr u/M (qv). The two differed only in minor details; the M 1869 had a cleaning rod, where the u/M did not, and there were minor deviations in the machining of the two receivers.

Only a few thousand M 1869 pioneer rifles had been made by 15 July 1870, when the Prussian armies were mobilized to meet the French. The Garde-Pionier-Bataillon and all regular units—eleven Prussian and one Saxon (Nr. 12, continuing the Prussian sequence)—were equipped with Dreyse needle-rifles during the fighting, but it is uncertain which of the units had u/M rifles and which the M 1869. It seems likely that the former predominated, since thirteen pioneer units would have required substantially more than the two thousand pioneer rifles Lehmann[1] credits with being on the inventory in July 1870.

1. Gustav Lehmann, *Die Mobilmachung von 1870/71*, Anlage 8, p. 235.

Production of M 1869 rifles continued after the Franco-Prussian War, a few being converted—or newly-made—to Beck's improved bolt system, which had been officially adopted early in 1870. They lasted in the hands of the pioneer troops until replaced by the metallic-cartridge firing Mausers in the late 1870s.

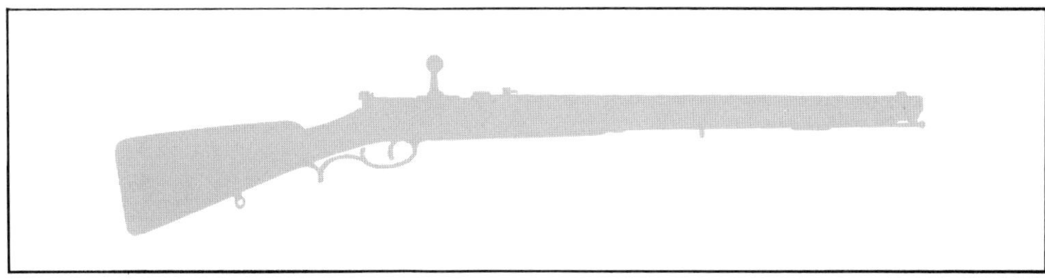

Right: the M 1869 pioneer rifle, which was really of carbine length.

Production history
The M 1869 Zündnadel-Pioniergewehr seems to have been made exclusively by the Prussian government arsenal in Spandau. The exact quantity made in the period 1869-72 remains unknown, but probably exceeded ten thousand; rifle 6076 dates from 1871, indicating that production considerably exceeded the 2,202 guns Lehmann claimed to have been on the Prussian inventory in mid-1870. M 1869 specimens with serial numbers in the 9000s have been reported but, as yet, are not authenticated. An unknown number of pioneer rifles may have been converted (or newly-made) for Beck's bolt head, which was adopted on 10 March 1870—although 6076, despite being made in 1871, has a standard bolt.

Markings
The marks on the Pioniergewehr M 1869 follow those of the other Dreyse rifles. The stampings on the left rear of the receiver include a spread or displayed eagle above the name of the manufacturing arsenal—usually 'SPANDAU'—which, in turn, appears above the designation 'Z.P.G.M69.' in fraktur (gothic script). Most guns bear the mark 'STAHL' across the 'flat' of the barrel immediately in front of the receiver, behind the back sight, showing that the barrel was made of steel rather than wrought iron. The monarch's cypher, a crown over FW before 1871 or W thereafter[2], is usually found on the left side of the barrel below the back sight and the date of manufacture ('1871' on rifle 6076) on the right rear side of the receiver.

2. Since the Prussians seem to have used the FW cypher as late as the mid and late 1880s, guns with a W cypher may have been used in Württemberg.

There are usually proof eagles ('Beschussadler neuer Art') on the barrel and receiver, and the full serial number on the left side of the barrel and receiver at the breech, and also on the bolt-handle base. Parts of the serial numbers, two or three digits, and crowned gothic letter inspectors' marks may be found on most of the parts.

A cypher and two large inspectors' marks may be found on the right side of the butt, while pioneer battalion marks may be stamped into the top surface of the butt plate.

Mechanical description and variations
The Zündnadel-Pioniergewehr M 1869 is a typical Dreyse breech-loader, sharing most of the characteristics of the other guns in the series. It has a short action similar to that of the u/M pioneer rifle, except that there are noticeable differences in the machining on the top of the receiver. The mechanism makes use of the standard cone-type obturation system. Apart from rifles fitted with Beck's improved bolt head, no mechanical variations of the M 1869 have yet been recorded.

Appearance, distinctive features and data
The M 1869 greatly resembles the u/M pioneer rifle, adopted four years earlier (qv). It has a plain fore-end, the barrel being retained by a transverse barrel-retaining screw which runs through special screw anchored steel washers and also holds the front sling swivel. A bayonet lug appears on the right side of the muzzle, behind the brass nose-cap. A conventional

cleaning rod is carried under the fore-end in two cast brass pipes, which is one easy way of distinguishing the M 1869 from the u/M—as the latter has no rod. The second sling swivel lies on the underside of the butt, a short distance behind the rearward finger-rest extension of the cast brass trigger-guard bow. The one-piece walnut stock lacks the cheek-piece found on the left side of u/M butts, although the guns share the other fittings apart from the cleaning rod. A simplified single-leaf back sight may be found on the short octagonal section of the barrel, which is otherwise a slightly tapering cylinder, immediately in front of the breech.

The M 1869 generally weighs about 200gm more than the converted u/M, because of the slightly different stock and the provision of the rod.

DATA

Calibre: 15.43 ± 0.13mm.
Rifling: concentric, 4 grooves 0.78mm deep and 6mm wide; 1 turn in 732mm (pitch of 3° 47').
Magazine: none—single-shot only.
Loading system: manual insertion of cartridge in chamber.
Length overall: 1,105mm.
Barrel length: 675mm.
Weight: about 3,875-3,900gm without sling.
Sights: (front) unprotected barleycorn; (back) a combined block and leaf sight, with a standing 'battle sight' for 200 paces and a single leaf for 300.
Performance: see cartridge data (Appendix 2).

Accessories

BAYONET

The pioneer rifles, regardless of pattern, were issued with the large and heavy Pionierfaschinenmesser M 1869 (TGB, pp. 27-29), whose saw-backed blade was 48.5cm long and 3.7cm broad. The crossguard was of wrought iron or steel, while the hilt was a one-piece brass casting.

OTHERS

The same as those of the Pioniergewehr u/M (qv).

Right: Dreyse rifles altered in accordance with the Beck Transformation can be identified by their sights and bolt-head design.

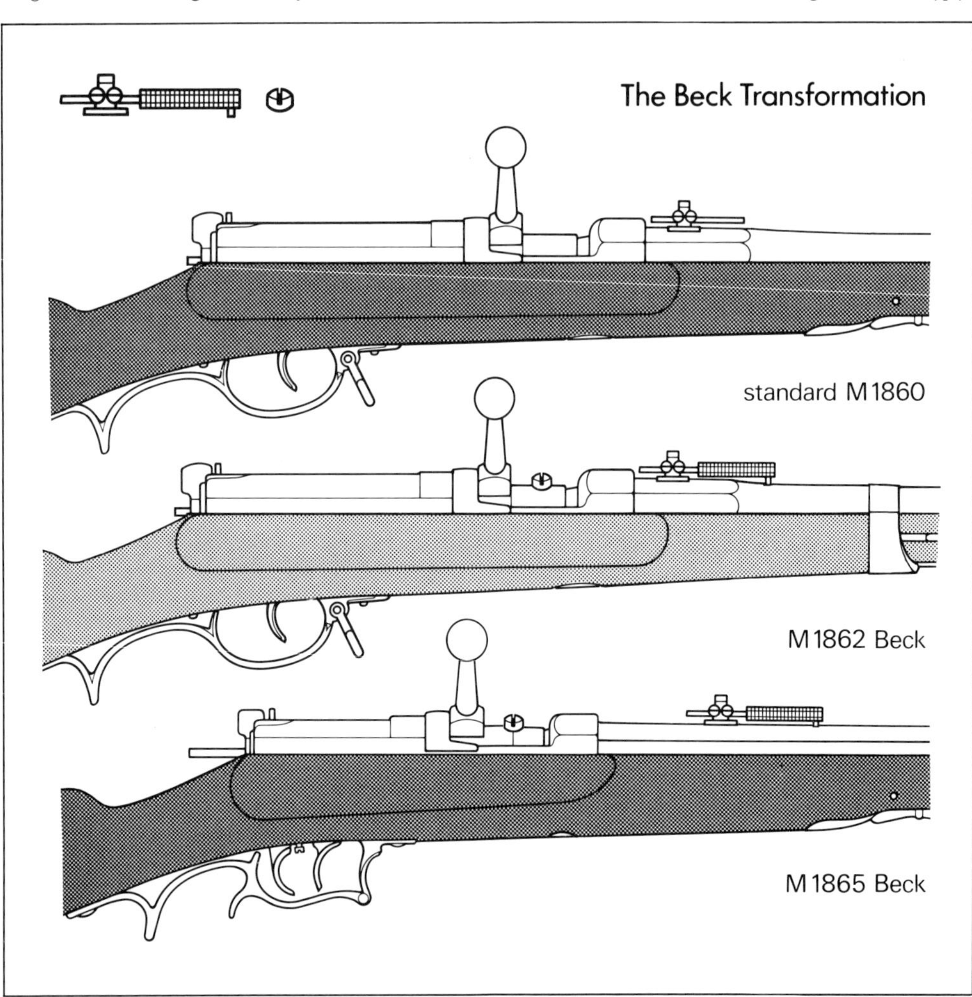

The Beck Transformation

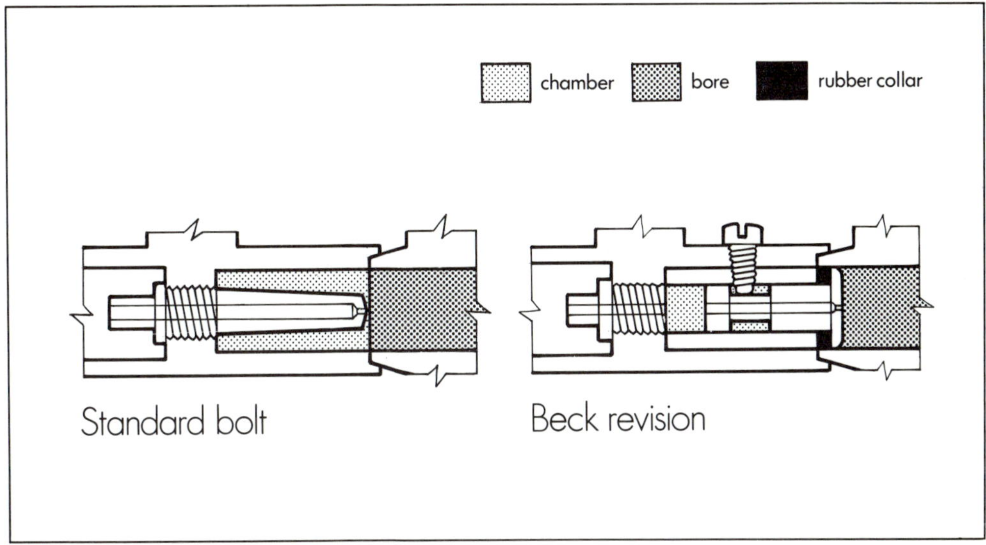

Right: constructional details of the Beck-system bolt-head. Note the annular indiarubber 'expansion collar', the design of which was virtually copied from the Chassepot.

The success of the French Chassepot needle-rifle showed the Prussians that the basic Dreyse action needed improving. The most important difference between the rival needle-guns lay in their ballistics, since the Dreyse bullet, the heavier of the two, attained a muzzle velocity of only 295m/sec compared to about 435m/sec for the French Mle 1866. The German bullets, consequently, had a high and looping trajectory which placed the troops at a distinct disadvantage, as they could ill-afford to make excessive range-gauging errors. It was also a fact that the accuracy of Dreyse's oddly-shaped oviform projectile was considerably impaired by it being of markedly less diameter than the bore. The sabot in which the bullet was seated engraved the rifling, instead of the bullet itself. The French design fired a paper-patched bullet that engaged directly in the rifling and, as a result, gave better accuracy and increased range.

The Prussians decided to seek a short-term means of improving the Dreyse needle-guns by the simple expedient of reducing the projectile weight, altering its shape and increasing the muzzle velocity. It was quickly established that the increased chamber pressures consequent on increased muzzle velocity made some kind of bolt-head improvement necessary, and, on 10 March 1870, King Wilhelm I signed the orders adopting a modified bolt system credited to Ludwig Beck[1]. It owed a great deal to the French Chassepot pattern and could almost be called a blatant copy. But it did permit the muzzle velocity to be raised from 295m/sec to 340m/sec and improved the flight-path of the bullets considerably.

1. Beck was an employee of the government arsenal in Spandau.

Production history

Conversion work began in May/June 1870 on the four chosen gun models, the Füsiliergewehr M 1860, the Infanteriegewehr M 1862, the Jägerbüchse M 1865 and the Pioniergewehr M 1869. Although the work proceeded slowly, enough converted infantry rifles had been completed to equip three regiments—4. Garde-Regiment zu Fuss, and infantry regiments 71 and 94—during the Franco-Prussian War. Work continued after hostilities had ceased, although the exact quantity transformed remains in dispute. Martin[2], quoting the Italian journal *Italia Militaire*, states that no less than 729,703 Dreyse needle-rifles had been altered by the end of 1873: a highly suspect figure since, even allowing for limited post-war production of the four models concerned, the total amount of guns available for improvement could scarcely have exceeded 750,000. It even seems possible that the figure may have been a misprint for 129,703.

2. Jean Martin, *Armes à Feu de l'Armée Française 1860 à 1940*, p. 210.

Markings

The Beck guns bore no marks other than those applied when they were first made (see the relevant sections elsewhere in this book).

Mechanical description and variations

The basic functions of the modified Dreyse needle-rifles remained practically unaltered. A new bolt head was fitted inside the old gas expansion chamber, where it was held by the large screw visible on top of the bolt ahead of the bolt handle; it functioned in much the same manner as the French Mle 1866, from which it may well have been copied. A leather washer was placed between the bolt head and the bolt body, and, when the gun fired, the pressure of the propellant gas forced the bolt head backwards sufficiently far to squeeze the annular washer out against the chamber walls. This provided a reasonably effective gas seal until the washer material deteriorated; however, as the guns chosen for conversion all had cone-type obturation systems, the bulk of leaking gas was deflected forwards and upwards. A few minor alterations were made to the interior of the bolt body, but were of little significance. No variations are known.

Appearance, distinctive features and data
The converted rifles resembled the unconverted types (qv), but could be identified by the prominent slotted-head screw on the top of the bolt body in front of the operating handle. The rifles also had new back sights of a wholly different design from the originals.

DATA
M 1860, M 1862 and M 1865: as unconverted weapons (qv), except—*Sights:* (front) unprotected barleycorn; (back) a combined block and two-leaf sight, with a standing 'battle sight' for 200 paces, a small leaf for 300 and a large one—with a sliding body—graduated to 1,200 paces.

Accessories

OTHERS
Men carrying guns modified to the Beck system ('aptierte Zündnadelgewehre') were issued with four spare leather washers in addition to the normal two needles.

BAYONET
The same as the original firearms where issued.

Right: men of Jäger-Bataillon Nr. 5 overrun a French artillery position during the Franco-Prussian War. The weapons are Jägerbüchsen M 1865. From an engraving by E. Zimmer. Courtesy of Anthony Carter.

The German Rifle

Part two

The Mauser and other metallic-cartridge weapons

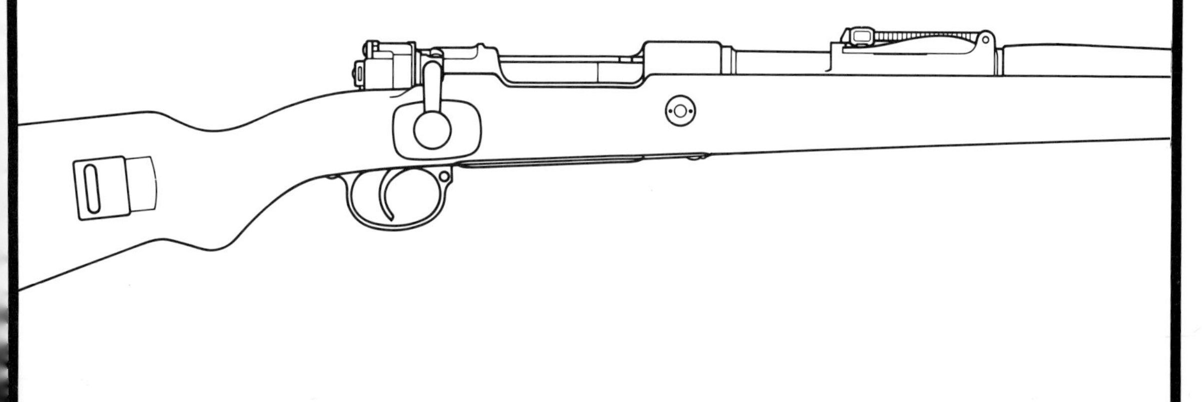

Infanteriegewehr Modell 1871 Mauser

The tortuous early history of this gun begins with the development in 1868 of a self-cocking derivation of the Dreyse needle-rifle. This was the work of Peter Paul Mauser, a then unknown employee of the Württemberg government armoury at Oberndorf. His alterations greatly increased the speed of fire, since the Dreyse's needle mechanism had to be manually retracted before the bolt could be opened for loading; the Mauser-Dreyse could be operated simply by raising the bolt handle and pulling it backwards, since the needle was cocked as the bolt was pushed forwards to re-load. He subsequently approached the authorities with his plans but, as the Minié rifle-musket was well-established in the Württemberg Army, very little interest was shown in the improved prototype.

Undaunted, Mauser returned to his work and had developed a modified rifle chambering a self-contained metal-case cartridge by the beginning of 1867. This, too, was exhibited before the Württemberg army ordnance department; but at Prussia's insistence, a Dreyse-type needle-rifle conversion had just been adopted[1] for the standard rifle-musket (the so-called 'Dorn Gewehr'), and a further change was not considered. Mauser then approached the Prussian ambassador to Württemberg, who was so convinced of the efficiency of the Dreyse guns, which had just obtained such good results in Bohemia, that he refused even to bring the Mauser rifle to the attention of the Prussian military. In desperation, Mauser turned to the Austrian ambassador in the belief that the Austrian Army, known to be searching for an efficient breech-loader in the wake of the disastrous Austro-Prussian War, might actually submit the new bolt-action rifle to trial.

1. There were two patterns of Württemberg's Dreyse infantry rifles. The M 1867 was a conversion, while the similar M 1868 was newly-made.

The Austrian ambassador was sufficiently astute to see that the Mauser had some potential, and forwarded it to Vienna early in 1867 for trials against the newly-adopted Wänzl breech-loading conversion system[2]; he was also well aware that the Wänzl was considered little more than a stop-gap, and that, as a result, an entirely new design was

2. Adopted on 5 January 1867.

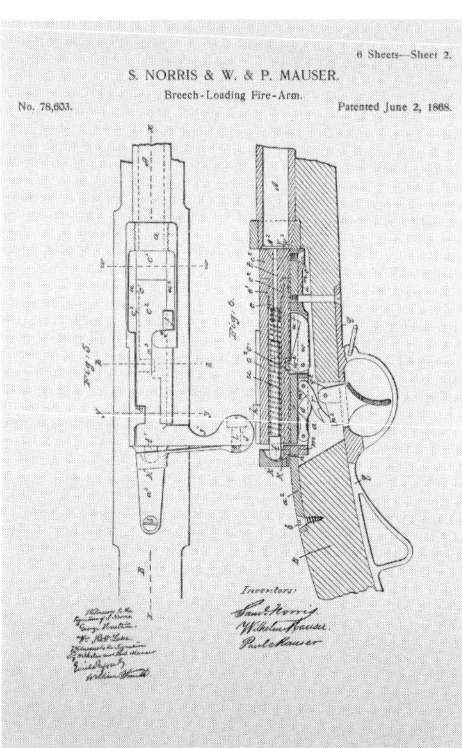

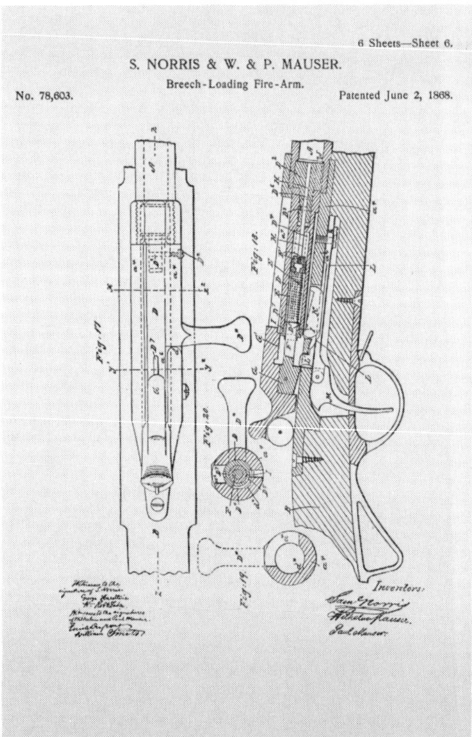

Right: some of the illustrations from Mauser's original US Patent, 78,603, granted in 1868.

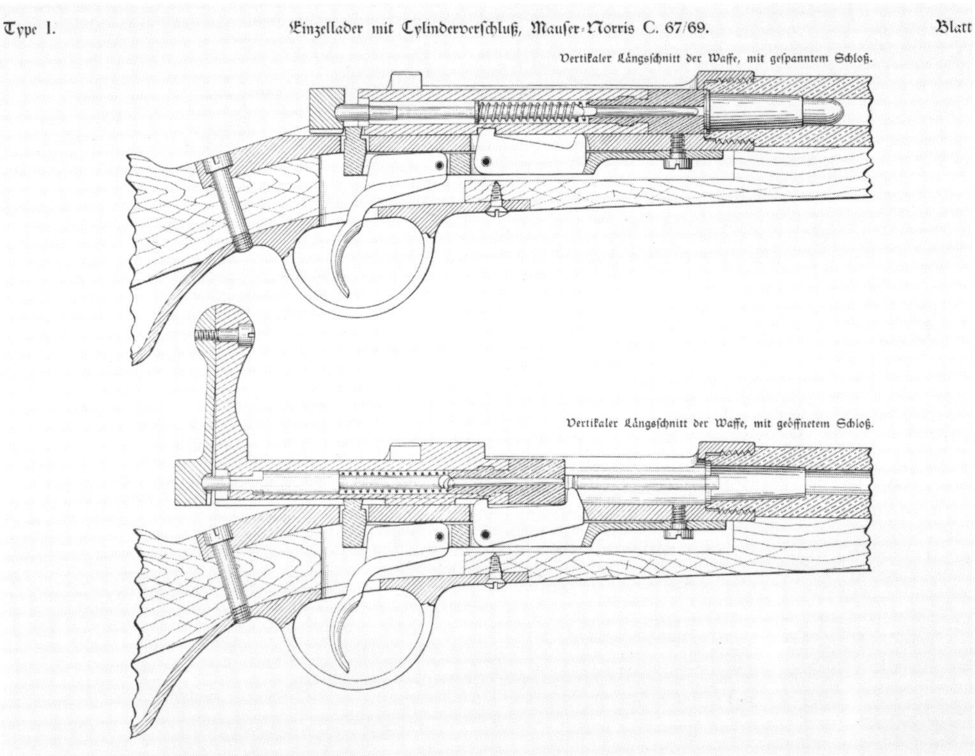

Right: the action of the 'Mauser-Norris' or C 67/69 rifle, built on a Württemberg rifle-musket. From Korn's *Mauser-Gewehre und Mauser-Patente* (1908).

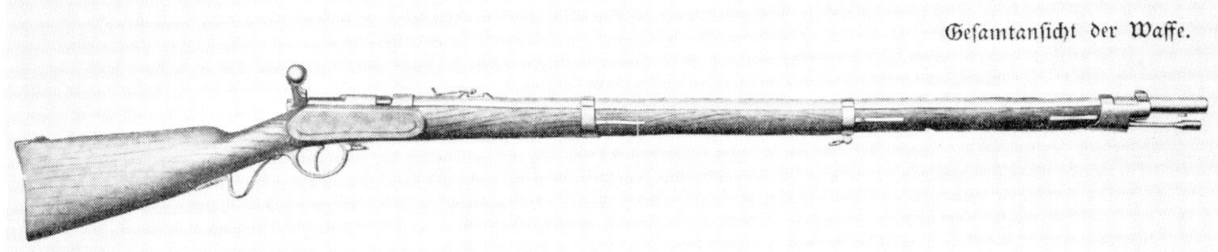

Right: a full-length view of the C 67/69.

being sought. However, the trials had proceeded far enough for the merits of two of the rivals at least—the Austrian Holub-Werndl and the American Remington—to be clearly evident and, although the advantages of the Mauser were acknowledged, the Artillerie-Comité preferred a block to a bolt-action[3].

Mauser then had a stroke of good fortune. In midsummer 1867, the existence of his prototype rifle was mentioned to Samuel Norris by General Arthur Graf Bylandt-Rheidt, who was then president of the Artillerie-Comité and later became Minister of War. Norris was the European sales agent of Eliphalet Remington & Sons, a very successful salesman with an entrée to most European ordnance circles, and sufficiently astute to see the potential in the Mauser prototype. So, with scant regard for business morality and the rights of his employers, Norris entered into private discussions with the French Artillerie-Comité to see if a means of converting the then-new Chassepot needle-rifle was wanted. The French, perhaps understandably, showed great interest: such an improvement would give them a vast technological advantage over the Dreyse-armed Prussians.

Equipped with this knowledge, Norris sought the Mauser brothers. Peter Paul Mauser had been laid off by the Württemberg armoury in the spring of 1867, because the

3. This was by no means an uncommon opinion; many other trial boards in many other countries reacted in the same way, believing bolt actions to be dangerous. See, for example, V. D. Majendie & C. O. Browne, *Military Breech-Loading Rifles*, p. 43, and the *Treatise on Military Small Arms and Ammunition*, 1888, (HMSO), pp. 36-38.

adoption of a Dreyse conversion, which seems to have been undertaken by the Dreyse factory in Sömmerda, had reduced production of rifle muskets in the factory and the work force had been commensurately reduced. Norris first met the Mausers in the second week of September 1867[4], and quickly ascertained that they would agree to his plans. By the last week of the month he had taken them to Liège ('Luttich' in German). There, Norris, the Mauser brothers, interpreters and lawyers drew up a provisional patent on what has since become known—wrongly, since it was already in existence—as the Mauser-Norris or C 67/69 rifle. A contract[5] between the principal interested parties, dated 28 September 1867, was drawn up in French—a language neither Mauser brother understood—and smacks greatly of exploitation. The cunning arms entrepreneur had ensured that, for the payment of a mere pittance spaced over several years, he controlled the exploitation of the Mauser rifle. He seems to have reasoned that two peasant-artisans, after all, would be so overcome by the legal subtleties and 'generous' financial provisions in the contract that they would hardly understand, far less question, each of the clauses. Virtually the only point in the brothers' favour was that Norris' rights to exploit the invention lapsed if he failed to pay the annuities.

4. W. H. B. Smith, *Mauser Rifles and Pistols*, p. 32, contains a copy of Norris's letter dated 13 September.

5. W. H. B. Smith, *Mauser Rifles and Pistols*, pp. 34-36.

The patents were sought late in 1867 and granted in 1867-68; the Austrian Privilegiums 17/684-XIX/9 (24 December 1867) and XIX/26 (15 January 1868), and US Patent 78,603, granted on 2 June 1868 although application had been made in 1867, are typical of the many sought in Austria, France, Spain, Germany and the USA. They each protect a bolt-action modification of the original Württemberg rifle-musket and an improvement to the French Mle 1866 Chassepot needle-rifle, adapting it for a metal-cased cartridge.

Then Eliphalet Remington & Sons found out about the dealings of Norris who, after all, was its salesman. Whether Norris told Remingtons himself, or whether the details simply leaked out, is neither known nor particularly relevant. The company was understandably incensed and nothing further was done with the plans, although Norris indicated that the idea had always been to purchase rights to a possible competitor to the Remington rolling-block military rifle and that the company was to be the maker of the Mauser-Norris. Remington's reasoned, quite justifiably, that it was bad policy to tool for the production of a wholly new and untried design when the rolling-block rifles were selling in the hundreds of thousands right across the world.

In addition, the French government was becoming increasingly anxious about the prospects of a war with Prussia, which was imagined to be imminent, and was issuing Chassepot needle-rifles as fast as possible; converting them to fire metal-case ammunition had become unthinkable in the circumstances. Norris thereafter lost interest in exploiting the Mauser rifle until, on the non-payment of the first instalment of the third annuity (1870), the rights reverted to Peter Paul and Wilhelm Mauser.

The brothers had intelligently watched Norris' dealings with the various governmental and military departments, and elected to try their own hand at negotiations. The burden of these fell on Wilhelm, who later proved to be an excellent salesman and a skilled diplomat. The first approaches to the Prussian Army are believed to have been made early in 1870[6], when an improved rifle was sent to the Militär-Schiess-Schule in Spandau. The Gewehr-Prüfungs-Kommission, which was responsible for the development of the German army small arms, quickly saw that the Mauser was a far better gun than the Dreyse, the efficiency of which was being increasingly questioned after the success of the French Chassepot in pre-1870 campaigns.

6. Some writers have maintained that this was done, at the Mausers' insistence, by Norris as a parting gesture.

Trials began in Spandau in midsummer 1870, the Mauser being only one of several competing designs. The onset of the Franco-Prussian War interrupted the experiments, but they began again in the spring of 1871 and by the early summer it had become clear that the choice lay between the Mauser and the Bavarian Werder. By September, the Werder had been rejected on several grounds, including difficult cleaning and

Right: the butt and breech of the Mauser infantry rifle, the M 1871, compared with those of the Dreyse rifle it replaced—in this instance, an M 1862 with Beck's bolt-head. RSAF collection, photograph by Fred Aldeslade.

Below: the M 1871 rifle. From Schott's *Grundriss der Waffenlehre* (1876).

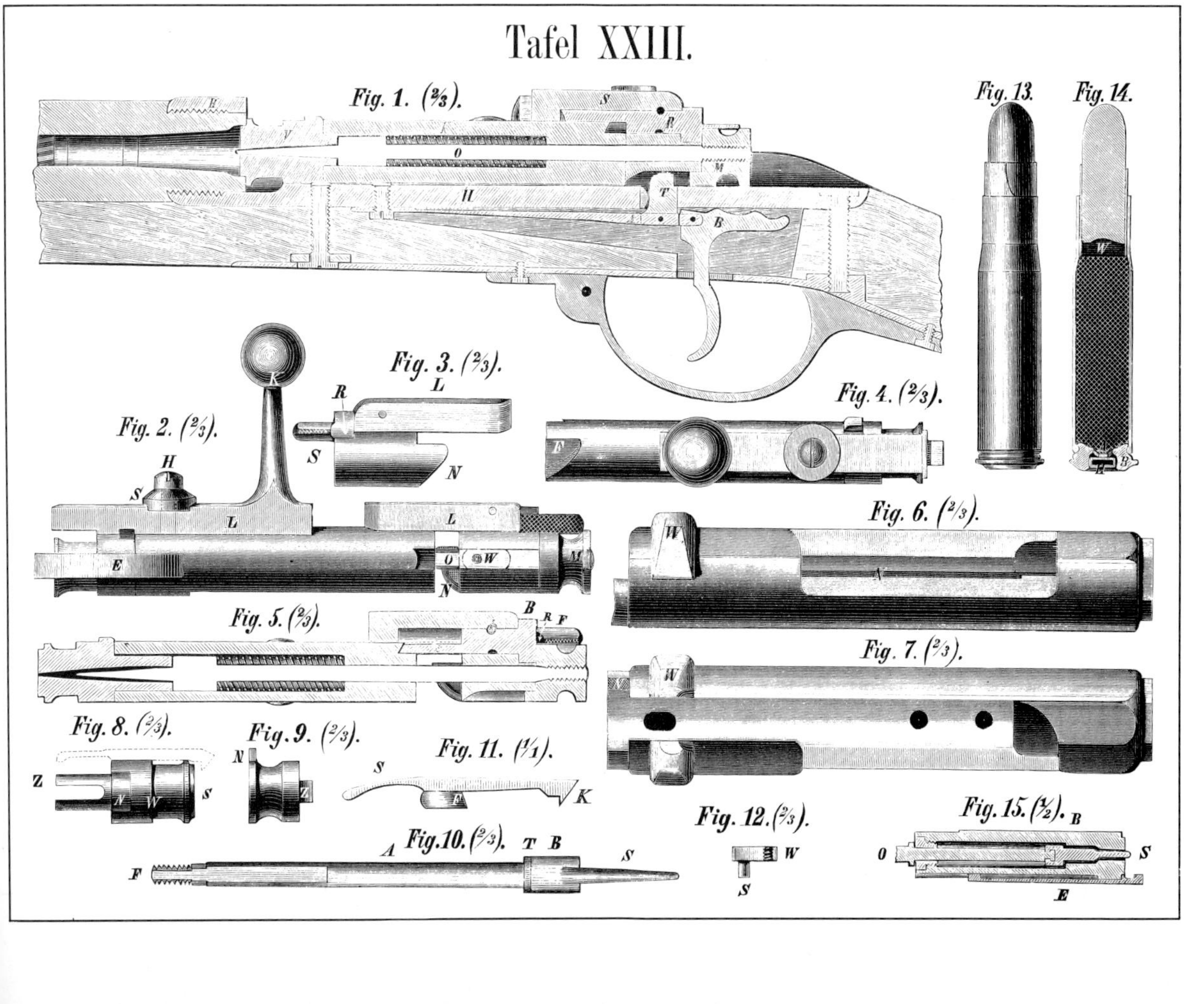

Tafel XXIII.

Fig. 1. (2/3). Fig. 2. (2/3). Fig. 3. (2/3). Fig. 4. (2/3). Fig. 5. (2/3). Fig. 6. (2/3). Fig. 7. (2/3). Fig. 8. (2/3). Fig. 9. (2/3). Fig. 10. (2/3). Fig. 11. (1/1). Fig. 12. (2/3). Fig. 13. Fig. 14. Fig. 15. (1/2).

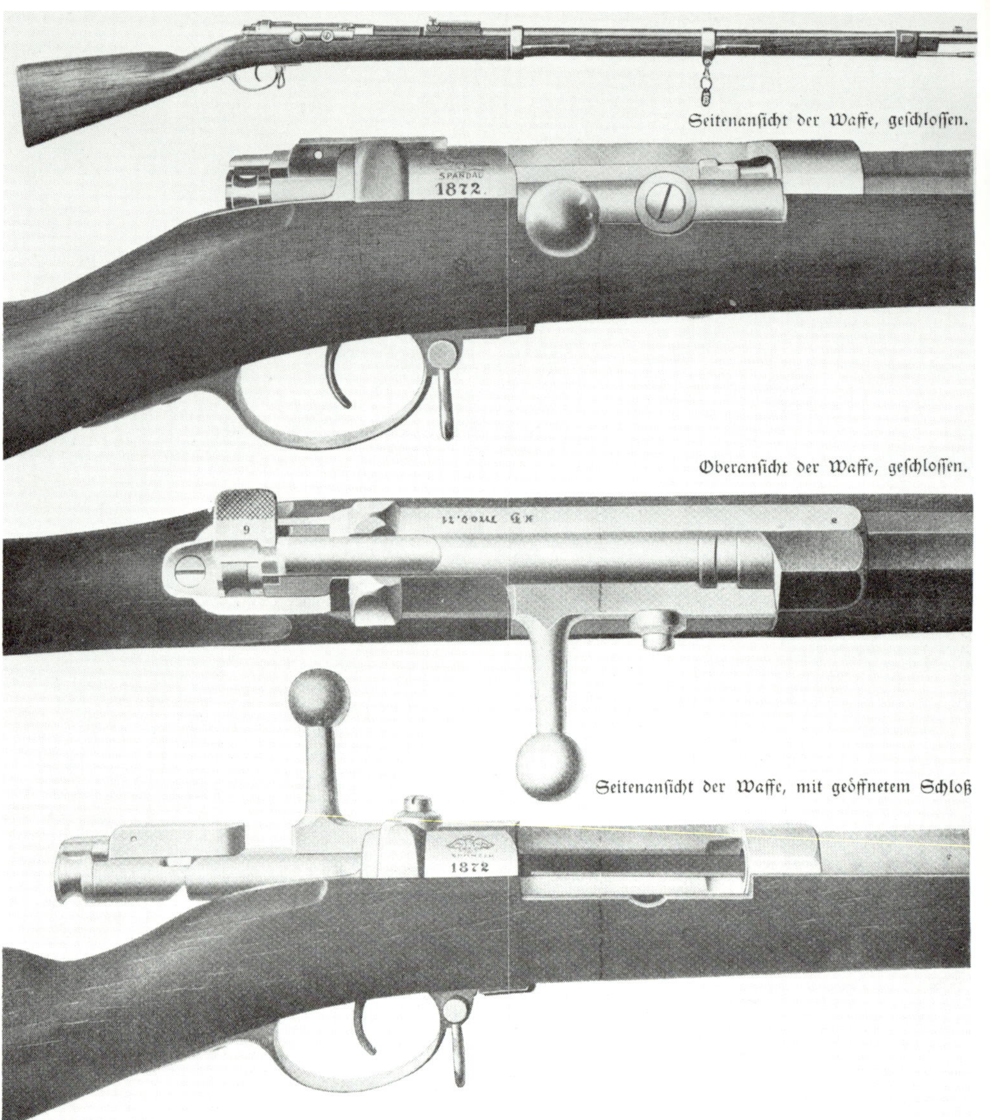

Right: three views of an early M 1871 rifle, from Korn's *Mauser-Gewehre und Mauser-Patente.* Note the markings.

maintenance, excessive barrel fouling and structural weakness in the breech. On 7 November, the GPK had decided on the length of the barrel and the stock fittings, and had settled the calibre as 11mm. Alarm was expressed about the lack of a suitable safety mechanism, but Mauser asked for two months in which to develop one and his rifle was provisionally adopted on 9 December 1871 as the Infanterie-Gewehr Modell 1871. Pending the perfection of the safety mechanism, the government arsenal in Spandau was ordered to manufacture 2,500 of what has since become known as the Interims-Modell for large-scale troop trials.

Wilhelm Mauser demonstrated two alternative safety catches to the GPK on 14 February 1872, and one, the now widely-known 'wing' pattern, was subsequently adopted. Finally, on 22 March 1872, the Kaiser signed the decree adopting the perfected rifle for the German armies. Only the bolt mechanism was Mauser's responsibility, because the barrel and rifling design had simply been pirated from the Chassepot, the trigger unit from the M 1862 Dreyse infantry rifle and the stock and its fittings had been designed by the GPK. The development of the 11mm centrefire cartridge and the resulting substantial changes to the original Mauser extractor and ejector have been credited to a governmental committee led by Oberst von Kalinowski.

With the design agreed, production plans were readied. The slow delivery of parts for the production line, much of which had been ordered from Pratt & Whitney, meant that the first series-made rifle was not presented to the emperor until the third anniversary of its adoption, on 22 March 1875[7]. Small numbers of pre-production weapons, however, had been made in the intervening period (see Production history).

7. According to the French periodical *Le Spectateur Militaire* for that year.

As with all new guns, problems were encountered after the Mausers had been issued. They included the *non-ignition of cartridges*, because of weak strikes; *poor accuracy* caused by the asymmetrical breech-locking and the design of the nose-cap assembly; and a tendency for the *bolt-stop washer screw* to come loose. Moves to rectify these faults were made in the period 1876-82, but only the latter was completely eradicated. The certainty of ignition was considerably improved, but the rifles were always dogged by accuracy problems. Fortunately for the Germans, they were not bad enough to cause the rifles to be withdrawn fro wholesale modification.

The Infanterie-Gewehre M 1871 served the regular armies until sufficient supplies of the M 1871/84 began to filter through in the mid-1880s. After serving with the second-line troops, such as the pioneers and the train, they were handed to the Landwehr and, ultimately, the Landsturm. However, many survivors reappeared in non-combatants' hands during the First World War. A few are believed to have had their barrels bored-out to 13mm and issued, as anti-balloon guns, with incendiary ammunition. Many other rifles were sold on the export markets in the late nineteenth century (notably to South America and the Far East) and a modified version, chambering the 6.5mm Daudetau cartridge, was used in Uruguay for some years[8].

8. They were altered versions of 1871-type German infantry rifles, contract—made by OEWG. Known as 'Dovitiis' conversions, after the inventor, they were modified in France in the 1890s. Their bolt handles were bent downwards.

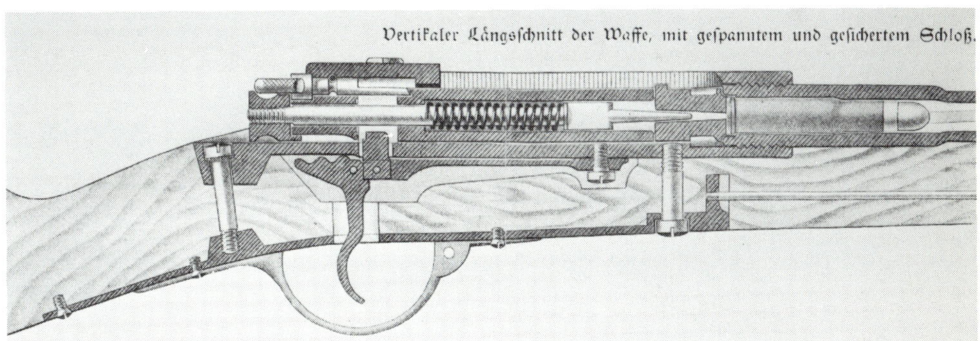

Right: a longitudinal section of the M 1871, from an original factory drawing reproduced by Korn.

Production history

The Prussian government arsenals in Danzig, Erfurt and Spandau were supposed to begin production of the Infanterie-Gewehr M 1871 in 1872-73, but the late arrival of production machinery (mainly drop-forges and grinding equipment) from Pratt & Whitney of Hartford, Connecticut, delayed work for a considerable period. Spandau, for example, was not readied for production until the beginning of 1874 rather than the autumn of 1872. Once manufacture had begun, the Germans had initial problems maintaining acceptable tolerances and quality control; the parts-fit of the relatively complicated Mauser was much more critical than on the older Dreyse types, which had been made by more traditional methods of production, relying very greatly on hand-work. This delayed production so much that the Prussian government, realizing that its target of complete re-armament in five years could not be attained, recruited some additional contractors.

A hundred thousand rifles had been ordered from the Bavarian government's factory in Amberg in May 1872, but the existing facilities were occupied converting Werder rifles for the Reichspatrone until the mid-1870s and nothing came of the Mauser contract. No M 1871 rifles were made in Bavaria until 1877, so a contract for 500,000 guns was placed in mid-1873 with Österreichische Waffenfabrik-Gesellschaft in Steyr[9]. The Württemberg government ordered 100,000 rifles from the Mauser brothers in December 1873, and it was this that was responsible

9. According to the company history, *Fünfundsiebzig Jahre Steyr-Werke* (1939), the contract was worth 8,894,500 gulden (about 17 million marks).

for the success of Gebrüder Mauser & Co.; the last gun was delivered in July 1879. A Prussian contract for 180,000 went to the Productionsgenössenschaft Spangenberg & Sauer, Schilling & Haenel in February 1876; another for 100,000 to Österreichische Waffenfabrik-Gesellschaft in mid-1876; and a third, for 75,000 to the British Birmingham-based National Arms & Ammunition Co. in the same period. Each of the original Amberg-contract guns had been estimated to cost about 57 marks (28.50 gulden) without any consideration of profit, while those delivered from Britain each cost 55 marks (55/-); the first 15,000 of the Württemberg order required about 66 marks (22 taler) each, while the remainder were delivered for 55 marks (18.55 taler). In addition, Mauser sent 26,000 rifles and carbines to China in 1876, and Serbia ordered 100,000 of a slightly modified pattern—the so-called M 78/80 or Mauser-Koká—in 1878.

Many smaller orders were subsequently placed with the major contractors, although it is not known exactly how many M 1871 rifles were made. The total, however, must have exceeded a million; Österreichische Waffenfabrik-Gesellschaft alone had delivered 474,622 rifles, 60,000 carbines, 150,000 bolts, 55,963 receivers and 52,000 barrels to Prussia and Saxony prior to 31 December 1877[10].

10. According to the French *Revue d'Artillerie*, 1878.

Markings

The first Infanterie-Gewehre M 1871, made in the Spandau factory in 1872 (largely by hand), seem to have been marked with a spread eagle and 'SPANDAU' over the date '1872' on the right side of the receiver behind the feedway—if the illustrations in Korn's book[11], which have been extensively re-touched, can be trusted. Later guns had the maker's mark on top of the octagonal breech portion of the barrel, taking the form shown in following table.

11. R. H. Korn, *Mauser Gewehre und Mauser Patente*, in the picture section. Also used by W. H. B. Smith in his *Mauser Rifles and Pistols*, pp. 57-58. The rifle apparently bears the serial number 6.

GOVERNMENT ARSENALS

DANZIG	Prussian arsenal, Danzig
ERFURT	Prussian arsenal, Erfurt
SPANDAU	Prussian arsenal, Spandau
AMBERG	Bavarian arsenal, Amberg

PRIVATE CONTRACTORS

G&B	Greenwood & Batley Limited, Leeds, Yorkshire, England
AGH	Arbeitsgemeinschaft C.G. Haenel, Suhl
MAUSER	Gebrüder Mauser & Co., Oberndorf am Neckar, Württemberg
ŒWG	Österreichische Waffenfabrik-Gesellschaft, Steyr, Austria
	National Arms & Ammunition Company Limited, Birmingham, Warwickshire, England
Sp.& Sr.	Spangenberg & Sauer, Suhl
VCS	V.C. Schilling & Co., Suhl

The designation mark 'I.G.MOD.71' is stamped, in gothic script, on the rear left side of the receiver, while the date of manufacture may be found on the right. There may occasionally be two dates, particularly on Bavarian rifles, but the first is generally that of manufacture while the second is the issue (re-issue in some cases?) year.

The serial number (18937, 91402), apparently without letter suffixes[12], may be found on the left side of the barrel octagon and on the left front side of the receiver. A calibre mark may be found on the left side of the barrel octagon immediately in front of its joint with the receiver, and takes the form of '10,95' for 10.95mm or '11' for 11mm. It represents the actual rather than nominal bore diameter. A monarch's cypher, a crown over FW in Prussia or a crown over L in Bavaria, may also lie on the left side of the barrel at the breech.

Parts of the serial number are repeated on most of the components, including the bolt guide rib, the bolt head, the striker, the safety 'wing', the cocking piece, the striker head and the extractor[13]. Standard inspectors' marks—taking the form of small crowned letters—may also be encountered on virtually all of the parts, including whole strings of them alongside the breech. On one gun examined, these took the form of P, U and *L* on the receiver and *M*, *M*, F, U and *C* on the barrel; some were in gothic script, while the others (shown here in italic) were cursive.

Cyphers and inspectors' marks may be struck into the right side of the butt, while unit marks may be located on the top surface of the butt plate. A typical example reads '16.R.E.3.197.'; made at Amberg in 1877, this gun was later issued to the third company of the Ersatz-Bataillon of Infanterie-Regiment von Sparr (3.Westfalisches) Nr. 16.

12. One gun made by the National Arms & Ammunition Co. has been seen with what may be an 'H' suffix.

13. The full serial number may sometimes be found on the bolt guide rib and the bolt head.

Mechanical description and variations

The Mauser was the first perfected bolt-action weapon developed for a metal-cased cartridge, since the gun patented in 1867 was substantially the same as that adopted in 1871-72. The major differences lay in the design of the mainspring, the locking lug, the ejector and other parts, but tended to concern details rather than the basic concept.

The M 1871 receiver is a one-piece forging, bored-out to accept the bolt and cut away on the right side to permit loading single cartridges into the feedway. The barrel screws into an octagonal reinforce at the front of the receiver body, the rear part of which is slotted to permit the bolt handle to pass through it. A prominent built-up bridge, on top of the rear part of the receiver, is specially designed to act as a bolt-stop.

The bolt consists of three major components: the bolt head, the bolt body and the cocking piece assembly. The removable *bolt head* is held in the

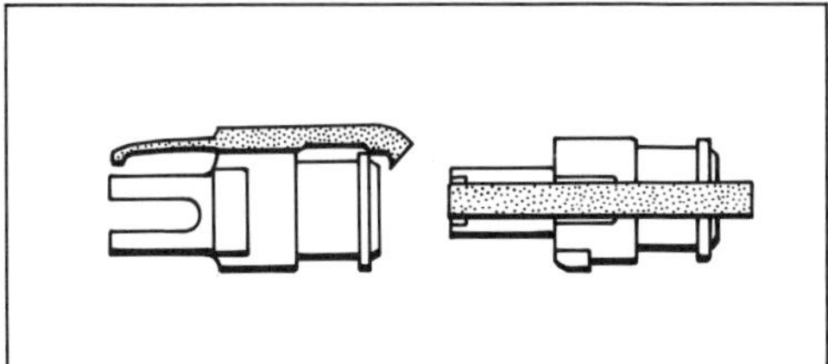

body by means of a small lug engaging in a recess cut in the underside of the long guide rib extending forward from the base of the bolt handle. On the left side it carries the claw-pattern extractor, which rides in a longitudinal slot cut in the receiver wall to prevent the bolt head rotating as the bolt handle is raised. A bifurcated rearward extension on the head engages 'flats' on the striker nose to prevent the striker and striker head, which are not attached directly to the cocking piece, from rotating.

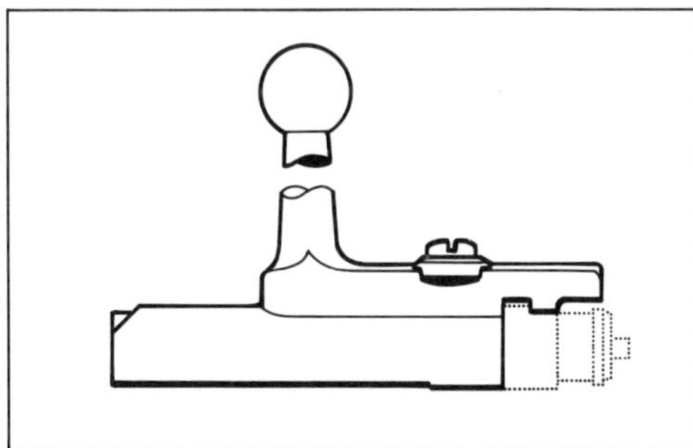

The *bolt body* is hollowed from the front to receive the striker and its spring, and carries the bolt handle and its prominent forward base-extension (bolt guide rib). The rear of the body cylinder has a short cut-out to engage the stem of the safety lever (mounted in the cocking piece body) and an indented cut-out to cam the cocking piece and striker assemblies backwards as the bolt handle is raised.

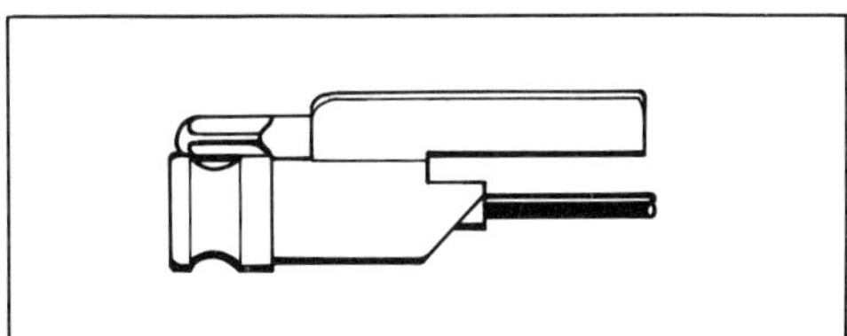

The *cocking piece assembly* consists of the cocking piece itself, the safety lever and the striker retaining nut or striker head. A long forward extension on the cocking piece runs between the sides of the receiver bolt-way to prevent the cocking piece turning as the bolt is operated. There is an approximately triangular projection on the front right side of the cocking piece body that meshes with the cam cut-out in the rear of the bolt cylinder to ensure that the striker is withdrawn from contact with the chambered cartridge as the bolt is opened. The safety mechanism consists of a special cylindrical spindle with a 'wing' or 'flag' head, and can be revolved so that the solid portion of the spindle enters a groove on top of the bolt body, thus keeping the cocking piece and bolt cylinder apart and preventing the bolt being opened or the striker being released.

The operation of the M 1871 is relatively simple. Starting with the gun in its fired condition, the shooter raised the bolt handle and the camming action of the bolt guide rib on the angled breech face began extraction. When the bolt reached the vertical position, the rear of the guide rib, which acted as the locking lug where it abutted the receiver, could slide backwards through the split portion of the receiver behind the feedway. The cocking piece body also had been cammed backwards to withdraw the nose of the striker from the base of the cartridge.

The bolt was retracted until the very prominent annular bolt stop, attached by a screw to the top of the guide rib, came into contact with the cut-outs in the receiver bridge. It was then returned to load the chamber—after the extracted case had been manually removed from the feedway, since the action surprisingly omitted an ejector—and, as the bolt handle was turned down, the camming action of the locking surfaces gently seated the cartridge. As the bolt was returned, the mainspring was compressed while the cocking piece was being held back against the sear. The gun was then cocked, loaded and ready to fire.

Several problems were encountered with the Mauser rifle after it had been introduced into service, and a few modifications ensued. The principal problems fell into several categories. *Poor accuracy*, discussed in several contemporary papers[14], was ultimately traced to the design of the muzzle and the bayonet attachment assembly. The science of ballistics was very much in its infancy during the 1870s and very little was understood about the effects of harmonics set up in the barrel during firing. Most barrels were snugly bedded in the stock and were retained by several clamping barrel bands, the position of which could have critical effect on accuracy. It was subsequently realized that variations in humidity, effects of barrel heat and many other factors could alter the pressure of the bedding—or the areas in which it made contact with the barrel surface—in such a way that the bullet trajectory was changed. At great distances, even a fractional change of direction at the muzzle could cause considerable deviation from the target.

The method of attaching the M 1871 nose-cap to the barrel (rather than the stock) by a transverse screw running through a special block brazed to the underside of the muzzle was found to be poor. The nose-cap was a close fit over the wooden fore-end, but was nonetheless allowed a little movement: on a damp day, if the stock swelled slightly, thus altering the pressure of wood on metal, the nose-cap could be forced fractionally out of line in almost any direction and accuracy suffered accordingly.

Firing with the bayonet fixed to the muzzle could also have serious effects, since its lateral attachment placed the nose-cap under asymmetrical stress. Accuracy was also impaired by the design of the locking system—a single lug on one side of the bolt,

14. For example, 'Die verschiedene Lage der Treffpunkte zum Haltepunkt bei Gewehren M/71', by the Militär-Schiess-Schule in Spandau; and Major Petersen's 'Abweichen der Treffpunkte der Gewehre M/71 bei gleichen Haltepunkten'.

which could again set up asymmetrical stress patterns in the barrel and the receiver. The accuracy problems were never really overcome during the rifles' service life but were never sufficiently bad to make a solution vital.

Non-ignition of cartridges was also apparent during the mid-1870s and was rectified by strengthening the mainspring and revising the design and metal-thickness of the primer walls. Various other suggestions were made—changing the weight and design of the striker nose, for instance—and a few guns were altered to a slightly modified bolt mechanism suggested by Premierleutnant Wind (see variations) in 1875.

A few alterations were made in 1882. A small coil-spring was added to the hinge of the small back sight leaf, to make its operation more positive; a hardened bolt extension piece was retained in the rear of the bolt guide rib (by a cross-pin) to prevent excessive wear in the locking shoulder; and the screw securing the annular bolt-stop, which occasionally worked loose and got lost, was given a retaining cross-pin so that it could be loosened but not removed.

VARIATIONS

Apart from the Jägerbüchse and the cavalry carbines, which are considered separately, and the minor pre- and post-1882 manufacturing variations, very few special M 1871 rifles have been reported. Experiments were made in the mid-1870s to ensure satisfactory cartridge ignition—as mentioned above—and in 1875 a Prussian army officer, Premierleutnant Wind, proposed altering the Mauser's lock-work so that the striker, the striker retaining nut and the cocking piece were made in a single unit. The cost of conversion was estimated to be between 3 and 4 marks per gun, and five hundred were converted by the Spandau arsenal in October/November 1876. The trials proved that the certainty of cartridge ignition increased with the heavier weight of the Wind striker assembly, but the lock-time also increased and nothing further was done.

Several experimental magazine conversions were developed in the late 1870s and early 1880s, but none attained service. Korn[15] pictures two, one dated 1879 with a curious side-mounted box magazine, and another (1880) with a saddle pattern running down

15. R. H. Korn, *Mauser-Gewehre und Mauser Patente*, picture section.

Right: two of the many magazines developed for the essentially single-shot M 1871 rifle. These, developed by Mauser, date from 1879-80.

Far right: Mauser's top-feeding box magazine, from DRP 41,375.

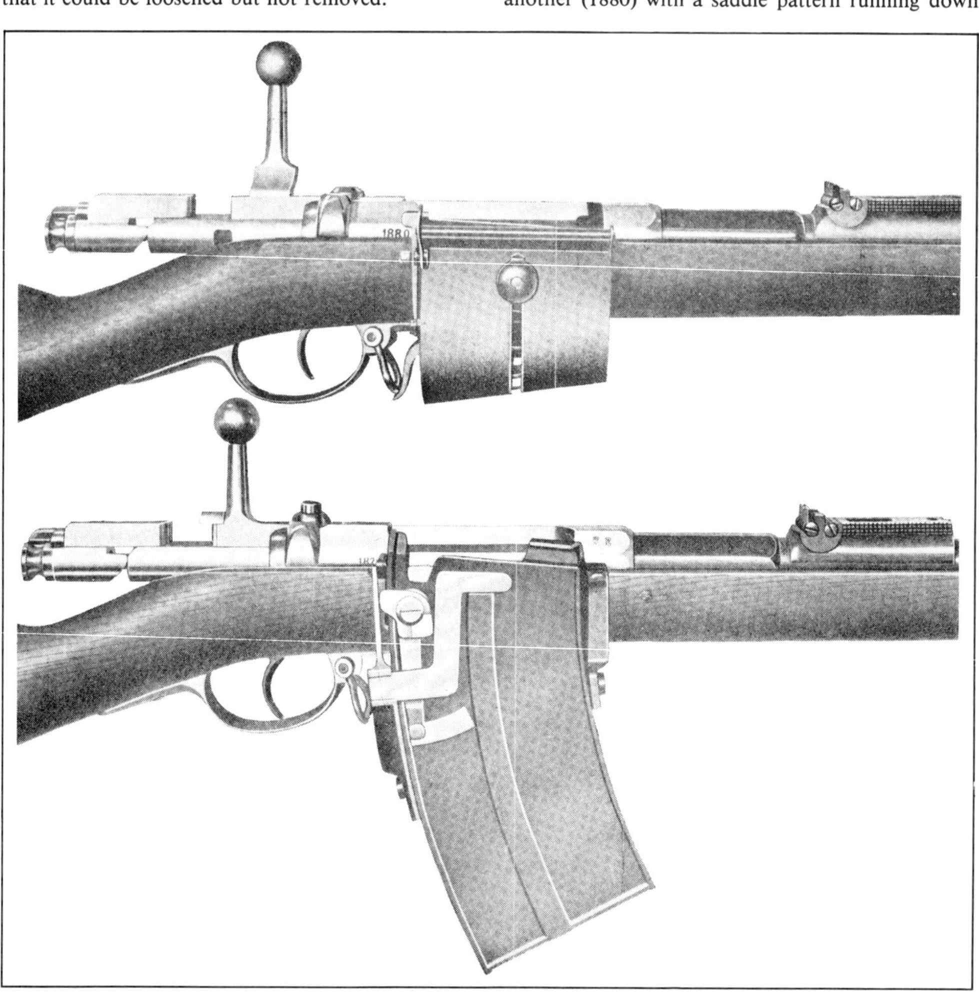

and under the stock. Among the other inventors to try their hand at developing a magazine for the Mauser were Karl Holub, inventor of the Austrian Werndl rifle, who patented a tubular type in 1878; Franz von Dreyse, son of the inventor of the needle-rifle, who developed a tube magazine in 1879 and a more conventional box pattern in 1882; Louis Schmeisser, who developed a drum unit in 1881-82; Ludwig Loewe & Co., a saddle unit in the early 1880s; and Edward Lindner came up with the idea of a downward-feeding box in 1883.

Appearance, distinctive features and data

Despite its much more efficient design, the Infanterie-Gewehr M 1871 still has an archaic air about it, especially when compared with the French Mle 1866 (Chassepot), which is distinctly more elegant and generally better finished. The proliferation of breech markings adds to the messy appearance of the Mauser rifle, and the overall effect suggests that the Germans were not as industrially advanced as the French [16].

The M 1871 resembles the preceding M 1862 (Dreyse) infantry rifle in some respects, being a long and somewhat clumsy large-calibre weapon with a long slightly tapering cylindrical barrel with a prominent octagonal-section reinforcement at the breeech. The leaf-type back sight lies immediately in front of the juncture of the cylindrical and octagonal parts of the barrel.

The barrel is attached to the stock by three iron fixtures: two bands, retained in position by leaf springs, and the special nose-cap. The last-named fitting is attached to the barrel rather than the stock, as a transverse bolt runs through its sides and through a reinforcing block brazed to the underside of the muzzle. A T-lug for the sword bayonet lies on the right side of the nose-cap body, and 1cm of the muzzle crown is turned to a smaller diameter to accept the bayonet muzzle ring. One sling swivel lies underneath the intermediate barrel band, while the other is attached to the front of the crudely-shaped cast brass trigger guard, which is in turn attached to a long iron or steel floor plate that serves to anchor the action retaining screws.

The barrel was originally browned, the trigger-guard bow was brightly polished, the bolt and the receiver were left 'in the white', and the remaining metal parts were blued.

16. Although this may have been true in the 1870s, in a couple of decades the roles had virtually reversed.

17. J. A. Carter, *German Ersatz Bayonets*, vol. 1.

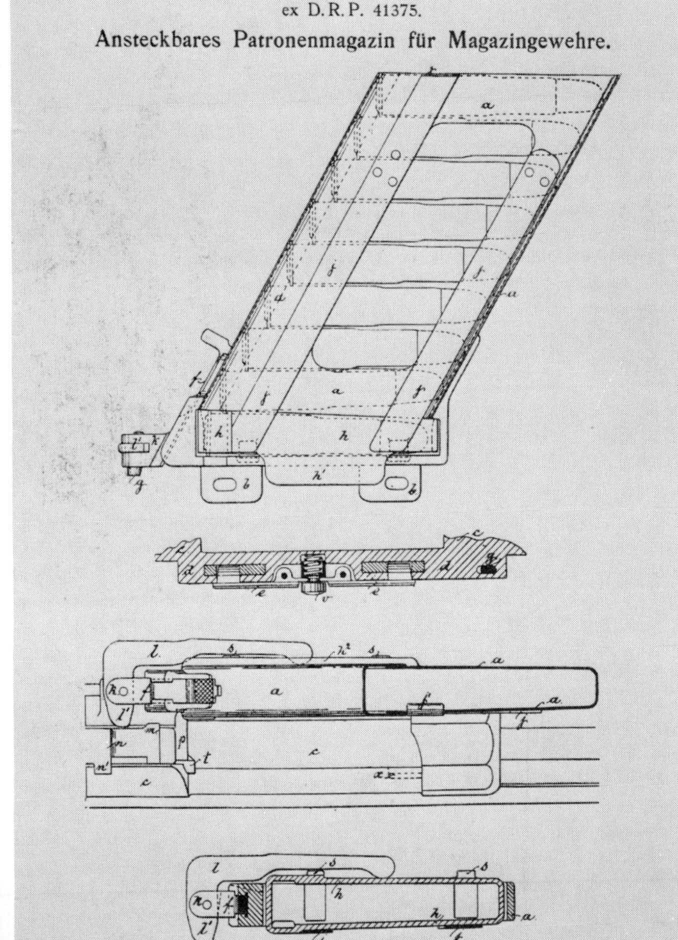

DATA

Calibre: 11mm (nominally, it was permitted to be between 10.95 and 11.10mm).
Rifling: concentric, 4 grooves 0.3mm deep and 4.5mm wide; 1 turn in 550mm, right hand (pitch of 3° 36').
Magazine: none—single-shot only.
Loading system: manual insertion of a cartridge in chamber or bolt-way.
Overall length: 1,345mm.
Barrel length: 855mm.
Weight: between 4,500 and 4,650gm, without sling.
Sights: (front) unprotected barleycorn; (back) a combined block and leaf sight, with a standing 'battle sight' for 300 metres, a small leaf for 400, and a large leaf with a sliding extension for 500-1,600m.
Performance: see cartridge data (Appendix 2).

Accessories

BAYONETS

The Gewehr M 1871 was originally issued with the Seitengewehr M 1871 (TGB, pp. 34-36), which had a 47cm sword blade, a cast brass hilt, and a steel or wrought iron crossguard containing a muzzle ring. During the First World War, many all-metal Ersatz bayonets were adapted to the M 1871 and its derivations. These included Carter Numbers [17] 3-13, 23, 34-35, 38-45, 47, 49-53, 63-72 and 74-75; and there were also many modifications of non-German sword, sabre and knife bayonets (TGB, pp. 78-81, for some details).

OTHERS

A cleaning rod, a sling, a muzzle protector, a sight cover, a screwdriver, a spare striker spring and a spare extractor.

Apt. Chassepot-Karabiner Modell 1871 Prussia

Experience gained in the Franco-Prussian War showed the Prussians that all their cavalrymen found carbines useful—not just the hussars and dragoons, who had been issued with Zündnadel-Karabiner M 1857 since 1859. These horsemen were often sent on scouting and picket duties where firearms were essential, but the cuirassiers and Ulanen (lancers), who were generally considered purely as cavalrymen fighting with sword and lance, were given nothing but percussion-ignition pistols for personal protection.

By 1871, the Dreyse needle-carbines were quite rightly regarded as obsolescent. In any case, they embodied the short Dreyse action with a 'step' rather than cone-type obturation system, and had an unpleasant tendency to leak propellant gas into the firer's face. Many cavalry units were hastily re-armed during the Franco-Prussian War with captured French needle-rifles, many of which had their muzzles shortened and the lug-and-bar bayonet fixings removed. They were then re-issued with captured French combustible paper-case ammunition.

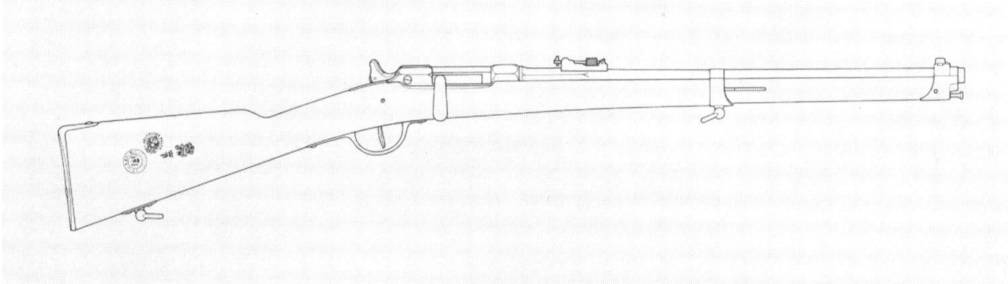

Right: the Prussian M 1871 Chassepot cavalry carbine, chambered for the 11mm Reichspatrone.

The development of the Mauser bolt-action rifle, which fired metal-cased cartridges, made it clear that a similar cavalry carbine would ultimately be adopted, but, equally, that work would be delayed until the government had built up sufficient stocks of infantry rifles. Consequently, most of the existing production facilities would be occupied and no new carbines would be made for several years. On 6 March 1873, Kaiser Wilhelm I signed a decree sanctioning production of cartridge conversions of the large stocks of French needle-rifles then in store. More than half a million guns had, after all, been captured during the war of 1870-71 and, if a suitable conversion system were found, they would provide a useful temporary solution to the carbine shortage. In March 1873, however, no such transformation had been finalized and so work began in unseemly haste. By the beginning of 1874, two possible alternatives had been forwarded: the Saxon Bremer-Einhorn pattern (M 1873, qv) and a similar Prussian type. By the autumn of 1874 the GPK had decided, after prolonged trials, that the Prussian carbine was stronger and more battle-worthy than its Saxon rival, which was made weaker in the barrel by the chosen method of re-chambering, and lacked a conventional barrel bedding system. The Prussian gun made use of the original Mle 1866 barrel, shortened from the muzzle rather than the breech as the Bremer-Einhorn type had been. A tubular liner or 'bush', complete with a chamber for the Reichspatrone 71, was inserted in the bored-out French cartridge chamber (in much the same way as the French elected to transform Mle 1866 to Mle 1874 standards in the 1870s). This conversion system had the merit of retaining virtually all of the metal surrounding the original chamber, unlike the Saxon pattern in which much of the metal was removed.

The Prussian transformation was approved late in 1874, the contracts were placed and first deliveries were made to the troops in 1875. Although issues of modified Chassepots had been made to the Ulanen by an AKO of 6 March 1873[1], the orders referred to 'Chassepot-Karabiner bzw. verkürzte Chassepot-Gewehre' (carbines or shortened rifles) and it is believed that they still chambered combustible ammunition. The metallic cartridge alterations did not enter service for at least two years, since the French journal

1. On the scale of 32 to each squadron.

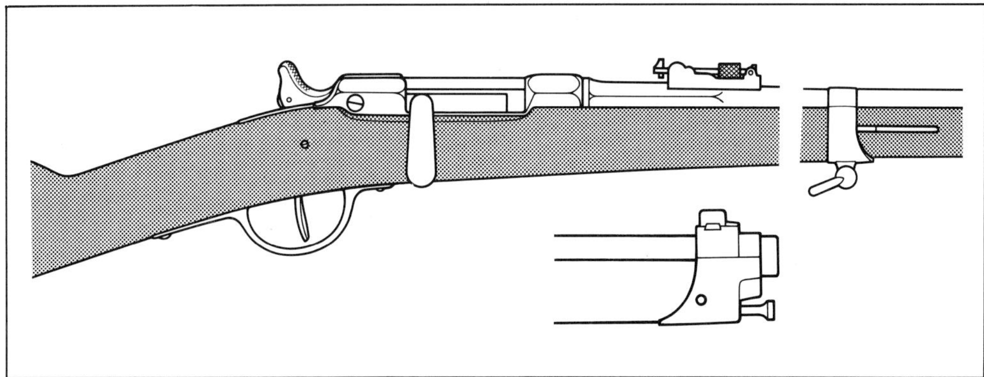

Right: the muzzle, nose-cap and back sight of the Prussian Chassepot carbine.

Le Spectateur Militaire (1875) notes that the first mass-produced Chassepot conversion and the first Mauser infantry rifle were displayed before the Kaiser on the third anniversary of the adoption of the Mauser system on 22 March 1875. An AKO of 31 August 1876 extended the issue of Chassepot carbines to all ranks of the lancers, with the exception of trumpeters and NCOs, and a further 25 were issued to each cuirassier squadron from 30 November 1880. In 1879, the French *Revue d'Artillerie* reported that all Prussian cavalrymen had been re-armed with the new Mausers, but was clearly being over-optimistic since the cuirassiers did not receive theirs until 1884.

Most of the converted Chassepots served until the mid-1880s, when they were passed to the Landwehr and, ultimately, to the Landsturm.

Production history

An unknown quantity of French needle-rifles was converted by the Prussian government workshop in Herzberg im Harz and innumerable contractors in Suhl[2]. Each cost the government between 18 and 24 marks. The Bavarians unsuccessfully tried to negotiate a conversion contract for 10,000 guns with Österreichische Waffenfabrik-Gesellschaft, but reluctantly sold the greater part of their captured French rifles in late 1876. Each gun—in original condition—was sold for 15 marks, according to Götz.[3] The Italian journal *Italia Militaire* recorded that 208,600 Chassepots were altered in 1875 and that they were then being carried by "the cavalry, the train, the siege artillery and the pioneers". And by the last day of 1877, Österreichische Waffenfabrik-Gesellschaft had despatched a further 54,900 carbines to Prussia and Saxony. It is clear, therefore, that the numbers altered ran into hundreds of thousands.

2. Few of whom bothered to leave their markings on the altered guns.

3. Hans-Dieter Götz, *Die deutschen Militärgewehre und Maschinenpistolen, 1871-1945*, p. 55.

Markings

The Prussians generally neglected to erase the original French manufacturers' markings and gun designation from the left side of the receiver, which, consequently, still displayed 'MANUFACTURE IMPERIALE' over Mutzig (for example) and 'MLE. 1866'. However, the marks on the upper 'flats' of the barrel octagon (the steel supplier, the arsenal code and date, and the 'poincons' of the Directeur de la Manufacture and the Contrôleur Principal) had all gone, to be replaced by standard German inspectors' marks and a large crown over the monarch's cypher FW. The French serial numbers were also retained, but the Prussians seem to have added numbers to some of the individual parts—possibly keyed to the dismantling procedure, since the barrel bears the number '11', the receiver '9' and the bolt '7'[4]. This has not yet been confirmed, however.

4. Similar numbers are found on some German pistols.

The original French butt mark, partly defaced by a Prussian inspector's letter punch, has been supplemented by a large crowned script *FW* cypher and a second inspector's mark. Unit designations may often be struck into the left side of the barrel band.

Mechanical description and variations

The Prussian Aptierter Chassepot-Karabiner M 1871 differs from the Saxon M 1873 (qv) in minor respects. Its new plug-type bolt head, for example, is retained by a flush-ground transverse pin rather than a slotted-head screw, and the front part of the bolt-handle base extension has been cut away. A long leaf-type extractor lies in the bottom of the bolt-way, where it is actuated by cam slots cut into the bolt body. A 2mm diameter gas escape hole is bored vertically down through the rear of the receiver ring into the chamber, the old firing needle has been replaced by a heavier and more robust striker, and the guide roller on the original cocking-piece head has been replaced by a brazed-on lateral semi-circular rib on the underside of the head body.

Probably the most important deviation between the Saxon and Prussian carbines lies in the method of re-chambering the barrel for the Reichspatrone 71. The Saxons cut away the original Mle 1866 chamber completely, reamed a new chamber in the remnants of the original barrel and re-seated the whole unit in the faced-off stump of the original breech; the Prussians simply bored-out the Mle 1866 chamber and inserted a tubular liner, containing a reamed-out chamber for the new metallic-case cartridge. The Prussian system was simpler, arguably the stronger, and had less radical effects on the stock, sights and barrel fittings. No variations are known.

Appearance, distinctive features and data

The Prussian Chassepot carbine, the barrel of which has the same appearance as the French original, may be recognized in several different ways. It has a short octagonal barrel-section near the breech, on which the original French tangent-leaf back sight is mounted; it is stocked to the muzzle; and it has a very distinctive brass nose-cap whose special dovetail-retained upward projections guard the front sight. The clamp-type barrel band is held in place by a spring, the nose-cap by a lateral screw, and there are sling swivels under the barrel band and under the butt. A short cleaning rod protrudes from the nose-cap beneath the muzzle.

5. Its leaf, however, was re-graduated for the new bullet, which had a flatter trajectory than the French Mle 1866 type.

DATA

Calibre: 11mm.

Rifling: concentric, 4 grooves 0.3mm deep and 4.5mm wide; 1 turn in 550mm, left hand (pitch of 3° 36').

Magazine: none—single-shot only.

Loading system: manual insertion of cartridge in chamber or bolt-way.

Length overall: 995mm.

Barrel length: 520mm.

Weight: 3,550-3,600gm without sling.

Sights: (front) unprotected barleycorn; (back) a combination tangent-leaf sight with a sight base for 200-400 metres and a single leaf graduated up to 1,300, although an upper notch for 1,500 metres was also provided.

Performance: see cartridge data (Appendix 2).

Accessories

BAYONET

None.

OTHERS

A sling, a cleaning rod, a muzzle protector and a sight cover.

Apt. Chassepot-Karabiner Modell 1873 Saxony

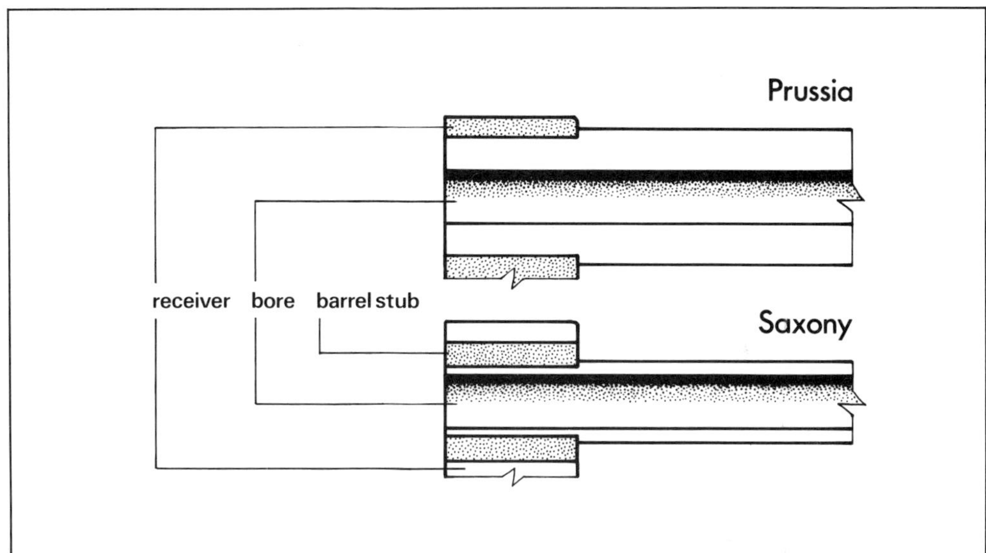

Right: a comparison between the Prussian and Saxon Chassepot conversions, the breeching systems of which were radically different.

Right: the Saxon M 1873 Chassepot carbine.

This rifle is known as the Bremer-Einhorn Transformation after its inventors, Hauptmann von Bremer of the Saxon Army and Oberbüchsenmacher Einhorn of the Dresden armoury, and dates from midsummer 1873. Although similar to the approximately contemporary M 1871 Prussian alteration (qv), there were radical differences in the re-chambering and stocking systems. Bremer and Einhorn decided that the easiest way to convert the Mle 1866 barrel for the Reichspatrone 71 was to simply cut off the existing chamber, ream out a new one in what had become the breech end of the new barrel, cut a thread on the outer surface of the new breech and screw it back into the existing receiver. However, the old breech had been of much greater diameter than the new, since the barrel had flared towards the breech to provide extra metal—and hence additional strength—around the chamber. The designers chose an ingenious solution by using the short portion of the original barrel that lay within the receiver as a 'bush'. It was simply bored-out and tapped to receiver the threaded breech of the new barrel.

Other alterations had to be made, including revising the back sight, replacing the existing bolt head with a solid plug-type and adding an extractor to remove the spent cases. Some guns (but not, apparently, all of them) may be found with a lever-pattern safety mechanism on the left rear of the receiver, operating against a long leaf spring anchored mid-way along the receiver wall immediately below the new designation mark. The much modified half-stock (see Appearance and distinctive features, below) is a good identifying feature of the Saxon Chassepot 'cavalry' carbine, which was actually issued to the State's Train-Bataillon, Nr. 12, by an order of 27 May 1875. The guns served until the 1880s, when they were replaced by the Karabiner M 1871. Apparently they were not very successful, since the new barrels were weak immediately in front of the breech where they lacked the thickness of metal found on even the original French Mle 1866 needle-rifles.

Production history

At least ten thousand French rifles were converted to the Bremer-Einhorn system in 1875-76, since examples have been seen with serial numbers as high as 9747. The alterations are assumed to have been undertaken by the government armoury in Dresden (the Dresdner Zeughaus).

Markings

The original French arsenal markings and designation stamp were somewhat crudely erased from the left side of the receiver, and replaced by the designation 'MOD.73' in fraktur (gothic script). Most of the other French marks remained intact, although all of those on the breech end of the barrel disappeared when the original chamber was cut off. New serial numbers, '5877' for example, may be found on the left side of the barrel, on the receiver at the breech and also on the rear portion of the bolt-handle base extension. The original French number may be encountered on the front portion of the rib, as erasure was only rarely attempted. The weapons also usually display standard Germanic inspectors' marks.

Mechanical description and variations

The operating system of the Saxon Mle 1866 conversion, while basically similar to that of the original French needle-rifle (qv), shows several important changes. The original bolt head was replaced by a new flush-headed plug pattern still retained by a transverse screw through the bolt handle base extension, and a conventional extractor was added. The original needle assembly was replaced by a more robust striker actuated by a more powerful coil-pattern mainspring. Most of the Saxon carbines retained the French-style cocking piece guide roller, while the Prussian M 1871 transformations (qv) did not. No mechanical variations of the Saxon Chassepot carbine have yet been encountered, apart from guns with or without the safety mechanism.

Appearance, distinctive features and data

In these respects, the M 1873 cannot be confused with the Prussian M 1871, although they share split-bridge receivers and turned-down bolt handles. The Saxon guns retain the original full-length bolt-handle base extensions, complete with a prominent screw retaining the new bolt heads, while the ribs on Prussian guns are partly cut away. They also lack the screw heads. The barrel of the M 1873 has been shortened by cutting away the original octagonal breech-reinforcing portion and no longer beds properly in the stock; there are, therefore, very noticeable gaps alongside the barrel immediately in front of the receiver. Bremer and Einhorn elected to use a virtually free-floating barrel; this decision was made in order to save time and money rather than to deliberately improve accuracy, since the significance of barrel vibrations was not fully understood in the early 1870s. Consequently, the original Mle 1866 stock was shortened to half length and fitted with a new nose-cap (which does, however, touch the barrel surface). One sling swivel lies beneath the nose-cap, while the other may be found on the underside of the butt.

The French-style tangent-leaf back sight has been replaced by a modified leaf type in which the hinge lies at the back rather than the front of the sight bed. The shortened barrel meant that the sight was of necessity sited nearer the muzzle.

Originally, the metal parts of the barrel and the receiver were browned, except for the bolt mechanism, which remained 'in the white'.

DATA

Calibre: 11mm.
Rifling: concentric, 4 grooves 0.3mm deep and 4.5mm wide; 1 turn in 550mm, left hand (pitch of 3° 36').
Magazine: none—single-shot only.
Loading system: manual insertion of cartridge in chamber or bolt-way.
Length overall: 955mm.
Barrel length: 477mm.
Weight: about 3,150gm without sling.
Sights: (front) unprotected barleycorn; (back) a leaf pattern, with a standing 'battle sight' for 200 metres and a single leaf graduated from 300 to 1,500 metres.
Performance: see cartridge data (Appendix 2).

Accessories

BAYONET
None.

OTHERS
A sling, muzzle protector and sight cover.

Jägerbüchse Modell 1871 Mauser

The first issues of the Mauser infantry rifle were made in 1875 and it soon became clear that a new firearm should be found for the Jäger-Bataillone—the élite riflemen, who had traditionally carried better weapons than the rank and file infantrymen. Their Dreyse-system Jägerbüchse M 1865 had, after all, been fitted with a special 'set' trigger and the GPK had acceded to a request for a distinctive Mauser-system Jäger gun as early as 1872-73. Trials began once supplies of the Infanterie-Gewehr M 1871 had been ensured, and the first production rifle was displayed before the Kaiser on 22 March 1875[1].

Very few problems were encountered in developing a Mauser Jägerbüchse, since the final pattern was little more than a shortened infantry rifle with a special finger-rest on the trigger guard bow. The weapon was adopted on 18 January 1876 and re-equipping had been completed by the end of the year, when most of the old Zündnadelbüchsen M 1865 were handed over to the navy and the Landwehr.

The Jäger-Bataillone, used to preferential treatment, had grounds for complaint against their new firearms, which had shorter barrels than the infantry types and were marginally less accurate, while the other alterations were almost exclusively cosmetic. The trigger mechanism remained that of the M 1871 infantry rifle, which, in turn, had simply been copied from the old M 1862 Dreyse design. Consequently, the M 1871 Jägerbüchse was almost a retrograde step, because its trigger mechanism lacked the finer design features found on the Jägerbüchse M 1865.

The Jäger rifles were also issued to other specialized troops who needed a short weapon: the foot artillery and the pioneers (who adopted it on 18 January 1876), the navy and, finally, the German colonial troops[2]. Many guns served in the hands of the last-named units until the First World War, in which a few others were bored-out and re-rifled for a special 13mm cartridge loaded with incendiary bullets and issued as anti-balloon guns.

1. The third anniversary of its final adoption.

2. The Schützruppe für Deutsche-Ostafrika; the Schützruppe für Kamerun; and the Polizeitruppen für Deutsche-Ostafrika, für Kamerun und für Togo.

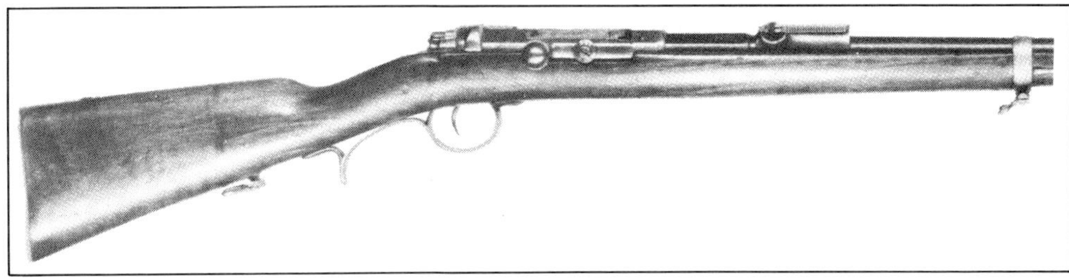

Right: the butt and breech of the M 1871 Jägerbüchse, showing the distinctive trigger-guard bow.

Production history

Jägerbüchsen M 1871 were made by several contractors, three of whom have been identified at the time of writing: the Prussian government's arsenal in Danzig, Gebrüder Mauser & Co. of Oberndorf am Neckar, and Österreichische Waffenfabrik-Gesellschaft of Steyr. The total quantity involved remains unknown. Danzig began production in 1876 and seems to have completed the contract in 1884; or, perhaps, simply stopped making 1871-system rifles on the introduction of the Gewehr 71/84.

Markings

These parallel the marks applied to the standard M 1871 infantry rifle (qv). The three manufacturers' stampings are discussed in the same section. The only major difference between the Jägerbüchsen and Infanterie-Gewehre M 1871 lies in the substitution of 'J.G.MOD.71' for 'I.G.MOD.71' on the left side of the receiver. (It is, however, very difficult to distinguish between the gothic 'J' and 'I'; but the other features of any rifle in question will make confusion unlikely.)

Many different types of unit marking may be found on the top surface of the butt plate; '10.J.3.25.', for example, represents the twenty-fifth rifle issued to the third company of Hannover'sches Jäger-Bataillon Nr. 10. Sometimes the mark is of a unit other than riflemen; '13.A.F.E.4.232.' shows that the gun was issued to the fourth company of the Ersatz-Bataillon of Hohenzollernsches Fussartillerie-Regiment Nr. 13, while 'Sch.D.O.A.347.' is the Schütztruppe Deutsche-Ostafrika.

Mechanical description and variations

The Jägerbüchse is mechanically identical with the standard M 1871, since the only ways in which the two differed concerned barrel length, stock fittings, the position of the sling swivels and the design of the trigger guard bow. Like the infantry rifle (and the carbine, for that matter), the Jägerbüchse does not have an ejector. No variations have been recorded apart from the large-calibre balloon guns produced during the First World War, which were converted simply by boring-out and re-rifling the barrel.

Appearance, distinctive features and data

The action of the Jägerbüchse M 1871 is identical with that of the standard M 1871 and is of the same appearance. The principal differences lie in the length of the barrel, which is about 10cm shorter but still has an octagonal-section portion at the breech and a very short (about 1cm) turned-down muzzle crown for the ring in the crossguard of the bayonet.

There are other minor differences: the Jägerbüchse has a special cast iron trigger-guard bow with a long rearward finger-rest extension, only a single iron barrel band, and flat-bottomed sling swivels on the band and under the butt behind the trigger guard. A small alteration has been made to the main back sight leaf, since the sliding extension is graduated for 1,150 and 1,250 metres rather than 1,100 and 1,200 metres; one wonders why the authorities bothered.

DATA

Calibre: 11mm.
Rifling: concentric, 4 grooves 0.3mm deep and 4.5mm wide; 1 turn in 550mm, right hand.
Magazine: none—single-shot only.
Loading system: manual insertion of a cartridge in chamber or bolt-way.
Length overall: 1,240mm.
Barrel length: 750mm.
Weight: between 4,450 and 4,525gm (without sling).
Sights: (front) unprotected barleycorn; (back) a combined block and leaf sight, with a standing 'battle sight' for 300 metres, a small leaf for 400, and a large leaf with a sliding extension for 500-1600m.
Performance: see cartridge data (Appendix 2).

Accessories

BAYONETS

The Jägerbüchse was issued with the Hirschfänger M 1871 (TGB, pp. 37-38), which had a steel pommel, chequered leather grips, a recurved steel crossguard and a 50cm swell-point sword blade of very distinctive style. However, some examples of the earlier Hirschfänger M 1865 (TGB, pp. 25-27) were bushed for the 1871-pattern rifles and re-issued while genuine M 1871 bayonets were in short supply. They could be recognized by their grip rivets; genuine M 1871 bayonets had five, the M 1865 only three. The Pioneers were issued with the Pionerfaschinenmesser M 1871 (TGB, pp. 38-41), which had a cast brass hilt, a steel or wrought iron crossguard, and a massive saw-backed blade measuring about 47.5cm × 3.7cm. The foot artillerymen were given the so-called Artillerie-Seitengewehr M 1871 (TGB, p. 41), which was little more than a bushed version of the standard Füsilier-Seitengewehr M 1860, but was distinguished by its 'pipe backed' blade.

OTHERS

A cleaning rod, a sling, a muzzle protector, a sight cover, a screwdriver, a spare striker spring and a spare extractor.

Karabiner Modell 1871 Mauser

Experience in the Franco-Prussian War convinced the Prussians and their allies that carbines were useful to all cavalrymen—not simply the dragoons and hussars—and to small patrols, pickets, outposts, personnel of the army postal services, and others who had been left to the mercies of the 'franctireurs' (what would now be called partisans) during the war. The obvious solution in 1872 was to develop a shortened version of the Infanterie-Gewehr M 1871, which had just been adopted. But all available production resources, in both public and private sectors, were concentrated on the new infantry rifle and it was realized that the Mauser carbine would have to wait. A short-term solution was found by converting large quantities of captured Chassepot infantry rifles to carbine length and issuing them to the cuirassiers, dragoons, hussars and lancers (Ulanen). In the event, the M 1871 Aptierter Chassepot-Karabiner (qv), adopted by the dragoons and the hussars early in 1875, was issued to the lancers from 31 August 1876 and, finally, to the cuirassiers in November 1880—four years after the Mauser carbine was approved.

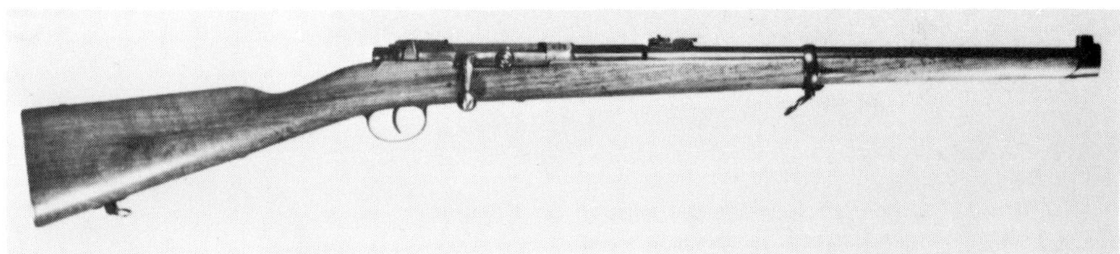

Right: the Karabiner M 1871. Courtesy of Frank de Haas.

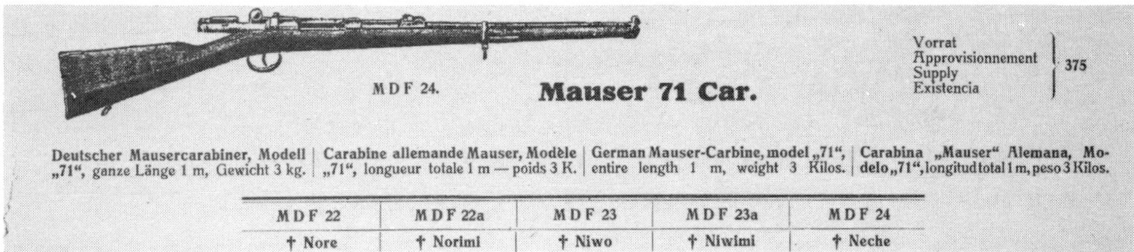

Right: the Karabiner M 1871, from the 1911 ALFA catalogue.

The prototype Karabiner M 1871 was developed by the GPK between January and May 1875, in accordance with a directive issued at the beginning of the year for a carbine a metre long, with the cylindrical and octagonal barrel form of the standard infantry rifle, a cleaning rod, a sight similar to that of the then experimental Jägerbüchse and a turned-down bolt handle. The final pattern appeared with a full-length stock, but discarded the cleaning rod and had a diminutive leaf sight of conventional design. The gun fired a reduced charge version of the full-power rifle cartridge, which had been developed at Spandau in 1875 to minimize the excessive muzzle blast and flash that was to be expected when firing rifle ammunition in such a short barrel. The muzzle velocity of the bullet dropped from 430 to about 395m/sec.

The trials proved to be leisurely affairs, since adoption (or, perhaps, issue) of the perfected carbine was delayed until 31 August 1876. It then became the weapon of all cavalrymen—dragoons, hussars, and lancers—apart from the non-commissioned officers and the trumpeters, who carried single-shot pistols[1]. The M 1871 carbines were first issued to the cuirassiers by an AKO of 12 April 1884, on the scale of 25 to each squadron; however, complete arming of these troops, apart from the non-commissioned officers and the trumpeters, was delayed until 1888.

The single-shot Mauser carbines served until the introduction of the Karabiner 88 (qv) in January 1890. Most had been handed to the Landwehr or discarded by the turn of the century, although many soldiers had been given the option of purchasing their carbines for two marks apiece. One thousand of these Mausers were sold to China in 1906. A. L. Frank Exportgesellschaft were still advertizing 375 of them for sale in 1911[2].

1. They were later issued with revolvers.

2. ALFA catalogue, 1911, p. 11.

Right: three views of the action of a standard Karabiner M 1871. Courtesy of Frank de Haas.

Production history

Most Mauser carbines were made by private contractors, since the Prussian government arsenals had very little spare manufacturing capacity. Götz[3] records that the first orders were placed by the Prussian government with Österreichische Waffenfabrik-Gesellschaft of Steyr in the summer of 1875. The quantity was sixty thousand, and all were delivered before the end of 1877. Each Steyr-made gun cost the Prussian government about 47 marks.

Gebrüder Mauser & Co. made three thousand carbines for Württemberg and an unknown number for Prussia and Saxony, while others were made by the Productionsgemeinschaft Spangenberg & Sauer, Schilling & Haenel in Suhl for between 36 and 38 marks each[4]. These contractors, despite being organized as a cartel, seem to have fulfilled their obligations separately, as carbines have been seen marked 'AGH' for Arbeitsgemeinschaft Haenel or 'V.C.S.' for Schilling. Total production probably exceeded 150,000.

3. Hans-Dieter Götz, *Die deutschen Militärgewehre und Maschinenpistolen, 1871-1945*, p. 45.

4. This organization was also known as the Handfeuerwaffen Produktionsgenossenschaft Suhl. The cost figures are those given by Götz.

Markings

A typical Karabiner M 1871 bears its maker's mark, 'GEBR. MAUSER & Co OBERNDORF' for example, along the top 'flat' of the barrel octagon. The designation 'K.MOD.71' is in fraktur (gothic script) on the left rear of the receiver. The serial numbers—'3995', for example, without letter suffixes—appear on the left side of the barrel, the left side of the receiver, the bolt head, and the bolt guide rib alongside the operating handle. The last two, or sometimes three, digits may be found on most of the components. There are the usual government inspectors' marks (small crowned letters) on most of the parts, and notably alongside the breech on the right side of the barrel and the receiver. Most carbines are dated on the right side of the receiver behind the bolt handle, and a large crowned FW or W cypher may be struck into the left upper face of the barrel octagon behind the back sight.

Unit markings often lie on the top surface of the butt plate, in the form of '5.D.3.32.': the thirty-second gun issued to the third squadron of Dragoner-Regiment Freiherr von Manteuffel (Rheinisches) Nr. 5. The key letters include D, H, K and U—Dragoner, Husaren, Kürassiere and Ulanen.

Mechanical description and variations

The carbine operates in much the same way as the standard 1871-system rifle and Jägerbüchse. The only difference is a purely cosmetic one: the bolt handle is turned down.

Few basic deviations from the basic Karabiner M 1871 design have yet been reported, although Götz[5] pictures one with a bayonet lug on the right side of the nose-cap. He theorizes that this weapon, which according to the receiver date was made by Gebrüder Mauser & Co. in 1876, may have been an experimental design for the Württemberg Army. However, he is probably wrong, because several such carbines have been reported and it seems that the bayonet they take is the so-called 'Marine-Seitengewehr M 1871' (identified wrongly, TGB, p. 41). The few known bayonets have all been dated 1880, and it is suspected that the carbines may have been issued to gendarmerie or border guards in Elsass-Lothringen. However, the theory awaits verification.

5. Hans-Dieter Götz, *Die deutschen Militärgewehre und Maschinenpistolen, 1871-1945*, p. 47.

GRENZ-AUFSICHTS-GEWEHR MODELL 1879

The identification of this weapon, forwarded by Hans-Rudolf von Stein[6] to explain the designation mark 'G.A.G.MOD.79' on the rear left side of the receiver, lacks any official confirmation. The Grenz-Aufsichts-Beamten are believed to have been part of the customs service, acting as border guards, and were not part of the armed forces. The two carbines examined were both made by V. C. Schilling of Suhl in 1880, and bear the 'V.C.S.' mark on the barrel; one is number '1', the other, '838'. The greatly resemble the standard Karabiner M 1871, but have 2 position rocking 'L' pattern backsights, Dreyse-style stock fittings and provision for a sabre bayonet.

6. In a letter to the author, 21 May 1977.

Appearance, distinctive features and data

The Karabiner M 1871 has a bolt mechanism almost identical with that of the M 1871 infantry rifle, although the bolt handle is turned downwards against the stock. The barrel is cylindrical, tapering slightly towards the muzzle, and has a short octagonal section at the breech. The leaf-type back sight lies immediately ahead of the octagonal portion. The one-piece walnut stock extends to the muzzle cap, which has upward projecting 'ears' to prevent the front sight snagging in the carbine scabbard. There is a single blued steel band, held in place by a spring and carrying a sling swivel. The second swivel lies on the underside of the butt. The butt plate and the plain trigger guard bow are steel or iron; like all the metal parts, apart from the browned barrel and the blued barrel band, they are left 'in the white'.

DATA

Calibre: nominally 11mm, actually 11.025 ± 0.075mm.
Rifling: concentric, 4 grooves 0.3mm deep and 4.5mm wide; 1 turn in 550mm, right hand (pitch of 3° 36').
Magazine: none—single-shot only.
Loading system: manual insertion of a cartridge in chamber or bolt-way.
Length overall: 995mm.
Barrel length: 505mm.
Weight: 3,350-3,475gm without sling.
Sights: (front) protected barleycorn; (back) a two-leaf sight with a standing 'battle sight' for 200m, a small leaf for 300 and a large leaf for 400-1200 metres.
Performance: see cartridge data (Appendix 2).

Accessories

BAYONET

Generally none.

OTHERS

A leather back sight cover, a sling, a screwdriver, a spare mainspring and a spare extractor. The carbines were also often issued with a saddle-mounted scabbard called the Karabiner-Futteral 71.

Gewehr 71/84 Mauser

The success of magazine rifles such as the Swiss Vetterli and the exploits of the Turkish Army during the Russo-Turkish War had eroded the widespread and deeply-held conviction that such weapons were simply a means of wasting ammunition and destroying fire discipline. The advantages of repeating rifles had been conclusively demonstrated, to those who were prepared to learn, at the Battle of Plevna in 1877[1].

1. See a quote from Todleben, the Russian commander, in Smith & Smith, *Small Arms of the World*, tenth edition, p. 68.

Conservatism was as much a part of the late nineteenth century German Army as any other, but it was clear by 1880 that the days of the single-shot Mauser infantry rifle were numbered. Several experimental magazines had been developed for the Infanterie-Gewehr M 1871 in the late 1870s and early 1880s, but none had been successful. Peter Paul Mauser, therefore, began development of a magazine version of his rifle and the first prototype emerged from the Oberndorf factory at the beginning of 1881. It was patented in March of the same year[2] and was based on the Serbian 1878/80-model infantry rifle, which in turn was derived from the German M 1871. The Probegewehr C/81 had a deepened receiver forging, which contained a bolt-operated tipping cartridge elevator fed from a tubular magazine under the barrel. This was hardly an innovation, as similar weapons had been in existence for fifteen years or more; however, Mauser's elevator was a more advanced design than most of its predecessors. The patent drawings

2. DRP (Deutsches Reichs Patent) 15,202 of 16 March 1881.

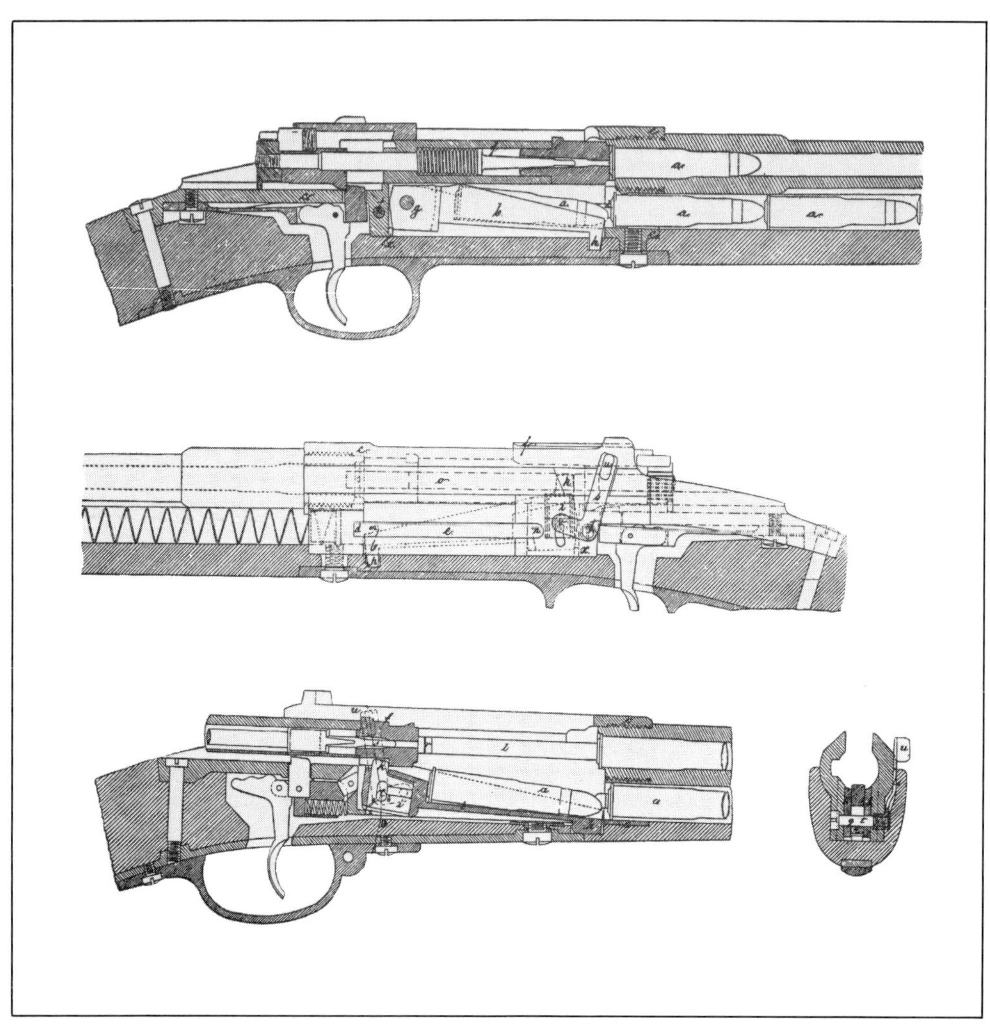

Right: one of Mauser's first tubular magazine designs. From the papers of DRP 15,202, granted in 1881.

illustrate several modifications to the elevator mechanism and it is clear that the inventor was still seeking inspiration in early 1881. The first prototypes were not especially successful, so Mauser filed another patent[3] in May 1882, the second part describing the mechanism which was to become part of the Gewehr 71/84. A modified ejector unit was patented in March 1884[4], before production of the finalized rifles had commenced.

3. DRP 20,738 of 7 May 1882.

4. The subject of DRP 30,035 of 30 March 1884.

Since the Kaiser had personally expressed interest in them, the trials proceeded as quickly as possible. Gebrüder Mauser & Co. delivered two thousand experimental Infanterie-Repetier-Gewehre C/82 to the GPK in the summer of 1882. These were promptly issued to four garrison battalions in Darmstadt, Königsberg in Preussen and Spandau. The rifles were understandably based on the existing Gewehr M 1871[5], although wholesale alterations had been made to the receiver forging to accommodate the cartridge elevator and the magazine. The trials proved to be very successful, but several instances of cartridges exploding in the magazine were reported. These explosions, which were often a feature of rifles using magazines of this type, even the French Mle 86 Lebel, were traced to the rounded nose of the bullet in the standard Patrone 71 slamming into and igniting the primer of the round lying ahead of it in the tube. This, of course, was a very dangerous feature, but it was quickly eliminated by

5. Five hundred of them had cleaning rods, the remainder had none.

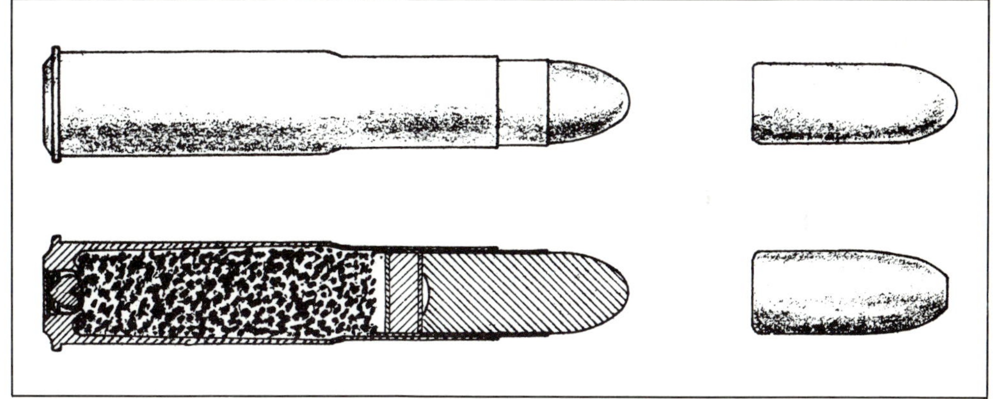

Right: the Reichspatrone M 1871 compared with the Patrone 71/84. Note that the bullet of the latter —the Geschoss 71/84— has its nose flattened.

introducing a new flat-nosed bullet (Geschoss 71/84) and a revised, recessed and more tightly-seated primer (Zündhütchen 71/84). The GPK had elected to retain the calibre of 11mm for the new rifle to save time and money, although highly revealing trials of smaller calibres had been undertaken in April 1879 and again in the autumn of 1883[6]. These had proved that 9mm was the minimum acceptable calibre for use with black powder propellant.

6. Calibres of 9mm, 9.5mm, 10mm, 10.2mm and 10.5mm had been among them. The guns were altered Gewehre M 1871.

Apart from these problems, and the inevitable change in the centre of gravity and the point of balance as the cartridges in the long tubular magazine were expended, the new rifle passed its tests with flying colours. With a few modifications it became the Infanterie-Gewehr M 1871/84, since the word 'Repetier' had been dropped for reasons of secrecy. The Kriegsministerium had stated at the end of January 1884 that, "His Majesty the King-Emperor . . . is pleased to order that future production of the M 1871 infantry rifle is to be suspended in favour of the new prototype demonstrated to Him on 17th January 1884 . . . It is [his] decision that, in the interests of secrecy, the designation of the new prototype will be M 71/84 and that the expression 'Repeater' will not be applied . . .".

The Gewehr 71/84 was adopted by an AKO of 31 January 1884 in Prussia, Saxony and Württemberg, but production did not begin until the midsummer of 1886 because most of the existing facilities were obsolescent. This forced the arsenals to re-tool completely. The Bavarian war ministry was given an example of the perfected magazine

7. Hans-Dieter Götz, *Die deutschen Militärgewehre und Maschinenpistolen, 1871-1945*, p. 67.

8. Normally credited to the arsenal's director, Major von Flotow.

rifle on 8 May 1884[7], although the Prussians had kept the Bavarians informed of progress throughout the developmental period. The Bavarian king, Ludwig II, signed adoption papers later in the same month.

Many engineering problems were encountered during the time in which the new production line was being developed, not least of which concerned the magazine tube. The latter was eventually solved by the arsenal in Danzig, where a cold-drawing process had been perfected for tubular lance-bodies[8]. This was applied to the magazines with great success, so much so that Danzig seems to have supplied them to the other contractors until sufficient experience of cold-drawing had been obtained.

The first issues of the Gewehre 71/84 were made in July 1886 to the two Prussian army corps, XV. and XVI., guarding the borders in Elsass-Lothringen. These men had been prepared for the new rifles by the distribution of about a thousand 'Demonstrations-schlosse' (sectioned actions to show how the 71/84 worked).

Mauser was keen to safeguard his rights, since the new rifle embodied a number of his patents. Eventually, a licensing agreement was concluded on 22 July 1885 between the Prussian government,. acting on behalf of the states of the German Empire, Peter-Paul Mauser and Waffenfabrik Mauser AG. A 3 mark royalty was to be paid on each of the first hundred thousand guns, and a sum of one mark on each rifle made thereafter. In return for a guaranteed sum of 300,000 marks, Mauser was to forego all royalties on the small numbers of guns made before the licence was signed and to indemnify the Prussian government against costs involved in correcting possible design faults in the action. In addition, no monies were to be payable on guns that failed proof.

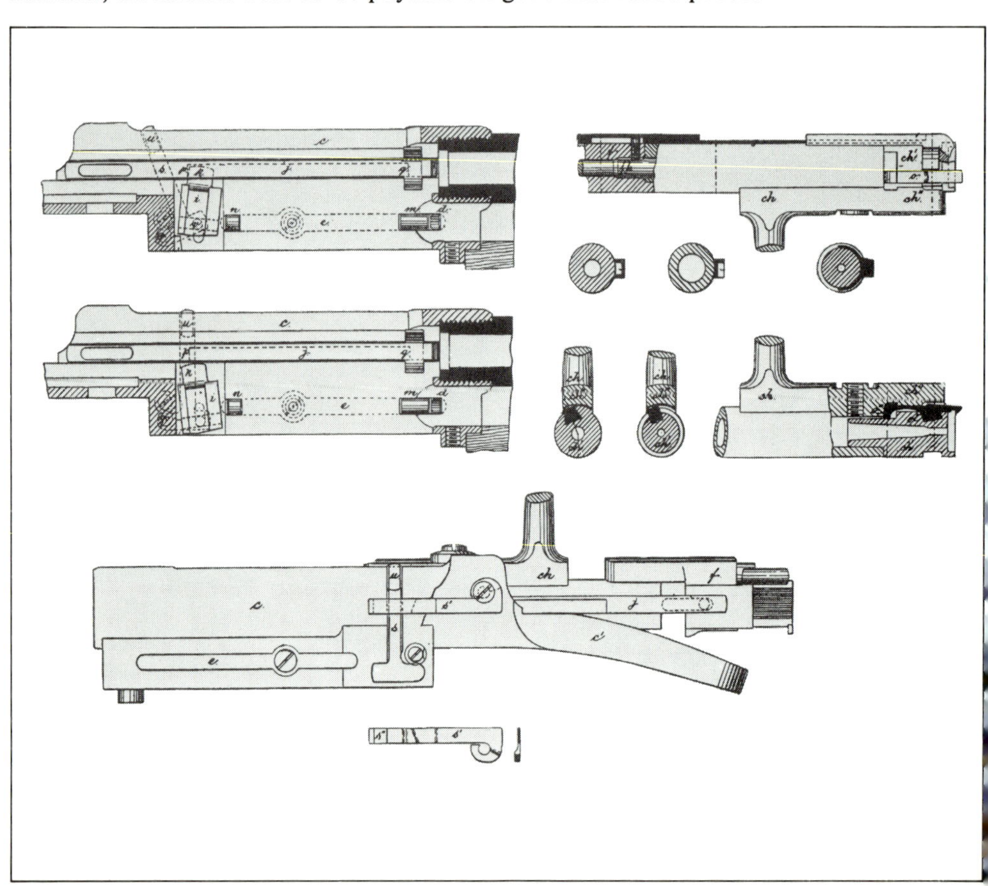

Right: Mauser's perfected tube-magazine bolt-action rifle design appeared in 1882. From the papers of DRP 20,738.

Once the rifles were in service faults became apparent, as was always the case with new designs. Small alterations were made periodically to the machining of the components, since binding problems had arisen during prolonged use. Also, a series of shooting trials undertaken by four Jäger-Bataillone in 1885-86 with the Gewehre M 1871 and 71/84 proved that the new guns shot consistently to the right. As a result, the front sight was offset 0.6mm to the right to correct the point of impact; and individual unit armourers were permitted to increase the lateral deviation to as much as 1.2mm to recify the occasional rifle that shot even more markedly to the right.

The shooting of the Gewehr 71/84 was found to be very sensitive to variations in temperature, whether atmospheric or because of the effects of barrel heating. This was blamed on the under-barrel tube magazine, the variations in the point of balance as the cartridges were used-up, and the consequent changes in the stress applied to the barrel by the stock. In addition, the stocks of many guns had not been seasoned for as long as usual[9] and occasionally warped, with disastrous effects on accuracy. The cut-off lever was also found to be weak and could break away, thus leaving the firer with a useless magazine if the lever had been positioned for single-shot fire.

9. They were stored for 3 years rather than 5.

The Gewehr 71/84 was robust and well-liked, despite being heavy, unwieldy and badly balanced. The last complaint, however, could be applied to virtually all tube-magazine military rifles, since the perceptible change in the point of balance as the cartridges were expended was an inevitable drawback in their design. But the 71/84 had a large magazine capacity, ten rounds could be inserted: eight in the tube, one on the cartridge elevator and the last directly in the chamber. On the debit side, the mechanism was more

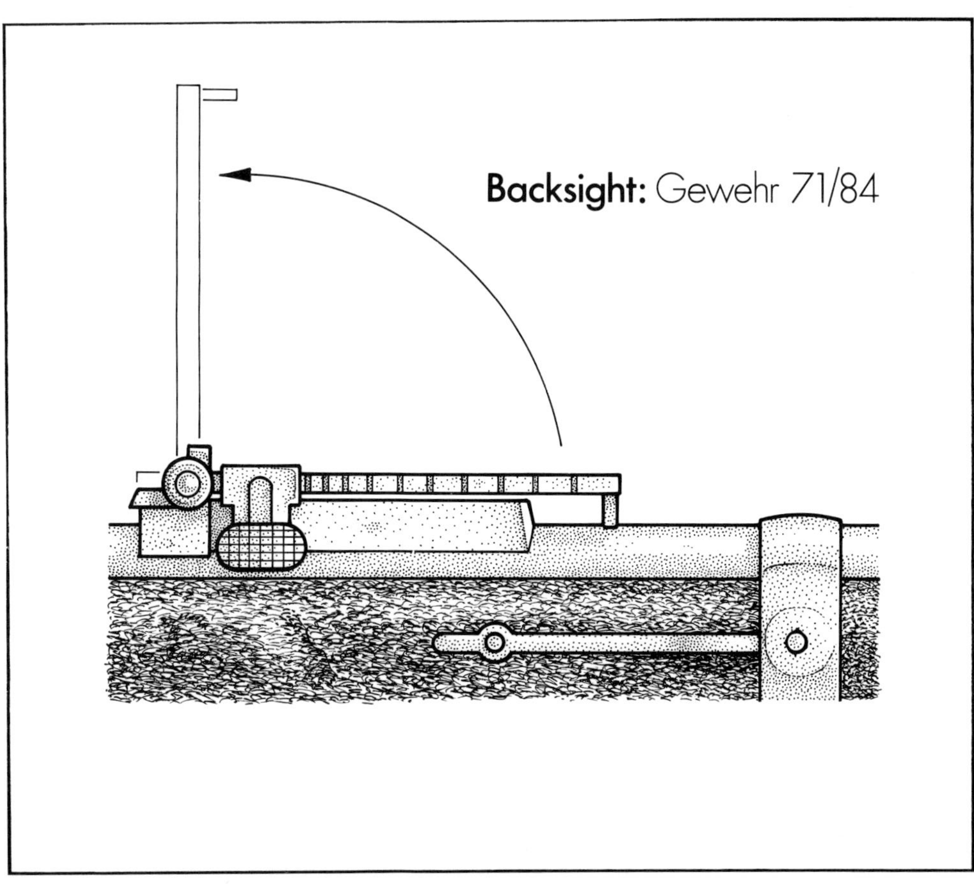

complicated and more difficult to dismantle compared with the M 1871, and could also be fairly easily jammed by dirt and dust.

The effective service life of the 71/84 was very short, since the appearance of the French Mle 86 Lebel rifle made it obsolescent virtually as production was beginning. Although its rival was only marginally superior mechanically, the 8mm French cartridge, with a charge of smokeless propellant, was infinitely superior ballistically. The French bullet attained a muzzle velocity of about 615-620m/sec compared with only 430m/sec for the German pattern, which led to a much flatter trajectory[10] and the consequent minimalization of inaccuracy owing to range-gauging errors.

The Germans developed the Gewehr 88 to counter the Lebel, in an atmosphere approaching blind panic. Had they not seen sense at the last moment, an 8mm version of the Gewehr 71/84, improved by the addition of a second locking lug[11], would have been adopted instead.

The surviving Gewehre 71/84 were gradually withdrawn as the more efficient Gewehre 88 entered service in large numbers. Many were relegated to the Reserve and the Landwehr, while others were sold for a few marks apiece; A. L. Frank Exportgesellschaft still had twelve thousand in stock in 1911. Those rifles that remained in the German armies at the outbreak of the First World War were re-issued to lines of communication, Landwehr, Landsturm and recruiting depot personnel. By 1914, many guns were chambered for the standard 8mm cartridges—generally by boring-out the barrels and inserting a new rifled liner—but this is believed to have been done during the early 1890s, to offset temporary shortages of Gewehre 88. (See Variations.)

10. With the sights set for 300m, the French Mle 86 bullet was 37cm above the bore at 150m; the figures for the 71/84 bullet was 82cm. For 600m, the figures were 2.50m at 300m and 4.80m at 300m respectively.

11. Patented in Austria-Hungary on 14 September 1887.

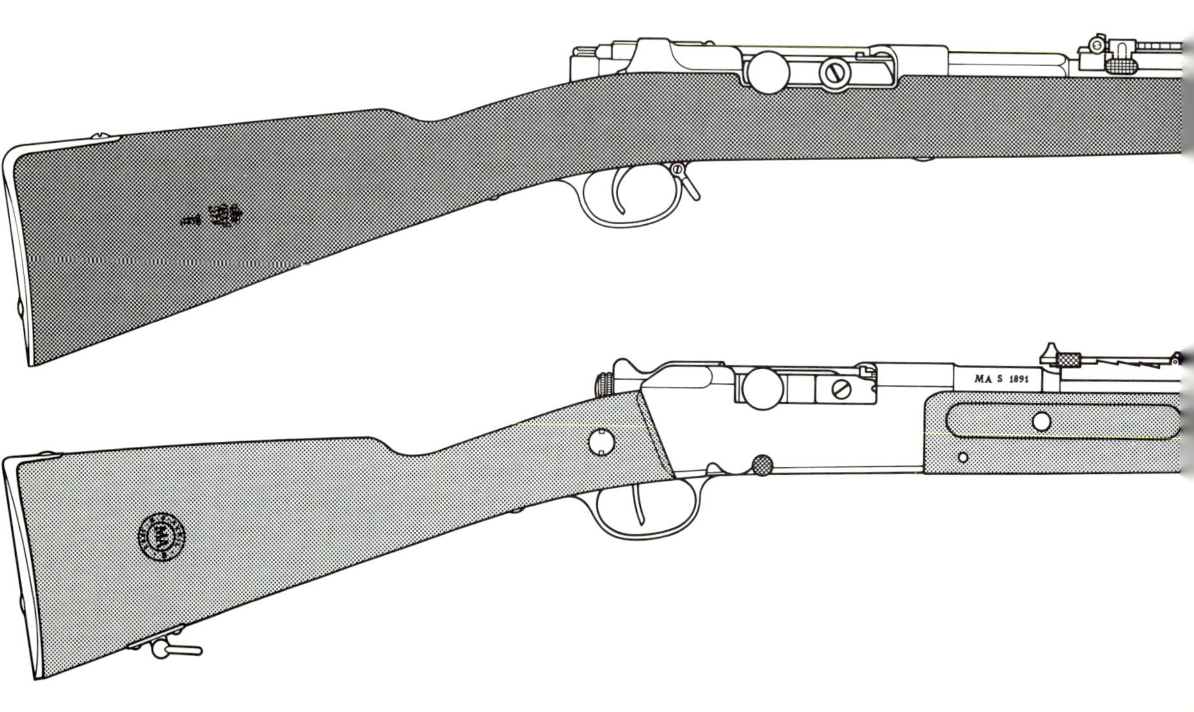

Production history

In 1884, the Prussian government granted a loan of 2.2 million marks to finance production of the Gewehr 71/84 in the three main arsenals in Danzig, Erfurt and Spandau. The sum did not prove to be enough and further grants were made in 1886-87. New production machinery was purchased from Ludwig Loewe & Co. of Berlin-Charlottenburg, Germany's premier machine-tool manufacturer, and installed in the arsenals during 1885. Götz[12] records that the three Prussian factories received 504 new machines, while 160 more went to Amberg.

The first new rifles were delivered, from Spandau, in March 1885. Erfurt's first followed in July, Danzig's in September, and Amberg's at the beginning of 1886. Each of the Prussian establishments ultimately attained a daily production rate of four hundred guns, while the smaller Amberg factory contributed an additional 200. The cost of each Prussian-made Gewehr 71/84 was estimated as 43 marks, without the royalty; Amberg calculated 42 marks, but the director of the factory noted that a fair price, including depreciation of the production machinery and royalties, was nearer 55 marks. Waffenfabrik Mauser AG made rifles for Württemberg, nineteen thousand being delivered in the summer of 1886 for 56 marks each, in addition to an unknown quantity despatched to Prussia and Saxony in the same period.

By April 1887, Amberg had delivered 16,000 rifles to the Bavarian Army; and by July, the three Prussian arsenals had completed their initial quotas, which may have run into the hundreds of thousands. In September, 99,000 rifles were delivered to Saxony, Württemberg and the Kaiserliche Marine (Imperial Navy). A further ten thousand were made in Danzig, Spandau and Erfurt in September-October 1887 and sent to Bavaria where, by the end of the year, there were 96,368 Gewehre 71/84 in service[13]. It is believed that about 950,000 Gewehre 71/84 were made between the beginning of 1885 and early 1889, when assembly probably ceased. Manufacture had been suspended in November 1888.

Markings

The Gewehr 71/84 bears its maker's mark on top of the barrel octagon, a short distance in front of the receiver ring. The following contractors have been identified:

DANZIG	Prussian arsenal, Danzig, Westpreussen
ERFURT	Prussian arsenal, Erfurt, Thüringen

12. Hans-Dieter Götz, *Die deutschen Militärgewehre und Maschinenpistolen, 1871-1945,* p. 67.

13. Hans-Dieter Götz, *Die deutschen Militärgewehre und Maschinenpistolen, 1871-1945,* p. 67.

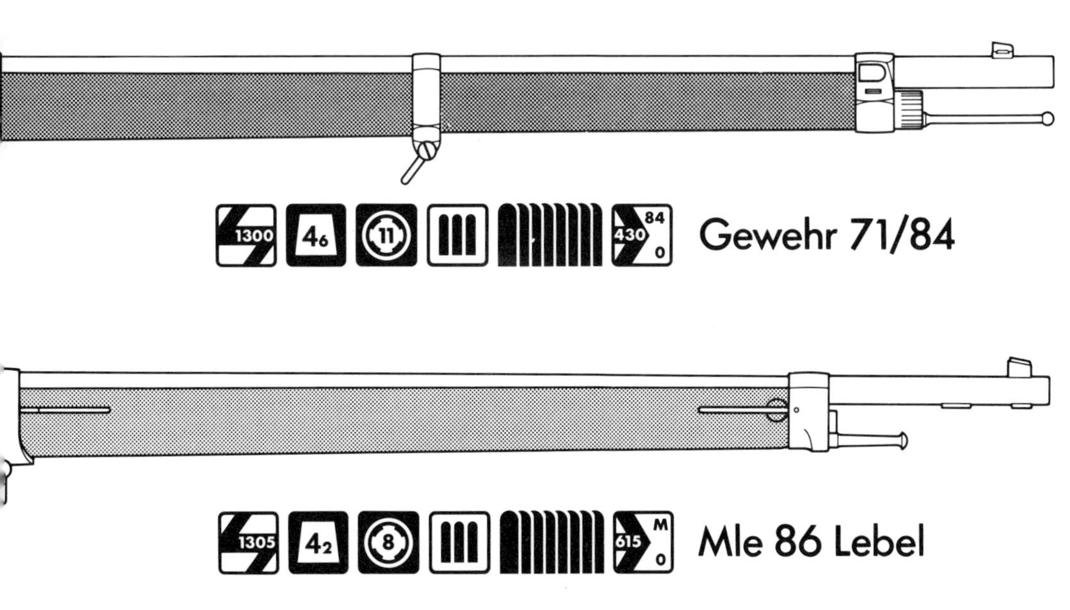

A comparison between the French and German infantry rifles of the late 1880s.

SPANDAU Prussian arsenal, Spandau

AMBERG Bavarian arsenal, Amberg

MAUSER Waffenfabrik Mauser AG, formerly Gebr. Mauser & Co. (under which title it had traded until April 1884), Oberndorf am Neckar, Württemberg

The designation mark 'I.G.MOD.71/84' in fraktur (gothic script) may be found on the left side of the receiver, while the date of manufacture often lies on the right side of the receiver bridge behind the bolt handle; occasionally, there may be two dates.

The serial number, apparently without letter suffixes, lies on the left side of the barrel octagon and the receiver, on the base of the bolt handle and on the removable bolt head. A calibre mark may be found on the left upper 'flat' of the barrel octagon immediately in front of its joint with the receiver. A monarch's cypher—a crown over FW or W in Prussia, or L in Bavaria—may also lie on the left side of the barrel octagon.

Parts of the serial number are repeated on most of the components, together with inspectors' marks in the form of small crowned letters. The letters are especially notable on the right side of the barrel, and the receiver at the breech. Cyphers and inspectors' marks may be struck into the right side of the butt, and unit marks are often to be found on the top surface of the butt plate. A typical example reads 'G.F.R.6.121.', the 121st rifle issued to the sixth company of the Garde-Füsilier-Regiment. '21.R.E.3.17.' would have been the seventeenth rifle issued to the third company of the Ersatz-Bataillon of Infanterie-Regiment von Borcke (4.Pommersches) Nr. 21.

Mechanical description and variations

Many of the features of the Gewehr 71/84 were the same as those of the earlier M 1871 (qv), although several important changes were made to accommodate the cartridge elevator and the tubular magazine. The upper part of the receiver is identical with the older design, but the forging has been deepened to provide a hollow housing or box for the cartridge elevator mechanism. The elevator, a U-trough, is operated by a cam lying in a recess milled in the left wall of the housing. The cam acts in conjunction with the spring-loaded magazine cut-off lever, the knurled head of which protrudes from the left rear of the receiver alongside the bridge. In its rearmost position, the cut-off raises the elevator-operating cam into the ejector channel milled longitudinally in the left side of the bolt-way; when pushed forward, the cut-off lowers the elevator cam to isolate the elevator from the operating stroke of the bolt.

The elevator is operated by the special ejector rib, running almost the entire length of the bolt body on the left side and retained by a spring collar[14]. The ejector rib has a groove milled along its lower edge, and this actuates the cartridge elevator as the bolt moves. The elevator rises as the bolt reaches the end of its backward travel, and depresses when the bolt is nearing the end of its closing motion. The front end of the ejector protrudes through a lateral slot in the bolt head and kicks the cartridges out of the bolt-way as the ejector rib is stopped by the elevator-operating cam, or by a stud on the cut-off spring if the cut-off lever is applied to interrupt the magazine feed.

14. The ejector was protected by DRP 30,035 of 30 March 1884.

A spring-loaded cartridge-stop device is fitted in the left side of the elevator housing, to hold the cartridges in the magazine when the elevator is in the 'up' position. The stop is released as the elevator drops and allows a new round to be pushed backwards out of the magazine tube.

Major adjustments were made to the 'wing' type safety lever and the trigger assembly—especially to the latter, which was completely redesigned—and the extractor claw was moved to the top right side of the bolt head.

VARIATIONS

Several of these were developed, the most important incorporating the so-called 'Mauser Kammer mit doppeltem Widerstand' (Mauser bolt with double locking lugs). This was patented in Austria-Hungary in September 1887[15] and, as the patent drawings show, had a new lug on the rear of the bolt body. This revolved into a recess milled in the left wall of the receiver immediately behind the cartridge elevator housing, and gave additional strength in an action normally locked only by the abutment of the bolt guide rib on the receiver bridge. The modified bolt was not adopted by the German armies, because its development coincided with the appearance of small-calibre cartridges loaded with smokeless propellant and the obsolescence of the Gewehr 71/84, but it was incorporated in the 1887-model Turkish rifle[16].

A few Gewehre 71/84 are believed to have served as test-beds for a bolt-mounted ejector patented in 1883[17], which necessitated small changes in the design of the bolt and the elevator-operating cam.

Many 71/84 rifles were converted for the standard 8mm cartridge, probably in the period 1890-95 when the Gewehr 88 was being introduced. It is, however, conceivable that the alterations were made during the First World War, although most of the guns examined showed little evidence of hard use and had unit markings that probably date from the end of the nineteenth century. The conversions were usually effected by boring-out the existing barrels, inserting and rifling a thin-walled liner, and replacing the existing back sight leaf. Small alterations were made to the stock in some instances, since some guns have been reported with additional recoil bolts running transversely below the chamber[18]. Modifications were made to the magazines to suit the 8mm cartridges, whose round noses could well have led to the re-appearance of the magazine explosion phenomenon.

Appearance, distinctive features and data

In many respects, the Gewehr 71/84 was the first German rifle to be made to what could be called modern standards, despite its unsophisticated design. There are still features that betray its age, however, including the long barrel and the three barrel bands.

Right: longitudinal sections of the Gewehr 71/84 action, from factory drawings reproduced in Korn's *Mauser-Gewehre und Mauser-Patente.*

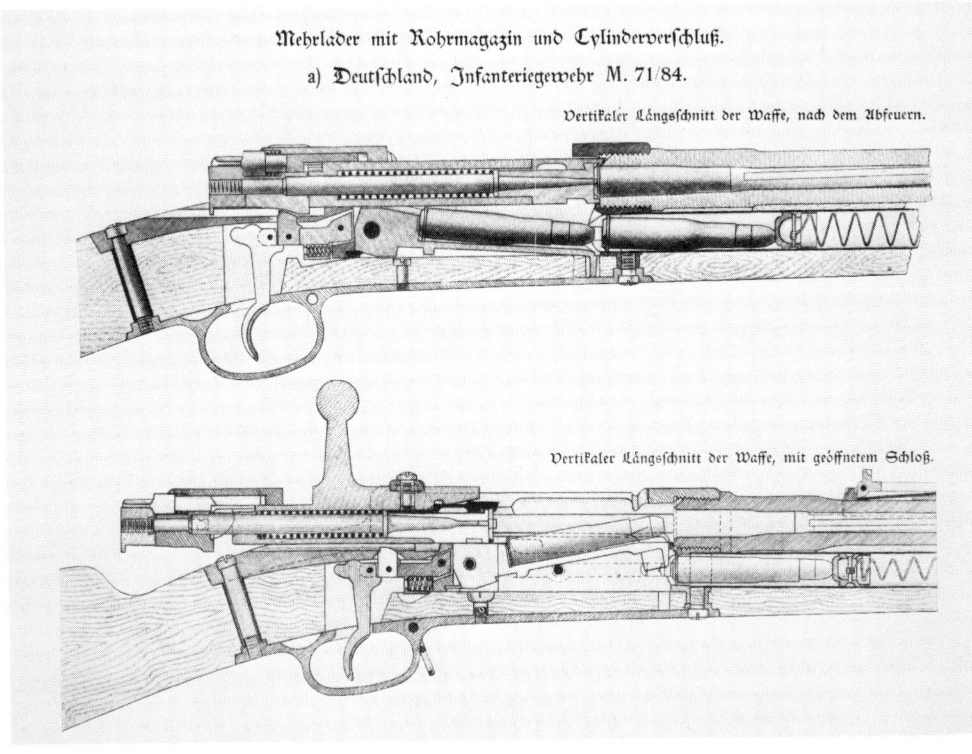

15. The subject of Privilegium (Austrian Patent) 37/1692 of 14 September 1887.

16. Small quantities of these guns were issued to the Württemberg Landsturm in the First World War.

17. DRP 28,109 was granted on 4 November 1883; the ejector was subsequently improved by DRP 44,393 of 29 February 1888.

Right: the breech of the Gewehr 71/84. Courtesy of Frank de Haas.

Right: the bolt action of the Gewehr 71/84, open. Courtesy of Frank de Haas.

18. It should be borne in mind that most 71/84 rifles made before 1886 had recoil bolts.

The rearmost band is retained by a long leaf spring[19] inlet in the right side of the fore-end, the underside of the middle band carries the sling swivel and the plain nose-cap has a bayonet attachment lug on its right side. The end of the tubular magazine protrudes below the muzzle and terminates in a robust screw-on cap. A straight ball-ended piling hook is attached to the magazine cap.

The one-piece walnut stock has a steel or cast iron butt plate and a much more modern-looking trigger guard, which is an integral part of the floor plate and is bored to accept the other sling swivel. The shape of the trigger itself was also improved.

The leaf pattern back sight was mounted on the barrel directly in front of the short barrel octagon, and came in two slightly differing patterns—the original infantry type and the modified 'Jäger-Visier' (see Data). The latter was ultimately adopted for all the guns, regardless of the part of the army to which they were issued.

19. Rifles made before 1886 have a screw-clamping rear band, as well as a recoil bolt through the stock beneath the chamber.

DATA

Calibre: nominally 11mm, actually 11.025 ± 0.075mm.
Rifling: concentric, 4 grooves 0.3mm deep and 4.5mm wide; 1 turn in 550mm, right hand (pitch of 3° 36'). However, the depth of the rifling grooves was reduced to 0.15mm on rifles made after 14 November 1885 in Prussia, Saxony and Württemberg, and after the end of 1886 in Bavaria.
Magazine: an under-barrel tube, 8 rounds capacity; one extra cartridge could be placed on the elevator, and a tenth in the chamber.
Loading system: manual insertion of cartridges through the floor of the bolt-way.
Length overall: 1,295-1,300mm.
Barrel length: 800mm.
Weight: 4,550-4,650gm without sling.
Sights: (front) open barleycorn; (back) (Infanterie-Visier) a combined block and two-leaf sight, with a standing 'battle sight' for 270 metres, a small leaf for 350 and a large leaf for 450-1,600 metres in 50m increments. ('Jäger-Visier') A combined block and two-leaf sight, with a standing 'battle sight' for 200 metres, a small leaf for 300 and a large leaf graduated from 400 to 1,600 metres in 50m increments.
Performance: see cartridge data (Appendix 2).

Accessories

BAYONETS

The Gewehr 71/84 was officially issued with the S 71/84 (TGB, pp. 44-46), which had a 25cm blade. However, the Prussian guard infantry retained the S 71 sword bayonet (TGB, pp. 34-36) and the Jäger units kept the Hirschfänger 71 (TGB, pp. 37-38). Many all-metal Ersatz bayonets were developed during the First World War, including Carter Numbers[20] 3-13, 23, 34-35, 38-45. 47, 49-53, 63-72 and 74-75; and there were also many modifications of non-German sword, sabre and knife bayonets (TGB, pp. 78-81, for some details).

20. J. A. Carter, *German Ersatz Bayonets*, vol. 1.

OTHERS

A sling, a muzzle protector, a back sight cover and suitable cleaning equipment.

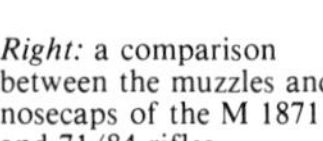

Right: a comparison between the muzzles and nosecaps of the M 1871 and 71/84 rifles.

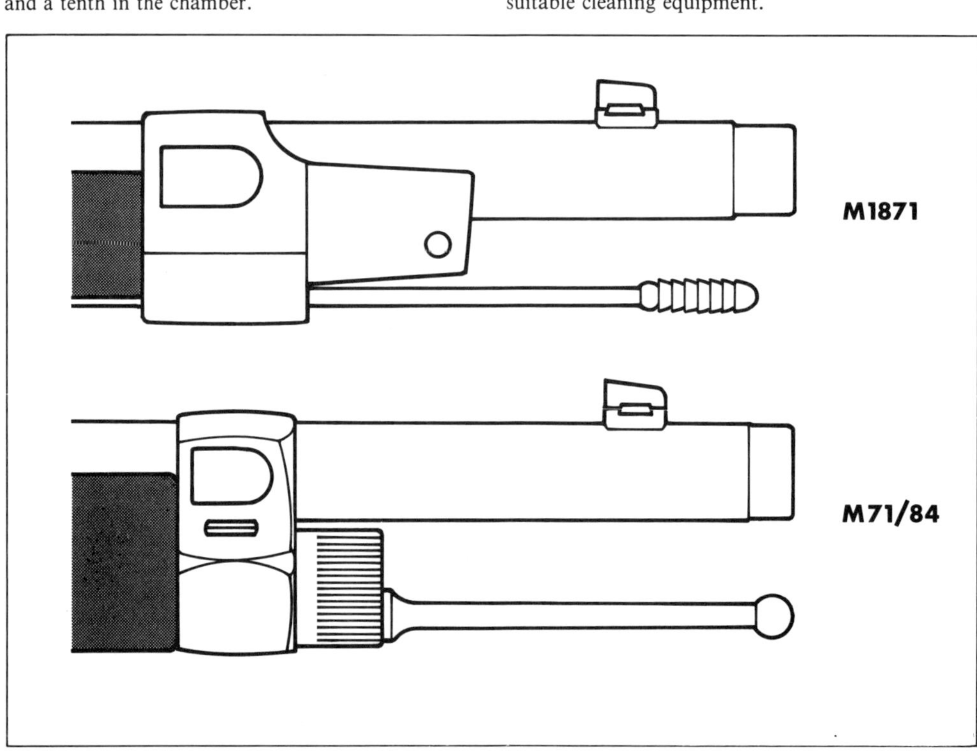

'Jägerbüchse 71/84' Mauser

It was normal German practice to develop a cavalry carbine and a Jägerbüchse, for the riflemen, shortly after each new infantry rifle had been perfected. The Karabiner M 1871 and the Jägerbüchse M 1871 had been developed in 1876, for instance, after supplies of the Infanterie-Gewehr M 1871 had been ensured.

It is logical to assume that the GPK considered introducing a carbine and a short rifle based on the 71/84 system, but, equally, that the production life of the infantry rifle (1885-88) had ended before any large-scale manufacture of the specialist weapons had begun.

None of the better books devoted to the subject, such as Götz, Baer and Von Menges, makes much mention of a Jägerbüchse 71/84, but some existing guns bear much the same relationship to the Gewehr 71/84 as does the Jägerbüchse M 1871 to the Gewehr M 1871. One is pictured in Lockhoven's *Waffen Archiv—Arms Archives—Archives d'Armes*[1] and another that has been examined is in the collection of the Royal Small Arms Factory. The Lockhoven specimen was made by Gebrüder Mauser & Co., Oberndorf, which may date it as before 1 April 1884 when the company name changed to Waffenfabrik Mauser AG[2]. It has a four-digit serial number (2842?) and typical 'Jäger' sling swivels on the underside of the barrel band and the under-edge of the butt, about 20cm from the butt plate. It also has a solid trigger guard bow, with no provision for the regular infantry-type sling swivel through the front of the bow, and the back sight of the Jägerbüchse M 1871. It is also about 6cm shorter than the standard 71/84 rifle, has only two barrel fixtures (band and nose-cap) and a magazine capacity of seven rounds rather than eight. The other detail differences are described later in this section.

1. Registration number C 0030.

2. Mauser may perhaps have continued the use of old marking dies for a few months after the changeover.

Lockhoven suggests that the guns were issued to the Württemberg Jäger units, but, as Hans-Rudolf von Stein has pointed out[3], the state army had no riflemen after 1871. It seems much more likely that the gun is one of several thousand supplied to four Jäger-Bataillone in 1885-86 for prolonged shooting trials, as the Prussian, Saxon and Bavarian Jäger formations were eventually issued with standard Gewehre 71/84.

3. In a letter to the author, dated 21 November 1970.

Right: the 'Jägerbüchse 71/84'. From Lockhoven's *Arms Archives.*

The gun in the RSAF collection, 1698, is in many ways comparable to Lockhoven's Mauser-made specimen, but was made at Spandau in 1886. It, too, is about 6cm shorter than normal but has standard sling swivels. Its exact purpose remains obscure, as its unit marking—probably applied at a later date—reads '29.R.E.3.40.', the third company of the Ersatz Bataillon of Infanterie-Regiment von Horn (3.Rheinisches) Nr. 29: not, of course, an élite rifle detachment.

Production history

The experimental Jägerbüchsen 71/84 seem to have been made exclusively by Gebrüder Mauser & Co. (Waffenfabrik Mauser AG after April 1884) between February and May 1884. The total quantity may have approached or even exceeded five thousand.

Markings

The guns display the maker's name 'GEBR. MAUSER & Co. OBERNDORF A/N. WURTTEMBERG' in a single line along the left side of the receiver. There is no designation mark on the action[4]. The full serial numbers lie on the left side of the barrel, the left side of the receiver at the breech, the bolt head, the bolt handle base, the cut-off lever spring, the safety 'wing' and elsewhere. There are no visible inspectors' marks, judging by Lockhoven's photographs, and no unit markings either.

4. Such marks are found on all 71/84 rifles other than the examples made by Mauser for Württemberg.

Mechanical description and variations

The Jägerbüchsen operate in exactly the same manner as the Gewehre 71/84 (qv). No variations have yet been reported, although some may have different sights.

Appearance, distinctive features and data

The guns greatly resemble the Gewehr 71/84 (qv), but are about 6cm shorter and have only two barrel fixtures: a screw-clamping barrel band, lacking a retaining spring, and a plain nose-cap with a bayonet attachment lug on its right side. The sling swivels lie underneath the barrel band and the butt, approximately 20cm from the butt plate.

The barrel is a conventional slightly-tapered cylinder, with a short octagonal section at the breech. The 1871 leaf-type back sight lies on the barrel immediately ahead of the octagonal portion. The magazine tube protrudes rather more below the muzzle than in the Gewehr 71/84, has a screw-on cap with a short ball-tipped piling hook, and there is a standard pre-1886 recoil bolt through the one-piece walnut stock below the chamber.

The barrel band and the nose-cap are blued, the barrel and the butt plate are browned, the rest of the metal parts are simply 'in the white', and the overall quality of the finish is excellent.

DATA

Calibre: nominally 11mm.

Rifling: concentric, 4 grooves 0.3mm deep and 4.5mm wide; 1 turn in 550mm, right hand (pitch of 3° 36').

Magazine: under-barrel tube, 7 rounds capacity—an eighth round can be placed on the cartridge elevator and another in the chamber.

Loading system: manual insertion of cartridges through the floor of the bolt-way.

Length overall: about 1,245mm.

Barrel length: 740mm.

Weight: about 4,450gm without sling.

Sights: presumed to be as the Jägerbüchse M 1871 (qv).

Performance: see cartridge data (Appendix 2).

Accessories

BAYONET

Assumed to have been the Hirschfänger M 1871 (TGB, pp. 37-39).

OTHERS

Assumed to be as those for the Gewehr 71/84 (qv).

'Karabiner 71/84' Mauser

This gun, the last and smallest of the 71/84 system, was purely experimental, although several hundred may have been made for troop trials. The provizion of a standard bayonet lug on the right side of the nose-cap indicates that the carbine may have been developed for foot artillerymen or the train rather than specifically for cavalry. Lockhoven's *Waffen Archiv—Arms Archives—Archives d'Armes*[1] illustrates a Bavarian weapon, made at Amberg in 1887 or 1888 (?) and apparently bearing a four-digit serial number; however, this may not indicate that more than a thousand carbines had been made, it is much more likely that the bolt mechanism was selected at random from the series production of infantry rifles, and that it had already been numbered. The carbine obviously dates later than 1886, as it has a 'Jäger-Visier' and lacks the transverse recoil bolt through the stock below the breech.

1. Registration number C 0029.

It has a magazine capacity of only five rounds, a single sling swivel on the front of the trigger guard bow, a turned-down bolt handle and only a single barrel band, but otherwise resembles a 71/84 rifle with about 21cm cut out of the barrel and fore-end. Since the basic design was virtually obsolete in 1887/8, no series production was ever undertaken and the Karabiner 88 (qv) was introduced instead.

Right: the 'Karabiner 71/84'. From Lockhoven's *Arms Archives.*

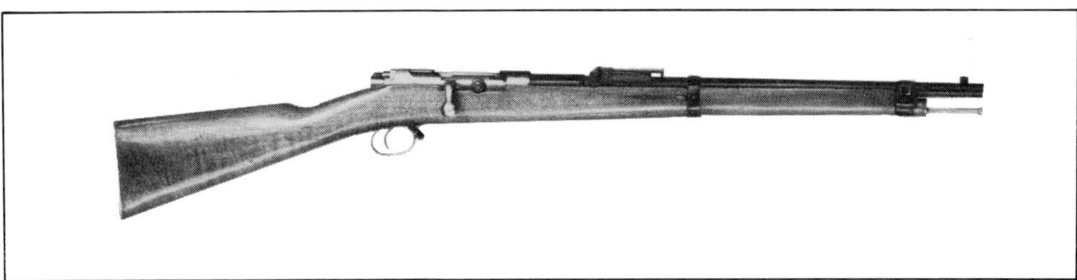

Production history
Uncertain, one Amberg-made gun is known to exist, and others may have been made by Mauser or the Prussian government arsenals.

Markings
Lockhoven's carbine bears the crown over 'AMBERG' mark on the top 'flat' of the barrel octagon, and the standard designation mark 'I.G.MOD.71/84' in fraktur (gothic script) on the left side of the receiver. There are, apparently, standard serial number, parts numbers and inspectors' marks; but the gun does not seem to be dated in the usual place on the right side of the action behind the bolt handle[2].

2. Lockhoven's photographs, however, are not too clear.

Mechanical description and variations
The carbine operates in the same fashion as the Gewehr 71/84 (qv), the turned-down bolt handle being of no significance.

Appearance, distinctive features and data
The Karabiner 71/84 is basically a shortened infantry rifle, of the post-1886 pattern, and lacks both the recoil bolt through the stock and an intermediate barrel band. A leaf spring is used to retain the remaining band. The bolt handle is turned-down against the one-piece walnut stock and has a spherical grasping knob. There is only a single sling swivel, in front of the trigger guard bow, and the barrel and the fore-end have been considerably shortened. The nose-cap has a bayonet attachment lug on the right hand side. The finish is the same as on the standard infantry rifles and the semi-experimental Jägerbüchse M 1871/84 (qv).

DATA
Calibre: nominally 11mm.
Rifling: concentric, 4 grooves 0.15mm deep and 4.5mm wide; 1 turn in 550mm, right hand (pitch of 3° 36').
Magazine: under-barrel tube, 5 rounds capacity; however, a sixth round can be placed on the cartridge elevator and another placed in the chamber.
Loading system: manual insertion of cartridges through the floor of the bolt-way.
Length overall: about 1,080mm.
Barrel length: about 580mm.
Weight: 4,000gm approximately, without sling.
Sights: (front) open barleycorn; (back) ('Jäger-Visier') a combined block and two-leaf sight, with a standing 'battle sight' for 200 metres, a small leaf for 300 and a large leaf graduated 400-1,600 metres in 50m increments.
Performance: see cartridge data (Appendix 2).

Accessories

BAYONET
Assumed to have been the S 71/84 (TGB, pp. 44-46).

OTHERS
Unknown.

Gewehr 88 hybrid Mauser-Mannlicher

1. Paul Pietsch, *Formations- und Uniformierungsgeschichte des preussischen Heeres 1808 bis 1914*, vol. 1, p. 272, gives the date of the Kriegsministerium order as 9 November; but it seems as though it received royal assent three days later. A date of 20 November has also been wrongly quoted.

The Gewehr 88, which was adopted in Prussia, Saxony and Württemberg on 12 November 1888[1], has been subjected to much abuse from writers who have compared it with the later and more effective German Mausers. In many respects, however, their criticisms are neither wholly justifiable nor especially accurate.

The rifle was conceived, designed, developed and introduced in less than year, to provide an effective counter to the French Mle 86 ('Lebel'), which was the first military rifle to chamber an efficient cartridge loaded with smokeless propellant. The Lebel, with its obsolescent tubular magazine, was not a particularly noteworthy design, but the power and flat trajectory of its cartridge conferred an advantage on the French troops. This naturally caused consternation in German ordnance circles. The Gewehr-Prüfungs-Kommission first made moves to redress the balance in November 1887, when letters were sent to interested officers and technicians attached to the governmental arms factories in Danzig, Erfurt and Spandau. They were asked to consider two alternatives: converting existing stocks of Gewehre 71/84 for a more battle-worthy 8mm cartridge, loaded with smokeless powder being developed by Rottweiler Pulverfabriken, or developing an entirely new weapon. Viewed in retrospect, and mindful of the great steps forward being made in contemporary France and Austria, the first alternative seems positively naive; it was undeniably cheaper, but it could not hope to be a long-term solution.

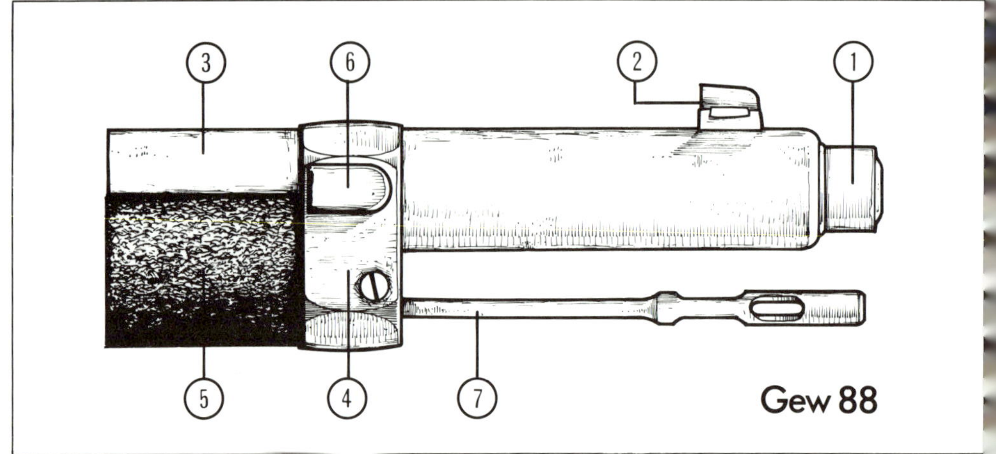

Right: the muzzle and nosecap of the Gewehr 88. Key: 1, barrel; 2, front sight; 3, barrel jacket; 4, nosecap; 5, stock; 6, bayonet lug; and 7, cleaning rod.

To save even more money, it was suggested that the tubular magazine of the 71/84 could be retained without modification if the new cartridge were little more than a necked-down version of the old 11mm Reichspatrone; only the sights would have to be revised. This, and the addition of a barrel jacket, was estimated to cost about twenty marks per gun—as events transpired, about half the cost of each new Gewehr 88.

After protracted consultations, which naturally included the Prussian War Minister von Schellendorf and his colleagues, it was decided to revise the Gewehr 71/84 by the addition of the 'Mauser-Verschluss mit doppeltem Widerstand' or 'Mauser-Kammer mit doppeltem Widerstand' (Mauser bolt system with double locking lugs). Previous Mausers, including the Gewehre 71 and 71/84, had only had one. Production machinery was ordered from Ludwig Loewe & Co., of Berlin-Charlottenburg, in December 1887.

As time dragged on, the personnel of the GPK and the leading German small arms experts became increasingly sceptical of the potential in the modified Gewehr 71/84. Disquieting rumours were appearing in the Press, and advances being made elsewhere by inventors such as Mannlicher were being mentioned in military circles. Worried, too, about the penny-pinching attitudes of the government, the German specialists suggested

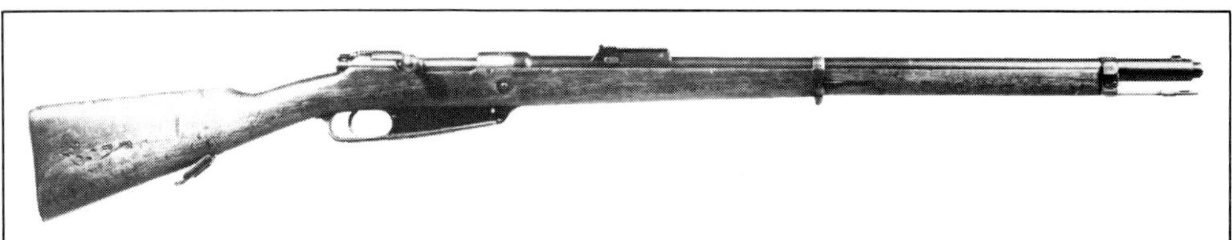

Right: the Gewehr 88/05. Courtesy of Ian Hogg.

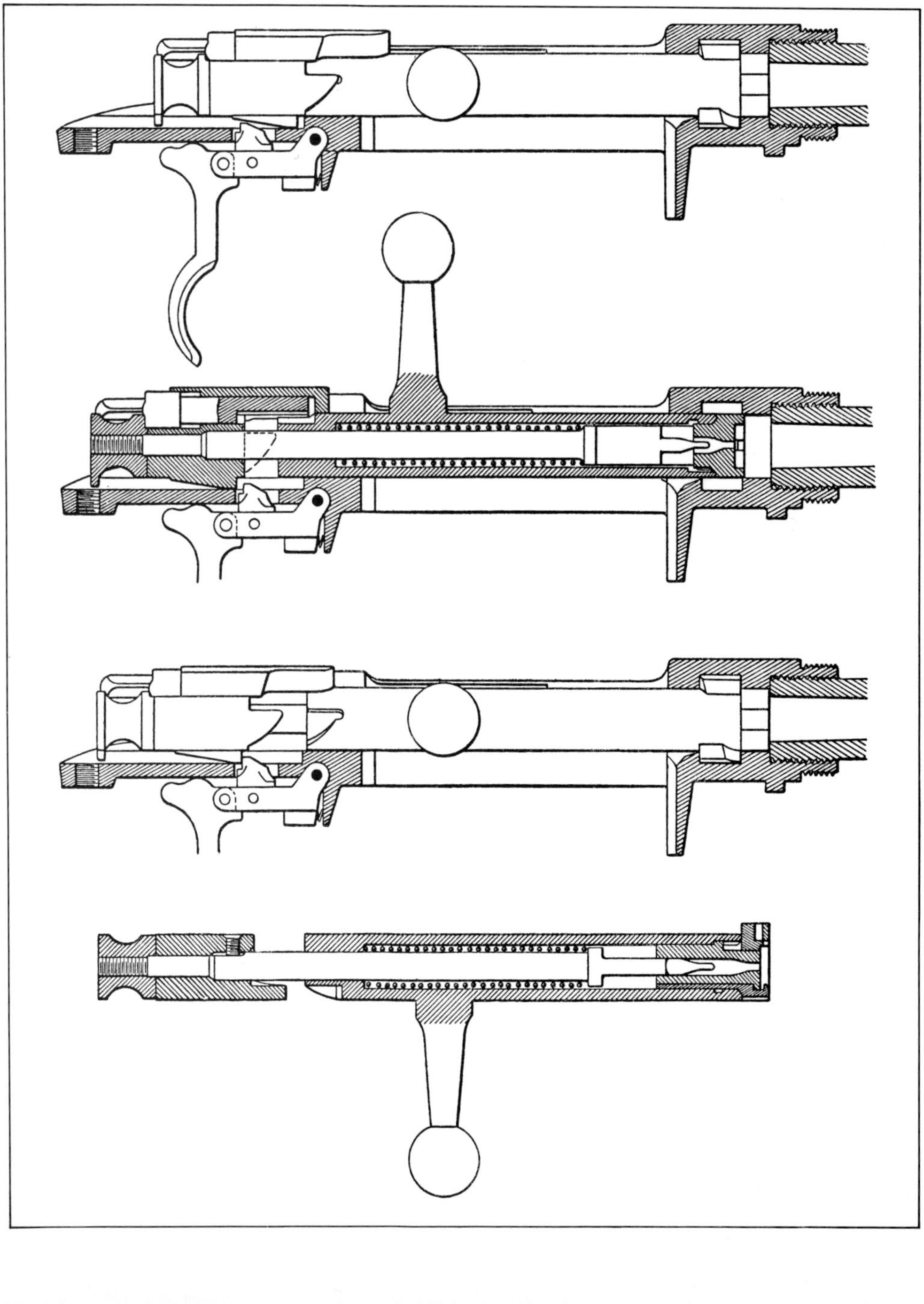

Right: the bolt mechanism of the Gewehr 88. The separate bolt-head was a bad feature, since it could easily be detached and lost.

that further trials should be undertaken with a view to developing a better and more efficient weapon.

So, taking the lock-work and bolt mechanism of the 71/84 as a basis, the GPK began work. Much of this has been credited to Louis Schlegelmilch[2], a technician attached to the Spandau arsenal, who was largely responsible for revising the bolt. The resulting prototype 'commission rifle' was a strange hybrid with a Schlegelmilch-Mauser action, a clip-loaded magazine inspired by Mannlicher (although modified by the GPK so that the clip would load either way up) and a barrel jacket designed by Armand Mieg[3]. The pitch and profile of the rifling were simply copied from the French Mle 86 rifle; this later proved to be a mistake but it at least minimized development time. The first experiments with the new German rifle were undertaken early in 1888 with rimmed 8mm cartridges adapted from the standard 11mm Reichspatrone 71. By midsummer, however, a modified Swiss-type rimless design ('Schweizer Art'), based on the doctrines of Eduard Rubin, had been developed and issued for trials. The Kriegsministerium was quickly made aware of progress and, by 23 March 1888, the Bavarian military observer in Berlin, General von Xylander, was able to report to his government in Munich that the rifle design had been virtually completed[4].

It quickly became apparent that the prototype was immeasurably superior to the obsolescent Gewehr 71/84 and its modification; it was also a potentially better weapon than the Lebel. But then the problems and controversy began, as Peter-Paul Mauser, the country's premier rifle designer, produced a new bolt-action prototype. This gun was patented in Germany on 18 April 1888 (DRP 45,561) and it has since been claimed that the Germans were wrong to choose the commission rifle at the expense of this Mauser prototype. But a study of the patent papers and photographs of the trials gun supplied to Belgium in 1889[5], and handling a similar rifle supplied to British trials at about the same time, confirms that the Mauser had several important weaknesses. These included the placing of the locking lugs behind the magazine (theoretically placing the front part of the bolt under great firing stress, as in the British Lee-Enfield); a clumsy bolt design with

2. Designer of the Schlegelmilch 'automatic' pistol. See Erlmeier & Brandt, *Handbuch der Pistolen- und Revolver-Patronen*, p. 140, for a longitudinal section.

3. Armand Mieg, 1838-1917, was an officer in the Württemberg Army. He is best remembered for his pistols (1890-93) and some embryonic automatic rifles.

4. Hans-Dieter Götz, *Die deutschen Militärgewehre und Maschinenpistolen, 1871-1945*, p. 90.

5. R. H. Korn, *Mauser Gewehre und Mauser Patente*, pp. 133-36 and illustrations in the photographic section; and also W. H. B. Smith, *Mauser Rifles and Pistols*, pp. 94-97.

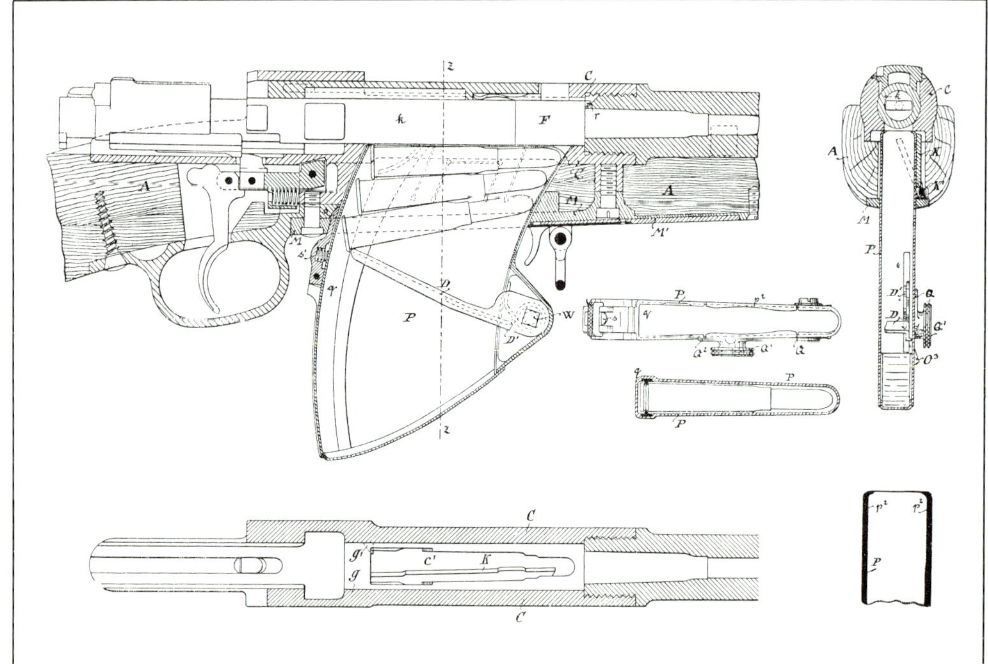

Right: the 1889-patented Mauser bolt-action rifle, showing the excessive distance between the small of the stock and the trigger—owing to the length of the cocking piece. From the papers of DRP 45,561.

so long a cocking piece that a normal hand could not grasp the stock and trigger satisfactorily; and a poorly designed magazine. Although this curious weapon was later developed into the efficient Belgian Mle 89 service rifle[6], it was in few respects superior to the commission rifle and the German military authorities—in my view, at least—were justifiably correct in rejecting it. Mauser is said to have been very unhappy with the decision.

6. Which, however, was not perfected until mid-1889; the first complete gun was not delivered to the Belgian Army until February 1892.

Trials with a pre-production series of commission rifles, about twenty having been hand-made in Spandau in April-May 1888, continued until the calibre question had been resolved in favour of 8mm (7, 7.5 and 8mm had all been tried). Work was completed by July, mass-production plans were readied, and limited series production began in October on machinery bought from Germany's leading machine-tool maker, Ludwig Loewe & Co. Large-scale field trials were devised and production of the Gewehr 71/84 was discontinued.

The field trials were completed by the beginning of November 1888 and the GPK recommended that the experimental rifle should be adopted immediately. The orders were signed by Kaiser Wilhelm II on 12 November 1888 and despatched to Bavaria, where they were received on the 23rd; acceptance, however, was delayed until 19 February 1889. Issues of the Gewehr 88 began in the spring of 1889 to XV. and XVI.Armeekorps, then stationed in Elsass-Lothringen. The first large-scale issues in Bavaria seem to have commenced on 22 October 1889, although small numbers had previously been distributed for troop trials. By 1 August 1890, all Prussian, Saxon and Württemberger line infantry regiments were carrying the new rifles, which were gradually replaced towards the end of the century by the Gewehre 98 (adopted on 5 April 1898[7]) and relegated to the Reserve, Landwehr and Landsturm. Many were converted to 88/05 standards in 1906-7 and stored for the Reserve (for the Landwehr by 1911), although large numbers of unaltered guns were sold to China in 1907. The 1911 catalogue of A. L. Frank Exportgesellschaft (ALFA), for example, notes that the company was trying to sell forty thousand Gewehre 88[8].

7. But 2 May 1901 in Bavaria.

8. 1911 ALFA catalogue (reprinted by Digest Books Inc. in 1972), p. 12.

By the outbreak of war in August 1914, the 88/05 was being stored for the Landwehr units not already issued with the Gewehr 98, and the surviving 88/S for the third-line Landsturm. It is estimated that about half a million Gewehre 88, of all types, were still serving the German armies, the remainder having been sold, converted to sporting rifles or scrapped. A shortage of guns caused many 88/05 rifles, together with the 'new' 88/14 conversions of the existing Gewehre 88/S, to be withdrawn from the Landwehr and Landsturm, who had to make do with older and captured weapons, and re-issued to line infantry regiments. Magdeburgisches Infanterie-Regiment Nr. 66, for instance, carried Gewehre 88/05 (?) in the period May-November 1915[9]. These were replaced by converted ex-Russian Mosin-Nagant rifles and finally, in late 1916, by Gewehre 98. The 88/05, 88/14 and surviving 88/S (mostly with a new upward ejecting clip system) were withdrawn from front line service at the end of 1915 and returned to the Reserve and Landwehr formations. By 1918, only the following remained in service:

9. As reported by Hans-Rudolf von Stein, in a letter to the author dated 14 December 1969.

State	**88/05**	**88/14**	**Total**
Bavaria	2,394	34,944	37,338
Prussia	55,309	10,885*	66,194
Saxony	2,579	0	2,579
Württemberg	10,050	2,601	12,651
	70,332	48,430	118,762

Note: the Prussian rifles marked with the asterisk (*) had been sent to Turkey, but remained nominally on the Prussian inventory. Virtually all the weapons had been discarded by 1920, many being sold to Ethiopia and the Balkan states.

The Gewehr 88 had a number of excellent features, including its excellent production quality and finish, a strong and simple mechanism, a good safety unit and a good dismantling system; but its best feature, arguably, was its superiority over all its contemporaries. The commission rifle is demonstrably more efficient than the Lebel (Fusil d'Infanterie Mle 1886) and the Austro-Hungarian Mannlichers of 1886 and 1888, which were the only comparable designs to be introduced before November 1888. Although the Belgian Mle 89 and the Mausers it inspired were undeniably superior rifles, they came later and drew heavily on the commission rifles' experiences. (Despite its 'Mle 89' designation, the Belgian Mauser rifle was not actually issued until February 1892.) In addition, the Rumanian M 1893, Dutch M 1895 and other Mannlicher rifles drew heavily on the commission rifle for their inspiration. So, too, did the Haenel military rifle and, arguably, the Portuguese Mauser-Vergueiro.

These positive factors must not be allowed to obscure the bad features of the commission rifle design, although many only became apparent when better weapons appeared. Initial problems included *double-loading*, with consequent explosions in the magazine, which was cured by re-designing the recessed bolt face; *barrel explosions*, caused by overloaded cartridges, partly cured by deepening the rifling grooves, strengthening the barrel in the chamber area, and improving cartridge quality control; *excessive bore wear*, cured by deepening the rifling grooves [10] ; and *excessive gas back-blast*, arising from ruptured primers and case-head flaws in many early cartridges. Blast problems were never entirely eradicated, since no proper gas escape holes were included in the bolt or receiver walls; however, lugs were added to the striker head to deflect gas from the firer's face.

10. After a series of trials, the GPK decided to increase the depth from 0.1mm to 0.15mm, the latter being found to give optimum barrel life.

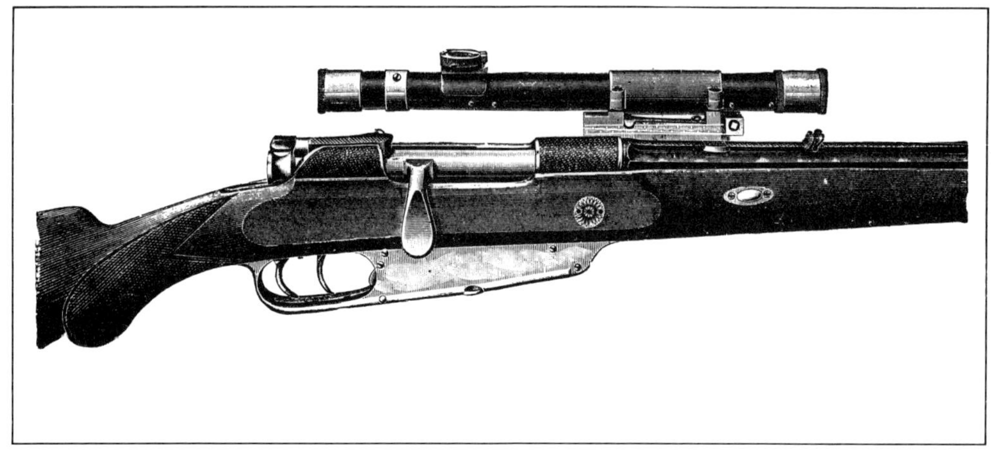

Right: a sporting version of the Gewehr 88. From the 1911 ALFA catalogue.

Despite protecting the barrel surface and insulating the firer from excessive barrel heating, the barrel jacket was easily dented and rusted at its joints. Also, it has never been satisfactorily proven that isolation of the barrel harmonics from the effects of warping and swelling in the wood bedding of the stock had any marked effect on barrel accuracy.

The split-bridge receiver is also held by many writers to be markedly inferior to the more common solid pattern. It is true that the former is often less rigid and that sloppiness is often evident in bolt retraction, but not in the Gewehr 88, where excellent construction and finish are evident. It is also popularly agreed that speed of firing is greatly improved by having the bolt handle as near as possible to the trigger, as in the British SMLE (Lee-Enfield) [11] . However, the action of the Gewehr 88 is easier to use than that of the later Gewehr 98, as the bolt handle is not drawn back as near to the cheek; this ensures minimum disturbance of aim when firing from the shoulder.

11. The advantages of the SMLE bolt handle, compared with those of other military rifles, are discussed in the British *Text Book of Small Arms 1904* (HMSO), pp. 128-29.

Minor flaws in the design of the commission rifle included a slow striker fall (lock-time) caused by the excessive weight of the striker head, cocking piece and safety unit; a detachable bolt head, which could easily be lost; and a small and weak extractor claw. The extractor was strengthened when the bolt face alterations were made in 1891.

The clip-loading magazine system, which prevents the gun being fired with single rounds unless the chamber is loaded by hand each time, is universally agreed to be inferior to charger patterns. The Germans ultimately accepted the validity of this argument, since the Gewehr 98 and its derivatives were charger-loaded and many thousands of Gewehre 88 were converted similarly between 1906 and 1915 (88/05, 88/14).

Production history

The Gewehr 88 was made by the three major Prussian arsenals—Danzig, Erfurt and Spandau—and by the smaller Bavarian establishment in Amberg. An assortment of private contractors was also recruited. The government's machinery, purchased from Ludwig Loewe & Co., was delivered in the autumn of 1888; first to Spandau, then to Danzig and lastly to Erfurt. The Amberg equipment was delivered after 1 July 1889, and by October the arsenals were working around the clock. The three Prussian factories soon each attained a maximum daily out-turn of six hundred guns, while Amberg contributed a further four hundred. The guns made in Prussia were delivered to a central store from which each of the army corps drew new weapons when the occasion arose.

The most important private contractor was to have been Waffenfabrik Mauser AG, of Oberndorf am Neckar in Württemberg, but the company was fully committed to a huge Turkish order[12] and could not spare the usual production facilities. Consequently, Ludwig Loewe & Co., whose experience of firearms production was exceedingly limited[13], entered large-scale rifle manufacture. As Loewe owned many Mauser shares, the business was kept within the same cartel. The original order for 300,000 rifles, dating from January 1889, was subsequently amended by the addition of a further 125,000. This undertaking seems to have weakened Loewe's resolve to supply machinery to Amberg, since the arsenal commandant, Oberstleutnant Freiherr von Brandt, complained that deliveries of equipment were proceeding very slowly[14].

Loewe-made commission rifles each cost the Prussian government about 49 marks, which was appreciably higher than the 35-36 marks estimated as the price of each government-made item. This led to allegations (largely unfounded) of rank profiteering[15]. More problems arose when the Prussians tried to order 300,000 rifles from Österreichische Waffenfabrik-Gesellschaft in Steyr. This was negotiated in October 1889, but all work stopped at the end of the month while legal wrangling over infringement of patents granted to Mannlicher and Mieg was sorted out. The clip-loaded magazine was clearly based on Mannlicher's, and no arrangements had been made to compensate Mieg for the Gewehr 88 barrel jacket, which had been developed for his experimental small-bore rifle in 1887 and patented in several countries. Mieg's backing syndicate attempted to negotiate a settlement of three hundred thousand marks for the time and trouble spent developing their experimental rifle, even though nothing had come of its extensive trials. On 20 March 1889, the Prussian government had granted Mieg 50,000 marks in recognition of his contribution to small arms design, but disputes over the use of his patents continued. This, and the setbacks at Steyr, greatly worried the Prussian government, but licencing agreements were ultimately concluded with the interested parties and the disputes were settled by the end of the year[16].

The three Prussian arsenals had delivered about 275,000 guns by the beginning of 1890; by the end of the year, the total had risen to 600,000[17]. Additional weapons were beginning to come from Amberg, Loewe and OEWG, and possibly from private companies in Suhl. (V. C. Schilling & Co. and C. G. Haenel & Co. are known to have made Gewehre 88-type sporting rifles, and military Karabiner 88 and Gewehre 91, but no Schilling or Haenel-made service-pattern Gewehr 88 has yet been reported.) The first issues of the new rifles were made to the border corps in Elsass-Lothringen in the autumn of 1889 and, by 1 August 1890, all Prussian, Saxon and Württemberger infantry regiments had been re-equipped. Production of the Gewehr 88 finally ceased in 1897. The totals, by contractor, are believed to have been:

Prussian government arsenals (Danzig, Erfurt, Spandau)	750,000 +
Bavarian government arsenal, Amberg	100,000?
Ludwig Loewe & Co., Berlin-Charlottenburg	425,000
Österreichische Waffenfabrik-Gesellschaft, Steyr	300,000
Private contractors in Suhl (Haenel, etc.)	100,000?
Total	1,675,000?

About 370,000 guns were converted to Gewehre 88/05 in 1906-7; 75,000 were converted to upward clip-ejection in 1914-15; perhaps 75,000 Gewehre 88S were converted to 88/14 standards in 1914-15; and 120,000 remained nominally on the army inventories in 1918 (Gewehre 88/05 and 88/14).

Markings

Among the standard marks applied to the Gewehre 88 were the manufacturers' marks, inevitably found on top of the receiver above the chamber with the production date. The following have been noted:

12. For 500,000 1887-model rifles and 50,000 carbines, placed in February 1887.

13. A large number of Smith & Wesson-type revolvers had been made in the mid-1870s.

14. Hans-Dieter Götz, *Die deutschen Militärgewehre und Maschinenpistolen, 1871-1945*, p. 93.

15. It must be borne in mind that the governmental costs were often calculated without regard to depreciation of the production machinery or the payment of royalties. They could not, therefore, be compared directly with those of private contractors.

16. Hans-Dieter Götz, *Die deutschen Militärgewehre und Maschinenpistolen, 1871-1945*, p. 95.

17. Götz states that the total was 660,000, which may be a misprint.

GOVERNMENT ARSENALS

DANZIG	Prussian arsenal, Danzig
ERFURT	Prussian arsenal, Erfurt
SPANDAU	Prussian arsenal, Spandau
AMBERG	Bavarian arsenal, Amberg

PRIVATE CONTRACTORS

LOEWE	Ludwig Loewe & Co., Berlin-Charlottenburg
ŒWG	Österreichische Waffenfabrik-Gesellschaft, Steyr
HAENEL	C.G. Haenel Waffen- & Fahrrad-fabrik, Suhl, Thüringen(?)

The designation 'GEW.88' is stamped into the rear left side of the receiver, while the serial number—'1588', '3829e'—appears on the left side of the receiver and the barrel clamping ring alongside the breech, and on the base of the bolt handle. The last two digits were repeated on the majority of the removable components such as the safety lever 'wing', the striker, the striker head, the cocking piece, the bolt-retaining catch and the many screws. Most of these parts also display small inspectors' marks in the form of tiny crowned gothic letters.

Many guns examined have had Turkish numerals and inspectors' small crescent marks on the parts, apparently substituted for the original German ones, which must, therefore, have been ground away. Gewehre 88 were also sold in large number in the Balkans and the Far East, and also, by Österreichische Waffenfabrik-Gesellschaft, to Peru and Brazil. Some were used during the First World War by the Austro-Hungarian Army under the Designation 8mm Repetiergewehr M 13. An assortment of stampings may be found above the chamber, including:

• 2mm diameter	Modified barrel contours, post-1891.
Z 3mm high	Deepened rifling grooves, post-1896. A large 7mm 'Z' may also be present on the right side of the butt.
S 3mm high	Suitably altered for S-Munition, 1903-5. An additional 7mm crowned 'S' may be found on the right side of the butt.
n 2mm high	Signifies an 88/14 conversion, 1914-15.

Unit markings are generally located on the left side of the barrel band, but may occasionally be struck into the top surface of the butt plate. Typical examples read '132.R.5.116.', '1.G.R.E.2.57.' and 'B.7.R.2.58.'; the first was applied by the fifth company of 1.Unter-Elsassisches Infanterie-Regiment Nr. 132; the second by the second company of the Ersatz-Bataillon of Grenadier-Regiment Kronprinz (1.Ostpreussisches) Nr. 1; and the third by the second company of 7.Bayerisches Infanterie-Regiment Prinz Leopold.

Mechanical description and variations

The basic action of the Gewehr 88 was a simplified form of the old 71/84 (Mauser) pattern. The receiver is a one-piece forging of the so-called 'split-bridge type', in which the bolt handle locks down in front of the bridge portion. A small pivoted bolt-stop, based on earlier Mauser designs, lies on the rear left side of the receiver and pivots outwards to release the bolt.

The bolt is an elegant, slender forged tube with an integral handle terminating in a spherical grasping-knob. There is no separate bolt sleeve. The spring-loaded striker slides inside the hollowed bolt body, shoulders towards the rear of which provide a ready bearing for spring compression; the cocking piece and the safety mechanism attaches to the striker extension. The bolt body carries the two locking lugs, one solid and the other slotted longitudinally to allow a finger on the bolt-stop unit to ride into the bolt and

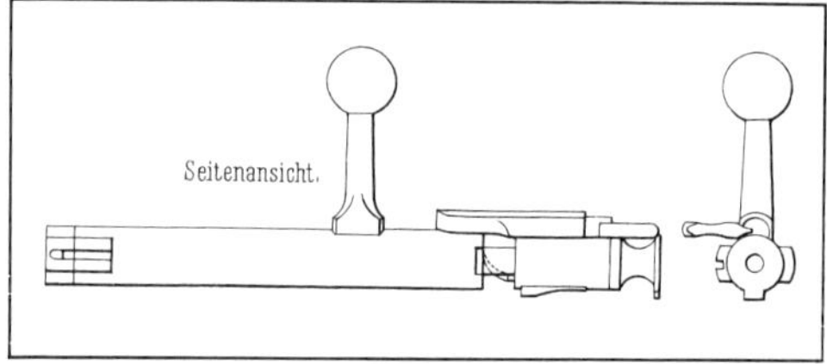

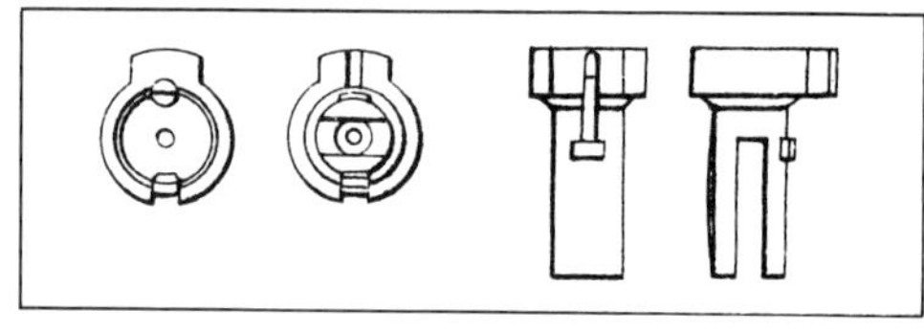

operate the ejector. The solid (bottom) lug is bevelled to match the contours of the face of the receiver ring and gives adequate primary extraction when the bolt handle is raised. The camming action of the bevel helps to pull a tight case out of the chamber. The bolt lugs lock horizontally in the solid receiver ring immediately behind the chamber, although the action would have been stronger had they rotated directly into an extension of the barrel. The separate bolt head is one of the weaker features of the Gewehr 88's design, since it can easily be lost when detached. It fits closely inside the front of the bolt body, and a lug on its small-diameter rearward extension matches a recess cut in the bolt in such a way that it can only be removed in one particular position. The extractor, a spring-steel claw, is much too small for its purpose and slides in a mortised groove on the right side of the bolt body. Some guns have a small screw added to retain the extractor, in addition to mere friction, and the extractor claw was widened when the bolt face was redesigned in 1891. The bolt-head face is recessed for the cartridge head; the recessing is completely circumferential on early guns, but is partly cut away on later ones to prevent double loading. The bolt head is prevented from rotating by 'flats' on the striker head.

Other features of the commission rifle's action include a standard Mauser-type 'wing' safety mechanism on top of the cocking piece—applied in the vertical position—which cams the cocking piece back out of engagement with the sear, and locks the bolt so that it cannot be opened or retracted. The sear and trigger units are simple, strong and arranged to give the widely favoured two-stage pull.

The trigger guard/magazine unit is formed from a single machining and extends forwards in a graceful sweep, to run up into the stock immediately below the crossbolt on which the recoil lug bears. The magazine is loaded with a five-round clip inspired by earlier Mannlicher patterns, but adapted by the Gewehr-Prüfungs-Kommission so that it will feed either way up; most Mannlicher clips can only be loaded in one way. The clip falls out of the underside of the magazine well when the last round has been stripped into the chamber. The cartridges are delivered to the bolt-feed by a follower arm, propelled by a spring-

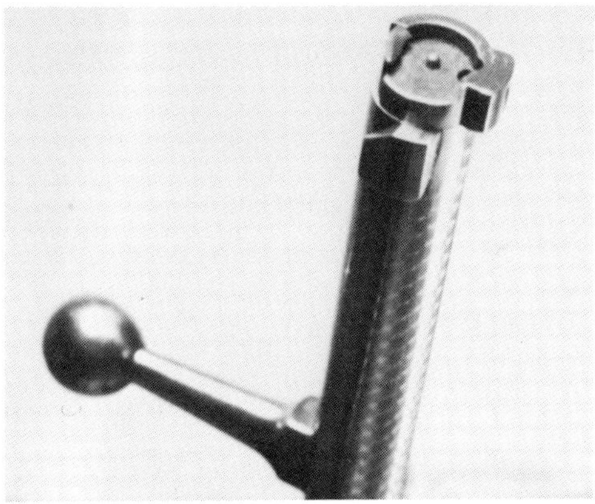

Right: the bolt-face of the Gewehr 88, the later pattern with a wide extractor claw and a partially cutaway bolt-head rim to prevent 'double loading'. Courtesy of Frank de Haas.

loaded pin in the front of the magazine body, while a spring-loaded clip retaining latch, which protrudes into the front of the trigger-guard bow, retains the clip when the bolt is open. Otherwise, the clip and its contents would be hurled upwards by the magazine arm—and out of the gun!

Troubles began as soon as the commission rifles entered service; Götz[18] reports a number of unfortunate incidents that occurred in the Bavarian Army almost as soon as the first rifles had been issued. These usually occurred when overloaded cartridges generated too much pressure, ruptured the chamber and the barrel, and often seriously injured the firers. Thirty-three incidents of exploding guns were reported in the Bavarian Army in two years; there were records of explosions in the magazine, as the action was operated; and of case-head and primer ruptures leading to excessive gas leakage. Even alterations made to the rifling groove depth (from 1896 onwards) failed to effect the necessary cure: nearly a thousand rifles were returned to Spandau with damaged barrels between March 1900 and March 1901. It was all supposed to be part of a Jewish plot to undermine the morale of the German Army[19].

Three major problems were eventually isolated and answers quickly sought. *Explosions in the magazine* were traced to double loading, when the extractor failed to slip into the extraction groove as the cartridge was pushed into the chamber. If this cartridge were not fired, and the firer attempted to re-load, the nose of the second round was struck into the primer of the one left in the chamber. If the blow were hard enough, the chambered cartridge ignited and the gun exploded in the firer's hands. The chance of serious injury was high, since the bolt was partly open and could easily be slammed back into the soldier's face with sickening force[20]. However, the problem was almost completely cured by cutting away part of the recessed bolt-head face so that the cartridges rose out of the magazine directly under the extractor claw, rather than hoping that the claw would slip over the case-rim as the bolt was pushed shut. This improved extraction and virtually eliminated double loading, as the chambered round was always being held by the extractor.

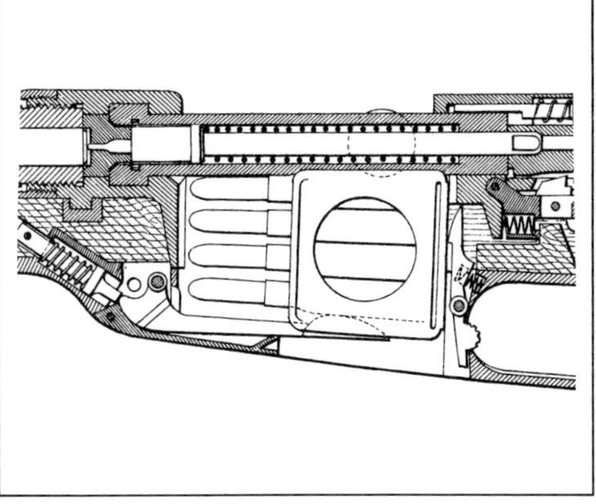

Explosions in the chamber were largely due to overload ammunition and were partly eradicated by improving cartridge quality control; the art of loading smokeless propellant, after all, was still in its infancy. In addition, from 9 January 1891, the barrel was strengthened by the substitution of a straight-sided cone for the original concave taper of the barrel surface directly in front of the chamber. This greatly reduced the number of incidents but did not cure the problems entirely.

Excessive gas leakage, usually caused by ruptured primers and flaws in the cartridge-case heads, was partly cured by the addition of two gas deflecting lugs on the striker head. The large lug on the left side (viewed from the rear) projected into the locking lug guideway, while the smaller (under) lug blocked the cocking-cam guideway. All service rifles were subsequently altered and original circular striker heads are very rarely encountered. The modification apparently dates from 1894.

18. Hans-Dieter Götz, *Die deutschen Militärgewehre und Maschinenpistolen, 1871-1945,* pp. 95-97.

19. See Götz's comments (p. 97 in his book) about the so-called 'Juden-flinten-Affäre' (Jewish Rifle Affair). The developer of the first German smokeless powder (Rottweiler Pulverfabriken) and Loewe, maker of many of the rifles, were Jewish-owned.

20. There are several properly authenticated instances of men being killed by the bolts flying out of rifles; notably the Canadian straight-pull Ross design, for which the reasons were very different. See H. V. Sent, 'The Ross Rifle Ruckus' in *Gun Collector's Digest*, vol. 2, pp. 30-37.

GEWEHR 88/•

This was simply the standard post-January 1891 version of the Gewehr 88, fitted with the improved and strengthened barrel. A large dot ('•') was struck into the top of the receiver and the side of the barrel.

GEWEHR 88/Z

The authorities soon discovered that there were serious problems with the rifling design that they had pirated from the French Mle 86 Lebel. The lands wore down with alarming rapidity, until, in spring-summer 1893, when most of the existing guns were less than three years old, a check of all Gewehre 88, Karabiner 88 and Gewehre 91 in the artillery depots and stores revealed that half needed new barrels. It became a matter of considerable urgency to develop a modified system of rifling to minimize barrel wear [21]. Trials were undertaken with modified bullets and different bullet-jacketing material, with no satisfactory results. The GPK subsequently began experimentation with differing rifling depths in the autumn of 1894 and these eventually provided the answer. Because the 8.1mm diameter of the standard bullet had to be reduced to a bore diameter of 7.9mm, the standard groove depth of 0.1mm was too shallow and led to unacceptable bullet squeezing. This, in turn, led to high chamber pressures and rapid bore wear, since the frictional forces between the bullet jacket and the bore walls was greatly increased by pressure. The bullet jackets tended to crack and excessive metal fouling was left in the barrel. The experiments with groove depths of between 0.125 and 0.2mm, with the standard 0.1mm pattern as a control, proved that 0.15mm gave the optimal combination of bore life, accuracy and chamber pressure. The modified rifling design was consequently introduced by a 'Höchsten Erlass' (Supreme Decree) on 7 July 1896, when the gauge for shot-out barrels was changed from 8 to 8.05mm[22]. Guns fitted with altered or newly made barrels—some existing specimens had been re-rifled satisfactorily—were marked with a 3mm letter 'Z' on top of the chamber, and sometimes with an additional 7mm 'Z' on the right side of the butt. A few barrels made during the early years of the twentieth century, however, seem to have been made without the distinctive 'Z' mark.

21. The British Army was among those that had similar problems, since Metford's segmental rifling also wore out rapidly and was replaced by an Enfield-type.

22. A shot-out barrel was one in which the rifling had lost much of its effectiveness, as the lands had been worn down.

GEWEHR 88/S

The introduction of the so-called S-Patrone[23]—on 3 April 1903—caused the existing Gewehre 88 to be altered. The bullet of the new cartridge had a diameter of 8.22mm, appreciably greater than the 8.1mm of the old Geschoss 88, and this meant increased chamber pressures; consequently, only guns with newly-made (rather than re-rifled) 'Z' pattern barrels were altered. The chamber was bored-out to accommodate the new bullets and the top of the receiver was marked with a large 'S'. A crowned 7mm high version was repeated on the right side of the butt.

The sighting arrangements were naturally altered to conform with the flatter long-range trajectory of the new pointed bullet. A new 2000m sight leaf was usually substituted for the old 2050m pattern, and the standing block 'battle sight' was intended for 400m rather than 250m. Eckardt & Morawietz [24] suggest that new sight leaves were added to the 88/S, but Götz [25] is adamant that the markings on the old sight leaves were simply ground away and replaced by new graduations. It may be that both ideas are half right and that the first guns had modified sight leaves, while later ones were newly-made. The small leaf of the original sight was officially abandoned at this time.

Many 88/S rifles survived to be used during the First World War, though up to 370,000 were converted to 88/05 standards in 1906-7. A magazine cover was developed in December 1914 to prevent dust, mud and sand from getting into the action through the opening in the bottom of the magazine well. These guns, 75,000 of them, were also fitted with a clip-ejector mechanism that threw empty clips

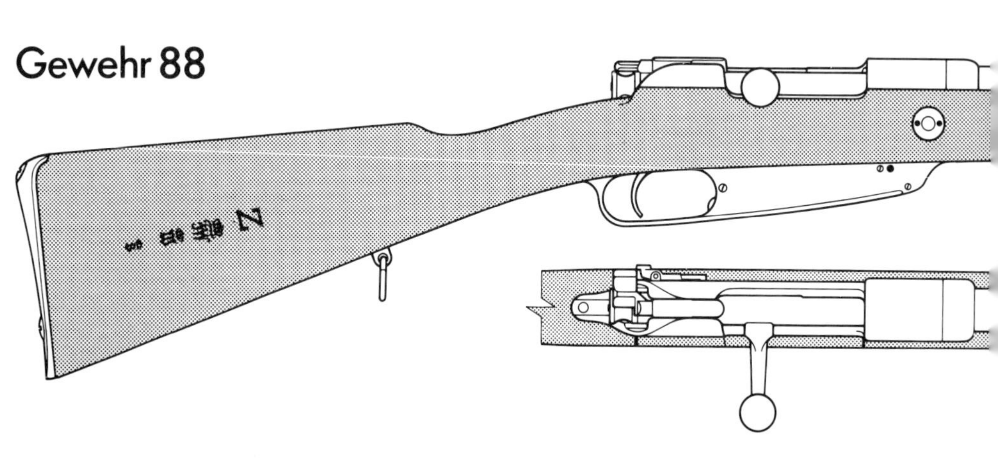

23. A cartridge loaded with a 'Spitzgeschoss', or pointed bullet.

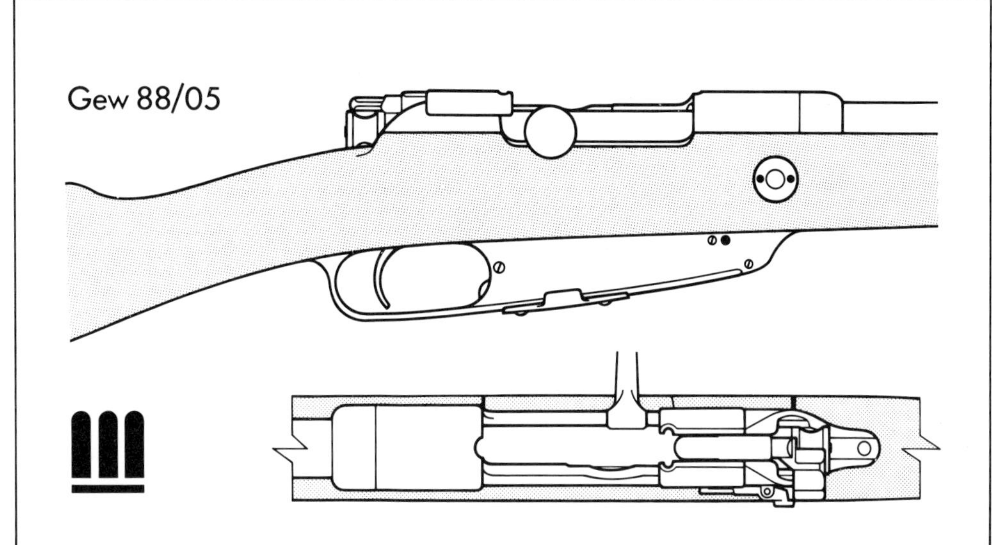

24. Werner Eckardt and Otto Morawietz, *Die Handwaffen des brandenburgisch-preussisch-deutschen Heeres 1600-1945,* p. 181.

25. Hans-Dieter Götz, *Die deutschen Militärgewehre und Maschinenpistolen, 1871-1945,* p. 100.

upwards out of the action when the bolt was opened to expel the last spent case; previously, they had simply fallen downwards out of the magazine base. The alterations to the magazine system are believed to have cost about three marks per gun and were undertaken exclusively by the government arsenal at Spandau in 1915.

GEWEHR 88/05

The 88/05, which was issued by an AKO of 3 January 1907, is essentially the same as the 88/S. It is often found with the chamber-top markings '•', 'Z' and 'S': modified barrel contours and deep-groove rifling suited to the S-Munition. The principal difference concerns the loading system: the 88/S uses the standard commission-developed clip, whereas the 88/05 has a pressed-tin charger whose five rounds are pushed downwards into the magazine well with the thumb before the charger body is discarded. Consequently, the 88/05 has blocks containing the charger guides screwed to the top of the receiver bridge, spaced to allow the bolt handle to pass through. The left side of the receiver wall is ground out to enable the thumb to press the cartridges fully down into the magazine well and a semi-cylindrical channel has been milled vertically across the breech face to allow the pointed nose of the S-Patronen to pass downwards into the magazine. This was very necessary, as the additional width of the charger body held the cartridges further forward in the magazine feed aperture than the old clip had done. The magazine was narrowed by the insertion of a pressed-steel strip and shortened internally by the addition of a small steel block, as there was no longer a wide clip

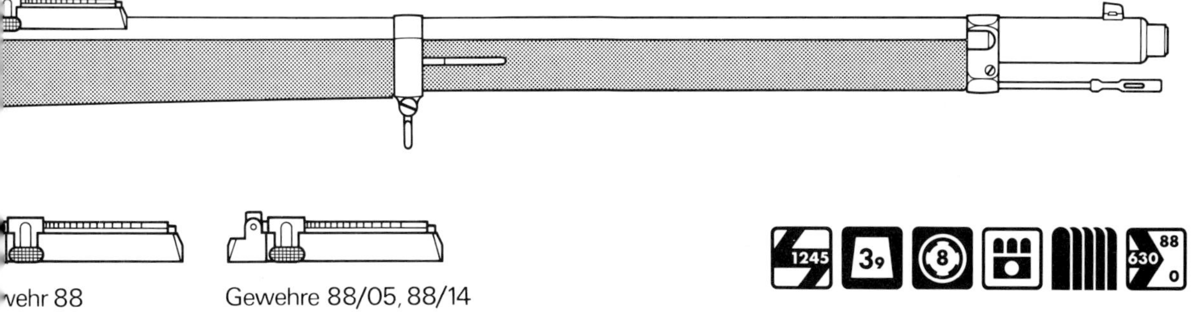

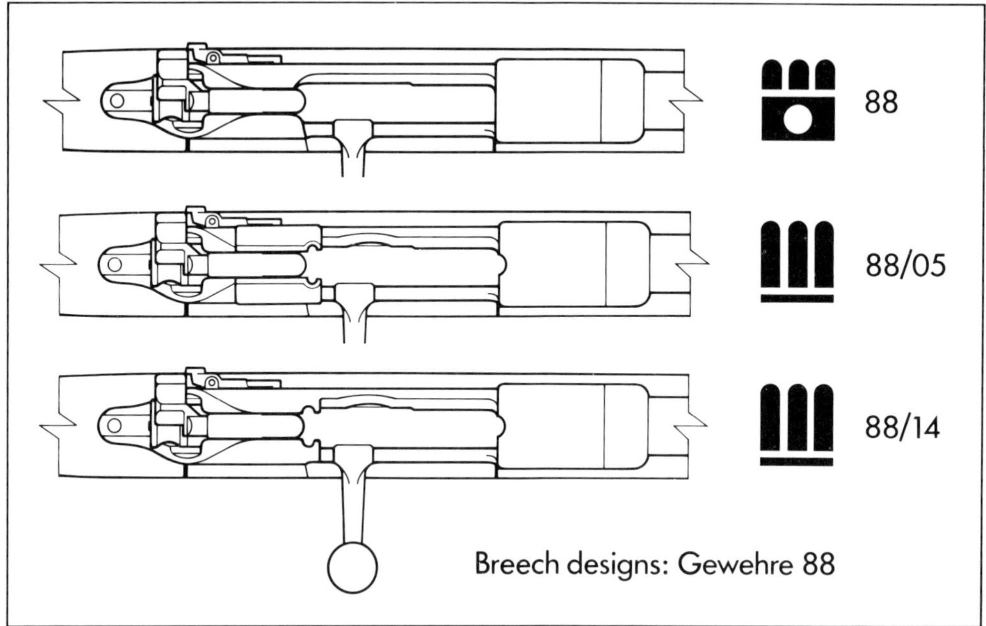

Breech designs: Gewehre 88

and the S-Patrone was slightly shorter than the old Patrone 88. Had modifications to the magazine not been made, the loose cartridges would have rattled around and failed to feed.

A spring-loaded cartridge retainer was fixed horizontally in the left wall of the magazine well and the opening in the bottom of the magazine was blocked by a pressed-steel cover, which prevented the incursion of débris.

The back sight was also revised. Eckardt & Morawietz suggest that the newly-made sight leaves were not interchangeable with those of the 88/S, but Götz states that the original graduations were ground away and replaced. There seems no good reason why the sight should have been modified at all, since the 88/05 and 88/S handled the same cartridges. The small (rear) sight leaf was generally removed from these guns. Götz[26] records that each 88/05 conversion, undertaken in Spandau, cost the government 8 marks.

26. Hans-Dieter Götz, *Die deutschen Militärgewehre und Maschinenpistolen, 1871-1945*, p. 103.

GEWEHR 88/14

These guns approximated to the earlier 88/05, but were altered from supplies of the 88/S, in considerable haste, between December 1914 and May-June 1915. Charger guides were provided by welding protrusions onto the front of the receiver bridge and shaping them upwards, noticeably crudely, into prominent curved 'ears'. The left wall of the receiver is cut away to permit the thumb to press the cartridges fully down into the magazine well, and a groove has been milled across the face of the chamber to allow the S-Patronen to enter the magazine satisfactorily. The opening in the bottom of the magazine was blocked by a sheet-steel cover and the spring-loaded cartridge retainer was angled forwards (rather than the horizontal 88/05 type). The magazine well was shortened and narrowed for the S-Patrone by welding in sheet-steel inserts, which also allowed for the omission of the original clip. It remains debatable whether the sights were revised at the same time.

The conversion work was carried out very hurriedly and the standard of finish is notably inferior to the peacetime 88/05 conversions. It is believed that less than 75,000 Gewehre 88/14, with a small 'n' mark on the barrel and the chamber top, were altered.

GEWEHR 88 N.M.

This variation remains an enigma, though many Gewehre 88 have been reported with an extra gothic letter 'n m' mark beneath the GEW.88 designation on the left rear of the receiver. No satisfactory explanation for its presence has yet been made, notwithstanding many enquiries and a perusal of official German documents. The most likely appears to be that 'n m' represents nitro-munition and would have been added to all guns surviving the introduction of the Munition 03, which was loaded with a new nitrocellulose-base propellant, the burning characteristics and pressure curve of which differed from its predecessors. Many Gewehre 88 had been discarded by 1903 and would have escaped re-marking, explaining why so many guns lack it. But, if the ammunition theory is correct, it is true that all 'n m' guns should also bear the standard chamber-top marks (•, 'Z' and 'S'), and that *all* 88/05 and 88/14 conversions should bear 'n m' marks, as they date from 1906-15. It has yet to be determined whether this is indeed the case. Most alternative explanations, however, have been discredited; 'n m' rifles have been noted with almost every possible combination of maker's mark and production date.

Appearance, distinctive features and data

The Gewehr 88 is one of the most aesthetically attractive military rifles to have been issued for service, a title it shares (in my view) with the French Lebel and pre-1915 Berthier rifles, the US Krag-Jørgensen and the Swedish Mauser. Its straight one-piece beech or walnut stock, which has a reinforced butt-toe to prevent breakage, sweeps gracefully up to the magazine. The latter—formed integrally with the elegant trigger guard bow—protrudes below the stock underneath the bolt mechanism. There is a single intermediate barrel band, retained by a leaf spring and carrying the front sling swivel, while the simple nose-cap has a conventional bayonet lug on its right side. A cleaning rod lies beneath the muzzle, which protrudes from the prominent barrel jacket. The rear sling swivel is positioned on the underside of the butt, although there is an alternative anchor position in the front portion of the magazine, which was used for parade use when the sling needed to be shortened. The bolt handle lies horizontally and locks down in front of the receiver bridge.

The 88/05 and 88/14 conversions have charger guides above the receiver bridge: the former's being carried on additional squared blocks and the latter's on prominent welded-on wings. These guns have several internal differences and (usually) sheet-steel covers over the clip-ejection port in the underside of the magazine body.

The original finish on Gewehre 88 was a lustrous polished blue of the highest quality and the standard of workmanship was virtually irreproachable—with very little play or sloppiness in the bolt-action, even when opened for loading. This quality was generally maintained in the 88/S and 88/05 conversions, but not on the 88/14 where the work was evidently hastily and crudely undertaken.

27. J. A. Carter, *German Ersatz Bayonets*, vol. 1.

DATA

Calibre: nominally 8mm.

Rifling: concentric, 4 grooves 0.1 or 0.15mm deep (the latter being for S-Munition) and 4.45 ± 0.05mm wide; 1 turn in 240mm, right hand (pitch of 5° 55').

Magazine: projecting in-line box, 5 rounds capacity.

Loading system: clip (originally) or charger (Gewehre 88/05 and 88/14 only).

Length overall: 1,245mm.

Barrel length: 740mm.

Weight: 3,850-3,950gm without sling.

Sights: (front) open barleycorn; (back) a combined block and leaf sight, with a standing 'battle sight' for 250 metres, a small leaf for 350 and a large leaf for 450-2,050 metres in 100m increments (NB: applies to Gewehre 88 only).

Performance: see cartridge data (Appendix 2).

Accessories

BAYONETS

The Gewehr 88 was originally issued with the brass hilted S 71 (TGB, pp. 34-36), which had a sword blade measuring 47cm and was re-introduced on 20 November 1888 for Prussian, Saxon and Württemberger infantrymen. The Hirschfänger 71 (TGB, pp. 37-38), which had a 50cm blade and a leather-gripped steel hilt, reappeared at the same time for the Jäger units. The Bavarians, however, retained the S 71/84 knife bayonet (TGB, pp. 44-46); this had a 25cm blade. During the First World War, many all-metal Ersatz bayonets were adapted to the Gewehre 88/S, 88/05 and 88/14, including Carter Numbers[27] 3-13, 23, 34-35, 38-45, 47, 49-53, 63-72 and 74-75; and there were also assorted transformations of non-German sword, sabre and knife bayonets (TGB, pp. 78-81, for some details).

OTHERS

These included two patterns of cleaning rod—the Wischstock 88 and Wischstock 93—and a muzzle protector. Screwdrivers were issued on the scale of one to every ten guns and lock spanners on the scale of one in every three. There was also a sling.

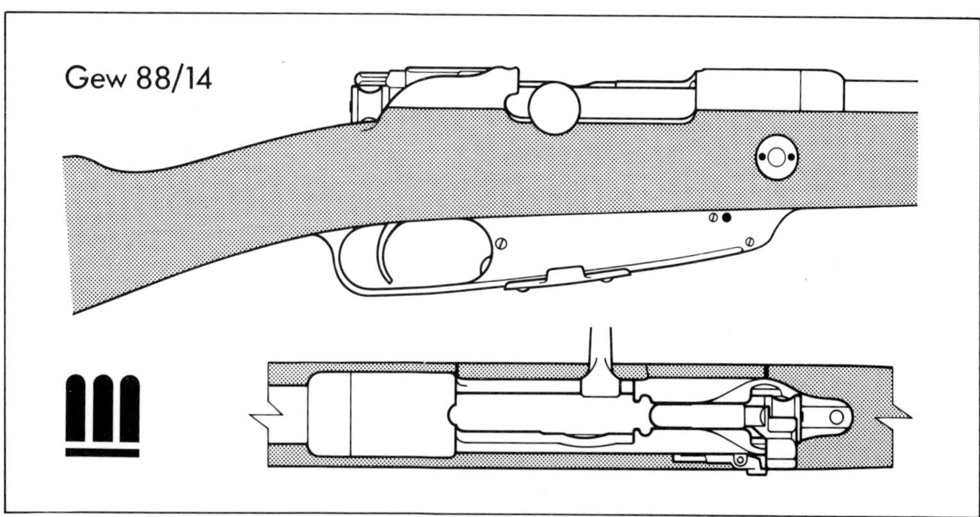

Karabiner 88 hybrid Mauser-Mannlicher

The development and widespread distribution of magazine rifles—exemplified in German service by the Gewehr 71/84 and, particularly, the Gewehr 88—made the single-shot M 1871 cavalry carbine obsolete. Ironically, issue of the carbines to the cuirassiers, the last cavalrymen to receive them, was completed in the very year in which the Gewehr 88 first appeared.

The GPK began to develop a shortened version of the new infantry rifle early in 1889 and had completed work by the autumn. The result was the Karabiner 88, adopted by Prussia, Saxony and Württemberg on 19 January 1890 and in Bavaria in about 1891. By March 1890, sufficient quantities had been delivered from the principal private contractors in Suhl to permit the first issues to be made to each Prussian cavalry squadron. The Karabiner 88 served the dragoons, hussars, cuirassiers and lancers, as well as the train and some other specialized units, until the adoption of the Karabiner 98 AZ (qv) in January 1908. Survivors were withdrawn in 1909-10, to be stored or sold; the 1911 catalogue of A. L. Frank Exportgesellschaft recorded that 8,200 were awaiting sale[1].

1. ALFA catalogue 1911, p. 12. Some guns had been fitted with new stocks, and others with 'set' triggers.

The 1888-system carbine suffered from many of the faults discovered in the Gewehr 88 (qv), which included rupturing of the barrels, excessive gas leakage from damaged primers or case-heads, and excessive rifling wear. The first was cured after January 1891 by modifying the barrel contours (the chamber top was marked •); the second by fitting new striker heads with gas deflection flanges; and the third by deepening the grooves in barrels made after July 1896 ('Z'). Many surviving carbines were converted for the S-Munition after 1903-5 and bore an additional chamber-top 'S'. However, because of

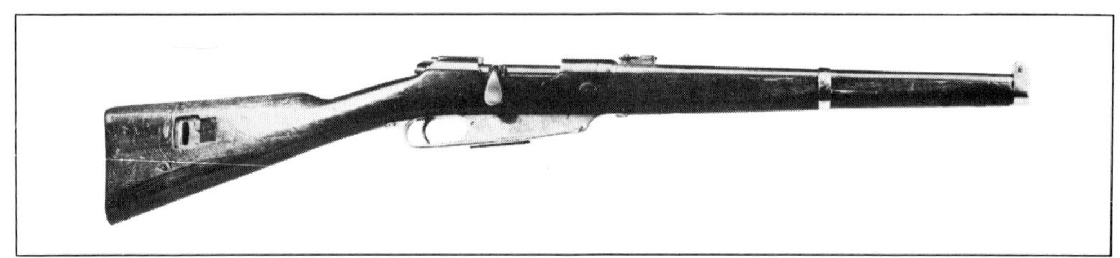

Right: an example of the Karabiner 88, made in 1891 by C. G. Haenel of Suhl. Courtesy of Ian Hogg.

M D F 29a. Seitengewehre dazu, 42 cm lang, in Lederscheide Mark | **M D F 29a. Bayonnette correspondante,** longue de 42 cm avec fourreau de cuir Mark | **M D F 29a. Original side-arms,** 42 cm long, in leather sheath Mark | **M D F 29a. Bayoneta original correspondiente,** en vaina de cuero, Marcos

M D F 30

Mauser Mod. 88 Car. Vorrat / Approvisionnement / supply / Existencia 5000

Original Deutscher Mauser-Karabiner, Modell 88, fünfschüssig, Gewicht, 3,150 kg, Länge 96 cm.

Wir liefern obige Waffe zum Preise von Mark **27.—** für überseeische Regierungen bei grossen Quantitäten aus Beständen der deutschen Regierung nach deren Bedingungen, die wir auf Wunsch mitteilen, in Holz und Zink, fob. Hamburg.

Carabine allemande Mauser Originale—Mod. 88 — à 5 coups — poids 3,150 kg — longueur 96 cm.

Nous livrons cette arme au prix de Mark **27.—** — pour les gouvernements d'outre-mer, par fortes quantités, des approvisionnements du gouvernement allemand et ce d'après les conditions du dit gouvernement, conditions dont nous envoyons exposé sur demande — marchandise emballée avec bois et zinc, fob. Hambourg.

Original German Mauser Carbine, Model 88, five shots, weight 3,150 Kilos, length 96 cm.

When large quantities for transoceanic governments are ordered, we deliver the above arm in wood and zinc packing fob. Hamburg at the price of Mark **27,—** from the supplies of the German government, according to the conditions of the latter, which will be specified on application.

Carabina Alemana original „Mauser", Modelo 88, de cinco tiros, peso 3,150 Kilos longitud 96 cm.

Entregamos esta arma al precio de Marcos **27,—** — para los gobiernos de ultramar, en grandes cantidades, de las existencias del gobierno alemán, y con arreglo á las condiciones de dicho gobierno, que enviamos según demanda, — mercancias embaladas con madera y cinc, fob. Hamburgo.

452/455

M D F 30 / a

Mauser Mod. 88 Car. Vorrat / Approvisionnement / supply / Existencia 1600

Derselbe Karabiner wie M D F 30, jedoch auf **neu** aufgearbeitet, extra eingeschossen, mit Riemenbügeln, Korn mit Silberpunkt etc.

La même carabine que le No. M D F 30, mais remise à **neuf** — spécialement éprouvée au tir avec anneau à bretelle — guidon à point d'argent etc.

The same carbine as M D F 30, but **renovated,** specially tested, with swivels, sight with silver point etc.

La misma carabina que le M D F 30, pero trabajada como **nueva**, probada para el tiro, con anillo de porta-fusil, guiador con punta de plata.

M D F 30 / b

Mauser Mod. 88 Car. Vorrat / Approvisionnement / supply / Existencia 1600

Derselbe Karabiner wie M D F 30a, jedoch **mit Stechschloss.**

Même caraubine que M D F 30a, mais **avec double détente.**

The same carbine as M D F 30a but with **hair trigger lock**

La misma carabina que M D F 30a, pero con **doble escape**

M D F 25	M D F 29	M D F 30	M D F 30 a	M D F 30 b
† Nerdon	† Olig	† Nimus	† Nimugu	† Nimuste

Right: sporting versions of the Karabiner 88, from the 1911 ALFA catalogue.

its short barrel, the carbine—and its near relation, the Gewehr 91—suffered from unpleasant muzzle blast and flash even with the original Patrone 88. Use of the more powerful S-Munition intensified the problems.

Production history

Most Karabiner 88 were made by the usual collection of private manufacturers in Suhl—notably C. G. Haenel and V. C. Schilling—since the production capacity of the principal government arsenals was fully occupied. The first contracts must have been placed in 1889, prior to the official adoption of the carbine in January 1890, since enough had been delivered by March 1890 to permit issue to begin.

It is believed that the Suhl manufacturers received orders for two hundred thousand firearms for Prussia, Saxony and Württemberg, and that the contract was completed in 1892. Each gun cost the government 47 marks 50 pfennige, but it is possible that some were completed as Gewehre 91 rather than Karabiner 88[2]. Production finally began in the Prussian arsenal in Erfurt in 1891 and continued, on a small scale, for five years. No Karabiner 88 seems to have been made after 1896.

The total production quantity of 1888-system carbines is not known, but may well have exceeded 300,000. Götz[3] records that 24,160 were on hand in Bavaria in May 1893—and Prussia, Saxony and Württemberg had about 75,000 between them in the same period.

Markings

The carbines were made by several contractors, whose marks (listed in the section devoted to the Gewehr 88) were stamped above the chamber. A typical example reads 'C.G. HAENEL/SUHL/ 1891', while the designation mark 'KAR.88' in fraktur (gothic script) lies on the left side of the receiver. The serial numbers appear on the left side of the receiver and the barrel clamping ring alongside the breech, and on the base of the bolt handle. The last two digits are repeated on most of the parts, which also display small inspectors' marks in the form of small crowned letters. An assortment of stampings may be found above the chamber, including:

•	2mm diameter	Modified barrel contours, post-1891.
Z	3mm high	Deepened rifling grooves, post-1896. A large 7mm 'Z' may also be present on the right side of the butt.
S	2mm high	Suitably altered for the S-Munition, 1903-5. An additional 7mm crowned 'S' may be found on the right side of the butt.

Unit markings, when present, are usually located on the top surface of the butt plate, since there is a fixed sling bar on the left side of the barrel band. A typical example reads '7.H.2.38.'—the thirty-eighth carbine issued to the second squadron of Husaren-Regiment König Wilhelm I (1.Rheinisches) Nr. 7.

Mechanical description and variations

The Karabiner 88 was mechanically identical with the standard Gewehr 88 (qv), from which it differed only in having a turned-down spatulate bolt handle.

There were several variations, complete descriptions of which may be found in the section devoted to the Gewehr 88. The Karabiner 88/• had the modified barrel contours introduced in January 1891, the Karabiner 88/Z had the deepened rifling grooves introduced in July 1896, and the Karabiner 88/S was chambered for the S-Munition. In addition, a few guns have been seen with additional 'n m' marks below the 'KAR.88' designation on the left side of the receiver; as related in the Gewehr 88 section, the precise meaning of this stamp has yet to be determined.

Appearance, distinctive features and data

The Karabiner 88 greatly resembles the standard Gewehr 88 but is considerably shorter, has a turned-down bolt handle, is stocked to the muzzle and lacks a bayonet lug[4]. The plain nose-cap has upward-projecting 'ears' guarding the front sight and there is a single spring-retained barrel band with a fixed sling bar on the left side; the other sling anchor point is cut through the butt. The small leaf-pattern back sight lies on the barrel jacket immediately ahead of the barrel clamping ring.

DATA

Calibre: nominally 8mm.
Rifling: concentric, 4 grooves 0.1 or 0.15mm deep and 4.45±0.05mm wide; 1 turn in 240mm, right hand (pitch of 5° 55').
Magazine: projecting in-line box, 5 rounds capacity.
Loading system: clip.
Length overall: 950-955mm.
Barrel length: 435mm.
Weight: 3,100-3,150gm without sling.
Sights: (front) protected barleycorn; (back) a combined block and leaf sight, with a standing 'battle sight' for 250 metres, a small leaf for 350 and a large leaf for 450-1,200 metres in 100m increments.
Performance: see cartridge data (Appendix 2).

Accessories

BAYONET

Originally, none; however, a few guns were fitted with auxiliary bayonet lugs.

OTHERS

A sling, a screwdriver, a lock spanner, and a leather muzzle protector. In addition, there were several different saddle scabbards, three of which (Futterale 88, 95, 96) are illustrated by Pietsch[5].

2. The sole difference lay in the addition of an under-muzzle piling hook to the Gewehr 91, which was really of carbine length.

3. Hans-Dieter Götz, *Die deutschen Militärgewehre und Maschinenpistolen, 1871-1945*, p. 107.

4. Bayonet attachment lugs were added to some guns in the First World War.

5. Paul Pietsch, *Formations- und Uniformierungsgeschichte des preussischen Heeres, 1808 bis 1914*, vol. 2, p. 302.

Gewehr 91 hybrid Mauser-Mannlicher

1. According to Ludwig Baer, *Die leichten Waffen der deutschen Armeen, 1841-1945,* p. 43; Hans-Dieter Götz, *Die deutschen Militärgewehre und Maschinenpistolen, 1871-1945,* p. 107, suggests that the date was 4 November 1891. Each lacks adequate confirmation at the time of writing.

This rifle, which was in reality of carbine length, was adopted for the foot artillerymen of Prussia, Saxony and Württemberg on 25 March 1891[1]. It was simply a derivative of the Karabiner 88, fitted with a special piling hook attached to a long steel plate inlet in the underside of the fore-end immediately behind the nose-cap; this permitted the guns to be stacked in pyramids. Other constructional details were the same as those for the Gewehr 88 (qv). The Gewehr 91 shared the same short-comings as the Karabiner 88, including excessive muzzle blast and flash on account of the extra-short barrel.

All Gewehre 91 were made with the revised or post-1891 barrel contours, which had been introduced some months before the rifle had been adopted. Service weapons were recalled in the mid-1890s and were retrogressively fitted with the post-1894 striker head, which had special gas deflection flanges. Those made or re-barrelled after mid-1896 had deepened rifling grooves (Gewehre 91/Z), and many were converted for the S-Munition in 1903-5 (91/S).

The guns were issued to the foot artillerymen and a few specialized detachments, such as the 'Luftschiffer' (airship) units, prior to the adoption of the Karabiner 98 AZ in early 1908. Most Gewehre 91 were withdrawn in 1909-10 and stored for the Reserve and Landwehr foot artillery, but were re-issued when the First World War began in August 1914. Many will be found with markings applied by munitions columns and other minor formations. Guns that survived the war were discarded after the Armistice.

Right: the fore-end of the Gewehr 91, with its distinctive stacking rod.

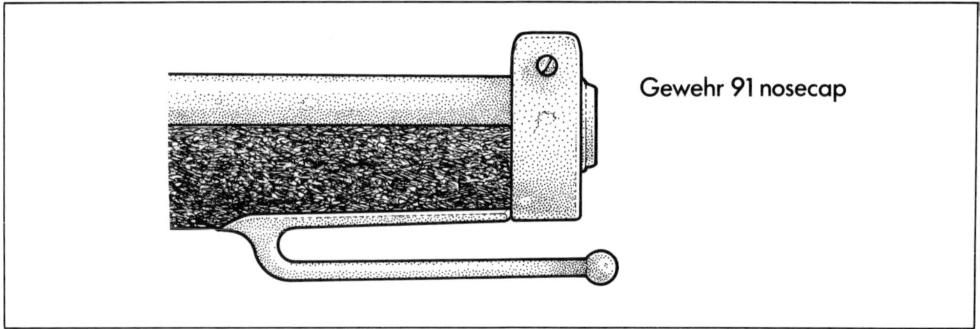

Production history

Like the Karabiner 88, the majority of Gewehre 91 were manufactured in Suhl by a handful of private contractors. Most of the rifles examined were made by C. G. Haenel or V. C. Schilling. The total quantity made between 1891 and 1896 is not known, even though Götz[2] records that 18,574 had been delivered to Bavaria by May 1893.

2. Hans-Dieter Götz, *Die deutschen Militärgewehre und Maschinenpistolen, 1871-1945,* p. 107.

Markings

The Gewehre 91 bear their maker's marks over the chamber, in typical German fashion. Most were made by either Schilling or Haenel and bear inscriptions such as 'C. G. HAENEL/SUHL/1892', or 'V. C. SCHILLING—SUHL/1894'. The designation mark 'GEW.91' in fraktur (gothic script) may be found on the left side of the receiver. There are standard German displayed eagle proof marks on the left side of the barrel and the receiver; and the serial numbers appear in full on the left side of the barrel and the receiver and on the base of the bolt handle. The last two digits are repeated on most of the components, along with standard crowned letter inspectors' marks. The marks on the front edge of the receiver ring include:

•	2mm diameter	Found on all guns. Denotes that the barrel has the strengthened contours adopted in January 1891, several months before the Gewehr 91 was introduced.
Z	3mm high	Deepened rifling grooves, post-1896. A large 7mm 'Z' may be present on the right side of the butt.
S	3mm high	Suitably converted for S-Munition, 1903-5. An additional 7mm crowned 'S' may lie on the right side of the butt.

Unit markings may be found on the side of the barrel band, or, in the case of second and subsequent stampings, on the top surface of the butt plate or the nose-cap. Typical examples read '5.A.F.2.57.' or '5.L.A.F.2.11.', signifying the fifty-seventh weapon issued to the second battery of Niederschlesisches Fussartillerie Regiment Nr. 5 and the eleventh gun belonging to the second battery of Landwehr-Fussartillerie-Bataillon Nr. 5. Some of the unit abbreviations can become very complicated: 'G.A.F.s. *M.* M.2.37.', for example, stands for the thirty-seventh gun issued to the second ammunition column (for 'schwere Mörser', or heavy mortars) of the Garde-Fussartillerie-Regiment.

Mechanical description and variations

The Gewehr 91 was mechanically identical with the Gewehr 88 (qv), from which it differed only in the turned-down spatulate bolt handle, its overall length, and the provision of a piling hook.

There were several variations of the Gewehr 91, details of which will be found in the section devoted to the standard infantry rifle. They included the Gewehr 91 or 91/•, all of which had the post-January 1891 strengthened barrel; the Gewehr 91/Z with post-1896 deepened rifling grooves; and the Gewehr 91/S re-chambered for S-Munition. Some rifles have been seen with the mysterious 'n m' mark below the 'GEW.91' designation on the left side of the receiver, but the significance of this has yet to be explained.

Appearance, distinctive features and data

The Gewehr 91 is identical with the Karabiner 88 (qv), stocked to the muzzle, with a turned-down bolt handle, a plain nose-cap with sight protecting 'ears', a single barrel band with a sling bar on the left side, a sling anchoring point through the butt, and a small leaf-type back sight. Its only distinguishing feature, apart from the designation stamp, is the piling hook under the fore-end.

3. However, the piling-hook base plate may have remained under the fore-end.

DATA

Calibre: nominally 8mm.

Rifling: concentric, 4 grooves 0.10 or 0.15mm deep and 4.45 ± 0.05mm wide; 1 turn in 240mm, right hand (pitch of 5° 55').

Magazine: projecting in-line box, 5 rounds capacity.

Loading system: clip.

Length overall: 990-995mm.

Barrel length: 435mm.

Weight: 3,175-3,250gm without sling.

Sights: (front) protected barleycorn; (back) a combined block and leaf sight, with a standing 'battle sight' for 250 metres, a small leaf for 350 and a large leaf for 450-1,200 metres in 100m increments.

Performance: see cartridge data (Appendix 2).

Accessories

BAYONET

Originally, none; however, some Gewehre 91 are said to have been fitted with auxiliary bayonet-attachment bars during the First World War. It is assumed that the piling hook was removed, and that the designation stamp on the left rear of the receiver then sufficed to distinguish the Gewehre 91 from Karabiner 88[3].

OTHERS

A sling, a leather muzzle protector, a screwdriver (one to every ten guns) and a lock spanner (one to every three guns).

Gewehr 88/97 Mauser

Experiments with modified Gewehre 88, embodying new Mauser bolt-actions and charger-loaded magazines, began as early as November 1894, when two hundred guns were issued for troop trials. These had conventional barrel jackets and a new tangent back sight credited to Oberstleutnant Lange, at one time director of the Spandau munitions factory. It was clear that advances made in contemporary rifle design—notably privately, by Mauser—had made the Gewehr 88 obsolescent; it was time that a more efficient weapon be found.

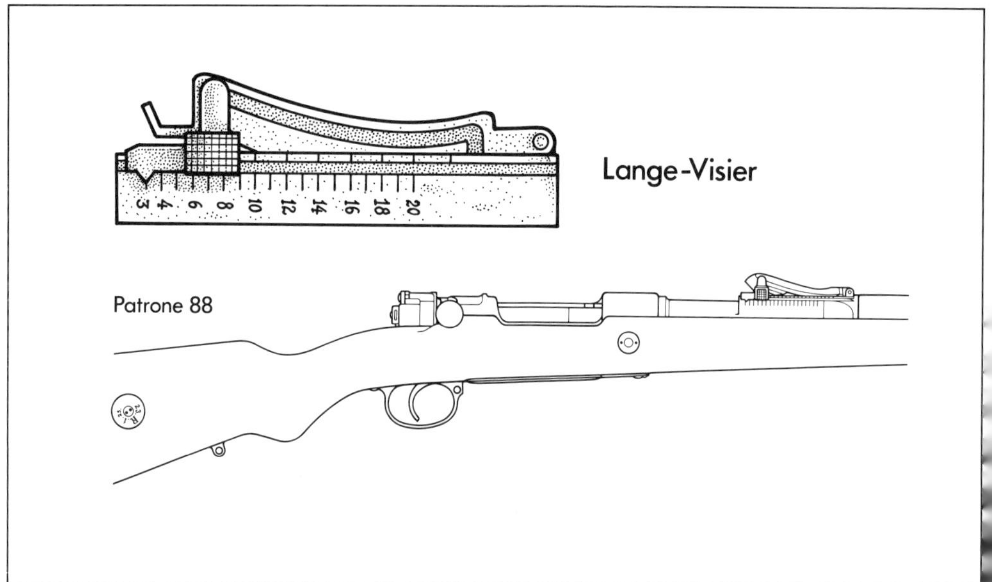

Right: the Lange-pattern tangent sight first appeared on the Gewehr 88/97; it was subsequently adapted for the Gewehr 98.

The GPK subsequently ordered two thousand rifles from Waffenfabrik Mauser AG in January 1895. A specimen gun appeared by 5 February according to Götz[1], who records correspondence from Oberst Hoffmann—the commanding officer of 6.Bayerisches Infanterie-Regiment—in which the prototype was mentioned. The rifles were delivered in the early summer of 1895—a thousand of each of two models, differing in the breeching arrangements—and were issued for trial on 1 August to the fusilier battalion of 1.Garde-Regiment zu Fuss, the Garde-Jäger-Bataillon, the third battalion of Füsilier-Regiment Königin (Schleswig-Holstein'sches) Nr. 86, and the Infanterie-Schiess-Schule in Spandau.

Predictably, the trials were a great success, as the new Mauser was much more efficient than the Gewehr 88. Its new 1895-patent action also proved superior to the 1893 model incorporated in the experimental rifles purchased from Mauser in 1896 (qv). Finally, the Kaiser signed the adoption orders on 11 March 1897; the Kriegsministerium recorded that "His Majesty the King-Emperor . . . commanded on 11 March 1897 that rifles with the modified lock shown him will be made in the arsenals during the Fiscal Year 1897/98, under the designation 'Gewehr 88/97' . . .".

This confirms two things: first, that the guns were officially adopted and, secondly, their official designation. The 88/97 was adopted in Bavaria on 21 April 1897 and production plans were readied. Erfurt was to attain a daily rate of 130 guns as soon as possible, but nothing was done and the Gewehr 98 was introduced instead. This weapon, which was a definite improvement compared with the 88/97, dispensed with the peculiar bayonet attachment assembly, had a pistol-grip (rather than straight-gripped) stock to help the firer control recoil, and an improved back sight. The barrel jacket was sensibly discarded.

1. Hans-Dieter Götz, *Die deutschen Militärgewehre und Maschinenpistolen, 1871-1945*, p. 121.

Production history

Two thousand Gewehre 88/97 were made in Mauser's Oberndorf factory between February and June-July 1895.

Markings

The gun illustrated in Götz's *Die deutschen Militärgewehre*, number 1729, bears 'WAFFENFABRIK/MAUSER/OBERNDORF A/N/1895' in four lines over the chamber. It is assumed that the serial numbers may be located in the usual places—on the barrel, the receiver and the bolt—and inspectors' marks can be clearly seen on many of the components.

Mechanical description and variations

The Gewehr 88/97 embodied a number of features new to the German army, many of which were the subject of Mauser patents. The most important was DRP 90,305 of 30 October 1895[2], which protected a modified bolt with a third locking lug, a cocking piece housing with integral gas deflector lugs, and several other new features. There were gas escape holes in the bolt body, and the escaping gases could escape along the left-hand locking lug guideway and out of the charger-loading cut-away milled in the left side of the receiver[3].

The rifle has a standard Mauser charger-loaded internal staggered-column box magazine[4]; and its operation is much the same as that of the Gewehr 98 (qv). No variations in its basic construction or operation have yet been reported. However, these were two minor variants, differing in the breeching arrangements.

2. It may have been applied for several months earlier.

3. The subject of DRGM ('Deutsches Reich Gebrauchs Muster', German utility design) 56,068 of 9 August 1895.

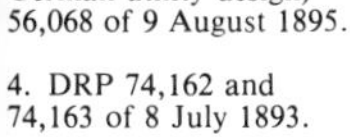

4. DRP 74,162 and 74,163 of 8 July 1893.

Appearance, distinctive features and data

The Gewehr 88/97 cannot be confused with any other Mauser rifle on account of its special features. Although the action, which has a straight bolt handle and the usual milled-out cut-away in the left side of the receiver wall, greatly resembles its 1898-system successors, the 88/97 rifle has a prototype Lange Visier mounted on top of the barrel jacket, no handguard above the stock, a straight-grip stock, and an extraordinary double-clamp nose-cap and bayonet bar assembly. This seems to have been based on a patent granted to Mauser in late 1895[5], with amendments made by the GPK. Certainly, the tube-hilted bayonets are unique to the 88/97.

5. DRP 85,365 of 30 October 1895.

There is a single screw-clamping spring-retained barrel band, which carries the forward sling swivel. There are positions for the second swivel through the front of the trigger guard bow and on the under-edge of the butt.

A half-length cleaning rod protrudes from the centre of the cylindrical bayonet attachment bar, and the true muzzle protrudes a short distance from the barrel jacket. The open front sight is mounted on top of the jacket.

DATA

Calibre: nominally 8mm.
Rifling: concentric, 4 grooves 0.10mm deep and 4.4mm wide; 1 turn in 240mm, right hand (pitch of 5° 55').
Magazine: internal staggered-column box, 5 rounds capacity.
Loading system: charger, or single rounds.
Length overall: 1,240mm.
Barrel length: 740mm.
Weight: about 4,000gm without sling.
Sights: (front) open barylecorn; (back) a Lange tangent sight graduated from 300 to 2,000 metres in 100m increments.
Performance: see cartridge data (Appendix 2).

Accessories

BAYONETS

The rifles were issued with a selection of experimental tube-hilt bayonets (TGB, pp. 48-51).

OTHERS

Not known.

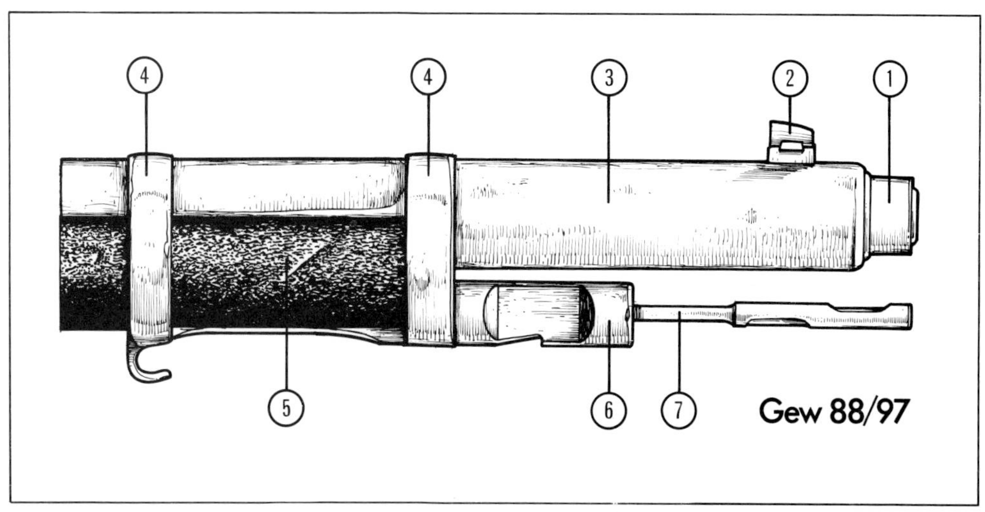

Right: the muzzle, nose-cap assembly and bayonet fitting unique to the Gewehr 88/97. Key: 1, barrel; 2, front sight; 3, barrel jacket; 4, bands; 5, stock; 6, bayonet boss; and 7, cleaning rod.

Kleinkalibriges-Versuchsgewehr Mauser, 1896

In 1892, the GPK began experiments with bullet diameters as small as 5mm, seated in cases measuring 67-68mm. These were developed by Polte of Magdeburg and, apparently, fired from modified Gewehre 88. The trials, however, had few lasting results[1], although they had shown that the existing German service rifles could be improved. Consequently, the GPK began to develop an improved gun based on the latest contemporary Mauser designs (see Gewehr 88/97) and ordered 2,185 experimental rifles from Waffenfabrik Mauser AG in October 1896[2]. Delivery was completed in 1897. The army was keen to assess the potential of small-calibre bullets, which is why the majority of the Mausers seems to have chambered a 6mm round, but there may have been other aims: the rifles differ considerably from the 1895-vintage 88/97 prototypes. However, so many of the 1896 rifles were re-chambered or tested to destruction that their development history is obscure. Rifle serial number 53 chambers a 6mm round, and 74 and 250 may have been similar—but Korn[3], listing their shooting results, describes them as 'Gewehre 98'. Number 9 seems to have fired a 7.65mm cartridge[4].

The experimental rifles of 1896 were based on legislation sought for the 1893-model Spanish rifle and others, and not on the patents granted in 1895 to protect the prototypes of the Gewehr 98. The GPK may have doubted the merits of the new 1895-patent action, wishing to undertake comparative trials. Not only do the Mauser rifles ordered in 1896 use the older action, but they also lack barrel jackets, have tangent-leaf back sights rather than Lange Visiere, comparable straight-grip stocks, and conventional bayonet attachment systems.

The special 6mm cartridge is generally believed to have been developed by Mauser and Deutsche Metallpatronenfabrik for the GPK, but its published dimensions suggest that it

1. It has not been determined whether these trials had any bearing on the development of the Mondragon 'piston cartridges' a few years later. These were also made by Polte and shared the designation '5.2mm × 68mm'; the same case dies may well have been used.

2. R. H. Korn, *Mauser Gewehre und Mauser-Patente*, p. 17.

3. *Mauser Gewehre und Mauser-Patente*, pp. 255-59.

4. This was service issue in Argentina, Belgium, Turkey and elsewhere.

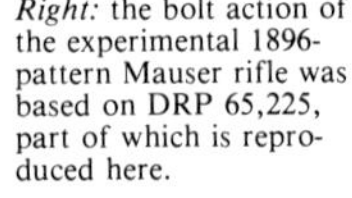

Right: the bolt action of the experimental 1896-pattern Mauser rifle was based on DRP 65,225, part of which is reproduced here.

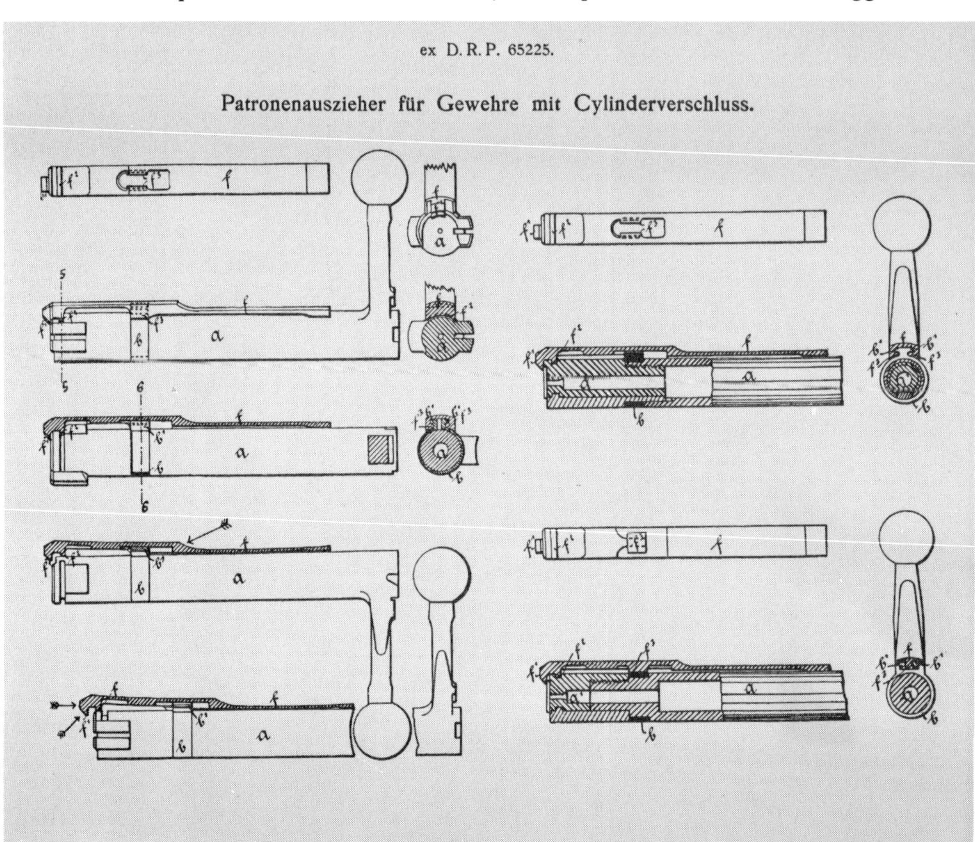

may have been a slightly modified copy of the US M 1895 (Lee Straight Pull) pattern. This bore the DM/DWM case number 425A and the same list states that case 425B was an experimental 6mm calibre German cartridge: because of the similarity of the numbers, the latter must have been at least based on the Lee-type[5].

The GPK's trials lasted from 1895 until about 1902, and had shown by the beginning of 1898 that the 1895-patent Mauser action was an improvement on the altered 1893-type embodied in the '1896' rifles. The Gewehr 98 was subsequently adopted in April 1898, but testing of different cartridges, rifling profiles and twist-pitches continued for several years. Calibres of 6mm, 6.5mm, 7mm, 7.65mm and 8mm are known to have been tried, and many of the experimental rifles were re-chambered to handle them. The GPK ultimately decided that the flat trajectory and high velocity of the 6mm bullets could not overcome their inferior lethality and wind-riding qualities, and the standard 8mm Patrone 88 was retained.

5. However, Mauser tested many cartridges during the 1890s, and the 6mm pattern could even have been a necked-down and slightly lengthened derivative of the standard 7mm or 8mm types (DWM case numbers 380 and 366). No gun is available for a chamber cast to be taken.

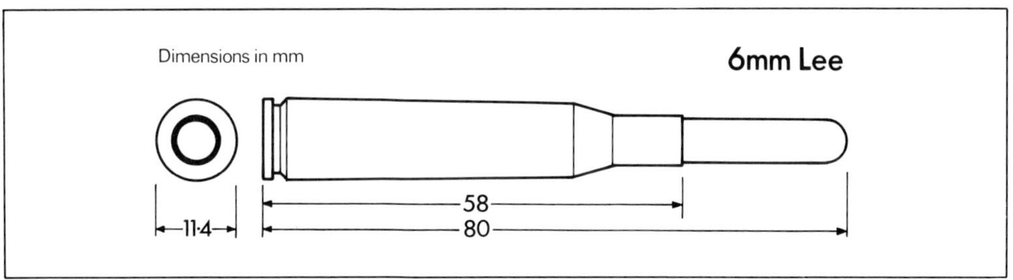

Right: the US .236 (6mm) M 1895 cartridge, for the Lee navy rifle, may have provided the basis for the 6mm German pattern.

Below: the tangent-leaf sight protected by DRGM 54,504 was a distinguishing feature of the 1896-type Mauser rifle, since a Lange tangent pattern was used on the Gewehr 88/97.

ex D. R. G. M. 54504.

Quadrantenvisier mit gleichmässiger Skalenteilung am Visierfuss und an der Visierklappe.

Production history

All 2,185 of the experimental 1896-pattern Mauser rifles were made by Waffenfabrik Mauser AG, of Oberndorf am Neckar, in 1896-97. They were delivered to the GPK by 1897.

Markings

The guns bear a standard Mauser chamber mark, consisting of 'WAFFENFABRIK MAUSER/ OBERNDORF A/N/1896,' and standard commercial proof marks on the barrel and receiver. The serial numbers lie on the barrel, the receiver, and the bolt handle.

Mechanical features and variations

The Mauser rifles delivered to the GPK in 1896-97 greatly resemble the 1896-model Swedish Mauser rifle but have a modified action based on several patents granted in the early 1890s. The most important was probably DRP 65,225 of February 1892, which protected the distinctive non-rotating extractor. The action is a standard Mauser, with two vertically locking lugs on the front of the bolt body, and a third lug (under the bolt body) that engages in a recess milled in the receiver behind the magazine well. The camming action of the bolt lugs as they are revolved out of their seats provides adequate primary extraction, and the nose of the striker is withdrawn into the bolt body as the handle is raised. This prevents the tip reaching the primer when the bolt is run forward to complete the re-loading stroke.

The left locking lug is slotted to allow the blade type ejector, which, with a bolt-stop, lies on the left rear of the receiver, to kick the extracted cartridge out of the bolt-way. The bolt head is partly shrouded, there are two (perhaps three) gas escape ports, and the non-rotating extractor is retained by a spring-collar around the bolt body. The safety lever is a Mauser 'wing' design[6] and has three positions: left, vertical and right. The rifle can be fired in the first instance, the striker is locked in the second, and the striker and the bolt are locked in the third.

The charger-loaded internal box magazine contains a staggered row of five cartridges and has a removable floor plate[7]. Charger guides are milled in the front portion of the solid receiver bridge to receive the C/94 charger, and a large thumb clearance cut-away is milled out of the left receiver wall. The trigger cannot be pulled until the bolt is securely locked, when a small lug on the sear bar enters a small recess in the underside of the bolt body; only then can the sear nose be rotated to release the striker.

The weapon is rarely seen, but variations in calibre and stock fittings may be encountered.

Appearance, distinctive features and data

The experimental rifles greatly resemble the Swedish M96 rifle, so far as their general appearance is concerned. Their bolt handles have spherical grasping knobs and are generally turned down against the stock. They lack barrel jackets, unlike the Gewehre 88/97. Walnut handguards run from the front of the receiver ring to just in front of the solitary barrel band, which is a spring retained screw-clamping pattern carrying a sling swivel. The second swivel lies underneath the butt. The nose-cap is a small clamping band, and carries a standard bayonet attachment lug on the right side. A tangent-leaf back sight[8] is carried on a short sleeve around the barrel and protrudes above the handguard. A half-length cleaning rod, for emergency cleaning and removing obstructions from the bore, is carried beneath the barrel. The one-piece walnut stock has a straight-grip rather than a pistol-grip, but it is believed that some rifles were later re-stocked in similar fashion to the Gewehr 98 (qv).

The metal parts are blued and polished, with the exception of the receivers, bolts and butt plates, which have a grey-pickled rust-resistant finish.

DATA

Calibre: 6mm.

Rifling: concentric, 6 grooves 0.1mm deep and of uncertain width; 1 turn in 165mm, right hand (pitch of 6° 31').

Magazine: internal staggered-column box, 5 rounds capacity.

Loading system: charger, or single rounds.

Length overall: 1,250mm.

Barrel length: 740mm.

Weight: about 3,630gm without sling.

Sights: (front) open barleycorn; (back) tangent-leaf sight with a standing 'battle sight' for 300m, and graduations from 400 to 2,000 metres.

Accessories

BAYONET

Unidentified. Possibly the S 71/84 (TGB, pp. 44-46).

OTHERS

Probably a sling, a muzzle protector, and others.

6. Protected by US Patent 547,932, granted in October 1895.

7. The magazine was protected by DRP 74,162; the floor plate by DRP 74,163. Both date from July 1893.

8. Protected by DRGM 54,504 of March 1896.

Mauser rifles and carbines: an identification guide

		Gewehr 88/97	Versuchsgewehr, 1896	Gewehr 98, pre-1915	Gewehr 98, post-1915	Radfahrer-Gewehr 98	Karabiner 98	Karabiner 98 A	Versuchs-Karabiner 98, 1906	Versuchs-Karabiner 98 Z, 1906	Karabiner 98 AZ (98a)	Karabiner 98b	Karabiner 98k
		1	2	3	4	5	6	7	8	9	10	11	12
ACTION	large ring	●	●	●	●	●	●	●				●	●
	small ring								?	?	●		
BOLT HANDLE	straight	●		●	●								
	turned down, ball knob		●			●			●	●	●	●	●
	turned down, spatulate						●	●					

Mausers			1	2	3	4	5	6	7	8	9	10	11	12
NOSECAP TYPE	see key		a	b	c	c	c	e1	d	e2	e1	f	c	c
BARREL BANDS			2	1	1	1	1	1	1	1	1	1	1	1
HANDGUARDS	none		●											
	breech to barrel band			●						●	●			
	breech to nosecap											●		
	backsight to barrel band				●	●	●		●				●	●
	backsight to nosecap							●						
BACKSIGHT	Lange tangent type	200-1200m						●						
		200-2000m			●	●	●							
		300-1800m							●					
		300-2000m	●											
		400-2000m			●	●	●							
	tangent-leaf type	100-2000m											●	●
		300-2000m		●						●	●	●		
SLING SWIVELS OR ANCHOR POINTS	butt edge		●	●	●	●								
	butt side						●	●	●	●	●	●	●	●
	trigger-guard		●		●	●								
	barrel band		●	●	●	●	●	●	●	●	●	●	●	●
STOCK FITTINGS, ETC.	marking disc				●		●	●						
	firing pin protection washer					●							●	●
	grasping groove					●							●	
	recoil bolts and/or transverse keys		1	1	1	1	1	1	1	1	2	2	1	1
	piling rod							●			●	●		
CLEANING ROD			●	●	●	●	●		●				●	●
BAYONET			●	●	●	●	●		●			●	●	●

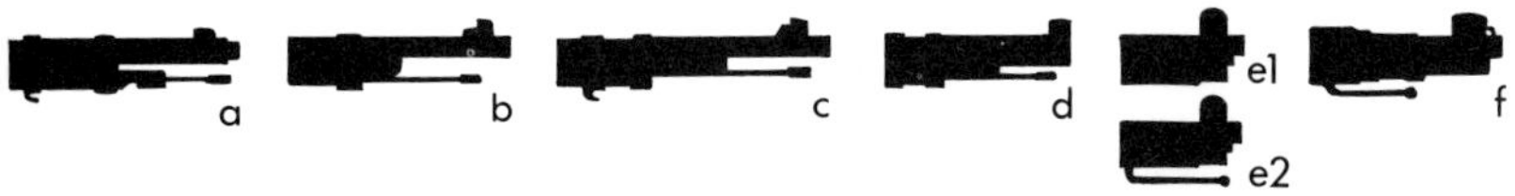

a b c d e1 e2 f

Gewehr 98 Mauser

Far right: two Mauser charger designs—DRGM 109,017 and 127,291 of 1898 and 1900 respectively—and the safety mechanism protected by DRGM 154,915 of 1901, in which the firing pin could not reach the primer of a chambered round until the bolt was safely locked.

This rifle was the third in a series of prototypes developed in the late 1890s to replace the obsolescent Gewehr 88, the others being the Gewehr 88/97 and the experimental Mauser 'Kleinkalibriges Gewehr' of 1896 (qv). Trials had been undertaken with many small-calibre cartridges in the same decade, including some as small as 5mm, but these had failed to challenge the supremacy of the standard 8mm Patrone 88; even though the trials Mausers of 1895-98 had been tested with bullet diameters of 6mm, 6.5mm, 7mm and 7.65mm.

The finalized Gewehr 98 differed greatly from the Gewehr 88. It had a solid rather than split-bridge receiver; a bolt handle locking behind the bridge rather than in front; a one-piece bolt with its double locking lugs forged integrally with the body, rather than a separate removable bolt head; a third locking lug in the receiver wall opposite the bolt handle; a special tangent sight, designed by Oberst Wilhelm Lange, rather than the old leaf type; a much modified bayonet attachment system; no barrel jacket; a pistol-grip rather than straight-grip stock; and, most importantly, a charger rather than clip-loaded magazine.

The Gewehr 98 was officially adopted on 5 April 1898, and large-scale troop trials were begun on 9 February 1899. These were undertaken by 1.Garde-Regiment zu Fuss, the Garde-Jäger-Bataillon, the Garde-Schützen-Bataillon and the Infanterie-Schiess-Schule in Spandau, and proved not only that the decision to adopt the new Mauser rifle was quite justifiable but also that the Gewehr 98 was a considerable improvement on the Gewehr 88. Plans for large-scale manufacture were readied immediately. The government voted an annual sum of 2.5 million marks to complete re-armament in five years, but the Kriegsministerium was well aware that the hurried development and introduction of the Gewehr 88 had, in the long term, led to serious problems. Finally, it was decided to spread the issue of the Gewehr 98 over more than a decade: all front line units were to be re-equipped by 1907, but the Reserve and the Landwehr would have to wait for a second production series to commence in 1912. The Prussian government had acquired rights to exploit Mauser's patents protecting the 'Mauser-Schloss und Magazineinrichtung' (Mauser lock and magazine design) as early as 16 November 1895, when Peter-Paul Mauser had signed a licensing agreement despatched from Spandau five days earlier. This was to last for seven years and a one mark royalty was to be paid on each of the first hundred thousand guns. Each gun thereafter was to be assessed at 50 pfennige (½ mark). Although the contract had been negotiated on the experimental Gewehr 88/97, it still applied to the Gewehr 98, which was, after all, little more than a refined version of the trials rifles of 1895-98.

Mass production of the new rifles began during 1900, and by February 1901 the three Prussian arsenals—Danzig, Erfurt and Spandau—were delivering 300 daily; Waffenfabrik Mauser AG began to supply rifles after 1904-5. About 90,000 had been received from all the contractors involved by late 1901, each costing the government about 54 marks. The first issues were made to the Kriegsmarine (navy) and the Ostasiatisches Expeditionskorps[1], and then to the first three Prussian army corps in the autumn of 1901; the next three were re-equipped in 1902, three more in 1903, and so on until issue was complete.

The Mauser rifle was not adopted in Bavaria until Prince Regent Luitpold signed the relevant papers on 2 May 1901. Machinery was installed in the Amberg factory in August and the first guns were completed in January 1903. Later, the total daily output reached eighty; these were delivered to the Ingolstadt fortress for subsequent distribution. The Bavarian army corps were re-armed between October 1903 and October 1907. A production agreement had been reached with Waffenfabrik Mauser on 17 September 1901, while the production machinery was being installed in Amberg, and was to run for four and a half years (ending, therefore, in March 1906[2]); royalties were set at one mark for each of the first twenty thousand guns and 50 pfennige for the remainder.

1. A German force sent to China to restore order in the wake of the Boxer Rebellion, and to safeguard German interests in the Far East. The guns may bear unit markings in the form of 'O.E.'

2. Hans-Dieter Götz, *Die deutschen Militärgewehre und Maschinenpistolen, 1871-1945,* p. 130, states this as 1905—a misprint?

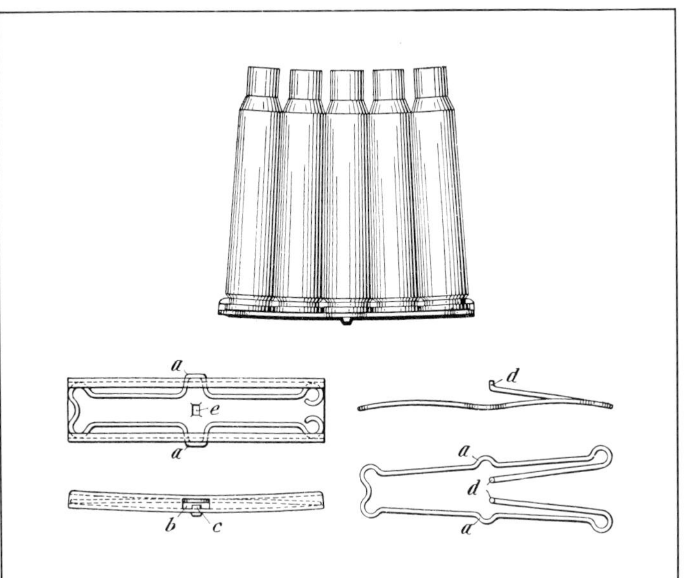
a
e
a
b
c
d
a
d
a

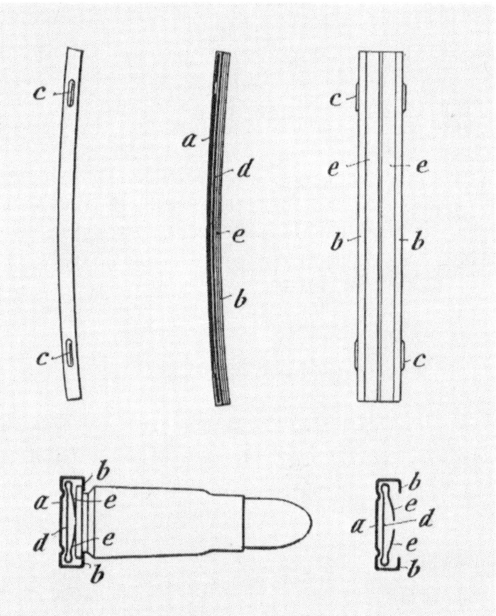
c
a
d
e
b
c
c
e
e
b
b
c
b
a
e
d
e
b
b
e
a
d
e
b

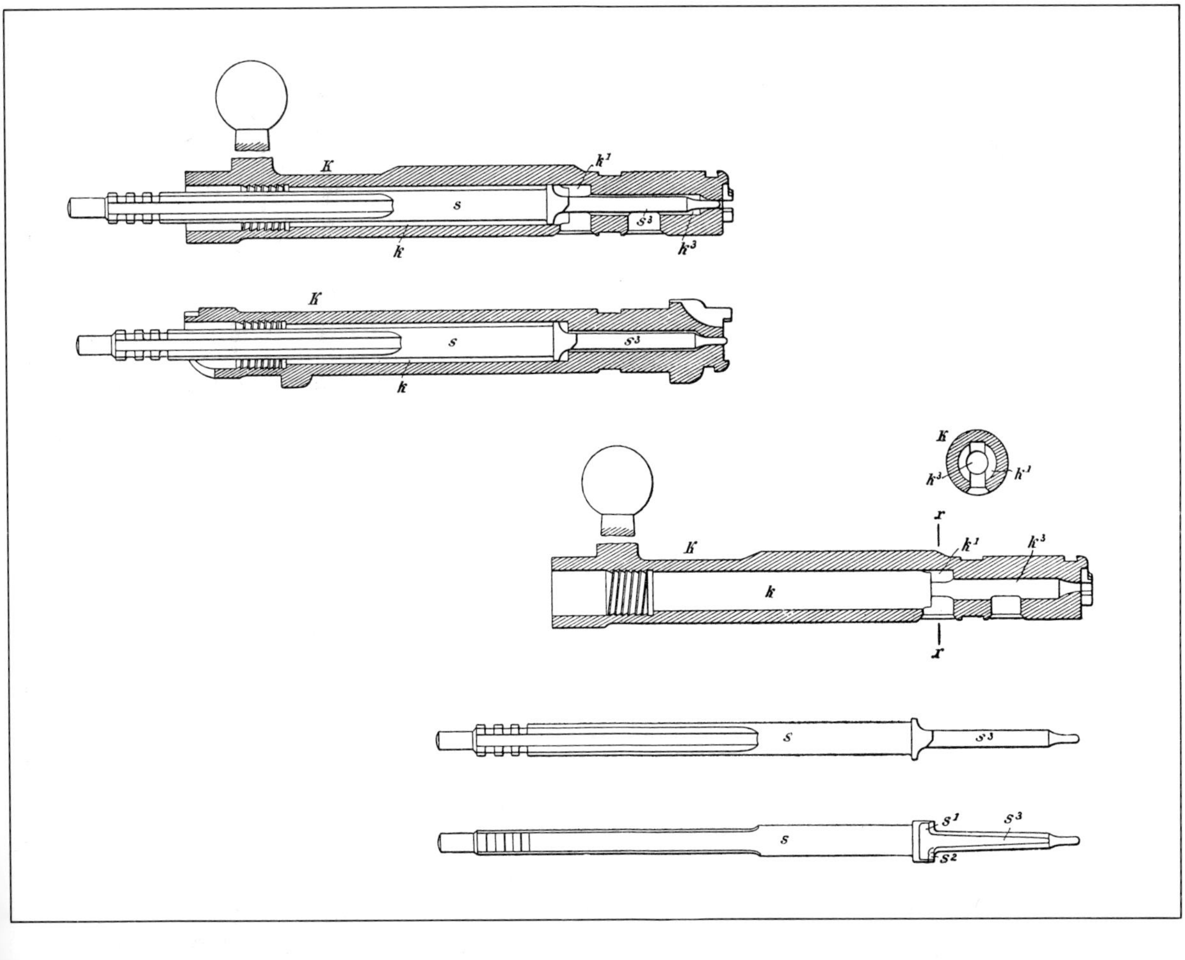

It will be appreciated that Mauser, quite apart from making thousands of the rifles and selling them directly to the authorities, was making large sums of money from the royalties since production was to run into millions before the First World War had ended.

Much work seems to have gone into designing the charger for the Gewehr 98. The original was designed by Mauser, protected by DRGM ('Deutsches Reich Gebrauchs Muster', German utility design) 109,017 of 20 December 1898 and comprised a steel body with a bent wire spring. A second pattern was then developed, with a flat leaf spring of the type pictured in Mauser's DRGM 127,291 of 23 February 1900. According to Götz[3], who credits its design to the GPK, it was introduced to the Prussian Army on 7 February. It was made of nickelled brass. Finally, a one-piece self-sprung brass bodied type was introduced in October 1904 and remained standard throughout the war. Very few other alterations were made to the Gewehr 98 or its accessories, although Mauser developed an improved safety feature—protected by DRGM 154,915 of 22 May 1901—which introduced lugs on the front portion of the striker head. These aligned with shoulders inside the bolt body when the action was unlocked, preventing the striker head from protruding out of the bolt face and contacting the primer of a live cartridge during the loading cycle.

3. Hans-Dieter Götz, *Die deutschen Militärgewehre und Maschinenpistolen, 1871-1945*, p. 135.

The Gewehr 98 initially fired the Patronen 88, but the sudden introduction in France of a pointed bullet for the Mle 86/93 Lebel rifle and the various Berthier carbines (the so-called 'Balle D', named after its designer Desaleux) caused the development of a comparable pattern in Germany. Experiments with the new pointed bullets, 'Spitzgeschosse', were undertaken in Spandau in the hope that streamlining would cut air resistance, increase range and improve accuracy. Götz[4] notes that the final experimental projectile, the so-called 'S2', weighed 10.3gm and had a diameter of 8.23±0.02mm[5]. The trials continued between October 1902 and June 1903 in the Prussian and Bavarian musketry schools—Spandau and Lechfeld respectively—until the new bullets were perfected. The final pattern, half-a-gram lighter than S2 at 9.7gm, was otherwise very similar to its forerunner. Several minor adjustments were made, and the thickness of the bullet's cupro-nickel jacket was increased from 0.3mm to 0.5mm in a bid to counteract a tendency to strip the jacket from around the lead core. This was caused by the increased frictional forces between the bore walls and the bullet surface, resulting from the commensurately increased muzzle velocity and the enlarged projectile diameter.

4. Hans-Dieter Götz, *Die deutschen Militärgewehre und Maschinenpistolen, 1871-1945*, p. 133.

5. Later standardized at 8.22mm.

Gewehr 98

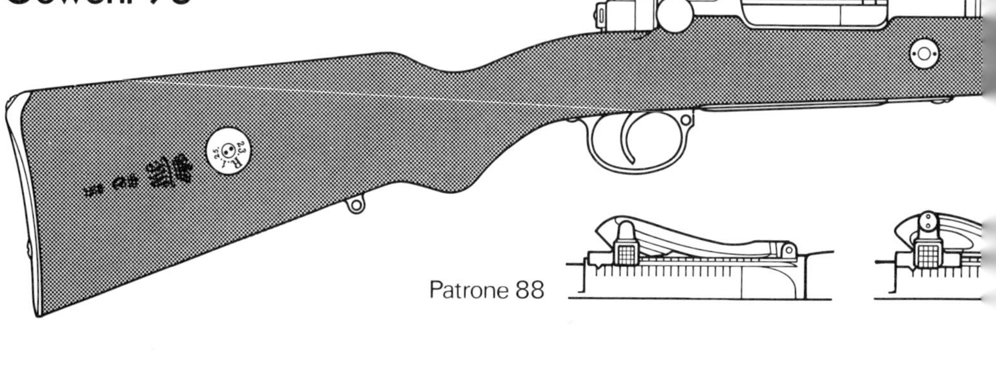

Patrone 88

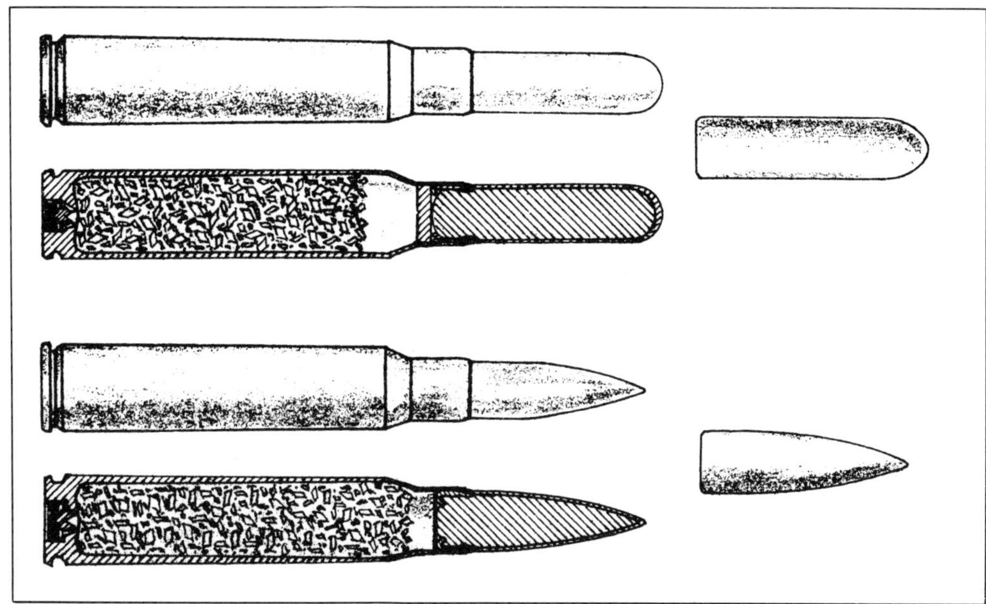

Right: a comparison between the Patr. 88 and the S-Patr. The latter is loaded with a 'Spitzgeschoss', or pointed bullet.

At about the same time, the old propellant—Blattchen-Pulver Typ 426[6]—was replaced by Spandauer-Pulver 682b with effect from 3 March 1903. The latter's propellant flakes were smaller and thinner, giving quicker and more complete burning, less fouling and more propellant in a given volume owing to the smaller grains[7]. The new cartridges were loaded with 3.2gm of Pulver 682b, compared to 2.63gm of Pulver 426 in Patronen 88 loaded between 1899 and 1903, and developed a muzzle velocity of 870 rather than 620m/sec. The chamber pressure was the greater at 3,100 atmospheres, compared to only 2,700 with Pulver 426, but was still appreciably less than the 3,350at. obtained in original Patronen 88 loaded with Gewehr-Blattchen-Pulver. The bullet weight was stabilized at 9.8gm.

By 1904, with cartridge production well under way, the government factories were delivering S-Patronen at 97 marks per thousand[8]. Bavarian ammunition was being loaded by the Hauptlaboratorium in Ingolstadt; Prussian, by the Government arsenals

6. The sides of the flakes measured 1.7 ± 0.1mm, and their depth was 0.375 ± 0.025mm.

7. The sides measured 1.35 ± 0.15mm; the depth, 0.30 ± 0.05mm.

8. Compared to 200 marks per thousand for commercial cartridges of similar type; ALFA catalogue, 1911, p. 450.

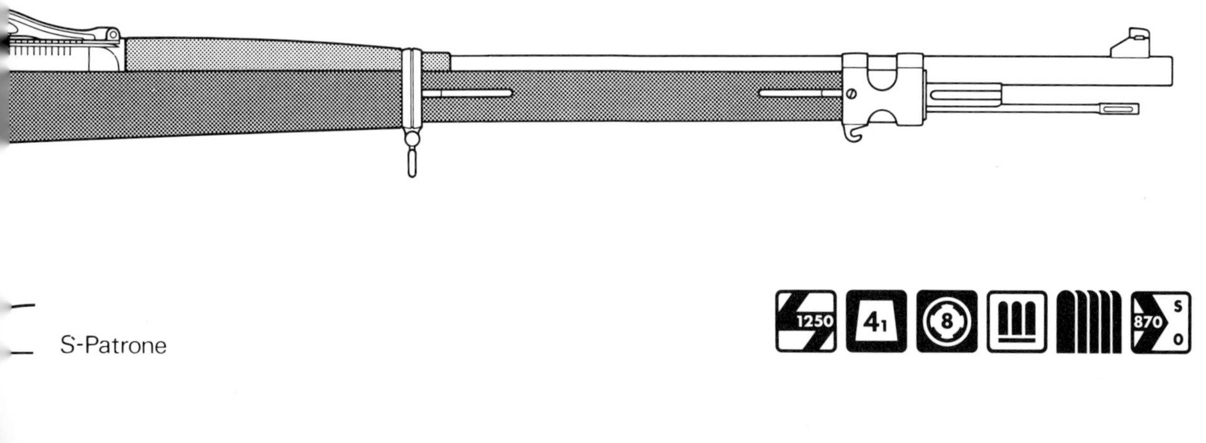

and a handful of private contractors, with propellant supplied by the Rottweiler Pulverfabriken and Westfälisch-Anhaltische Sprengstoff AG. Stocks of Patronen 88 were gradually exhausted after the official 'changeover day' to the S-Patrone, which occurred on 1 October 1905, although the newer cartridge had been adopted as early as 25 March 1903. There were 163 million Patronen 88 and 197 million S-Patronen in store on 1 October 1906, but the figures had altered to 110 million and 250 million respectively within three years; all post-1907 shooting practice was undertaken with old cartridges regardless of the fact that all the rifles had been converted for the new!

All existing service rifles, whether Gewehre 88 or 98, were converted for the new ammunition between 1903 and 1905. The Prussian arsenal in Spandau and the smaller Bavarian establishment in Amberg soon became very efficient at converting them—revising, inspecting and cleaning one every four minutes until daily production rates of 800 or more were reached[9]. Converted guns were given a 2.5mm high letter 'S' on top of their chambers and on their barrels, behind the back sight base. It seems that many (all?) new guns made during the period in which others were being converted were also given the special 'S' marks, and that marking continued even after all existing rifles had been altered; as all the guns then chambered the S-Patronen, the distinction became unnecessary and it mattered little whether the guns were 'S' marked or not.

9. Hans-Dieter Götz, *Die deutschen Militärgewehre und Maschinenpistolen, 1871-1945*, p. 137.

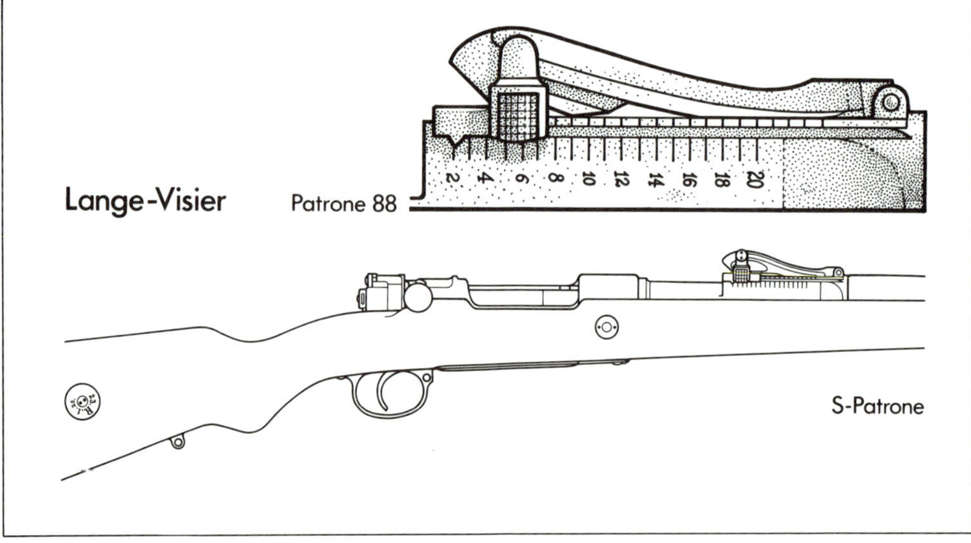

Right: the Lange tangent backsight of the Gewehr 98.

Far right: the action of the Gewehr 98. Key: 10, barrel; 11, receiver; 12, receiver bridge; 13, bolt; 14, bolt handle; 15, extractor collar; 16, extractor unit; 17, cocking piece housing; 18, cocking piece; 19, safety catch guide; 20, charger guides; 21, trigger; 22, trigger guard and magazine housing; 23, magazine floorplate; 24, sling swivel hole; 25, stock; 26, recoil bolt; and 27, grasping groove.

The back sights were naturally revised at the same time, since the bullet of the S-Patrone had a flatter trajectory than that of the Patrone 88. Most of the weapons were returned to the regimental depots at a convenient moment, where their sight leaves were removed and sent to the government workshops. New leaves were sent back to the regimental armourers on a one-for-one basis, fitted to the rifles as quickly as possible, and the guns were issued once more. The old sight bases had been graduated from 200 to 2000 metres, but when the new sight leaves were fitted, the 200m and 300m marks could not be used. Newly-made sights, as opposed to those that had simply been modified, had their bed-graduations beginning at 400 metres. During the First World War, this modified Lange-system sight was found to be very inefficient; the guns shot very high at ranges of 50m or 100m, since the minimum sight setting was 400. Unfortunately, most fighting was done at much closer ranges than had been envisaged and an auxiliary sight ('Hilfskorne') was developed to fit behind the existing front sight in order to lower the sight line. The guns were then sighted for 100 metres.

The Gewehr 98 proved to be one of the world's most successful military rifles, but was by no means flawless. For example, it was much too long and unwieldy—as many German soldiers were to find to their cost in the trenches of the First World War. A few years after the Mauser rifle had appeared, the British began to issue the Rifle, Short, Magazine Lee-Enfield Mark 1 (SMLE)[10], which was long enough to be an adequate infantry rifle, short enough to be an acceptable cavalry carbine, and destined to prove very handy in the trenches despite its badly-shaped stock. The US Army had followed the British lead with the acceptance of the Rifle .30 M 1903, which, ironically, was a slightly modified Mauser[11]. The US government even purchased rights to the seven Mauser patents it infringed, five in the bolt mechanism and two in the charger.

10. Adopted on 1 July 1903, but re-adopted after a few minor changes had been made on 14 September 1903.

11. This rifle was adopted on 19 June 1903, a few days before the SMLE, but the design was not really finalized until 1905.

The Germans subsequently toyed with the idea of an 'Einheitswaffe' (a short rifle for universal issue) and even developed a series of long and short carbines before concluding that the advantages in such weapons were largely illusory. They scarcely merited re-equipping the German armies at a time when large-scale distribution of Gewehre 98 were just beginning, and the authorities did not wish to shorten the length of their rifle/bayonet combination in case of a war with France. The French had a long rifle (the Mle 86/93 Lebel) and a long épée bayonet, and it was thought that the German troops would be at a severe disadvantage if a short rifle were issued universally. That was long

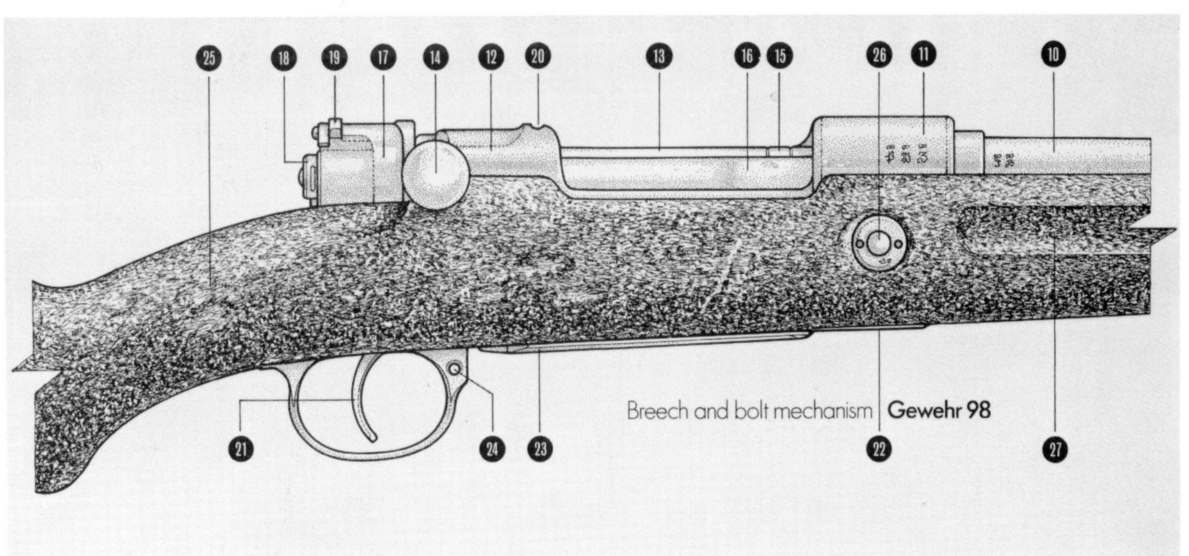

Breech and bolt mechanism **Gewehr 98**

before anyone realized how the First World War would be fought, however, and many military tacticians still had in mind the outmoded en masse bayonet charge. The Germans chose to retain the full-length Gewehr 98 for the infantry and riflemen, but introduced a cavalry carbine and a short rifle—the latter being confusingly known as the 'Karabiner 98' or 'Karabiner 98 AZ'—in June 1902 and January 1908 respectively. Ultimately, the short rifles replaced the carbines; both are described separately.

The horizontal handle of the Gewehr 98's bolt is, in the opinion of many experienced marksmen, very badly placed for rapid shooting, although even the British *Text Book of Small Arms 1904*[12] grudgingly admits that it is easily grasped without taking the eyes off the target. However, the position of the handle when fully retracted means, almost inevitably, that the firer has to move his cheek away from the butt, and, consequently, disturb his aim. The bolt handle of the SMLE, turned downwards and lying just above and behind the trigger, is much better adapted to rapid shooting. By way of proving this, many have pointed to the famous incident on the Marne in 1914, where the German

12. Page 128.

Right: German infantrymen pose confidently for the camera in 1916/17. From a contemporary picture postcard.

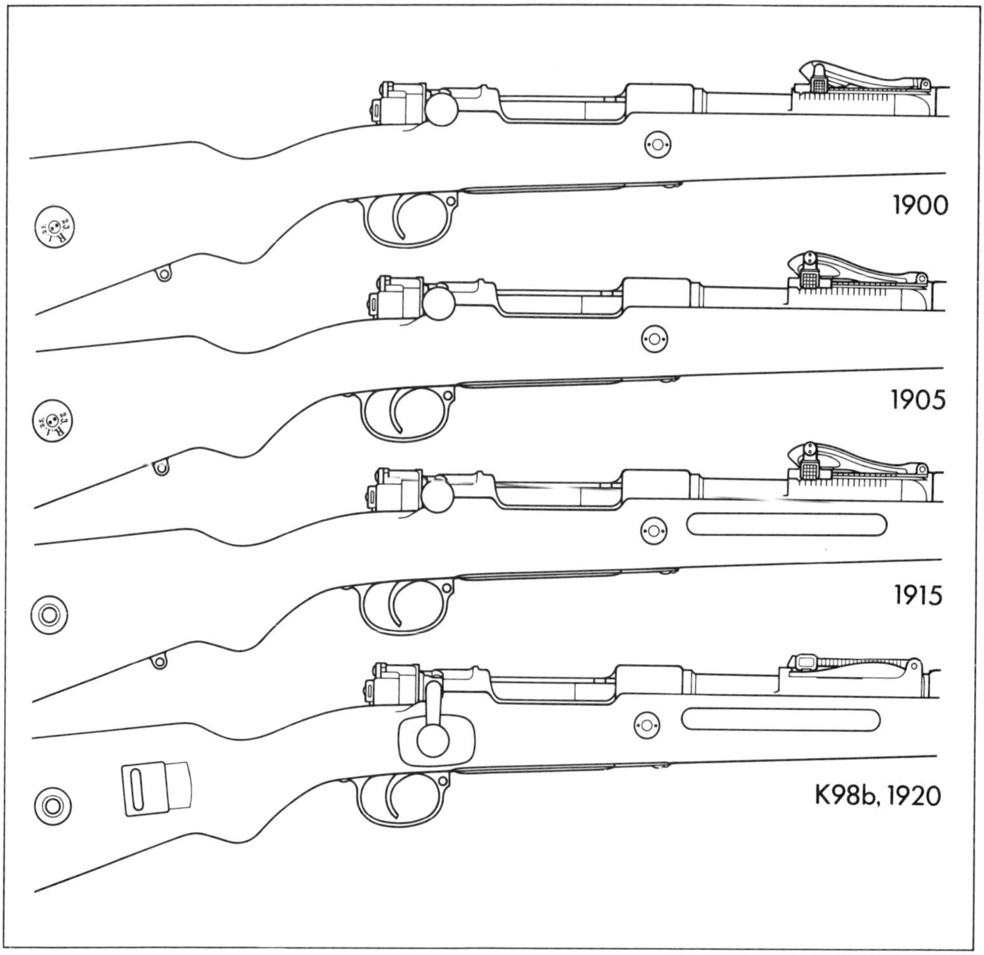

Right: stages in the evolution of the Gewehr 98, 1900-16.

1900

1905

1915

K98b, 1920

infantrymen were so impressed with their British opponents' speed of fire that they believed they were faced by automatic rifles. However, some German writers have since suggested that this was noticed simply because the Germans were not trained for rapid fire, rather than because the Lee-Enfield could be operated faster than the Gewehre 98. Hans-Rudolf von Stein once noted[13] . . . "I don't deny the merits of the Lee-Enfield, but I have never heard of difficulty caused by the position of the bolt handle in the Mauser. This is . . . only a matter of training. And, concerning the rapidity of fire of the British Expeditionary Forces on the Marne, please remember that they [the British] were professional soldiers with much experience of overseas campaigns. The German army opposing them was formed of conscripted men, trained for only two years. In our army, there was no rapid-fire training—our soldiers being taught only aimed fire, to make every shot count, and anything else was regarded by the authorities as a waste of ammunition . . .". It is quite probable that the Lee-Enfield can be fired faster than the Mauser, but I believe the differences to be so marginal as to be insignificant.

3. In a letter to the uthor, 17 November 971.

There is a minor weakness in the design of the Gewehr 98 receiver, which may, very rarely, crack below the thumb clearance cut-away milled in the left receiver wall in front of the bridge. This, though, does not seem to have been a very common occurrence during the First World War, since no notes of it could be found in any German contemporary source.

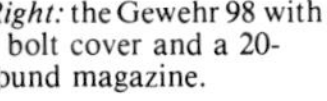
ight: the Gewehr 98 with bolt cover and a 20-ound magazine.

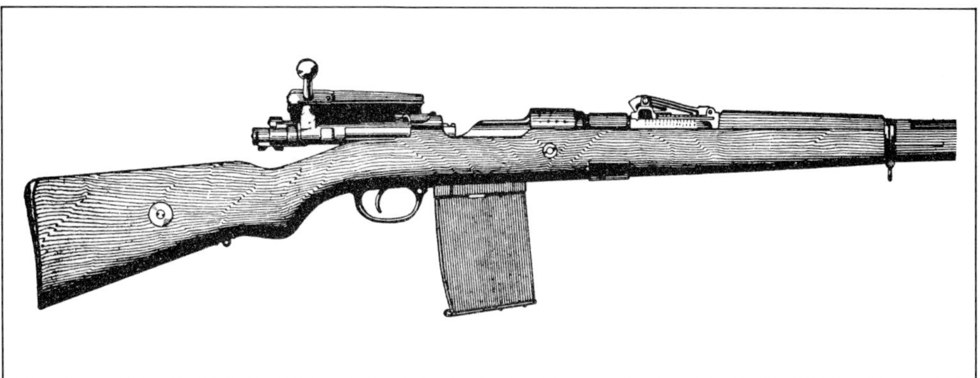

The long Mauser rifle was being carried by the regular infantry regiments and the greater part of the Reserve in August 1914, but the supplies were inadequate to arm even part of the numerous front line formations raised during and shortly after mobilization. Consequently, various adjustments of weaponry were made from time to time. Large numbers of Gewehre 88S, 88/05 and 88/14 appeared in the front line in the early stages of the fighting, while many captured rifles (particularly ex-Russian Mosin-Nagants) were pressed into service as well. Typical of the confusion was the case of Magdeburgisches Infanterie-Regiment Nr. 66, which according to the regimental history was armed with Gewehre 98 until 1915, received ex-Russian rifles in 1916, then a supply of Gewehr 88/05 (?) and finally another consignment of Gewehre 98. But although weapons came and went, the German troops—unlike their Russian opponents, for example—were never short of efficient magazine rifles and ammunition on anything other than a purely temporary local basis.

Wartime production of the Mauser rifles was accelerated as quickly as practicable, as more and more sub-contractors were recruited. In addition to the major government arsenals and the large private manufacturers such as Waffenfabrik Mauser and Deutsche Waffen & Munitionsfabriken, and the smaller companies such as Schilling and Haenel, many tiny workshops joined the production programmes in 1916-17. Virtually every uncommitted metalworking company—particularly around Suhl, centre of the German firearms industry—was ordered to make parts for the Gewehr 98 or other weapons, and subsequently supplied large numbers of small parts such as extractors, ejectors, bolt-stops, magazine floor plates and trigger-guard bows to the government arsenals. There, teams of experienced inspectors assembled the usable parts in complete rifles called 'Stern Gewehre' (star rifles), so-called because there was a large ★ struck into the top of each chamber. The parts were not completely interchangeable.

Few mechanical changes were made to the Gewehre 98 between 1914 and 1918, despite the introduction of several new cartridges. The S.m.K.-Patrone, which appeared in or shortly before March 1915 and was loaded with a 'Spitzgeschoss mit Kern'[14], was reserved for snipers' use in the Scharfschützen-Gewehr 98 since it was expensive to make; and the heavy 'sS' ball[15], introduced on 28 July 1918, was initially reserved for heavy machine-guns. It was issued with rifles only after the end of the war.

On 19 November 1915, the markings disc attached to the right side of the butt was altered to provide an easy means of dismantling the firing mechanism. The new butt fixture consisted of two washers connected by a short hollow tube in which the nose of the firing-pin was rested during dismantling to prevent distorting the tip, which had often been damaged formerly. A grasping groove was added to the fore-end at about the same time.

Several modified sights were developed during the war, as the need arose; there was an auxiliary front sight blade ('Hilfskorne') to reduce the minimum sighting distance from 400 to 100 metres; an anti-aircraft 'lead' sight attachment; three different front sights of varying height, intended to correct the shooting of guns whose points of impact had altered owing to bore wear or altered barrel bedding; a special night sight ('Leuchtvisier') fitted with luminous radium sight inserts to improve accuracy in twilight or dusk; and a 'Gewehr mit Spiegelkolben', which was a Gewehr 98 with a special hinged stock and a periscopic mirror-sight assembly. The last device was designed to permit firing from a trench without the firer exposing himself[16]. Few of these developments were of any real significance, and even the luminous night sights, which the troops had been anxious to receive, were abandoned after a short trial.

14. A pointed bullet with a special steel core, giving better penetration.

15. 'sS' meant 'schweres Spitzgeschoss', or heavy pointed bullet.

16. Similar guns were developed by the British, the Americans and the French. Some had hinged stocks, while others had standard rifles in special cradles fitted with periscope sights. None was successful, since problems of loading and recoil could not be overcome satisfactorily.

Right: the Mondragon semi-automatic rifle, issued in small numbers during the First World War. Courtesy of Ian Hogg.

Right: the Mauser Flieger-karabiner, sometimes called the 'M 1916', was developed experimentally during the First World War—but was never successful. Courtesy of Rolf Gminder.

A bolt cover and several auxiliary magazines were developed for use in the trenches, but never became common. The modified Gewehr 98/17 and the Mauser-Gewehr 18, too, failed to make any impression on the millions of Gewehre 98 still serving at the war's end.

A minor alteration was made to the locking system of the forward action retaining screw, which ran up through the front end of the trigger guard bow extension/magazine floor plate assembly. Only one lock-screw position (instead of three) was provided after about 1916, principally to speed up manufacture. The bolt mechanism was browned after 1917 rather than properly finished and polished, for much the same reasons, and finish gradually deteriorated. Alternatives to the standard walnut stock blanks, which had to be seasoned for at least three years before they could be used, were eagerly sought and a selection of accelerated drying processes were tried without lasting success. Elm and copper-beech stocks and handguards were made, the latter in appreciable quantity, and various laminated patterns were developed experimentally. Some guns also had separate butt-toes, which were attached by glueing and a dovetail joint in the Japanese manner so that stock blanks that might otherwise have been rejected could be used.

After the war had ended, many millions of rifles were discarded, destroyed, or converted into sporting rifles and shotguns. The few retained by the Reichswehr (Armed Forces), which the Treaty of Versailles had limited to 100,000 men, had their Lange sights replaced by simpler tangent-leaf types with a minimum sighting distance of 100 metres, their bolt handles turned down, their barrel bands revised, and their designation changed to 'Karabiner 98b' (qv).

Right: a typical pre-1915 Gewehr 98.

Production history

Mass production of the Gewehr 98 began in the Prussian government arsenals during 1900, previous trials weapons having apparently emanated from Waffenfabrik Mauser AG. By February 1901, Danzig arsenal had attained a daily delivery rate of 140 guns; Spandau, 107; and Erfurt, a mere 54. By the autumn of the same year, the three arsenals had made about 90,000 Mausers at about 53-55 marks apiece and issues to the first three army corps was made towards the end of 1901. The 100,000th government-made Gewehr 98 appeared in February 1902.

Production in the Bavarian arsenal in Amberg began in the late summer or early autumn of 1902 and the first guns were assembled in January 1903; production soon reached a daily rate of 70-80. Issue began in October 1903 and was to be completed in four years. By 1907, when front line re-equipment was supposed to have finished in Bavaria, Prussia, Saxony and Württemberg, at least a million rifles had been made: Götz[17] notes that Waffenfabrik Mauser's share of the first commercial contract, placed in 1904, had been 290,000. The remaining 210,000 were made by DWM. A second production series was planned to begin in 1912, but it is unlikely that there was such a large gap. Much more research into the production history of the Gewehr 98, contractor by contractor, has yet to be done, but rifles have been examined with dates *between* 1907 and 1912, as the Table below shows.

17. *Die deutschen Militärgewehre und Maschinenpistolen, 1871-1945*, p. 131.

Production was accelerated during the First World War, as contractors galore joined in the production chain. The Stern Gewehre (see Mechanical description and variations) were made in the government factories by assembling thousands of parts supplied by small metalsmithing companies whose capacity fell a long way short of making complete rifles. Some of these components were relatively badly-finished and would ordinarily have failed inspection owing to erratic adherence to the tolerances on the Gewehr 98 blueprints; the government assemblers and inspectors lowered the standards, accepting virtually any part that was structurally sound and operated satisfactorily. The penalty for this was that complete interchangeability amongst the components of the Stern Gewehre could not be guaranteed.

Peak production was reached in 1917, when several of the major manufacturers—the Erfurt arsenal, for one—used the entire first set of serial number suffix letters ('a-z') and began the second ('aa-zz'), which indicates that more than 270,000 rifles had been made in the twelve months. Even in 1915, Deutsche

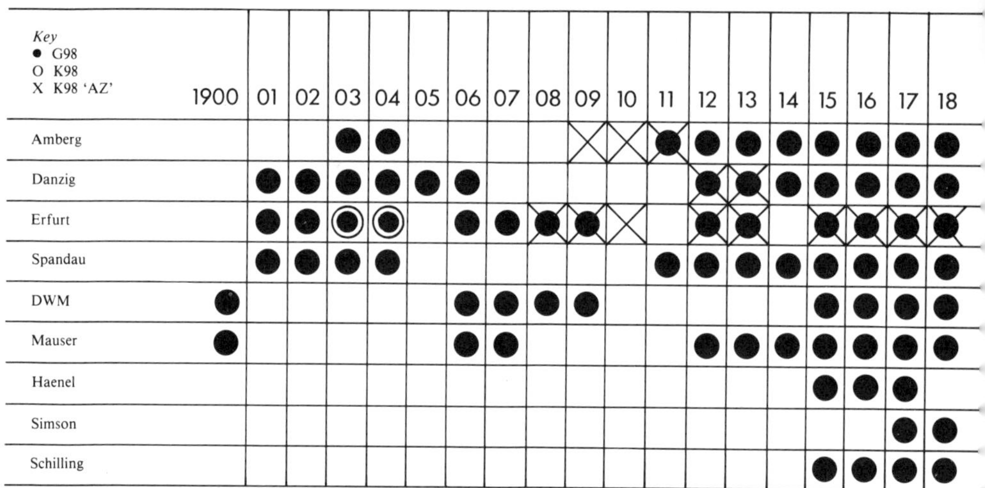

Key
● G98
O K98
X K98 'AZ'

	1900	01	02	03	04	05	06	07	08	09	10	11	12	13	14	15	16	17	18
Amberg				●	●					X	X	● X	●	●	●	●	●	●	●
Danzig		●	●	●	●	●	●						● X	● X	●	●	●	●	●
Erfurt		●	●	● O	● O		●	●	● X	● X	X		● X	● X		● X	● X	● X	● X
Spandau		●	●	●	●							●	●	●	●	●	●	●	●
DWM	●						●	●	●	●						●	●	●	●
Mauser	●						●	●					●	●	●	●	●	●	●
Haenel																●	●	●	
Simson																		●	●
Schilling																●	●	●	●

Waffen- & Munitionsfabriken had been making 1,400 rifles and two million rounds of 7.9mm ammunition daily[18]. Mauser had received a contract for 800,000 Gewehre 98 in mid-1915, the order was never completed. DWM's company history records that 930,000 Mauser rifles (Gewehr and Karabiner 98AZ) were made between 1 August 1914 and 11 November 1918.

Exactly how many rifles were made between 1898 and 1918 remains a mystery, but the total probably exceeded five million.

Markings

The infantry rifles bear standard German military markings, very similar to those found on the earlier Gewehre 71, 71/84 and 88. The maker's mark, together with the date, may be found above the chamber. The following have been noted:

GOVERNMENT ARSENALS

DANZIG Prussian arsenal, Danzig

ERFURT Prussian arsenal, Erfurt

SPANDAU Prussian arsenal, Spandau

AMBERG Bavarian arsenal, Amberg

PRIVATE CONTRACTORS

DWM Deutsche Waffen- & Munitionsfabriken AG, Berlin-Charlottenburg and Berlin-Wittenau

MAUSER Waffenfabrik Mauser AG, Oberndorf am Neckar, Württemberg

HAENEL C. G. Haenel Waffen- & Fahrradfabrik AG, Suhl, Thüringen

Schilling V. C. Schilling & Co., Suhl, Thüringen

SIMSON Simson & Co., Waffenfabrik, Suhl, Thüringen

Kornbusch Waffenwerke Oberspree, Kornbusch & Co., Berlin-Niederschönweide; this company was purchased by DWM in 1916 and is known to have made rifles.

★ Stern-Gewehre

The designation mark 'GEW.98' is struck, in fraktur (gothic script), into the left side of the receiver in front of the thumb clearance cut-away while proof eagles ('Beschussadler') may be located on the left side of the barrel and the receiver in the area of the chamber. The complete serial numbers—2457, 9753g, 1846bb, etc.—may be found on the left side of the receiver, the left side of the barrel at the breech, on the bolt handle, and sometimes on the left side of the stock immediately below the breech. The numbers initially lacked a suffix, until ten thousand had been made. An 'a' suffix was added to the next block of ten thousand, then proceeded to 'b' and so on to 'z'. When the last gun in the 'z' group had been completed, the sequence began at 01aa and ran on, ultimately, to 9999zz[19]. This would indicate a production of about 530,000 guns in a single year, as numbers reverted to 1 on 1 January; none of the contractors is known to have reached the 'zz'-block, although Erfurt reached (and possibly passed) the 'cc' group in 1917.

The last two or three digits of the serial number, without the letter suffix, appear on most of the removable parts together with small crowned inspectors' letters. There is an 'S' on the chambers and barrels of all guns converted for the S-Patronen prior to 1905, and on all barrels made subsequently[20]. Unit markings were stamped on the butt marking-disc prior to November 1915, and thereafter on the top surface of the butt plate. The following are typical of the many that can be found:

18. According to the company history, *75 Jahre Deutsche Waffen- und Munitionsfabriken Aktiengesellschaft.*

19. Or, perhaps, to 10000zz.

20. The mark is not found on the Karabiner 98 AZ, whose handguard extended to the breech-ring.

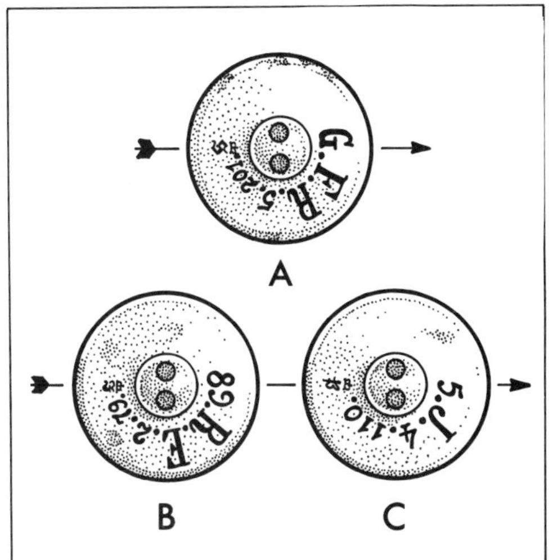

Right: typical butt-marking discs, pre-1915.

Far right: the bolt of the Gewehr 98. Key: 1, locking lugs; 2, extractor; 3, extractor collar; 4, gas vents; 5, safety lug; and 6, bolt handle.

The first mark, 'G.F.R.5.201.', signifies the 201st rifle issued to the fifth company of the Garde-Füsilier-Regiment; the second, '89.R.E.2.79.', was the seventy-ninth rifle to be issued to the second company of the Ersatz-Bataillon of Grossherzoglich Mecklenburgisches Grenadier-Regiment Nr.89; and the last, '5.J.4.110.', was the 110th to be issued to the fourth company of Jäger-Bataillon von Neumann (Schlesisches) Nr. 5.

A cypher, usually a crowned 'FW', and two large inspectors' marks will usually be found on the right side of the butt behind the marking disc or the firing-pin washer.

Mechanical description and variations

The action of the Gewehr 98 was the culmination of a long series of experiments that could, perhaps, have been said to start with the perfected Belgian Mauser rifle of 1889-90. This had led to the Spanish Mauser of 1893, which was the first to feature the internal staggered-row box magazine patented in July 1893[21], and finally to the experimental German Army rifles of 1895-98.

The receiver is a one-piece forging of the so-called 'solid-bridge' type, since the bolt handle locks down behind the bridge rather than passing through it as in the case of the Gewehr 88. A standard Mauser-pattern dismantling catch lies on the rear left side of the receiver body and can be pivoted outwards to release the bolt. The barrel screws into the front of the receiver and its base abuts a specially-machined collar, the rear edge of which is bevelled to assist the loading of a cartridge into the chamber. The mass of the collar surrounds the bolt head, apart from the extractor passage. The lugs on the bolt head lock into the receiver immediately behind the collar unit.

The bolt[22] is a solid machined forging, with an integral handle and guide rib. There are three locking lugs: two on the bolt head (which, unlike that of the Gewehr 88, is an integral part of the bolt body) and a third on the underside of the bolt body in front of the handle. The first two lock vertically in the receiver directly behind the breech face, while the third acts as a safety lug; lying in a well in the receiver bridge behind the magazine, it does not normally touch the back of its recess and only operates should both the frontal lugs shear away—a very unlikely occurrence! The lower of the two bolt-head lugs and the safety lug are solid, while the upper bolt-head lug is slotted to allow the ejector to kick a spent case or extracted cartridge clear of the bolt-way. The bolt face is partially rimmed to support the cartridge case and has a small projection around the slot through which the ejector works (diametrically opposite the extractor claw), to ensure that the cartridges do not drop as the bolt is retracted.

The long extractor, a single piece of sheet-steel, is attached to the bolt body by a collar lying immediately behind the locking lugs[23]. It is prevented from moving longitudinally by a small projecting lip behind the extractor claw engaging a short under-cut groove on the bolt body ahead of the locking lugs.

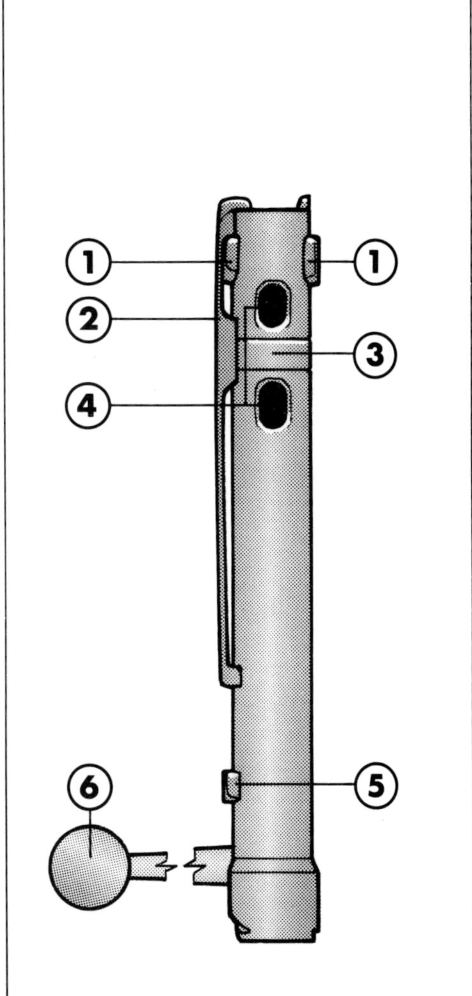

21. DRP 74,162 and 74,163 of 8 July 1893.

22. Protected by Mauser's German patent 90,305 of 30 October 1895.

23. The subject of Mauser's German patent 65,225 of 16 February 1892.

Right: the action and components of the Gewehr 98. From the *Text Book of Small Arms,* 1929, by permission of the Comptroller, HMSO. Crown copyright.

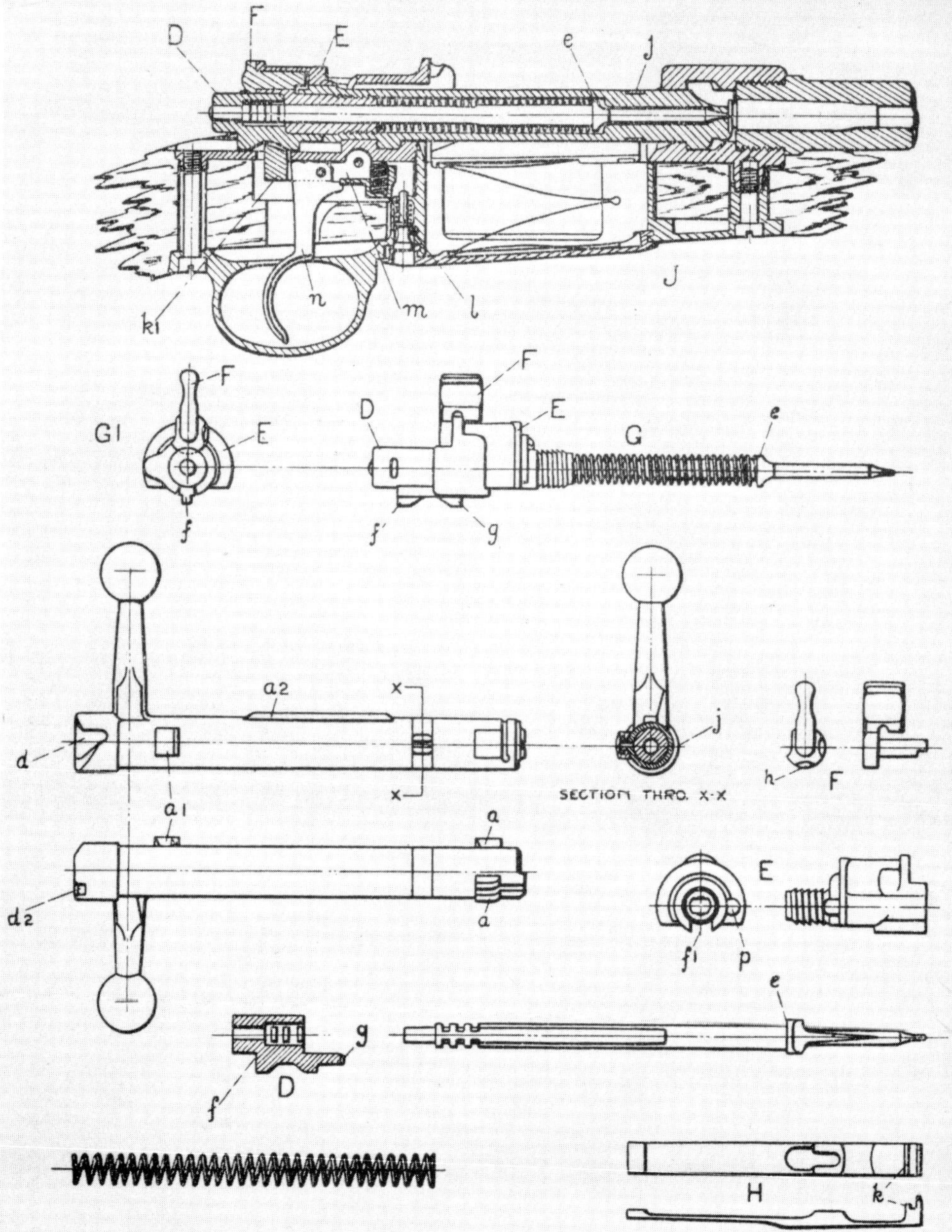

PART I, CHAP. I, FIG. 1.

MAUSER (MODEL 1904).

The bolt is bored-out from the rear to accept the striker and the mainspring assembly. Bolts made after May 1902[24] had lugs on the striker nose that mated with shoulders cut inside the bolt head, to prevent the striker nose from reaching a cartridge primer until the bolt handle was securely locked. The bolt is closed from the rear by the cocking piece guide or bolt-plug, which screws into the bolt body and provides an efficient bearing for mainspring compression. It also serves as a mounting for the 'wing'-pattern safety mechanism and carries a large deflection flange to divert gases that may escape from a ruptured primer. These pass through two large oblong ports in the underside of the bolt body[25] and into the guideway for the upper (left) locking lug. Much of the gas may subsequently escape through the thumb clearance cut-away in the receiver wall, but some can perhaps run back through the receiver bridge and out into the firer's face. The cocking piece is attached to the striker, which runs into the bolt body through the cocking-piece guide or bolt-plug.

24. When DRGM 154,915 of 22 May was granted to Mauser.

25. Mauser's DRGM 54,786 of 9 August 1895, DRGM 56,068 of 18 August 1895 and Belgian patent 120,477 of 12 March 1896 are all relevant.

The 'M98' magazine—a light sheet-steel box—is contained entirely within the stock, the staggered cartridge column being lifted by a light steel follower powered by a flat leaf W-spring mortised into the detachable magazine floor plate. The magazine can be loaded from a charger through the open action, because the charger guides are milled into the receiver bridge. The empty charger is automatically thrown clear as the bolt is closed and the left wall of the receiver is cut away to allow the firer's thumb to push the cartridges far enough into the magazine-well to be caught by the feed lips.

The Gewehr 98 operates in much the same way as most other contemporary magazine rifles. Starting with the weapon fired, the bolt handle is raised, revolving the locking lugs out of their recesses, camming back the cocking piece and—because of the curved receiver face against which the bolt handle works—giving adequate primary extraction to the spent cartridge case. When the bolt handle is vertical, the bolt can be drawn back through the receiver bridge, supported by its guide rib, until progress is stopped as the left (upper) locking lug comes to rest against the bolt-stop. At the same time, the ejector, which is contained in the bolt-stop mechanism and works in the locking lug guideway, passes through the slotted lug and kicks the spent case upwards and out of the right side of the gun. The bolt is then returned to strip another cartridge out of the magazine well

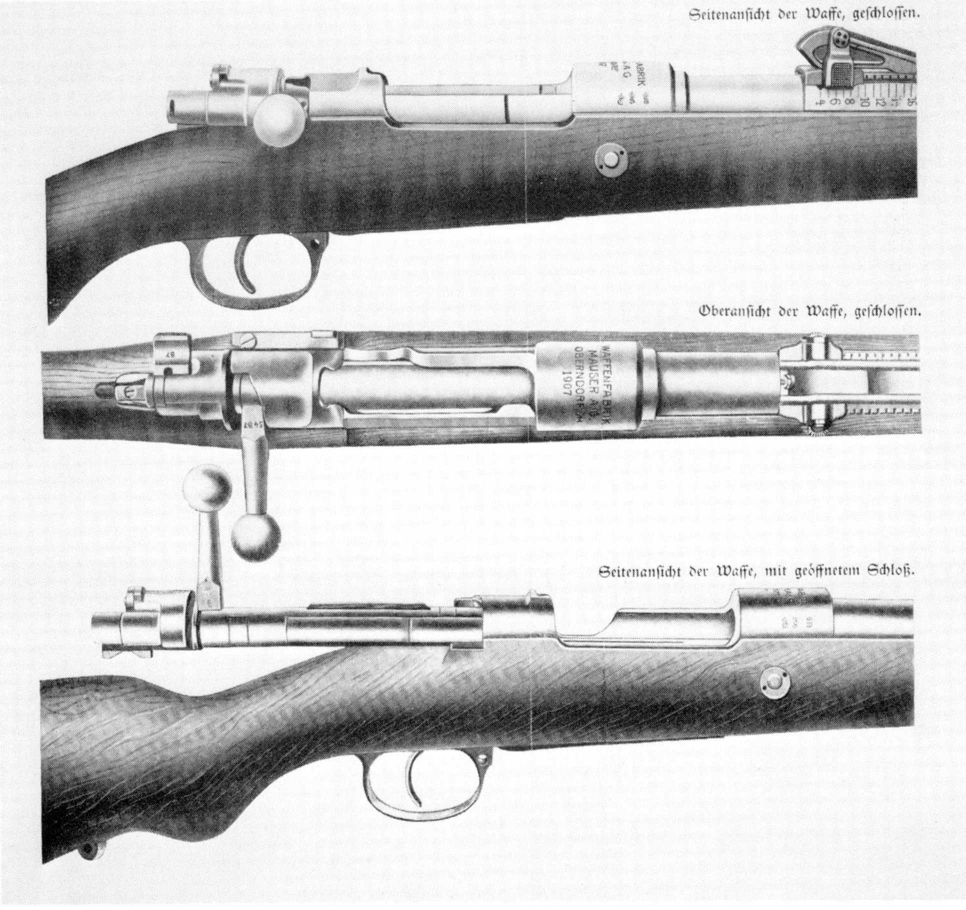

Right: a typical Gewehr 98, made by Waffenfabrik Mauser AG in 1907. From Korn's *Mauser-Gewehre und Mauser-Patente.*

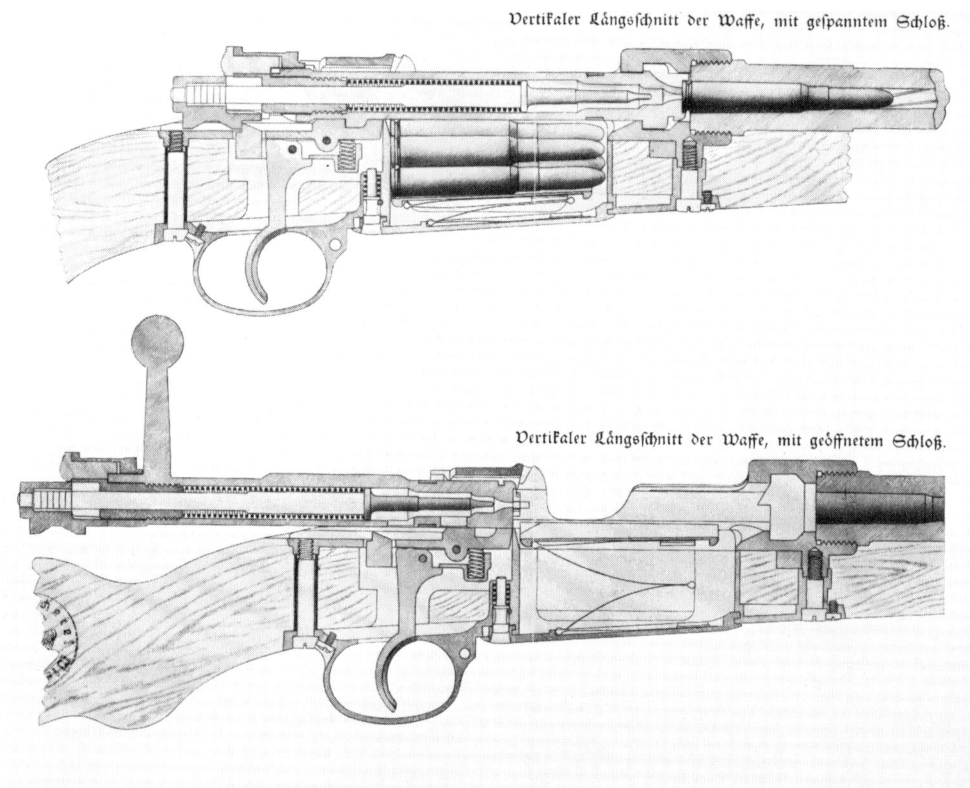

Right: longitudinal sections of the Gewehr 98.

and into the chamber. The cocking piece is held back by the sear, and final mainspring compression—and the gentle seating of the new cartridge in the breech—is accomplished by the camming action of the bolt handle as it is turned down, and by the locking lugs as they seat in the receiver. The gun was then loaded, cocked and ready to fire. However, if the magazine was empty, the bolt, owing to the absence of any hold-open mechanism, closed on an empty chamber. This was a bad feature of the basic design and was rectified in the Gewehr 98/17 and the Mauser-Gewehr 18 described below. The Gewehr 98 proved to be a very efficient design; and, consequently, very few alterations were made prior to 1918. A modified striker was developed as an additional safety feature in 1901, to prevent the striker nose reaching out of the bolt face until the bolt was locked; and a special washer to prevent the striker nose being damaged during dismantling was added to the butt in late 1915, but virtually nothing else was done. The only poor feature to become apparent during the service life of the Gewehr 98 was the slight weakness below the thumb clearance cut-out in the left wall of the receiver.

26. Hans-Dieter Götz, *Die deutschen Militärgewehre und Maschinenpistolen, 1871-1945*, p. 141.

RADFAHRER GEWEHR 98 (R.GEW.98)
This version of the Gewehr 98 was issued to cyclists, but was virtually identical with the standard infantry pattern apart from having a turned-down bolt handle and sling swivels on the side of the butt and the barrel band rather than underneath. It was discontinued on the introduction of the Karabiner 98 AZ in January 1908.

GEWEHR 98/S
An alternative definition for the rifles chambering the S-Patronen, issued with effect from 1 October 1905.

SCHARFSCHÜTZEN GEWEHR 98 (S.GEW.98)
With the rise of trench warfare, the Germans quickly became aware that they needed suitable snipers' rifles. The first to be acquired were standard hunting rifles ('Jagdgewehre') fitted with commercial Gérard, Goerz and Zeiss telescope sights, although a few standard Gewehre 98 were fitted with 4X Goerz 'Certar Kurz' sights as an experiment. Götz[26] records that sniper rifles were first issued to the Bavarian Army in December 1914.

The 'civilian' rifles all chambered the obsolescent Patrone 88 rather than the improved S-Munition and so, to prevent accidents, a stamped tin plate was added to the left side of their butts; the plate bore a silhouetted Patrone 88, with its distinctive round-nosed bullet, and the warning 'NUR FÜR PATRONE 88, KEINE S-MUNITION VERWENDEN' ('only for Patrone 88, unsuitable for S-Munition'). These guns were not altogether suitable for trench usage, since many were fitted with delicate commercial 'set' triggers which reacted badly to mud. It became clear that a modified version of the standard infantry rifle was required and the GPK promptly ordered fifteen thousand rifles, known as Zielfernrohr-Gewehre 98 or later Scharfschützen-Gewehre 98, in late 1914. It was estimated that 18,421 guns were needed for the Prussian, Saxon and Württemberg armies. Bavaria ordered 750 guns, reckoned to be half the requirements, at about the same time.

The guns seem to have been issued—in Bavaria at least—on the scale of one to each infantry and Jäger company, rising to three per company by August 1916. The Prussians, however, organized their snipers as independent operators, detaching them from their units and allowing them virtual freedom of movement along the entire Front. One official document states: "With the manufacturing of the K [S.m.K.] bullet being difficult and expensive, this cartridge must only be used for precision shooting when great penetration is sought. The S.m.K. cartridge is only being distributed to marksmen supplied with the Gewehr 98 and telescope sight . . . There are two kinds of telescope-sighted rifles in the German army: (a) the standard Gewehr 98 to which a telescope has been fitted. The first order (placed in late 1914) was for 15,000 rifles. (b) Hunting rifles with telescope. All of these . . . have been requisitioned. These rifles have less strength than the Gewehr 98 and can only fire the Patrone 88. The weapons . . . are very accurate up to 300 metres. They must only be issued to qualified marksmen who can guarantee results when firing from trench to trench, and especially at dusk or during clear nights when ordinary weapons are not satisfactory . . . The marksman will use his telescope sight to watch the enemy front, recording his observations in a notebook, as well as his cartridge consumption and probable results of his shots. Marksmen are exempt from additional duties."

The Scharfschützen Gewehr 98 was a specially selected and finished Gewehr 98, capable of great accuracy. Its bolt handle was bent downwards and a Goerz or Zeiss 4X telescope sight was fitted in two ring mounts, offset to the left to permit charger-loading of the magazine. The guns were otherwise identical with the standard infantry weapons, but are now rarely seen since their owners often destroyed the guns before capture. The sights had knurled range drums, graduated for 200/400/600 metres in Bavaria, and from 100 to 1000 metres in 100m increments in Prussia, Saxony and Württemberg.

STERN GEWEHR 98

This was simply an 'emergency' version of the standard rifle, dating from 1916 or later. Many of its minor parts were supplied by innumerable sub-contractors and were rarely interchangeable. The chambers were marked with a large star (★), from which the rifles took their name.

GEWEHR 98/17

This was a GPK-inspired revision of the standard Mauser infantry rifle, intended as a better close-combat weapon. The barrel was altered from conical to cylindrical—to save weight and make production easier—and the sights were modified to give a minimum sighting distance of 100 metres. A tangent-leaf back sight replaced the Lange Visier. An improved stamped-steel bolt cover was developed, adapted to permit quick-loading from the chargers, an altered magazine follower held the bolt open when the last cartridge had been fired and extracted, and the upper part of the trigger was ribbed for better grip. It is assumed that most of the other features remained unaltered, but no surviving gun is known to exist. The GPK ordered five thousand Gewehre 98/17 from Simson & Co. of Suhl in 1917, the first guns being delivered in March 1918. They were to have been issued for large-scale trials in the summer and autumn of 1918, but nothing seems to have been done before the end of the First World War.

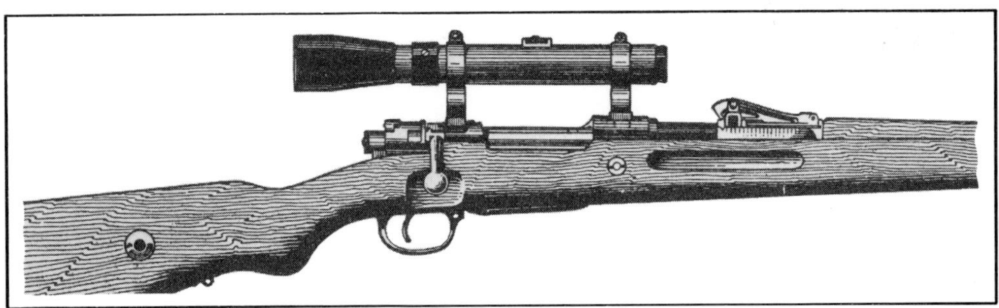

Right: the Scharfschützen-Gewehr 98.

MAUSER-GEWEHR 18

Officially known as the 'Mauser Schützengraben- und Nahkampfgewehr 18' (Mauser trench-shooting and close-combat rifle), this was a private development undertaken by Waffenfabrik Mauser AG of Oberndorf shortly before the end of the First World War. Several improvements were made in the basic design of the Gewehr 98, the most important being the addition of a detachable box magazine, for 5, 10 or 25 rounds. The magazines had stamped vertically-ribbed sides and were retained by a spring catch in the front of the trigger-guard bow; they could be loaded through the open action from the standard chargers, or, separately, before being inserted in the gun. The magazine follower actuated a separate mechanical hold-open, which held the bolt back when the last spent cartridge case had been ejected, and a linkage between the trigger and the bolt catch meant that magazines could be removed only when the bolt was open. The design of the mainspring was altered and

Right: a typical Mauser-made sporting rifle (Jagdgewehr), many of which were pressed into emergency service during the First World War.

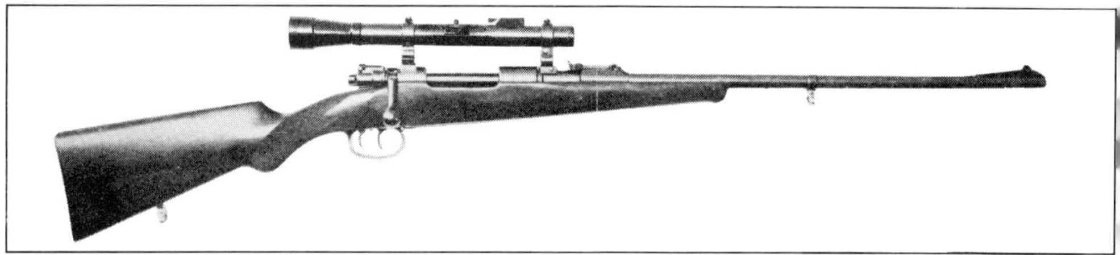

the bolt-stop, which had formerly lain on the rear left side of the receiver behind the thumb clearance cut-away, was included in the trigger mechanism. The Mauser-Gewehr 18 had an improved bolt cover and a modified stock with a strengthened pistol-grip, and, presumably, modified sights. It is also believed to have been made in several barrel lengths, but no lasting results came from the trials; the development of the Bergmann MP 18, the first true submachine-gun, virtually put an end to development of the experimental 'trench carbines'.

HYBRID GEWEHR-KARABINER 98

Small numbers of these 'rifles' were delivered to the Turkish Army in 1918, probably in an attempt to boost the Turks' morale. Some seem to have been made from damaged full-length Gewehr 98, the barrels and fore-ends of which were considerably shortened, but others were newly-made. One example —serial number 3571a, which is in the collection of the Royal Small Arms Factory at Enfield Lock— displays the designation mark 'GEW.98' on the rear left side of the receiver, and the maker's mark 'WAFFENFABRIK/MAUSER A.G./OBERNDORF A/N 1918' over the chamber. A large Turkish crescent is struck above the maker's mark. The very short barrel must have caused a very unpleasant muzzle blast, which had also been common to the original 1898-system cavalry carbine.

Appearance, distinctive features and data

The Gewehr 98 is a typical infantry rifle of the 1890-1910 period, long and somewhat elegant, but clumsy in the hand, particularly when fitted with its long bayonet. It has a bolt action of the solid-bridge pattern, with a long straight handle locking down horizontally behind the bridge—except in the Radfahrer- and Scharfschützen-Gewehre, where the handles turn down against a well in the stock. Prominent charger guides are milled in the front of the bridge and a large thumb clearance cut-away appears in the left receiver wall. The one-piece stock, originally walnut but sometimes beech or elm on wartime guns, has a well-shaped pistol-grip. The magazine lies entirely within the stock and has a special detachable floor plate. A marking disc or dismantling washer appears on the side of the butt. There is a wooden handguard running from just ahead of the back sight to a short way in front of the barrel band, which is retained in position by a leaf spring. The nose-cap and bayonet bar assembly is unusual, but typical of most post-1898 German rifles: a long under-muzzle bar—which does not interfere with the barrel—is attached to an integral nose-piece,

Right: a comparison between the bayonet attachments of the Gewehr 98 (top) and the Karabiner 98 AZ (bottom).

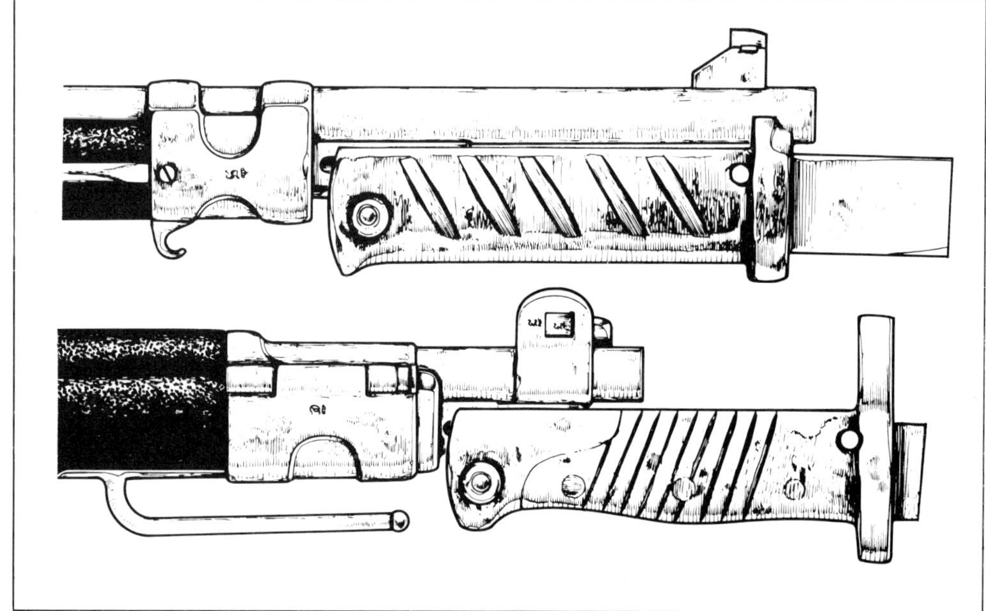

Far right: the muzzle and nosecap of the Gewehr 98. Key: 1, barrel; 2, front sight; 3, nosecap; 4, stock; 5, nosecap retaining spring; 6, bayonet bar; and 7, cleaning rod.

which is in turn clamped to the stock fore-end by a very distinctive barrel band. The latter is retained by a cross-pin and a leaf spring. A half-length cleaning rod may be found beneath the muzzle, threaded so that any two may be joined to make a full length one.

There are sling swivels under the butt behind the pistol grip and under the barrel band on all except the Radfahrer-Gewehre, whose swivels are on the side of the butt and band. A small hook under the nose-cap was used to shorten the sling when necessary.

DATA

Calibre: nominally 8mm, actually 7.92±0.02mm.
Rifling: concentric, 4 grooves 0.125mm deep (0.15mm for S-Munition) and 4.4mm wide; 1 turn in 240mm, right hand (pitch of 5° 54').
Magazine: internal staggered-column box, capacity 5 rounds.
Loading system: charger, or single rounds.
Length overall: 1,250mm.
Barrel length: 740mm.
Weight: 4,075-4,150gm without sling.
Sights: (front) unprotected barleycorn; (back) a Lange pattern tangent sight, graduated from 200-2000 metres for the Patronen 88, or 400-2000m for S-Munition.
Performance: see cartridge data (Appendix 2).

Accessories

BAYONETS

The Gewehr 98 was issued with a wide selection of bayonets. The first to be issued was the Seitengewehr 98 (S 98), which was adopted in April 1898 in Prussia, Saxony and Württemberg, and in May 1901 in Bavaria (TGB, pp. 51-56). It had a long slender blade with a pipe-back, a wood-gripped steel hilt and a vestigial crossguard with a quillon, but no muzzle ring. The machine-gunners had the KS 98 (TGB, pp. 56-58), introduced in all states, except Bavaria in March 1901; the pioneers, telegraph troops, and the field artillerymen had the S 98/05-one version of which was saw-backed—from November 1905 (TGB, pp. 63-71); while the Reserve and a few others had the S 84/98 (TGB, pp. 60-63), which seems to have been introduced in about 1903 although a new version of the same bayonet was approved for cavalry use in December 1914. There were many novel Ersatz all-metal bayonets dating from the First World War, including Carter Numbers[27] 1—19, 21-53, 55-57 and 61-79. There were also assorted transformations of non-German knife, sword and sabre bayonets (TGB, pp. 78-81 for some details).

27. J. A. Carter, *German Ersatz Bayonets*, vol. 1.

OTHERS

A sling, a cleaning rod, a muzzle protector and a screwdriver were among the standard accessories. Others appeared during the First World War, including a grenade-launcher, a telescope sight for the Scharfschützen-Gewehre 98, luminous night sight attachments, an anti-aircraft 'lead' light, auxiliary box magazines and a stamped-steel bolt cover. The last-named was developed to prevent trench mud getting into the bolt mechanism and consisted of a light sheet-steel body fixed over the receiver. Retained by a clip under the bolt handle shank, it reciprocated with the action, as a long rod extended forward from the front left side of the cover to slide in a special fitting attached around the barrel and the fore-end by a powerful spring clip. The bolt covers are usually marked W-CO/D R P, indicating that they were patented in Germany (since DRP represents Deutsches Reich-Patent); their maker has yet to be identified, however.

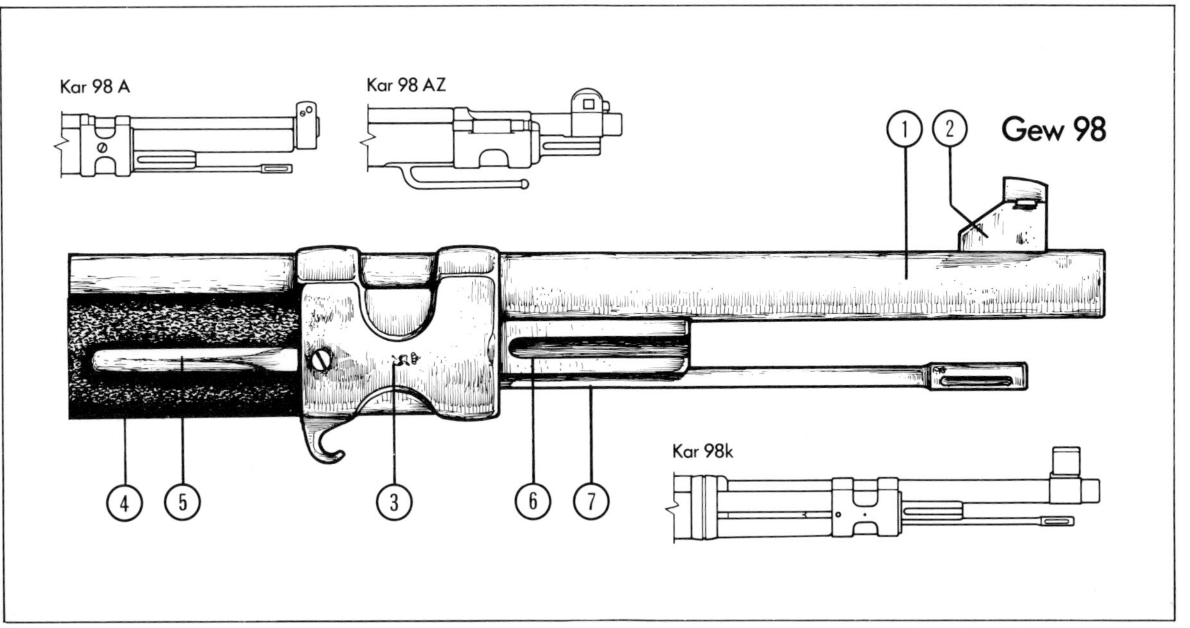

Karabiner 98 Mauser

1. Hans-Dieter Götz, *Die deutschen Militärgewehre und Maschinenpistolen, 1871-1945*, p. 144.

The adoption of the Gewehr 98, and its subsequent success, caused a suitable cavalry carbine derivative to be sought. This was to replace the obsolescent Karabiner 88 and the essentially similar Gewehr 91, issued to the cavalry and the artillery respectively. The GPK developed a short version of the 1898-pattern infantry rifle in the late autumn of 1899 and had submitted it to the Kriegsministerium by April 1900. Götz[1] records correspondence from the latter, dated 20 April, stating that the carbine had been examined. A few examples of a pre-production series were made in the government arsenal in Erfurt and issued to two cavalry squadrons and a foot artillery company for field trials, but the production pattern was not finalized until June 1900. The first carbine was not considered to be an outstanding success and, although limited production was undertaken for about eighteen months, it was subsequently replaced by the Karabiner 98 A of 1902 (qv); this should not be confused with the Karabiner 98 AZ, later known as the Karabiner 98a, which dated from January 1908.

Surviving Karabiner 98 A were withdrawn in 1902-3, and those that remained serviceable were converted to 'Zielkarabiner' (practice carbines) firing 5mm primer-propellant cartridges for short-range target practice.

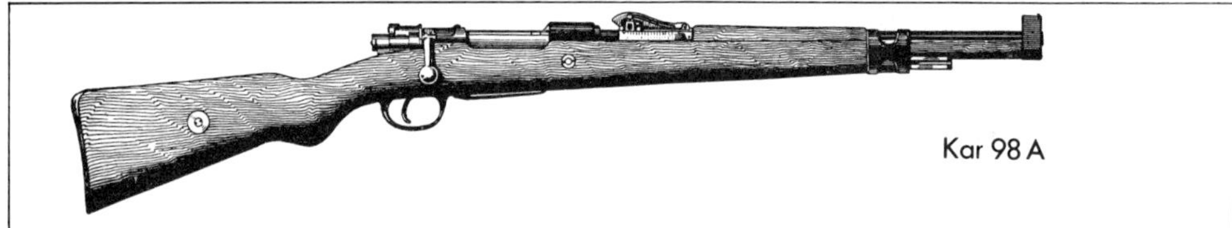

Kar 98 A

Production history
Between 2,500 and 3,000 examples of the first-type Karabiner 98 are believed to have been made in the Erfurt arsenal in 1900 and 1901. The highest reported number, however, is 1993.

Markings
These were much the same as found on the Gewehre 98 (qv), except that the chamber mark reads crown/ERFURT/1900 (or 1901) and it is assumed that the designation stamp on the left side of the receiver simply read '98'. The serial numbers have no suffix letters, since production did not begin to approach ten thousand.

Mechanical description and variations
The 1898-pattern carbines worked in exactly the same way as the standard Gewehre 98 (qv). No variations have been reported, apart from the guns chambering the 5mm Zielpatronen.

Appearance, distinctive features and data
The first 1898-system carbine shares much the same butt profile as the infantry rifles, unlike the later Karabiner 98 AZ and its prototypes whose butt-shapes were modified. The differences are mainly concerned with the pistol-grip radii, which are much tighter in the post-1907 carbines than in the pre-1902 varieties. The barrel and fore-end of the Kavallerie-und Artillerie-Karabiner 98 are much shorter than the rifle types, there is a special nose-cap protecting the front sight, a stacking device has been added beneath the muzzle, the turned-down bolt handle has a spatulate form, and a special small Lange Visier has been developed. The carbine is stocked virtually to the muzzle, only a tiny section of which protrudes from the nose-cap. The sling swivels have been replaced by a special sling aperture cut through the butt and a sling bar on the left side of the single barrel band; in consequence, the butt marking disc has been moved upwards and back until it lies only a short distance in front of the butt plate.

The carbine is otherwise much the same as the infantry guns, but has a walnut handguard running the entire length of the barrel from the nose-cap to the back sight.

DATA
Calibre: nominally 8mm, actually 7.92 ± 0.02mm.
Rifling: concentric, 4 grooves 0.125mm deep and 4.4mm wide; 1 turn in 240mm (pitch of 5° 54').
Magazine: internal staggered-column box, capacity 5 rounds.
Loading system: charger, or single rounds.
Length overall: 945mm.
Barrel length: 435mm.
Weight: about 3,325gm without sling.
Sights: (front) protected barleycorn; (back) a Lange system tangent sight graduated from 200 to 1200 metres in 100m increments.
Performance: see cartridge data (Appendix 2).

Accessories

BAYONET
None.

OTHERS
A sling, a cleaning rod (carried separately), a muzzle protector and a screwdriver.

Karabiner 98 A Mauser

The original carbine derivative of the Mauser infantry rifle, dating from early 1900, was not greeted with universal acclaim. It was, therefore, subjected to considerable re-design and was re-introduced on 26 February 1902[1] as the 'Karabiner 98 mit Aufpflanzvorrichtung für das Seitengewehr 98' (1898 model carbine with attachment for the 1898 model bayonet). This gives a clue to its principal distinguishing feature, which is a standard 4cm bayonet bar beneath the fore-end. Other design changes are described below.

1. Ludwig Baer, *Die leichten Waffen der deutschen Armeen 1841-1945*, p. 46, gives the date as '26.6.1902'. This is a misprint, as the February date is confirmed by the official (1908) adoption order for the perfected 98 AZ carbine.

The Karabiner 98 A was mechanically identical with the 1900-pattern Karabiner 98, and the maximum setting of its original Lange Visier is believed to have remained at 1,200 metres. The carbines originally chambered the Patrone 88, since they were introduced and placed in production in 1902, but experiments to adapt them to the more powerful S-Munition began in 1904. The results were an altered chamber, deepened rifling grooves and an altered Lange Visier graduated from 300 to 1,800 metres.

By the beginning of 1905, the GPK and the Kriegsministerium were having doubts about the efficacy of converting the existing carbines for the S-Patronen, as the results included excessive recoil, fearful muzzle flash, which blinded the firers during night shooting, and strong muzzle blast. The plans were subsequently abandoned and production of the 98 A carbine stopped while the GPK developed a weapon with a longer barrel. The result was the Karabiner 98 AZ, which was introduced in January 1908.

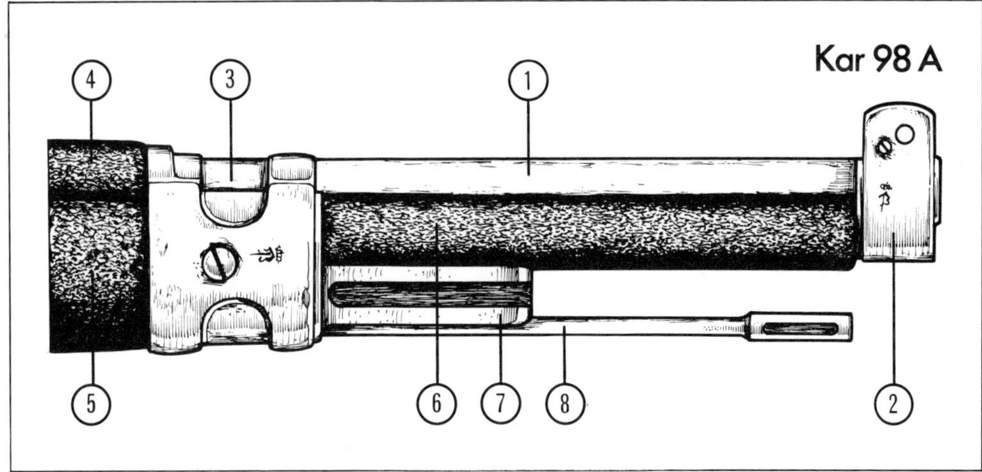

Right: the muzzle and nosecap of the Karabiner 98 A. Key: 1, barrel; 2, nosecap; 3, barrel band; 4, handguard; 5, stock; 6, fore-end; 7, bayonet bar; and 8, cleaning rod.

The Karabiner 98 A had been considered as a universal firearm ('Einheitswaffe') for the cavalrymen, the foot artillery and other specialized units, but was ultimately considered to be a failure. The guns were withdrawn in 1908-9 and many were then converted to Zielkarabiner for short-range target practice. They had never been issued for much more than large-scale troop trials.

Production history

The carbines were made exclusively by the government arsenal in Erfurt, total production exceeding six thousand in 1902-5. The highest number yet reported is 6573, on a carbine dated 1904. Götz[2] records that the specimen sent to the Bavarian war ministry on 24 October 1904 was numbered 1834, but it need not have been newly-made. Each Karabiner 98 A was estimated to have cost the government about 68 marks—approximately fifteen more than an infantry rifle—although the figure would undoubtedly have been less had true mass production been undertaken.

2. Hans-Dieter Götz, *Die deutschen Militärgewehre und Maschinenpistolen, 1871-1945*, p. 146.

Markings

The carbines inevitably bear their manufacturer's markings—a crown/ERFURT/1903, for instance—above the chamber. The designation stamp appears on the left side of the receiver in front of the thumb clearance cut-away; originally, it simply read '98' (as on gun 794, Erfurt, 1903) but was later changed to 'KAR.98'. The proof and inspectors' marks, and the positions of the serial numbers, remained unchanged from the standard Gewehr 98 (qv). Unit markings appeared on the top surface of the butt plate, as the special butt marking-disc had been discarded. A typical mark reads 'M.G.A.10.41.', the forty-first gun to be issued to the Maschinengewehr-Abteilung Nr. 10, which was an independent machine-gun unit drawn from Jäger-Bataillon Nr. 8 and attached to XIV. Armeekorps.

Mechanical description and variations
These carbines worked in exactly the same way as the Gewehr 98 (qv). No variations are known to exist, apart from the Zielkarabiner conversions.

Appearance, distinctive features and data
The Karabiner 98 A greatly resembles the original carbine derivation of the infantry rifle, insofar as its action and turned-down spatulate bolt handle are concerned. Originally it may have had a similar Lange Visier graduated to 1,200 metres, but this was replaced by a slightly larger pattern on guns chambering the S-Patronen. The stocking arrangements, however, changed considerably, although the sling aperture through the butt and the sling ring on the left side of the barrel band remained unaltered. The Karabiner 98 A has a wooden handguard stretching from ahead of the back sight base as far as the back of the barrel band, which is combined with a special bolt-retained nose-cap very similar to that of the Gewehr 98. A standard 4cm bayonet bar lies in front of the nose-cap unit, below a narrow wooden fore-end stretching to the muzzle. 'Ears' on the muzzle block, from which the muzzle itself scarcely protrudes, are continued upwards to protect the front sight. (This was necessary to protect the front sight blade from the inside surface of the saddle 'boot'.) A half-length cleaning rod lies beneath the muzzle.

There is no butt marking-disc, and the armourers consequently struck their marks on the butt plate.

DATA
Calibre: nominally 8mm, actually 7.92±0.02mm.
Rifling: concentric, 4 grooves 0.125mm deep (0.15mm for S-Munition) and 4.4mm wide; 1 turn in 240mm (pitch of 5° 54').
Magazine: internal staggered-column box, capacity 5 rounds.
Loading system: charger, or single rounds.
Length overall: 945mm.
Barrel length: 435mm.
Weight: about 3,425gm without sling.
Sights: (front) protected barleycorn; (back) a Lange system tangent sight graduated 300-1,800 metres for S-Patronen.
Performance: see cartridge data (Appendix 2).

Accessories

BAYONETS
The Karabiner 98 A can be fitted with virtually any of the standard bayonets described under the Gewehr 98 (qv)—including the S 98, KS 98, S 98/05 n.A. and the S 84/98—with the exception of the S 98/05 a.A., which has too much of a muzzle ring on its guard. Any Ersatz bayonet without the standard double-diameter ring will also fit, depending on the protrusion of the ring remnants (i.e.: Carter Numbers 1, 15-19, 25, 30-34, 46, 48, 55-57). But the carbines ought to have been withdrawn by the time the Ersatz bayonets appeared during the First World War, and, therefore, ought not to be displayed with them.

OTHERS
A sling, a cleaning rod, a muzzle protector and a screwdriver.

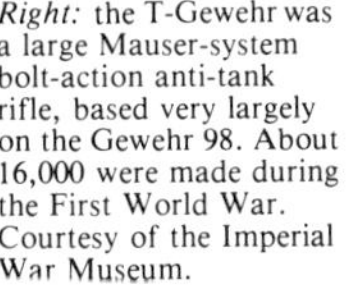

Right: the T-Gewehr was a large Mauser-system bolt-action anti-tank rifle, based very largely on the Gewehr 98. About 16,000 were made during the First World War. Courtesy of the Imperial War Museum.

Karabiner 98 AZ Mauser

The excessive muzzle blast, flash and recoil encountered in the two short 98 system carbines forced the GPK to develop an experimental gun with a barrel of 59cm rather than 43.5cm, as the latter had proved to be much too short for use with S-Munition. The new carbine was stocked to the muzzle and had a nose-cap of standard German pattern, a single spring-retained barrel band and two transverse recoil bolts—one below the chamber and the other, the smaller, some 15cm behind the barrel band. The bolt handle was changed from spatulate to a half-sphere, the flattened underside of which was chequered to improve grip, and a recess was cut into the stock beneath the bolt-knob to make its operation easier. A sling aperture was cut through the butt from the left side, a sling ring lay on the left side of the barrel band, and the trigger-guard bow was entirely plain (differing from that of the Gewehr 98, which had a transverse hole through it for a sling swivel). A new tangent-leaf sight, graduated from 300 to 2,000 metres, was substituted for the Lange Visier and the contours of the pistol-grip were revised so that—in theory—the firer's right hand could exert greater control during recoil.

These prototype carbines remained mechanically much the same as the contemporary Gewehre 98. Götz[1] records that the first large-scale field trials began in June 1906 with 806 (800?) of them: 706 (700?) were fitted with a special stacking device, or 'Aufpflanzvorrichtung', similar to that of the obsolescent Gewehr 91, and a hundred with a plain nose-cap. There was also a small number—Götz says 70—of the short-barrelled Karabiner 98 A for comparison. The trials ended in the summer of 1907, having shown that the muzzle blast, flash and recoil were more tolerable in the long-barrelled weapons than in the short, but the troops demanded some kind of suitable bayonet attachment as they had become used to the Karabiner 98 A.

1. Hans-Dieter Götz, *Die deutschen Militärgewehre und Maschinenpistolen, 1871-1945*, p. 148.

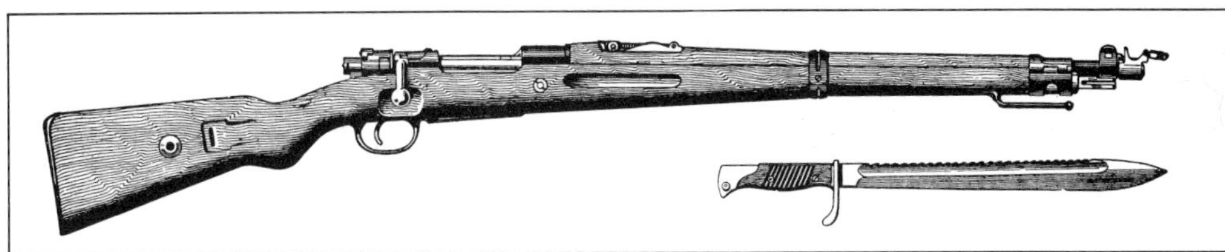

Right: the Karabiner 98 AZ. Note the design of the stock, the back sight and the handguard.

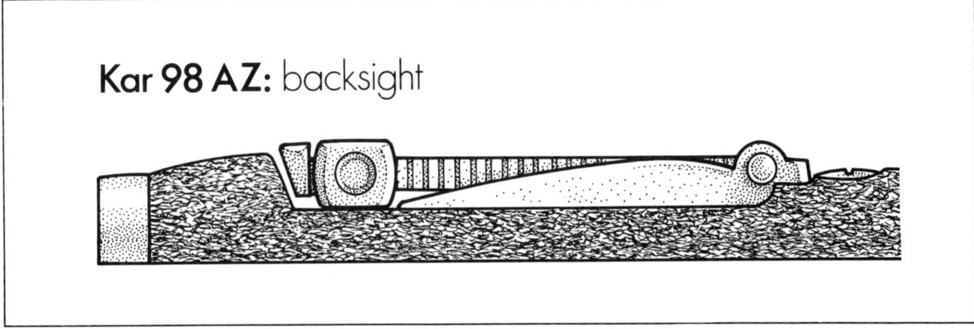

Right: the back sight of the K 98 AZ.

In the autumn of 1907, the GPK developed a fourth prototype, which was to become the 'Karabiner 98 mit Aufpflanz- und Zusammensetzvorrichtung' (with bayonet attachment and piling hook) or Karabiner 98 AZ[2]. This differed from the preceding third prototype principally in the design of the nose-cap and the handguard. The former took the form of a special hinged band—something like that on the Gewehr 98—clamping a standard 4cm bayonet bar that lay beneath the muzzle, yet was not in direct contact with the barrel itself. The wooden handguard ran the length of the barrel from in front of the receiver ring to the back of the nose-cap, and a stacking hook was placed under the fore-end.

2. Known as the Karabiner 98a in the Reichswehr.

The Karabiner 98 AZ otherwise greatly resembled the preceding prototype. It was adopted by Kaiser Wilhelm II's decree of 16 January 1908, to replace the earlier carbine dating from February 1902, and the first issues were made to the cavalry in the middle of 1909. The foot artillery received its first guns in the autumn of 1910, and by the outbreak of the First World War in August 1914 Karabiner 98 AZ were being carried by the cyclists ('Radfahrer') of the infantry, riflemen, sharpshooters and pioneers; by the independent machine-gun units; by the telegraph and field telephone units; by the airship and motor transport detachments; by most cavalrymen (see Appendix 3); and by the foot artillerymen and parts of the train.

The carbines served with distinction during the war and large quantities were made. There was still rather too much muzzle blast for the troops' liking, but this, common to all short firearms firing full-power ammunition, was offset by the handiness of the Karabiner 98 AZ compared with the longer and clumsier Gewehr 98. Complaints were also made about the new tangent-leaf sight, which, it was claimed, was difficult to operate and made the firer crane his neck at maximum elevations.

Most of the surviving guns were sold or destroyed after the 1918 Armistice, although small numbers were retained for the post-Versailles 100,000-man Reichsheer (German Army). There, they were known as Karabiner 98a to distinguish them from the '98b', which was a modified version of the full-length Gewehr 98 with a turned-down bolt handle and a new tangent-leaf back sight.

3. Hans-Dieter Götz, *Die deutschen Militärgewehre und Maschinenpistolen, 1871-1945*, p. 150.

4. Frank de Haas, *Bolt Action Rifles*, p. 38.

Production history

The Prussian, Saxon and Württemberg Karabiner 98 AZ were acquired, according to Götz[3], from the Prussian government arsenal in Erfurt. However, Danzig-made specimens have been reported and it is clear that while the initial contracts may have been placed exclusively with Erfurt, later ones were not. The Bavarians bought their weapons from Amberg, although production was very slow: most of the production facilities had been committed to the Gewehr 98. At a daily rate of fifty carbines, only 30,000 had been delivered to the Bavarian Army in the first two years. Each was estimated to have cost between 51 and 55 marks without accounting for depreciation of machinery and royalties.

The total number of Karabiner 98 AZ made between 1908 and 1918, when production stopped once and for all, remains unknown, however, it comfortably exceeded 1.5 million.

Markings

These take standard German form. A typical chamber mark reads crown/ERFURT/1913, while 'KAR.98' may be found on the left side of the receiver immediately in front of the thumb clearance cut-away. The serial numbers, part-numbers and inspectors' marks remain much the same as those applied to the Gewehr 98 (qv). Unit markings were struck into the top surface of the butt plate, since the 98 AZ was never made with the special pre-1915 butt marking-disc. Typical examples read '12.H.5.37.', or '3.A.F.1.195.'; the former was applied by the fifth squadron of Thüringisches Husaren-Regiment Nr. 12, the latter by the first company of Fussartillerie-Regiment General-Feldzeugmeister (Brandenburgisches) Nr. 3.

Some guns may, conceivably, be found with unit marks applied during the Weimar Republic; examples of these, which differed slightly from those applied during the First World War, may be found in the section devoted to the Karabiner 98b of 1920-23.

Mechanical description and variations

The Karabiner 98 AZ operated in exactly the same way as the infantry's Gewehr 98 (qv), the only major difference lying in the external diameter of the receiver. Frank de Haas[4] says of this, ". . . Model 98 actions with a receiver ring diameter of about 1.410" [35.8mm] are commonly called 'large ring' Mausers. Most M98 sporting and military rifles made up to the end of WW II are based on this large ring action . . . The 'small ring' Mauser actions have a receiver ring diameter of about 1.300" [33mm]. A lot of early M98 carbines, like the 98a [98 AZ], were based on the small ring action . . . The differences between the large and small ring actions is readily discernible by sight or touch, and there is no need to use a caliper to identify them. On the small ring action the left side of the receiver is straight, including part of the bridge, the wall and the ring. However, on the large ring action this surface has a notable jump where the receiver wall merges with the ring, which can be seen and felt".

No important variations of the Karabiner 98 AZ have been noted apart from a version with a bolt cover developed during the First World War; this, however, remained mechanically identical with the standard guns.

Appearance, distinctive features and data

The 98 AZ differs from the earlier Karabiner 98 and 98 A (qv) principally in the length of its barrel, the design of its stock, and the substitution of a simple tangent-leaf backsight for the Lange Visier. The action looks exactly like that of the Gewehr 98, apart from the half-sphere bolt handle turned downwards against a recess in the stock. The underside of the bolt grasping-knob is chequered to facilitate grip. The one-piece stock is made of walnut (sometimes beech or elm on guns made during the First World War) and has revised pistol-grip radii, tightened to give the firer's right hand more control over recoil, and the butt has an aperture in which to anchor the sling. The second sling anchor-point comprises a fixed ring on the left side of the single barrel band, which is held in place by a screw rather than a leaf-spring. A wooden handguard runs from the receiver ring to the nose-cap, the latter being a special hinged pattern that clamps the 4cm bayonet attachment bar to the stock. There is no under-muzzle cleaning rod, but a special piling hook (a long, bent ball-tipped rod) is attached to a metal plate running backwards from the nose-cap under the fore-end.

A tangent-leaf back sight has replaced the Lange Visier of the earlier carbines of 1900-5, and a grasping groove was cut into the fore-end of Karabiner 98 AZ made after about 1915. This appears immediately ahead of the recoil bolt through the stock, directly below the chamber, and runs half-way to the barrel band. The Karabiner 98 AZ muzzle has a barleycorn front sight surrounded by a distinctive 'eared' protector. This also mounts a small forward projection, under which the muzzle protector ('Mündungsschoner') locks.

. J. A. Carter, *German* *rsatz Bayonets*, vol. 1.

DATA

Calibre: nominally 8mm, actually 7.92 ± 0.02mm.
Rifling: concentric, 4 grooves 0.15mm deep and 4.4mm wide; 1 turn in 240mm, right hand (pitch of 5° 54').
Magazine: internal staggered-column box, capacity 5 rounds.
Loading system: charger, or single rounds.
Length overall: 1,090mm.
Barrel length: 590mm.
Weight: between 3,600 and 3,800gm without sling, depending on the stocking wood.
Sights: (front) protected barleycorn; (back) a tangent-leaf pattern, graduated 300-2,000 metres in 100m increments.
Performance: see cartridge data (Appendix 2).

Accessories

BAYONETS

These depended on the units to which the Karabiner 98 AZ were issued. The cavalry, for example, had the S 84/98; the foot artillery, the S 98/05; and the independent machine-gun units, the KS 98 (TGB, pp. 60-63, 63-71 and 56-58 respectively). In addition, many all-metal Ersatz bayonets were manufactured during the First World War. Those that fitted the 98 AZ included Carter Numbers[5] 1-19, 21-53, 55-57 and 61-79. There were also assorted transformations of non-German knife, sword and sabre bayonets.

OTHERS

A sling, a muzzle protector, a screwdriver; some guns were fitted with bolt covers—of the type described under the Gewehr 98—during the First World War.

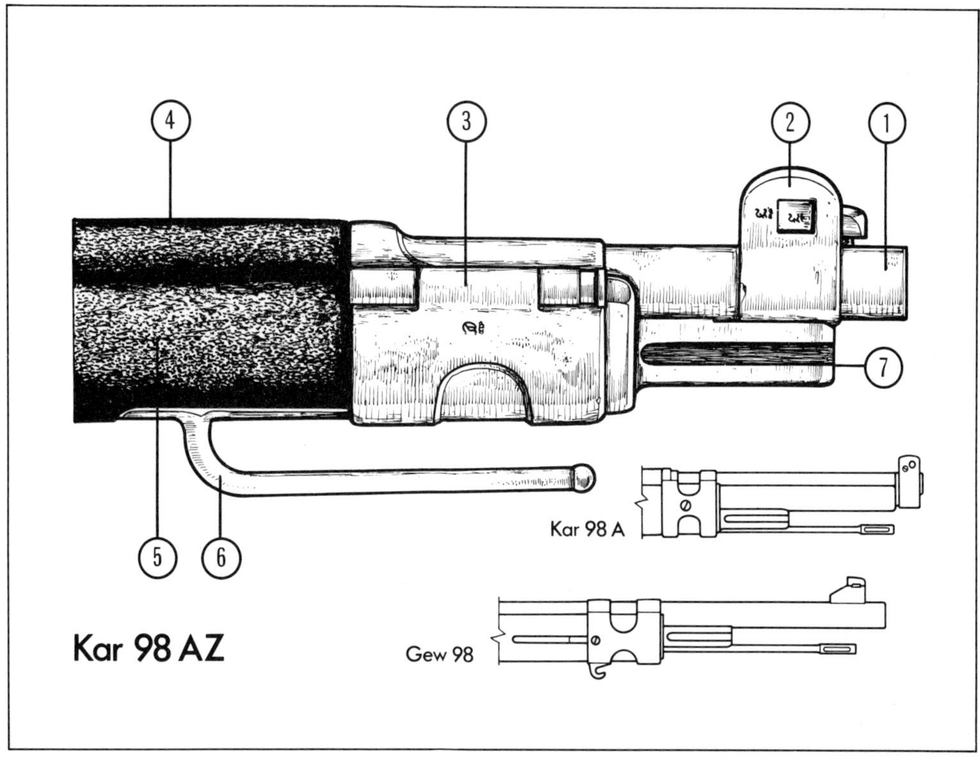

ight: the muzzle and osecap of the Karabiner 8 AZ. Key: 1, barrel; 2, ront sight protector; 3, osecap; 4, handguard; 5, tock; 6, piling rod; and 7, ayonet bar.

Karabiner 98b Mauser

The capitulation of the German armies in 1918 caused huge quantities of Gewehre and Karabiner 98 to be stockpiled, awaiting sale or destruction. The Treaty of Versailles restricted the German Army ('Reichsheer') to a mere hundred thousand men and, since more than thirteen million had been mobilized and armed during the First World War, the short-term weapons requirements were easily satisfied from war surplus. Consequently, small numbers of pre-1918 firearms were retained and the vast remainder discarded. Article 180 of the Treaty permitted the Reichsheer to retain 84,000 Gewehre 98, 18,000 Karabiner 98 AZ, 1,926 machine-guns, 252 mortars and 288 assorted field-guns and howitzers[1]. However, though the Treaty articles listed the permitted quantities of many warlike stores, items such as swords, lances, bayonets and grenades had been omitted and alterations were later made. These led to the inclusion of a further fifty thousand rifles, which were to be stored for the Reserve. Each infantry company also had—possibly in defiance of the regulations—a dozen 'Zielfernrohrgewehre 98 oder Zielfernrohrkarabiner 98b mit Zeiss-Zielvisier' (snipers' rifles with telescope sights)[2].

1. Hans-Dieter Götz, *Die deutschen Militärgewehre und Maschinenpistolen, 1871-1945*, p. 158, gives the quantity of machine-guns as 1,863. The figure quoted here is from Musgrave and Oliver, *German Machine Guns*, p. 6, where it is also noted that the Allies subsequently permitted an increase to 2,336 guns.

2. Eckardt and Morawietz, *Die Handwaffen des brandenburgisch-preussisch-deutschen Heeres 1600-1945*, p. 223.

No alterations were made to the Karabiner 98 AZ, now renamed Karabiner 98a as no examples of the original 1902-vintage 98 A type remained in service, but the surviving Gewehre 98 were modified after about three years' service and re-issued as Karabiner 98b—somewhat confusingly, since they were not shortened. The unmodified spherical bolt-handle grasping knob was turned down into a recess cut in the stock side, the existing Lange Visiere were replaced by simpler tangent-leaf sights, and broad 98 AZ-pattern barrel bands were substituted for the narrower rifle type. This permitted the Karabiner 98b to use a standard side-mounted sling, since a fixed sling ring lay on the left side of the new barrel fixing. These features apart, the 98b and the original Gewehr 98 were identical in all respects. Some of the former have been examined with 98a-type bolt handles, whose half-spherical grasping knobs have chequered under-surfaces, but these are assumed to have been replacements.

The first Karabiner 98b are believed to have been converted and issued in 1923 though a few have been reported with the additional Versailles 'permission' date (1920 or 1921) above their chambers. Guns officially issued in the Reichswehr had to be specially inventoried under Allied supervision and were given a second chamber date before being released for service. Karabiner 98 AZ and Gewehre 98 were treated

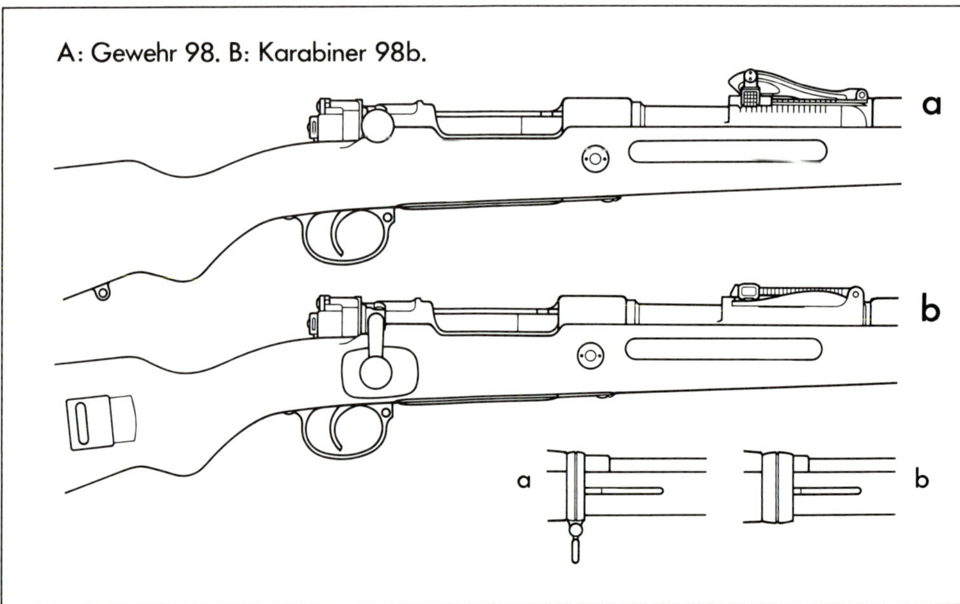

Right: the differences between the Karabiner 98b and the original Gewehr 98. Despite the designations, both weapons were full-length rifles.

similarly. A few Karabiner 98b were subsequently converted from Gewehre 98 without erasing the original chamber marks, although many others were completely re-finished and can have the appearance of new guns; this was greatly helped by the apparent absence of pre-1918 manufacturers' or Versailles 'permission' stampings.

There has always been controversy as to whether any new 98b carbines were manufactured during the 1920s, rather than simply converted from pre-1918 infantry rifles. It is likely that Simson & Co., who acquired large numbers of surplus parts from the Prussian government arsenal in Erfurt along with some production machinery, did assemble a few thousand weapons from unused parts between 1923 and 1928, and these would have looked new, despite having been made from parts some years old.

The guns were supposedly issued to the cavalry and the motorcyclists, according to Baer[3], or to the armoured and cavalry units according to Smith[4], but some have been reported with infantry, pioneer and other unit markings and it is clear that issue was wider than often believed.

3. Ludwig Baer, *Die leichten Waffen der deutschen Armeen 1841-1945*, p. 52.

4. W. H. B. Smith, *Book of Rifles*, 4th edition, p. 204.

5. The Allies were keen to prevent firms such as DWM and Mauser making weapons, as a reprisal for their contributions to the German war effort in 1914-18, and consequently favoured the previously unimportant Simson company.

Production history

By far the majority of Karabiner 98b was converted from Gewehr 98 standards during the early 1920s, probably mostly by Simson & Co. of Suhl, who were granted an exclusive licence by the Allies to supply weapons to the Reichswehr[5]. It is also believed that the company made small numbers of new guns—perhaps no more than fifteen thousand—in the period 1923-28. The total production quantity of Karabiner 98b may not have exceeded 150,000, although the (deliberate?) erasure of some chamber marks may indicate that Article 180 of the Versailles Treaty was not being honoured.

Markings

These paralleled the marks applied to the original infantry rifles (qv), with chamber marks reading 1920/crown/ERFURT/1918, or crown/ERFURT/1921, applied while the rifles were still unaltered Gewehre 98. The first mark has an additional date applied under Allied supervision, while the second has a replacement date; this it must be, since the Erfurt arsenal had ceased operating three years previously. Some guns 'made' from pre-1918 unused components and many of the post-1923 conversions bore chamber marks such as 'SIMSON & Co/SUHL/1925'. Others were completely unmarked, since the chamber legend had been totally erased. The proof and inspectors' marks, and the serial and parts-numbers, generally remained unchanged.

Original pre-1918 unit markings may occasionally be found on the butt plate of Karabiner 98a and and 98b, or—even more rarely—stampings governed by the 1923 regulations. These took the form of '4./J.R.12.39.', '2./Pi.5.128.', '2./R.R.2.15.' and 'Ü.Pl.Mu.35.', applied by the fourth company of Infanterie-Regiment Nr. 12, the second company of Pionier-Bataillon Nr. 5, the second squadron of Reiter-Regiment Nr. 2, and the Truppenübungsplatz-Kommandantur Munster.

Mechanical description and variations

The Karabiner 98b operated in exactly the same manner as the original Gewehr 98 (qv), since the bending of the bolt handle had no effect on the functioning of the action.

Appearance, distinctive features and data

The Karabiner 98b greatly resembles the post-1915 version of the Gewehr 98, with a grasping groove cut into the fore-end and the special firing-pin nose guard washer inlet in the butt. However, the bolt handle is turned downwards against a recess cut in the stock side, there is a new broad spring-retained barrel band with a fixed sling ring on its left side, and a tangent-leaf sight has replaced the original Lange Visier. The sights were graduated for the S-Patrone until it was decided to standardize on the boat-tailed 'sS' bullet, which had been introduced late in the First World War for use in heavy machine-guns. Modified sight-curves were developed for the sS-Patrone and could be changed for the S-type originals when desired. The minimum sighting distance on the 98b sight was reduced to 100 metres as a result of the experience of trench warfare.

DATA

Calibre: nominally 8mm, actually 7.92 ± 0.02mm.
Rifling: concentric, 4 grooves 0.15mm deep and 4.4mm wide; 1 turn in 240mm, right hand (pitch of 5° 54').
Magazine: internal staggered-column box, 5 rounds capacity.
Loading system: charger, or single rounds.
Length overall: 1,250mm.
Barrel length: 740mm.
Weight: 4,150gm without sling.
Sights: (front) unprotected barleycorn; (back) a tangent-leaf sight graduated from 100 to 2,000 metres in 100m increments.
Performance: see cartridge data (Appendix 2).

Accessories

BAYONET

The soldiers of the Reichswehr—regardless of unit or service branch—were issued with the S 84/98 (TGB, pp. 60-63), which had a short single-edged 25cm blade.

OTHERS

A sling, a cleaning rod, a muzzle protector and a leather breech cover.

Karabiner 98k Mauser

The Reichsheer, restricted to a hundred thousand men shortly after the end of the First World War, was forced to re-equip with pre-1918 rifles and carbines: the Karabiner 98 AZ and the Gewehr 98, later known as the Karabiner 98a and 98b. It was soon obvious that a new weapon would be needed to replace them as they wore out, and the army was keen to standardize on the sS-Patrone[1], which was introduced in mid-1918 to improve the long-range accuracy of the Maxim heavy machine-guns. It was pointless retaining the S-Patrone for rifles and the sS-Patrone for machine-guns if it could be proved that the latter was suitable for all the rifle-calibre firearms in service, particularly as the streamlined 'sS' bullet, despite being considerably heavier than the S-type, gave much better range and velocity retention[2].

1. The 'sS' notation stood for 'schwere Spitzgeschoss', or 'heavy pointed bullet'.

2. The initial velocity of the S-Geschoss was 895m/sec, compared to only 785m/sec for the 'sS' type. At a range of 300 metres, however, the velocities were virtually equal (649m/sec 'S', 642m/sec 'sS') and by 700 metres, the 'sS' bullet was travelling at 481m/sec, compared with 394m/sec for the S-Geschoss.

Experiments began with modified examples of the Karabiner 98a (the old pre-1918 98 AZ) in 1924, when a number of different barrel lengths were tested. Most were shorter than the standard 59cm barrel fitted to the 98a 'carbine'. The results were predictable, since the firers complained bitterly of excessive muzzle blast, muzzle flash and recoil, just as they had when the original 98 AZ carbine had been introduced in early 1908. However, the Germans were well aware that the Czechs and the Belgians, among others, had started production of short Mauser rifles chambering cartridges as powerful as the 8mm German service patterns. Ironically, many of these guns were being made on ex-German production machinery; the Allies had confiscated Mauser's Oberndorf production lines immediately after the Armistice and had distributed the machinery in Czechoslovakia and Yugoslavia as war reparations, while the rifle-making equipment from the Prussian arsenal in Danzig had been given to Poland and was moved to Radom.

Right: the FN Mle 1922 infantry rifle, manufactured in small numbers after the First World War and typical of the guns made before the introduction of 'short rifles' in the mid 1920s. Courtesy of Fabrique Nationale.

Right: FN's 'Carabine de Gendarmerie Mle 1935', typical of the very short Mauser-system weapons produced between the wars. Courtesy of Fabrique Nationale.

The ČZ vz.24 and FN Mle 24 short rifles both had 60cm barrels. By the end of the decade, the Czechs had introduced an even shorter weapon with a barrel measuring a mere 45.5cm, much the same as the original German carbines of 1900-2. Naturally, the muzzle blast of this weapon was terrible, as the German solidery was to discover when the OKW (Oberkommando der Wehrmacht, Armed Forces High Command) adopted the Czech vz.16/33 carbine in October 1940 (see Gewehr 33/40, page 141).

Protracted experiments proved to the Reichsheer's experts that a 60cm barrel gave the best compromise of short overall length, maximum handiness, and minimal muzzle blast and flash, and development of a modified Karabiner 98b proceeded quickly. The result was the Karabiner 98k, in which the letter suffix represented 'kurz' or 'short', introduced either in late 1934 or early 1935[3]. The Karabiner 98k was little more than a 98b with 14cm of the barrel and fore-end removed between the nose-cap and the barrel band, since the Germans were keen to retain the standard bayonet fitting and cleaning

3. The precise date has not yet been found.

rod. The bolt handle was still turned downwards into a recess on the stock side, the tangent-leaf back sight was retained and the sling attachments remained the same. Mechanically, too, the 98k and the 98b were identical.

Experiments with various types of stock had been undertaken in the early 1930s, when many had been considered: walnut, beech, laminated, and even a hollow bakelite-covered metal type[4]. Most guns made before 1940 were stocked in solid walnut or beech, but the laminated pattern, which had the advantages of improved warp resistance and strength, predominated by the end of the war as properly seasoned wood blanks had run short. Plastic stocks were developed experimentally and issued in small numbers for trial.

4. One example of this may be found in the collection of the Royal Small Arms Factory at Enfield Lock, England. The gun is a standard Erfurt-made Gewehr 98, number 242a, dating from the First World War (most of the chamber mark is hidden by a telescope sight mount), and this has been taken to date it prior to 1918. However, the stock may not be original.

Mauser began production of ČZ/FN-type short rifles in about 1931, as a few export orders had been negotiated and a production line had been installed in the Oberndorf factory. A typical commercial rifle, with a straight bolt handle and a standard German tangent-leaf back sight, has been examined with the company banner and the date, 1933, over the chamber. Its finish, like that on most pre-1939 Mauser rifles, is immaculate; the blueing, particularly, being of very high quality. Many guns of this type, some of which have turned-down 98k-pattern bolt handles, will be found with the Ethiopian Lion of Judah mark struck into their barrels and the cypher of Haile Selassie above the chamber.

The first deliveries of Karabiner 98k were made to the Wehrmacht in 1935, as the old restrictions on German arms-making had been openly repudiated and a full-scale programme had begun to re-equip the armed forces at the greatest possible speed. This had been overtly acknowledged by the opening of the Zentralburö für deutsche Aufrüstung (Central Office for German Rearmament) in Margarathenstrasse, Berlin, in

Right: Mauser-Werke's Oberndorf am Neckar factory, as it looked in the early 1930s. Courtesy of Rolf Gminder.

1934. Rifle production was initially entrusted to the Mauser factories in Oberndorf and Berlin-Borsigwalde—the latter being opened specially in 1934—until other contractors were recruited during the war, when it was realized that Mauser-Werke could not cope with the enormous demands. The Oberndorf factory alone made something approaching four million Karabiner 98k between 1934 and 1945, but the total rifle procurement in the same period exceeded fifteen million discounting captured guns.

Many millions of Karabiner 98k were made for the Wehrmacht by Mauser-Werke, Steyr, Waffenfabrik Brünn and others, despite the introduction of automatic rifles and Maschinenkarabiner in the last years of hostilities. The 98k shared the same action as the original Gewehr 98 and, therefore, the same strengths and few weaknesses. The quality of the weapons made towards the end of the war declined considerably, but, by and large, all were soundly-made even if their external finish left a lot to be desired. Being a bolt-action, the Karabiner 98k was obsolescent by the end of the war, as the automatic and assault rifles had been developed to a point where they were being introduced for general service; the Germans themselves had the Gewehr 43 and the MP 43/StG 44 series[5], and had made extensive use of captured Russian Tokarevs. And the US Army had had the Rifle .30 M1 (Garand) since 1936.

Although Mauser-system rifles and carbines were made in the immediate post-war years in Belgium, Czechoslovakia, Iran, Israel, Yugoslavia and elsewhere, the design had no future.

Production history

The production history of the Karabiner 98k is difficult to assess satisfactorily, since a lot of detailed research has still to be done concerning the principal contractors and the many sub-contractors recruited to the production programme during the Second World War. This, indeed, may be essential for even a reasonably accurate summary to be made of the whole story. The Germans themselves managed to camouflage parts of it by introducing many types of code, which were constantly changed in the period 1935-42. (See Markings.)

It has been estimated that 11.485 million Karabiner 98k were made between 1934 and the end of the Second World War[6], and no data have yet been produced to make this figure untenable, or, for that matter, to confirm it. However, a few fragments have now been found, since Götz[7] gives figures that indicate the delivery of 8.48 million Karabiner 98k in 1940-44. These break down as:

1940	1,351,700
1941	1,358,800
1942	1,363,400
1943	2,149,300
1944	2,262,300

The sudden rise between 1942 and 1943 is probably explained by the incorporation of new principal contractors, such as Steyr-Daimler-Puch and Waffenwerk Brünn, and, perhaps, some important sub-contractors. Alternatively, it could be due simply to the introduction of the 98k Kriegsmodell to simplify and accelerate production, although the increase of about 58 per cent makes this a little unlikely.

The CIOS report[8] on Mauser's Oberndorf factory states that 3.67 million Karabiner 98k were made in the decade 1935-45, together with 86,000 additional Zielfernrohr-Karabiner 98k in 1942-45 and about 279,000 sporting guns between 1935 and 1944. The figures are:

	Kar 98k	Z-Kar 98k	sporting guns
1934	(45,000*)	—	(60,000*)
1935	150,000	—	60,000
1936	200,000	—	60,000
1937	250,000	—	60,000
1938	250,000	—	60,000
1939	300,000	—	30,000
1940	350,000	—	1,000
1941	420,000	—	1,000
1942	450,000	10,000	800
1943	550,000	40,000	800
1944	665,000	35,000	5,200
1945	85,000	1,000	—
Total	3,670,000	86,000	278,800

Figures marked (*) are approximations, and are excluded from the totals.

The totals given in the CIOS report look sufficiently imprecise to be very considerable approximations, and may even be target figures rather than actual deliveries. Consequently, they should be considered with a certain amount of caution pending further work.

The contribution of the Mauser-Werke factory in Berlin-Borsigwalde is unknown, but may have reached several million rifles. Similarly, Steyr-Daimler-Puch and Waffenwerk Brünn contributed appreciable quantities. Their participation has still to be fully investigated since, for instance, it is not clear whether the Germans drew a distinction between the Steyr-made Gewehre 29/40 (ö) and Karabiner 98k in

5. The first examples of what are now termed assault rifles.

6. John Walter, *The German Bayonet*, p. 87.

7. Hans-Dieter Götz, *Die deutschen Militargewehre und Maschinenpistolen, 1871-1945*, p. 162.

8. R. D. Shephard, *Visit to Mauser-Werke AG, Oberndorf am Neckar and Mauser Personnel at Lager Haining, Otzal, near Innsbruck*. CIOS Report XXXIII-IV, page 329.

their procurement figures. Waffenwerk Brünn apparently commenced manufacture of the 98k in the third quarter of 1943, in factories in Brno and Povaška Bystrica. The quantity made for the Oberkommando des Heeres (Army High Command) was:

1943, third quarter: 117,000
1943, fourth quarter: 170,532
1944, first quarter: 172,720
1944, second quarter: 165,125
1944, third quarter: 198,769
1944, fourth quarter: 197,365
1945: very few (none?) Total: 1,021,511

Markings
These were similar to those applied to the older German rifles, particularly the Gewehr 98, although their form changed considerably. The manufacturers' marks remained above the chambers, but were coded to disguise the companies concerned.
The chambers are invariably dated, in full until 1941-42 and with only the last two digits thereafter. Guns made by Mauser's Oberndorf factory are said to have used a year-code 'MB' on rifles made with the 'svw' code group in late 1944/early 1945. The Steyr-Daimler-Puch plant, however, continued to use the standard two-digit date until it was overrun by the Russians.

Karabiner 98k: principal manufacturers, 1934-45

S/237, 237

Berlin-Lübecker Maschinenfabrik AG, Werk Lübeck.

LL (LP)

Unknown, found on Karabiner 98k dated 1942. The code dates from October 1940, however.

dot

Waffenwerk Brünn AG (formerly Československá Zbrojovká), Brno, Czechoslovakia. Code granted in April 1941.

ch

Fabrique Nationale d'Armes de Guerre, Herstal-lèz-Liège, Belgium. Code granted in October 1940.

S/27, 27, ax

Feinmechanische Werke GmbH, Erfurt, Altonaerstrasse; use of the S-code and the number paralleled those applied by the Mauser factories. The 'ax' code group was granted in October 1940.

bcd

Gustloff-Werke, Werk Weimar, Weimar. This company had traded until 1935 as 'Simson & Co.', but had then been seized by the NSDAP. The code group was granted in February 1941.

S/243, 243, ar

Mauser-Werke AG, Werk Berlin-Borsigwalde, Eichborndamm. Use of these three codes paralleled those applied by the Oberndorf factory, as far as dating was concerned. The letter code 'ar' was granted in October 1940 and first seems to have been applied to guns in the following year.

S/42, 42, byf, svw

Mauser-Werke AG, Oberndorf am Neckar, Württemberg. The S/42 code was used in the period 1934-39, when it was replaced by the simpler 42. This in turn lasted until being replaced by the letter code 'byf' in 1942, although the latter had been granted to Mauser in February 1941. The last code, 'svw', seems to have been granted very late in 1944.

S/147, 147, ce

J. P. Sauer & Sohn Gewehrfabrik, Suhl, Thüringen. The letter code 'ce' was allocated to Sauer in October 1940.

660, bnz

Steyr-Daimler-Puch AG, Werk Steyr, Oberdonau, Austria. The number code dates from 1938, the three-letter type from February 1941, although it does not seem to have been applied to Karabiner 98k until 1943. It is believed that only Gewehre 29/40 were made with the '660' mark.

The designation 'MOD.98', in ordinary (roman) letters, lies on the left side of the breech ahead of the thumb clearance cut-away milled in the receiver wall. There are distinctive proof eagles on the left side of the barrel and receiver in the chamber area, while the complete serial number may be found on the left side of the barrel, the left side of the receiver, and the bolt handle base. The last two or three digits, or often the complete number without the serial suffix letter, appear on virtually all the individual parts. Gun 3803c for example, made by Mauser's Oberndorf factory in 1938, has the full number (3803) repeated on the magazine floor plate; the trigger guard bow-extension, in front of the magazine unit; the cocking piece support or bolt-plug; the safety 'wing'; and the left side of the nose-cap. The last two digits lie on all the screws and bolts.

The numbers initially lacked a suffix, and each contractor seems to have reduced the sequence to 01 at the end of each calendar year. When about ten thousand guns had been made, the numbers began again at 01a ran up to 9999a or 10000a, and then re-commenced at 01b. What happened when the last 'z' number had been reached remains unconfirmed, though it is logical to expect that the series reverted to 01aa and began once more. If the figures given in the CIOS report are correct, Mauser's Oberndorf factory exceeded the 01aa-9999zz series in 1943 and 1944; did the numbers become 01aaa? The answer, it seems, is no; indeed, the contractors may not always have used double-letter suffixes[9]. Some may have distinguished the alphabet series by using different suffix-letter designs (i.e.: e and *e*); this has yet to be confirmed, but it seems quite feasible since some guns have been seen with suffixes in script.

9. At the time of writing, only one gun has been reported with such a number, 2905ee, made by Mauser's Oberndorf plant in 1942.

The old imperial inspectors' marks, small crowned gothic letters, were replaced by stamps applied by the inspectors of the many Waffenamt sub-bureaux, controlled by the Heereswaffenamt. These comprised tiny linear eagles over the sub-bureau number and, sometimes, the letters 'WaA'.

Principal sub-bureau marks on Karabiner 98k

63, 76	Waffenwerk Brünn AG, Brno
103, 140, 613	Fabrique Nationale d'Armes de Guerre, Herstal-lèz-Liège
26	Mauser-Werke AG, Berlin-Borsigwalde
63, 135, 655	Mauser-Werke AG, Oberndorf am Neckar
623	Steyr-Daimler-Puch AG, Steyr

Unit markings are very rarely found on Karabiner 98k, although a few unscrupulous individuals have made a fine trade out of falsely-applied SS runes. Few of these items are genuine.

Mechanical description and variations

The Karabiner 98k operates in exactly the same way as the original Gewehr 98 (qv), which its construction also greatly resembles. The magazine follower acts as a hold-open device after the last round has been ejected.

KARABINER 98K

This was the standard version, generally with a one-piece solid walnut stock, properly forged barrel bands and butt plate, and little evidence of declining manufacturing standards. The first guns of this type were made in 1934 or 1935; the last, in 1942-43 depending on the contractor involved. They generally have open front sights.

GEBIRGSJÄGER-KARABINER 98K

This was an experimental version of the standard 98k, fitted with a large cast-steel plate on the left side of the butt to assist mountain troops ('Gebirgsjäger') in climbing and to protect the butt from blows. Probably dating from 1939 or 1940, it was replaced by the Gewehr 33/40 (qv).

FALLSCHIRMJÄGER-KARABINER 98K

These guns were developed experimentally for the German parachutists. The earlier pattern has a swinging butt ('Klappschaft'), hinged on the left side of the small of the stock. A latch on the right allows the whole butt to be swung laterally towards the left and back against the fore-end. The two guns reported were both made by Mauser's Oberndorf factory in 1938, which may indicate when the first trials were carried out. The second type of parachutists' rifle—the sole example recorded being made by Mauser in 1942—has a detachable barrel ('abnehmbarem Lauf') with an interrupted-thread joint immediately in front of the receiver ring. The barrel has three groups of threads, and locks by turning through 60°. It is retained by a longitudinally moving bar that meshes with a recess cut in the bottom of the receiver ring. The bar is controlled by a long fluted-head lever on the left side of the fore-end ahead of the receiver/barrel joint. The chamber and barrel top are marked thus:

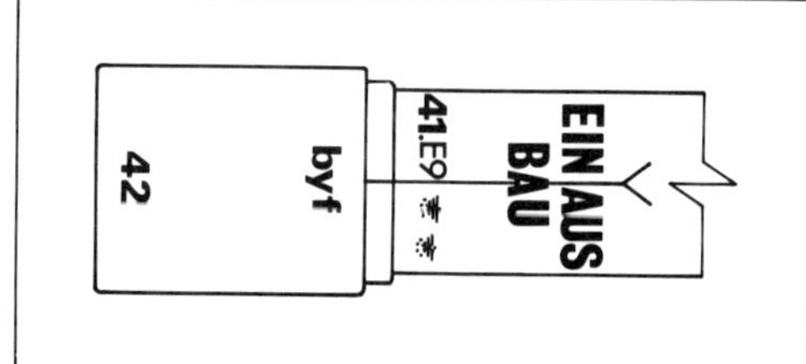

The parachutists' rifles do not seem to have been especially successful and neither was issued for anything other than trials.

KARABINER 98K KRIEGSMODELL

As the war progressed, and as things became more and more critical for Germany, the time allotted to rifle production became increasingly valuable. Quantity was wanted rather than quality, and resulted in what has come to be known as the 'war model' ('Kriegsmodell') of the Karabiner 98k. This differed from the original in several important details. The *stock* of the pre-1939 guns was inevitably made of a single piece of walnut, but trials had been undertaken with substitute materials in the early 1930s and a satisfactory beech plywood pattern had been developed. However, many weapons made after 1942 had laminated stocks made of whatever usable wood was available. One important, but unexpected advantage of using laminated wood stocks was that the stock-blank wastage during finishing dropped from 10 per cent to between 1½ and 2 per cent[10]. The laminated stocks were less susceptible to flaws in the wood grain and proved to be stronger than the one-piece varieties, although they were between 200 and 300gm heavier.

10. Eckardt and Morawietz, *Die handwaffen des brandenburgisch-preussisch-deutschen Heeres 1600-1945*, p. 227.

The *stock fittings*, originally properly machined forgings or castings, were simplified and stamped from low-grade material. The butt plate design was noticeably changed, the barrel band became a plain ring, and the typically German H-type nose-cap was replaced by what amounted to a plain steel cylinder. Most guns were issued with short tubular front sight guards, and the bayonet bar and cleaning rod were eliminated altogether on some Karabiner 98k made in 1944-45. Some also had their mounts, the barrel band and the nose-cap, retained by ordinary wood screws.

The *machining and finishing* processes were greatly simplified, among the results being prominent machine-marks and blemishes which had previously been polished away (thereby wasting time), and the introduction of phosphating on many of the metal parts. Short cuts such as simply circular-boring the gas escape holes in the bolt, rather than milling them into elegant ovals, were introduced wherever possible, while the development of all kinds of simplified production techniques—precision casting and stamping among them—greatly accelerated manufacture of certain key components.

ZIELFERNROHR-KARABINER 98K

Though desultory experiments with these telescope-sighted marksmen's rifles had been undertaken during the 1930s, and small numbers had been issued in the opening phases of the war, it took the effective mass use of snipers by the Red Army—particularly at Stalingrad—to convince the OKW that large-scale manufacture of comparable weapons was essential.

In 1942, therefore, the companies involved in making the Karabiner 98k were ordered to ensure that 6 per cent of their output was fitted with mounts for a suitable sight. Most of the rifles made prior to 1942 were fitted with the large Zielfernrohr 39 (Zf 39), which came in several patterns according to its maker: Zeiss, Leitz, Goerz, Hensoldt and others all delivered small numbers of sights to the Wehrmacht. The Zf 39 was used in conjunction with two ring mounts attached to 'turret' bases on top of the receiver bridge and the chamber, or, occasionally, in a one-piece two-ring mount locked by a clamping bar and sliding on a special rail attached to the left side of

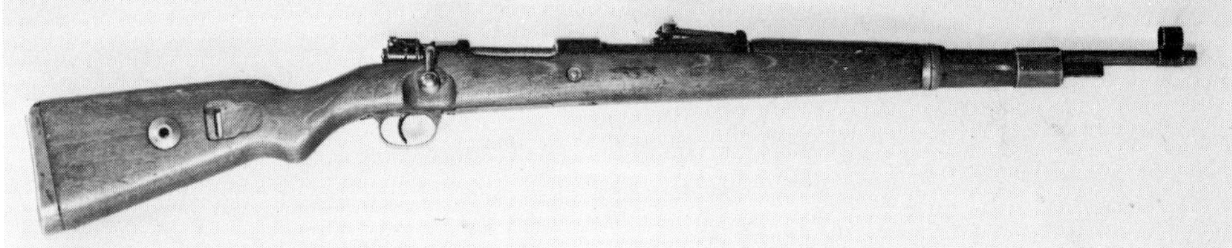

Right: an example of the 'Kriegsmodell' Karabiner 98k, with a stamped barrel band/nosecap assembly and a simplified buttplate.

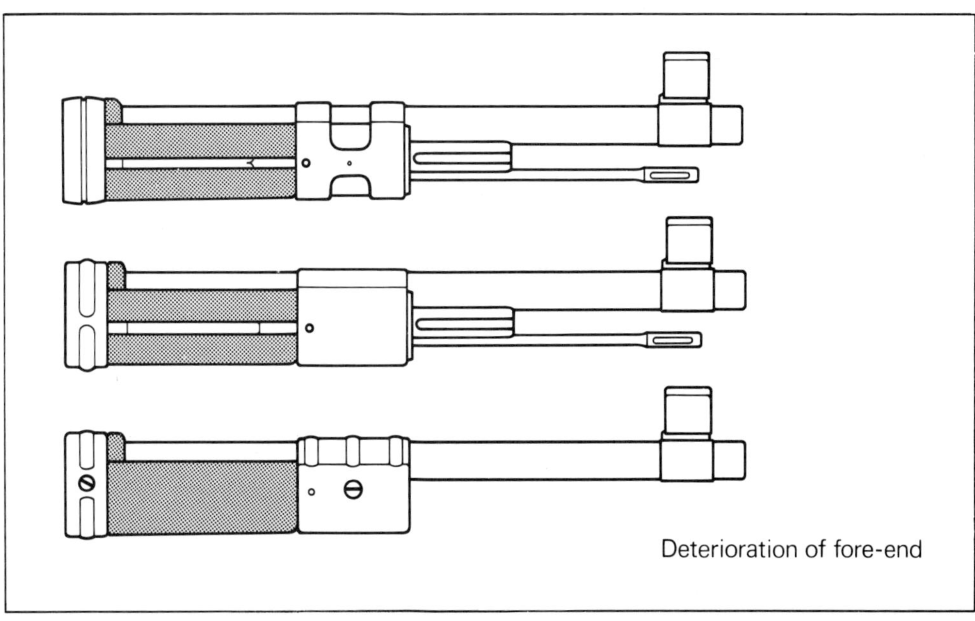

Deterioration of fore-end

Right: a Zielfernrohr-Karabiner 98k, with the small Zf 41 telescope sight.

the receiver ahead of the thumb clearance cut-away. The sights have a range adjustment drum, graduated from 100 to 800 metres, on top of their bodies. The drum could be locked in place by a thumbscrew.

Most post-1942 Zielfernrohrkarabiner 98k were issued with the essentially similar Zf 40, Zf 41, Zf 41/1 or Zf 41/2[11], small 1.5 × sights whose special two-ring side mount slid onto a distinctive rail on the left side of the back sight, where it was locked by a laterally moving spring-loaded catch. The sights, with their excessive eye relief, were not greeted with much enthusiasm and were widely regarded as optically inferior to the 4× Zf 39. The annular range drum of the Zf 40/41 series was placed around the centre of the body and graduated from 100 to 800 metres.

A few guns may be found with the Zf 4 sight, which was shared with the semi-automatic Gewehr 43, in a distinctive rearward slanted two-ring side mount attached to a rail on the left side of the receiver. This telescope unit resembles the Zf 39, but is shorter, stubbier and closer in design to a plain tube.

Many Zielfernrohrkarabiner 98k were specially made—Mauser's Oberndorf factory, for instance, made 86,000 between 1942 and the end of the war—but others were converted from existing rifles. Götz[12] pictures a 1938-vintage S/27 specimen mounting a Zf 41.

11. The differences between these are not clearly understood, but seem to have been relatively minor.

12. Hans-Dieter Götz, *Die deutschen Militärgewehre und Maschinenpistolen, 1871-1945*, p. 164.

VOLKSKARABINER 98

These were last-ditch weapons, which were produced in desperation during the last few months of the war. Genuine VK 98[13] can be distinguished by their standard, if badly finished, bolt-actions, but have crudely shaped half-stocks, stepped barrels and fixed standing-notch back sights. Most of those reported were marked 'bnz 45', indicating that they were made by Steyr-Daimler-Puch AG in 1945, but there may have been other contractors. However, since these firearms were destined for the Home Guard ('Volkssturm') rather than the regular army, they are not considered here in detail.

13. There were other 'Volksgewehre', such as the VG 1, using different types of bolt mechanism of varying degrees of crudity.

GEWEHR 40K

One example of this 'rifle', marked 'GEW.40K' on the left side of the receiver and 'byf' above the chamber, exists in the Aberdeen Proving Ground Collection. It has a 49cm barrel, a turned-down bored-out bolt handle, no barrel band, a special nose-cap with a sling swivel on the left side and a lightened trigger guard; though it is otherwise similar to the Karabiner 98k. The carbine—for carbine it is—is believed to have emanated from Mauser-Werke's Oberndorf factory in 1941. The Gewehr 40K was a short-lived experiment, perhaps intended as a competitor for the Gewehr 33/40. The 40k would have encountered fiendish muzzle blast/flash problems, owing to the use of such a powerful cartridge in so short a barrel, and the advantages in handiness compared with the Karabiner 98k would have been largely illusory. The carbine is about 990mm long, weighs 3,765gm and has a tangent-leaf back sight graduated from 100 to 1,000 metres.

Appearance, distinctive features and data

The standard Karabiner 98k greatly resembles the original Gewehr 98 (qv), though it is considerably shorter, has its bolt handle turned down against a recess in the stock in the manner of the Karabiner 98 AZ, and has sling attachment points through the butt and on the left side of the barrel band. There is a tangent-leaf rather than Lange-pattern back sight, the base of which may have a mounting rail for the Zf 40 or ZF 41 on the left side. Other guns have turret mounts on the receiver for the Zf 39, or rails on the left side of the receiver wall for the Zf 39 or Zf 4.

Early guns have one-piece walnut stocks, although solid and laminated beech, elm and other substitute materials are known to have been used. Plastic stocks were issued experimentally, but proved to be failures.

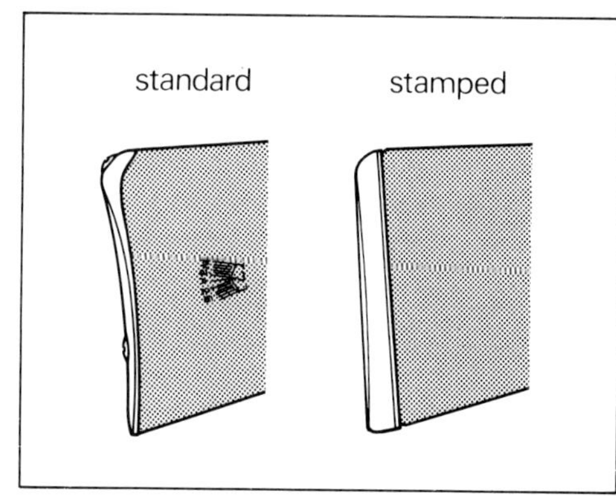

The post-1942 stamped butt plates differ visibly from the earlier types, since they form a 'boot' around the butt edge. The nose-cap may be a plain cylinder on late guns and a single leaf spring usually retains the barrel band and the nose-cap, though a few rifles made in 1945 simply held the mounts with wooden screws. Many rifles (notably those made after 1942) may be found with tubular front sight protectors.

DATA

Calibre: nominally 8mm, actually 7.92 ± 0.02mm.

Rifling: concentric, 4 grooves 0.15mm deep and 4.4mm wide; 1 turn in 240mm, right hand (pitch of 5° 54').
Magazine: internal staggered-column box, capacity 5 rounds.
Loading system: charger, or single rounds.
Length overall: 1,110-1,115mm.
Barrel length: 600mm.
Weight: between 3,800 and 4,100gm, depending on the stocking material.
Sights: (front) open or protected barleycorn; (back) a tangent-leaf sight graduated from 100 to 2,000 metres in 100m increments.
Performance: see cartridge data (Appendix 2).

Accessories

BAYONETS

The Karabiner 98k was officially issued with the S 84/98 (TGB, pp. 88-92), though small numbers of the S 98/05 (TGB, pp. 63-71) were issued in the mid-1930s to offset a temporary shortage of bayonets and some guns had their bayonet bars modified to use the ex-British P 07 sword bayonet. They were then issued to the Reichs-Arbeits-Dienst (Labour Service)[14]. Polish wz.29 and Czech vz.24 bayonets were often used with German rifles during the Second World War (TGB, pp. 92-4).

OTHERS

These included a sling, a muzzle protector, the 'Reinigungsgerät 34'[15], and, in some cases, a front sight guard. In addition, a number of special accessories were developed, among them being at least two types of grenade launcher, an infra-red night sight, a muzzle brake, a silencer, and a curved barrel attachment to enable the gun to fire round corners!

The *grenade launchers* included the Gewehr-granategerät 42 (Gw.Gr.Ger. 42), introduced in 1942, which consisted of a cup-type projector clamped to the rifle muzzle and fired with a special blank cartridge. The pre-rifled tail of the grenades, which came in several different patterns, engaged in the rifling cut in the inner surface of the discharger cup. A special sight was clamped to the rifle immediately behind the back sight, although the grenades were notoriously inaccurate at long range. However, they could penetrate up to 8cm of armour plate at a range of 75 metres. A typical launcher unit is marked 'GW.GR.GER/K98K' on top of the sight clamp and bears its maker's code 'aye' on the sight arm[16].

The second grenade-launcher is a spigot pattern, used to fire large finned anti-tank bombs, and consists of a plain surfaced tube held to the muzzle by a rearward bayonet-hilt extension that slides over the standard bayonet bar. There is also a catch on the left side of the launcher alongside the front sight. An auxiliary back sight (graduated from 25 to 100 metres in 25m increments) was clamped onto the stock ahead of the receiver ring.

The *infra-red night sight* was the IG 1229 Vampir ('IG., or 'Infra-rot Gerät', means infra-red equipment). It was developed as a night-driving aid, according to Ian Hogg[17], but was later adapted as a rifle sight, working in conjunction with a special telescope unit. It relied on the infra-red heat emission of an otherwise unseen target to provide a suitable image in the receiver. The Vampir attachment, resembling a large lamp, was mounted above the telescope sight.

The *curved barrel device*, unofficially known as the

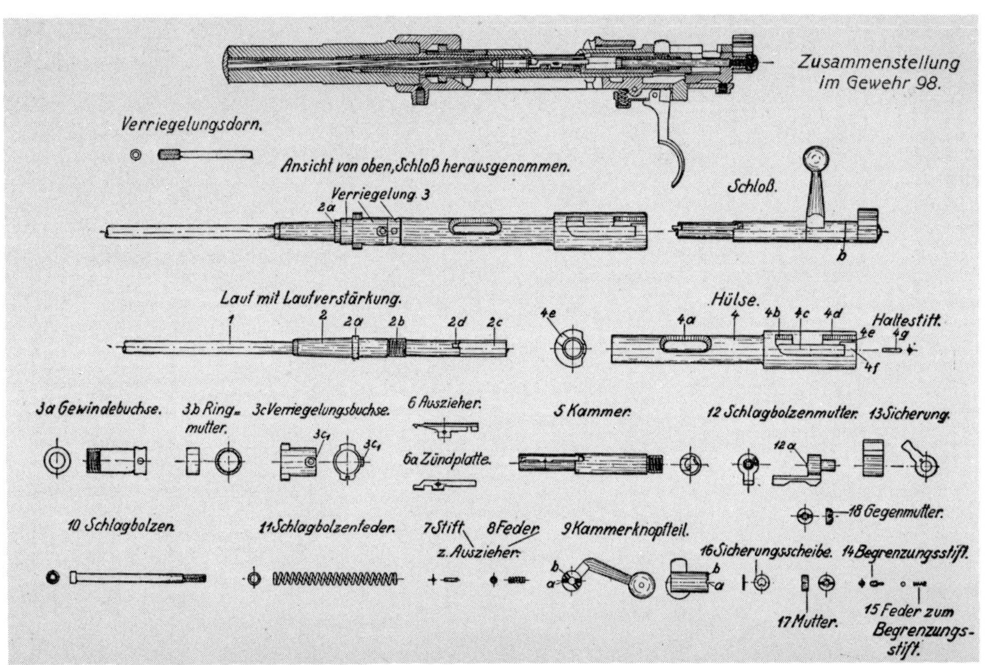

Right: the Erma-developed Einstecklauf 24, a sub-calibre training device chambering the 0.22in LR rimfire cartridge.

14. Not to the DAF (Deutsche Arbeits-Front, German Workers Front), as reported in *The German Bayonet*, p. 86.

15. Cleaning equipment.

16. Showing it to have been made by Olympia Burömaschinenfabrik AG of Erfurt.

17. Ian Hogg, *German Secret Weapons*, p. 63.

'Krummlauf' or 'K-Lauf', is another of the many examples of the OKW and the HWaA favouring technological 'advances' of highly dubious significance rather than pressing ahead with the mass production of standard weapons. This was especially important at such a late stage in the war, when the K-Lauf, which was never satisfactorily perfected, diverted developmental and production facilities while wasting valuable time and materials. Although modified Karabiner 98k were used during the first series of trials, the K-Läufen were only issued with the MP 43/StG 44 series of assault rifles.

A *sub-calibre training device* was developed in the early 1920s to permit low-cost target practice to be undertaken with rimfire ammunition. It was designed by Erfurter Maschinenfabrik Berthold Geipel GmbH (Erma-Werke) and adopted by the Reichswehr in about 1924. It was officially known as the 'Einstecklauf 24 mit Zielmunition Kaliber 5,6mm lfb' (barrel insert for practice cartridges)[18] and was originally capable of only single-shot firing, although a detachable box magazine was developed in about 1929. The unit consists of a small-diameter barrel liner, bored out and rifled for the 5.6mm bullet, and a special bolt mechanism inserted in a receiver—the external surfaces of which greatly resembled those of the regular Karabiner 98k bolt body. The standard bolt was removed and replaced by the Erma insert, which came in a special wooden case containing the adaptor, two box magazines and a tool to tighten the unit into the existing bolt-way. The top of the Erma insert is usually marked as shown.

18. The abbreviation 'lfb' stands for 'lang für Büchsen' or what is known as 'long rifle' in English-speaking countries.

A *winter trigger*, a *safety lever extension* and a *remote firing device* for the Karabiner 98k were also made in small numbers. The trigger consisted of an external lever on the right sideplate of two attached to the trigger-guard bow, and allowed the firer to wear gloves or arctic mittens. The safety extension consisted of a long lever replacing the original 'wing' on top of the cocking piece housing and permitted the firer to operate the safety easily even if the receiver of his rifle was fitted with a Zf 39 or Zf 4 telescope sight. The remote-control unit consisted of a Bowden cable attached to the trigger and operated by a pressure mechanism that could, for example, be half-buried in the ground to act as a booby trap.

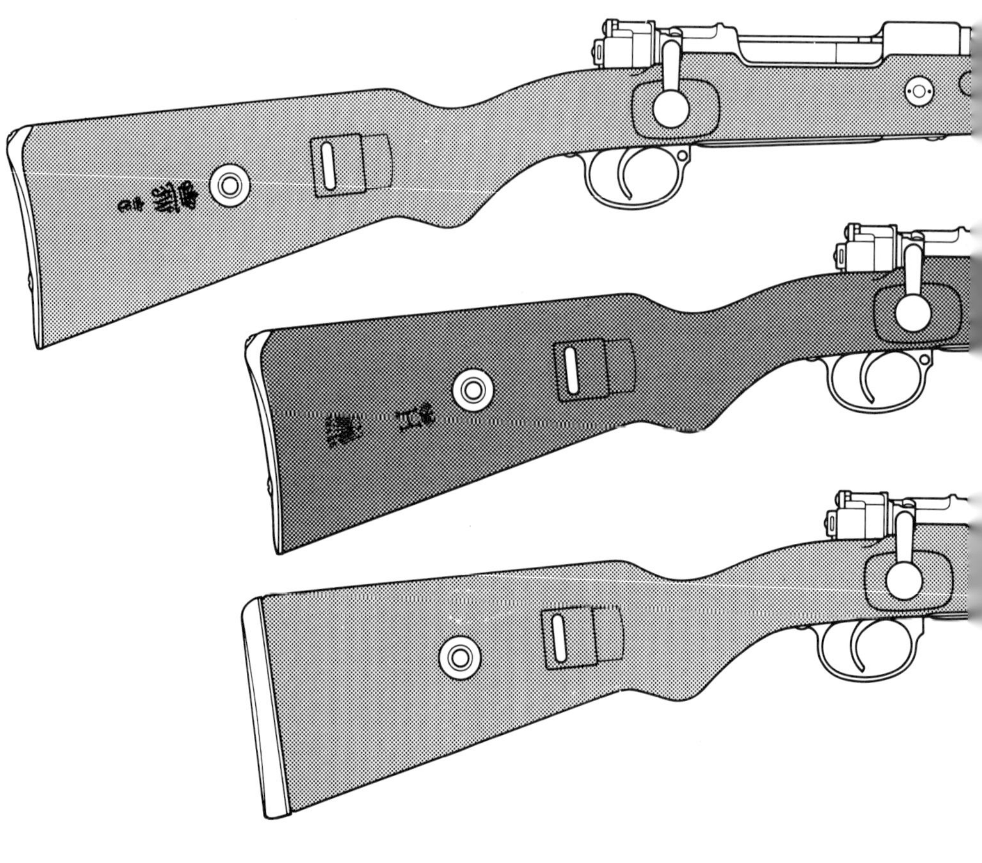

Right: two views of the magazine-fed derivative of the basic Erma sub-calibre trainer. Courtesy of Frank de Haas.

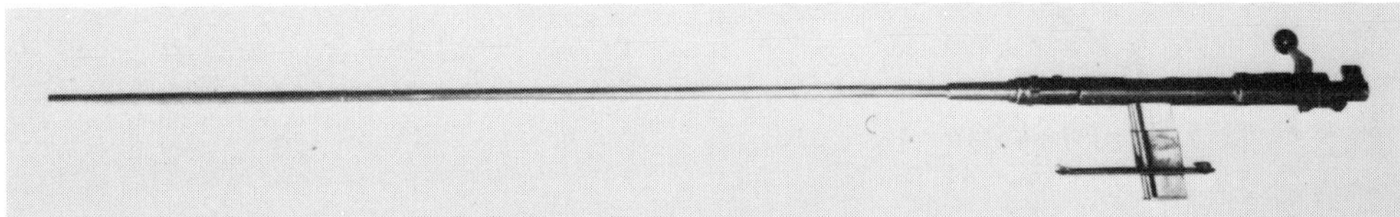

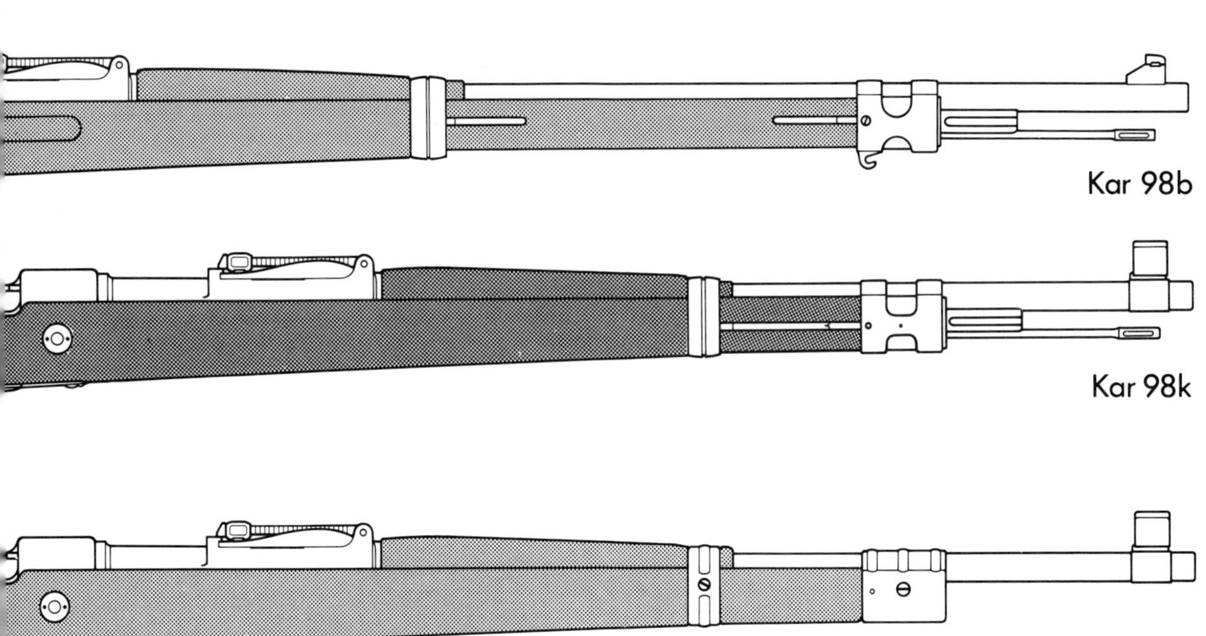

Karabiner 98b and 98k

KKW and DSM training rifles

After Versailles, the Reichswehr was limited to an ammunition expenditure of only 60 8mm rounds per soldier per year, which was scarcely enough to ensure that proficient marksmanship was maintained. During the 1920s and 1930s, when the German armed forces were secretly re-equipping and while the arms industry was theoretically banned from making large numbers of 8mm calibre service rifles, several methods of training recruits in the art of marksmanship were devised. Apart from the introduction of the Erma-developed Einstecklauf 24 (EL 24), described in the section devoted to the Karabiner 98k, several types of small-calibre training rifle were introduced in the 1930s. They included an air rifle (M 33) designed by Hugo Schmeisser and made by Haenel, some 4mm Zimmerstützen or parlour rifles, and the KKW and DSM 5.6mm rimfire military and sporting patterns. The KKW—Kleinkaliber-Wehrsportgewehr, or small-calibre military and sporting rifle—was virtually a rimfire version of the Karabiner 98k, as it shared the same design of stock, sling fittings and bayonet attachment. The position of its bolt handle, the back sight and the bolt-release catch all resembled the full-bore rifles. The DSM (or DSM-34), the Deutsches Sportmodell, was basically a sporting version of the KKW; it had a straighter bolt handle, a different back sight and a non-military nose-cap that lacked the bayonet bar. Although not specifically intended as a military trainer, it was widely used by the paramilitary formations such as the SA and the SS.

The rifles were single-shot patterns, but it is believed that magazine-fed derivations of the basic designs were also made in small numbers. The KKW and the DSM were accurate, well-made and well-liked, and trained thousands of German soldiers in handling the Karabiner 98k, which was in short supply in 1935 and remained so until the re-armament programmes bore fruit in 1938-39.

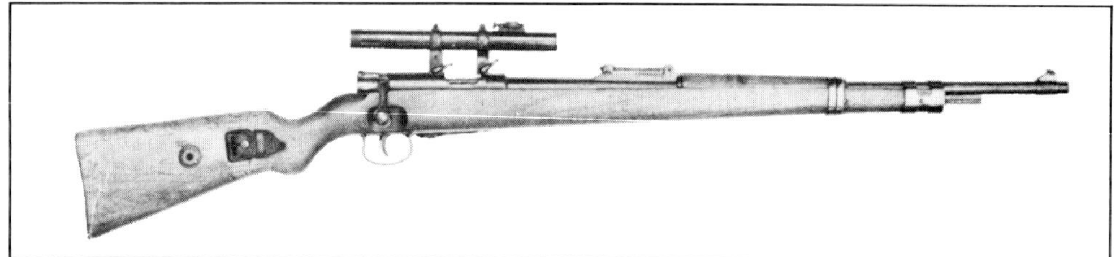

Right: a typical KKW, fitted with a 2.5× telescope sight. From the *World's Guns* catalogue, 1972.

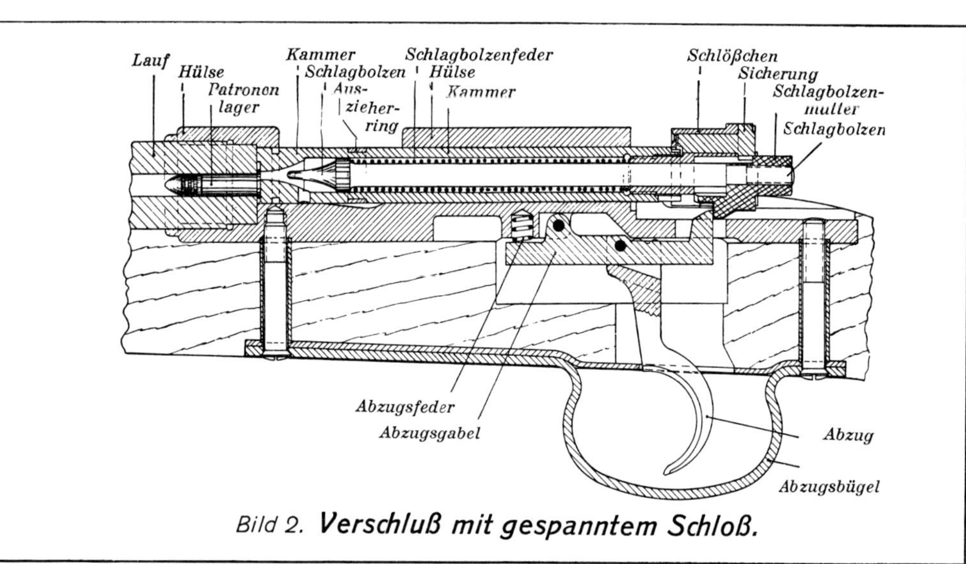

Right: a longitudinal section of the DSM 34.

KKW and DSM: makers

Although the quantity of KKW manufactured remains totally unknown, since so many contractors participated, it must have run into hundreds of thousands.

Production history
The KKW and the DSM were made by many different companies, many of whom had a long involvement in the firearms industry. They included:

Berlin-Suhler Waffen- und Fahrzeugwerk (BSW), Waffenfabrik-Abteilung; Suhl, Thüringen.

J. G. Anschütz, Germaniawaffenfabrik; Zella-Mehlis, Thüringen.

Bolte & Anschütz Jagdwaffenfabrik; Zella-Mehlis, Thüringen.

GECADO

G. C. Dornheim AG, Waffenfabrik; Suhl, Thüringen. This company is believed to have made some or all of the rifles marketed by Genschow.

ERMA

Erma-Waffenfabrik B. Geipel GmbH (vormals Erfurter Maschinen- und Werkzeugfabrik); Erfurt, Thüringen.

Gustav Genschow & Co. AG ('Geco'); Berlin-Treptow. These guns, according to some sources, were made by Dornheim.

C.G. Haenel Waffen- und Fahrradfabrik AG; Suhl, Thüringen.

Gustloff-Werke, Waffenwerk Suhl, Thüringen. This 'company', owned and operated by the NSDAP, had traded as Simson & Co. prior to 1935.

Mauser-Werke AG; Oberndorf am Neckar, Württemberg.

Bernh. Paatz Waffenfabrik und Maschinenbau; Suhl, Thüringen.

Carl Walther Waffenfabrik; Zella-Mehlis, Thüringen.

HWZ

Hermann Weihrauch Waffenfabrik, Zella-Mehlis, Thüringen.

SIMSON & CO.

Simson & Co., Waffenfabrik; Suhl, Thüringen. This company was seized by the NSDAP in 1935 and traded thereafter as Gustloff-Werke.

Oskar Will, Venus-Waffenwerk; Zella-Mehlis, Thüringen.

Markings

A typical KKW bears several marks. Above the chamber, for example, may be found the Gustloff-Werke shield-based 'G' trademark and the legend 'GUSTLOFF-WERKE/WAFFENWERK SUHL', while 'KK-WEHRSPORTGEWEHR' lies on the right side of the receiver behind the loading port. The calibre designation 'KAL. .22 LANG FÜR BÜCHSEN' is struck into the left side of the barrel.

A typical DSM displays the encircled Geco emblem above the chamber, 'GUSTAV GENSCHOW & CO. AKT. GES./ABTL. WAFFENFABRIK BERLIN-TREPTOW' on the left side of the receiver, and 'DEUTSCHE SPORTMODELL' in fraktur (gothic script) on the right side of the receiver in front of the bolt handle. The guns display standard German commercial proof marks—a crown over 'N' before 1 April 1940, an eagle over 'N' thereafter—but are not always visibly numbered, possibly to disguise how many were being made. Many may be found with butt markings supposedly applied by the various paramilitary organizations controlled by the NSDAP (such as those pictured below) but though some are genuine, most are spurious.

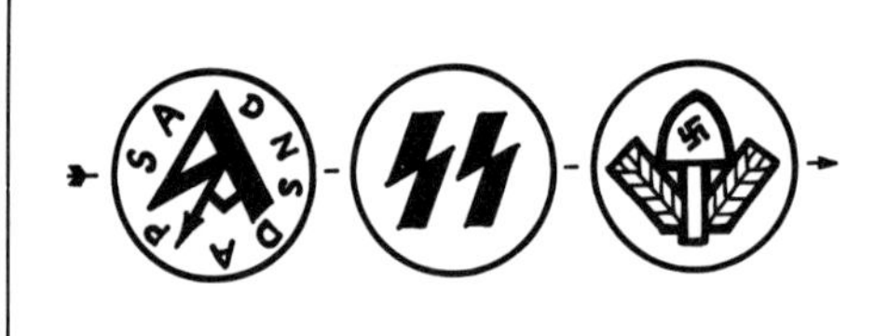

Mechanical description and variations

The KKW is a simple bolt-action single-shot rifle, and has a plain tubular receiver with a cut-away loading port behind the receiver ring. The bolt is locked by the base of the bolt handle as it turns down into its seat, and by a small lug diametrically opposite the handle which revolves into a cut-out in the receiver wall. The action is amply strong enough for the 5.6mm rimfire cartridges, especially as it is usually of excellent materials and finish. The bolt head is a

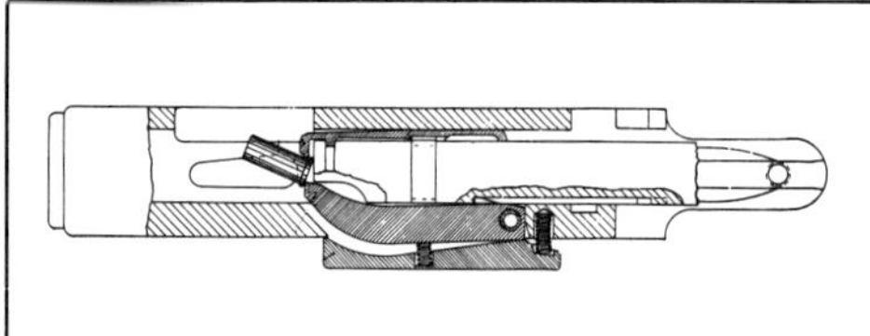

Right: the DSM ejector and extractor mechanism.

separate non-rotating type, has a leaf-pattern extractor on the right side and is cut laterally on the left to permit the ejector to kick extracted cases out of the bolt-way. The ejector is usually a spring-loaded blade mounted coaxially with the bolt-release catch, the design of which parallels that of the Karabiner 98k. An angled surface on the face of the receiver acts in conjunction with the bolt handle base to give adequate primary extraction, while raising the bolt handle cams the cocking piece backwards to withdraw the firing-pin nose into the body of the bolt. The safety is a Mauser 'wing' pattern mounted on top of the cocking-piece housing, where it can be used to lock the cocking piece and the bolt. The action cannot be opened with the safety applied.

The mechanical details of the KK-Wehrsport-gewehre varied slightly from maker to maker, though the description given previously, by and large, suffices for most of them. However, the ejector design in rifles made by Gustloff-Werke comprised a spring-actuated loading tray, over which the bolt slid during its forward stroke; and there were other minor differences.

There are many more design variations among the DSM guns, since some have actions in which the bolt handle lies much further forward of the trigger than in the KKW, and, often, in which the bolt handle base alone serves to lock the mechanism.

Appearance, distinctive features and data

The Wehrsportgewehr looks very much like the Karabiner 98k, but has a plain cylindrical receiver with a very short loading port and, of course, a complete absence of charger guides. The 98k-type back sight, the graduations on which differ considerably from normal, lies on the barrel at the same distance from the firer's eye as the standard pattern. Because the KKW has a shorter action, the sight appears to lie much further forward than on the 98k: in fact, it does not.

The KKW has a one-piece walnut or beech stock, recessed beneath the bolt handle, and has regular 98k-pattern fittings: an 'H' nose-cap, a single barrel band with a fixed sling ring on its left side, a slot cut through the butt, and a typical firing-pin dismantling washer on the butt side. The butt plate, the trigger-guard bow and the barrel bands are heavy steel stampings.

A standard 4cm bayonet bar and a half-length cleaning rod lie below the muzzle.

DATA

Calibre: 5.6mm.

Rifling: concentric, 4 grooves 0.09mm deep and about 2.6mm wide; 1 turn in 40-45cm, depending on maker (pitch of 2° 32' to 2° 15').

Magazine: none—single-shot only.

Loading system: manual insertion of cartridge in chamber or bolt-way.

Length overall: 1,110-1,115mm.

Barrel length: 600mm.

Weight: about 3,800gm, depending on maker.

Sights: (front) open barleycorn; (back) a tangent-leaf sight graduated from 25 to 200 metres in 25m increments.

Performance: see cartridge data (Appendix 2).

Accessories

BAYONET

The KKW were often issued with the S 84/98 (TGB, pp. 88-92).

OTHERS

A sling, a muzzle protector, cleaning equipment and, sometimes, a 2.5× telescope sight.

Gewehr 33/40 Mauser

The German invasion of Czechoslovakia, with the subsequent capitulation of the Czech armies and the capture of the great arms-making centre of Brno, presented the OKW with a new source of weapons. Although initially content to seize, re-finish and issue the available Czech vz.24 rifles[1], which were little more than minor variations of the Karabiner 98k, the HWaA ('Heereswaffenamt', Army Weapons Office) soon re-commenced production in the facilities of Československá Zbrojovka, which had been suitably renamed Waffenfabrik Brünn AG (Brünn was the German name for Brno).

1. These were known in the Wehrmacht as Gewehre 24 (t), the suffix representing 'tschechisch' or 'Czechoslovakian'.

The Germans concentrated on a small Mauser-system carbine, which was officially adopted on 16 October 1940 as the Gewehr 33/40: a very confusing designation, since it was appreciably shorter than the Karabiner 98k! The 33/40, sometimes known by its manufacturer's designation vz.16/33, had been adopted by the Czech police authorities and the financial guards as the 'Krátká četniká puška vz.33' (M 1933 gendarmerie carbine); and slightly over 25,000 had been acquired by the Czechs prior to the German invasion[2]. The Gewehre 33/40 were issued to the Gebirgsjäger, or mountain units, of the army and the Waffen-SS and had a special reinforcing plate on the left side of the butt to prevent damage when being used as a 'Bergstock' (mountain stick). The rifles were widely disliked on account of their horrendous muzzle flash and muzzle blast, but they were undeniably very handy. The problems of flash and blast were inevitable in barrels measuring a mere 49cm, since even the 60cm pattern fitted to the Karabiner 98k was considered to be too short to allow complete combustion of the propellant in the standard 8mm sS-Patrone.

2. 18,040 in 1933-34, and a further 7,271 in 1938? See Miroslav Šada, *Československé Ruční Palné Zbraně a Kulomety*, p. 144.

Right: the folding-butt version of the Gewehr 33/40.

Production history
The Gewehr 33/40 was made exclusively by the former Československá Zbrojovka factory in Brno, which was operated as Waffenfabrik Brünn AG and allocated the code letters 'dot' in April 1941. The OKW ordered 50,000 rifles in 1940, and the total acquisitions may have exceeded 150,000 before production at Brno seems to have been switched to the standard Karabiner 98k.

Markings
The 33/40 always bears the maker's code letters 'dot' above the chamber, which means that none was delivered before the code was granted in April 1941. A large date—1942 for example—also lies above the chamber. There is a standard German designation mark, G 33/40, on the left receiver wall in front of the thumb clearance cut-away, and the usual 'WaA' sub-bureau inspectors' stampings appear on the parts. Interestingly, some guns dated 1942 have been examined with the sub-bureau number accompanying the linear eagles altered from 76 to 63, which had once been allocated to the Oberndorf office[3]. This remains to be explained, unless personnel of what had once been WaA 63 were transferred to Brno to revise existing inspection procedures; they had, after all, considerable experience of Mauser rifle production. But it is clear that the '63' numbers have been stamped over the originals, and that, presumably, the rifles have been inspected twice. The guns have standard cyclical serial numbers with letter suffixes, such as 2581d, on the left side of the receiver, the left side of the barrel (covered by the handguard) and the bolt. Parts of the number are repeated on most of the components.

3. Between 1935 and 1939.

Mechanical description and variations
The Gewehr 33/40 is a standard bolt-action Mauser, which deviates from the design of the Karabiner 98k (qv) in essentially minor respects, mainly in matters of dimensions and manufacturing tolerances.

While no basic mechanical changes have been reported, aside from the occasional machining variations, a few guns were made with a sideways-hinging butt breaking at the small of the stock and controlled by a spring-latch on the right side. They were intended for parachutists' use, and probably date from early 1941, but were unsuccessful.

Appearance, distinctive features and data
The 33/40 cannot be mistaken for the Karabiner 98k, although the two share many points of similarity.

Both have their bolt handles turned down against a recess in the stock, and share similar stock and barrel fixtures—the nose-cap and a single barrel band—although the Gewehr 33/40 has its band retained by an adjusting screw under the stock. However, the ex-Czech firearm is noticeably the shorter (99 compared with 110cm) and has a wooden handguard extending backwards to the front edge of the receiver ring. It also has a lightened action.

The curves of the small of the Czech stock and pistol-grip also differ from standard German practice, and the 33/40 back sight is only graduated to 1,000 metres.

The principal difference between the original Czech vz.33 and the Gewehr 33/40 concerns the under-muzzle bayonet bar, since the Germans substituted their standard 4cm pattern for the shorter original. The vz.33 also lacks the sling anchor point cut through the butt, the sling swivel lies under the barrel band rather than being a fixed loop on the left side, and there is no firing pin dismantling washer on the butt side. Most 33/40 rifles also have a heavy steel plate on the left side of the butt.

DATA

Calibre: nominally 8mm, actually 7.92 ± 0.02mm.
Rifling: concentric, 4 grooves 0.15mm deep and 4.4mm wide; 1 turn in 240mm, right hand (pitch of 5° 54').
Magazine: internal staggered-column box, 5 rounds capacity.
Loading system: charger, or single rounds.
Length overall: 990mm.
Barrel length: 490mm.
Weight: about 3,775gm without sling.
Sights: (front) protected barleycorn; (back) tangent-leaf sight graduated from 100 to 1,000 metres in 100m increments.
Performance: see cartridge data (Appendix 2).

Accessories

BAYONETS

The standard German S 84/98 (TGB, pp. 88-92) was standard in the Gebirgsjäger units (mountain units), but the ex-Czech vz.24 pattern—generally minus its muzzle ring—was also widely used.

OTHERS

A sling, a cleaning rod, a muzzle protector and the Reinigungsgerät 34 (cleaning equipment). Baer[4] lists a telescope sight among the accessories, but no G 33/40 has yet been examined with any suitable mounts, whether turret or side-rail.

4. Ludwig Baer, *Die leichten Waffen der deutschen Armeen 1841-1945*, p. 54.

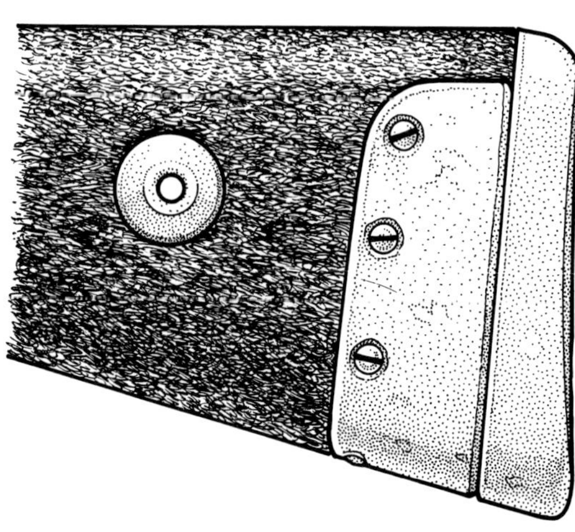

Right: the distinctive butt-protecting shoe, unique to the Gewehr 33/40 and the experimental Gebirgsjäger-Karabiner 98k.

Gewehr 98/40 Mannlicher

Shortages of rifles during the opening phases of the Second World War—despite the seizure of large numbers of Belgian, Czech, Polish and other Mausers and the continuation of production in Herstal, Brno and elsewhere—forced the RMRK (Reichsministerium für Rüstungs- und Kriegsproduction, Ministry for Armament and War Production) to explore every possible means of obtaining guns. The wholesale enlargement of the Wehrmacht and the loss of many rifles in Russia made it essential to find alternative supplies quickly.

The Germans had already captured most of the facilities from which, in different circumstances, weapons could have been obtained. Eventually, however, the RMRK realized that there was unused production capacity in pro-German Hungary and weapons were promptly ordered from the Hungarian state firearms manufactory in Budapest[1]. Production of pistols and rifles began under Heereswaffenamt supervision in 1941 and the factory—known to the Germans as Metallwaren-, Waffen- und Maschinenfabrik AG, Budapest—was granted the code group 'jhv' in the same year.

The rifle chosen for production was a modified version of the standard Hungarian Huzagol 35.M, a Mannlicher design, which could be said, indirectly, to have been derived from the original Gewehr 88 (see Mechanical details). It chambered an 8mm cartridge known as the 31.M, or 8mm × 56mm, and was easily adapted for the German sS-Patrone. Götz[2] states that the Hungarian weapons had a bore diameter of 7.87mm, whether 35.M or Gewehr 33/40, rather than the popularly accepted German standard of 7.90mm; Mathews[3], however, gives the rifling details of two examples of the 98/40, with bore diameters of 0.3120in and 0.3133in (7.925mm, 7.956mm). And de Haas[4] notes a

1. Fémaru Fegyver és Gépgyár, or 'FGGY'.

2. Hans-Dieter Götz, *Die deutschen Militärgewehre und Maschinenpistolen, 1871-1945*, p. 164.

3. J. Howard Mathews, *Firearms Identification*, vol. 3, p. 39.

4. Frank de Haas, *Bolt Action Rifles*, p. 111.

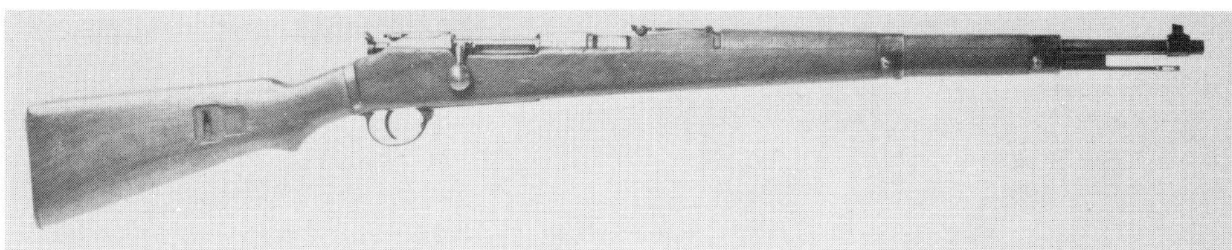

Right: the Gewehr 98/40, made exclusively in Hungary for the German armed forces. Courtesy of Ian Hogg.

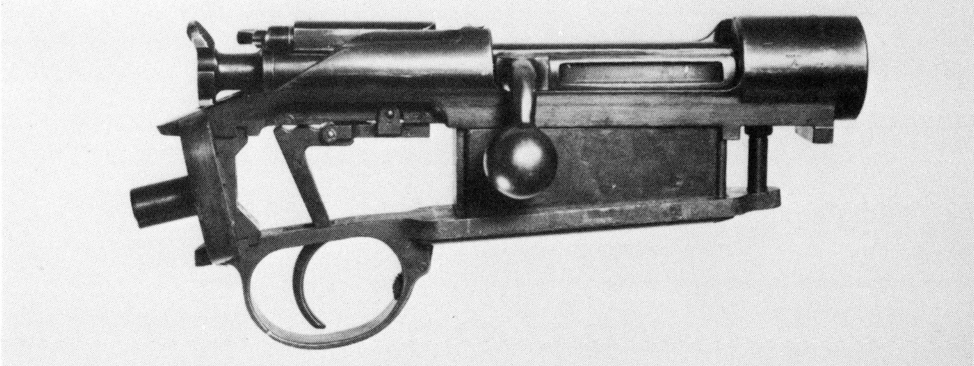

Right: the action of the Gewehr 98/40, which was a Mannlicher rather than a Mauser. Courtesy of Frank de Haas.

specimen with the barrel marked '7.91', which, even allowing for the fact that one of Mathews' examples had a shot-out barrel, suggests that the bore diameter of the Gewehre 98/40 was exactly the same as that of the Karabiner 98k. The Germans may have made minor adjustments to the original 35.M rifling for the 'sS' bullet. However, its diameter of about 8.22mm was less than that of the Hungarian 31.M bullet, which measured between 8.32 and 8.33mm according to figures given by Smith[5] and others. This suggests that a bore diameter of only 7.87mm would have been too tight for the Hungarian cartridge, and may even suggest that Götz's figure is a misprint.

5. W. H. B. Smith, *Book of Rifles*, 4th edition, p. 294.

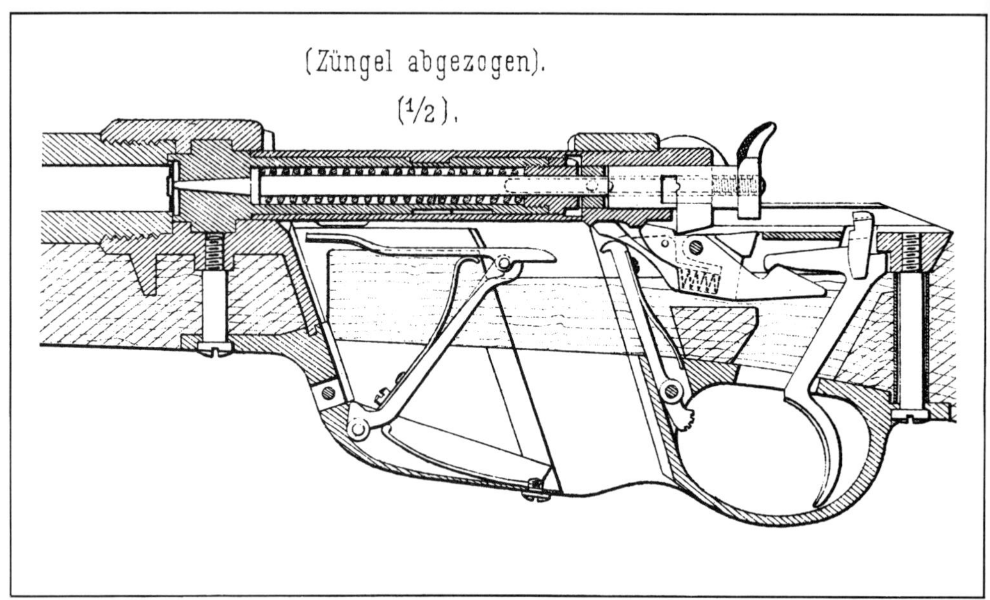

Right: the action of the M 1895 Austro-Hungarian Mannlicher rifle, on which the Gewehr 98/40 and its Hungarian predecessor—the Huzagol 35.M—were based.

The HWaA took the basic 35.M action, substituted an internal charger-loaded magazine for the original clip-loaded projecting Mannlicher pattern, and replaced the original Hungarian nose-cap assembly with a 4cm bayonet bar for the S 84/98. The modified rifle was known as the Gewehr 98/40 because it used the 98-system magazine, although the name '35/40' might have been more appropriate. It was finally adopted on 13 October 1941. Production began immediately and is assumed to have continued until the Germans began evacuating the Budapest arsenal's arms-making machinery in 1944, in the face of Russian advances. However, the German contract may have been completed in 1943, when the Hungarians, impressed with the 98/40, converted it back to the 31.M cartridge and adopted it as the Huzagol 43.M: Mauser-type magazine and all.

The Gewehr 98/40, issued as a universal rifle to all kinds of service units, was efficient and robust. Although theoretically inferior to the Mausers, on account of features such as its detachable bolt head and badly-placed bolt handle, it was well-liked by the troops. Its barrel measured 60cm and, therefore, avoided most of the muzzle blast and muzzle flash problems associated with the Gewehr 33/40 (qv). The worst fault of the Hungarian guns was an occasional tendency for the separate butt to work loose[6].

6. The stocks of the 35.M, 98/40 and 43.M were of a British two piece type.

Right: the action of the Gewehr 98/40, from the left. Note the long butt-attaching bolt running back from its recessed socket. Courtesy of Frank de Haas.

Production history
The Gewehre 98/40 were made exclusively by the Hungarian state arsenal in Budapest, known to the Germans as Metallwaren-, Waffen- und Maschinenfabrik AG. It was granted the code letters 'jhv' in September 1941. The first rifles were delivered to the Wehrmacht in the same year, but the bulk seems to have been made in 1942 and 1943. Manufacture is believed to have ceased in 1944, by which time several hundred thousand had been made.

Markings
A typical Hungarian-made rifle bears the code letters 'jhv' and a two-digit date ('42' for 1942, for example) above the chamber, and the designation G 98/40 on the left side of the receiver in front of the thumb clearance cut-away. Proof eagles may be found on the left side of the barrel and the receiver, and the true calibre—'7.91'—on the left side of the barrel shoulder where it meets the receiver. The serial numbers consist of from two to four digits over a letter suffix ('2861g'), and may be found on the left side of the barrel, the left side of the receiver and the base of the bolt handle. They are repeated, sometimes without the suffixes, on the trigger guard, the magazine floor plate and the butt socket. The last two digits are repeated on most of the components, along with the marks applied by the inspectors of Waffenamt sub-bureaux 58 or 173. The numbers seem to have been reduced to 01 at the end of each calendar year, but confirmation is lacking. Other marks are rarely found on Gewehre 98/40.

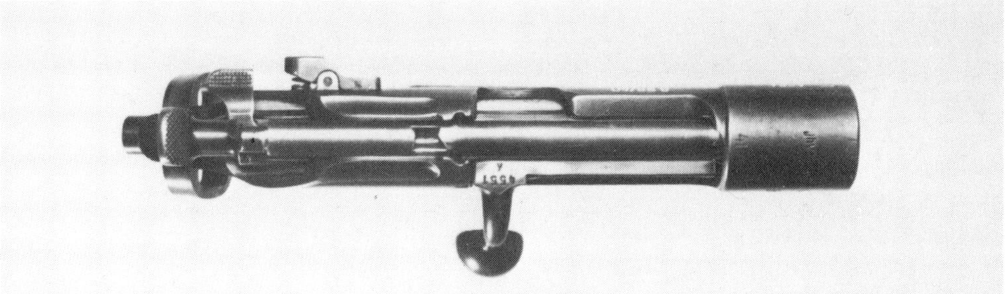

Right: a top view of the Gewehr 98/40 action. Courtesy of Frank de Haas.

Mechanical description and variations
The Gewehr 98/40 is a bolt-action 'short rifle' of conventional appearance. Unique among the German service rifles adopted in the twentieth century, it has a bolt handle lying in front of the receiver bridge, which is split longitudinally to allow the bolt guide rib to reciprocate through it during the operating stroke.

The receiver is a robust machined forging, and a clearance cut-away is milled out of the left receiver wall to permit the firer's right thumb to press cartridges out of the charger and down into the magazine-well. Suitable charger guides are milled in the front of the receiver bridge and seats for the locking lugs are cut inside the receiver ring. The lead-in to these seats contains the cam surfaces necessary to push the cartridge gently into the chamber as the bolt handle is lowered.

The barrel screws into the receiver, the underside of which carries a stout recoil lug; and the socket for the butt anchoring bolt fits around the rearmost part of the bridge portion of the receiver. The internal Mauser-pattern staggered-column magazine consists of a sheet-steel box unit underneath the receiver and has a detachable floor plate locked by a small spring-loaded catch in the front portion of the trigger-guard bow. The magazine follower acts as a hold-open when the last round has been extracted and ejected, and is powered by a W-spring mortised into the floor plate.

The bolt consists of three major components: the detachable head, the body and the cocking piece. The bolt head carries the two diametrically opposed locking lugs (which lock vertically), and the extractor and the ejector; the former lies on the right side, the latter on the left. Their undersides are rounded to allow the rim of the cartridge to rise up out of the magazine and under the extractor claw, thereby preventing the double-loading problems encountered in the first examples of the Gewehre 88 (qv). The extractor holds the separate bolt head to the body, as it could otherwise be detached and lost.

The bolt body consists of a steel tube bored-out to accept the coil pattern mainspring and has a large guide rib on the right side. The rear of the rib acts as an auxiliary locking lug, as it abuts the receiver bridge. The face of the rib is milled out in front of the integral bolt handle, which is a large half-sphere with a chequered underside. The camming action of the front of the guide rib against the curved surface of the breech face provides adequate primary extraction.

The cocking piece serves to anchor the striker and carries the safety unit, which is a 'flag' type similar to the Mauser, but which can lock the bolt and cocking piece when the action is not cocked. Swinging the safety to the right, with the mechanism cocked, locks the bolt and the cocking piece; swinging it to the right with the mechanism uncocked withdraws the nose of the striker into the bolt body and locks the bolt as well. The cocking piece has a prominent chequered thumb-piece to permit re-cocking in the event of a misfire without opening the bolt: a very useful feature, lacking in most Mausers.

Cam surfaces between the rear of the bolt body and the front of the cocking piece withdraw the striker nose into the bolt as the handle is raised, although the actual cocking process occurs on the forward stroke of the bolt when the sear catches and holds back the projecting nose of the cocking piece. The trigger cannot release the cocking piece, by way of the sear, until the action is securely locked—owing to a projection on the front of the trigger arm, which passes up through the receiver and into a recess cut in the underside of the bolt body. The two can only mate when the bolt is locked. Similarly, a cam-and-notch device between the cocking piece and the bolt body prevents the striker head reaching the primer of a chambered cartridge unless the bolt has been turned down as far as it will go.

The bolt-stop is a spring-loaded pivoting lever on the rear left side of the receiver, its nose projecting into the locking-lug guideway. Once removed, the bolt can be replaced simply by pushing it home: unless the detachable bolt head is missing, whereupon the bolt-stop blocks the bolt and warns the operator that something is wrong.

Despite its few bad features, the Gewehr 98/40 is a sound and practical military design. No variations are known.

Appearance, distinctive features and data

The 98/40 may be readily identified by the design of its bolt mechanism, in which the operating handle turns down ahead of the longitudinally split receiver bridge, and by the prominent chequered spur on the cocking piece. The guns also have a distinctive two-piece stock, with a separate British-style butt attached to a prominent steel socket (behind the cocking piece) by a bolt running through the pistol-grip. This is undeniably a stronger unit than a conventional one-piece wooden stock, though the butt of the Gewehr 98/40—and, for that matter, the 35.M and 43.M Hungarian rifles—occasionally worked loose. The fore-end is rebated into the front surface of the socket. A wooden handguard runs from the front of the back sight to the back of the nose-cap. The simple nose-cap and barrel band are plain sheet-steel cylinders retained by recessed-head bolts. The butt has a typically German sling anchoring aperture. There is also a fixed sling bar on the left side of the barrel band.

German 98/40 rifles have a standard 4cm bayonet bar under the muzzle, in addition to a half-length cleaning rod. Hungarian 35.M and 43.M guns have a small projecting stud on the otherwise plain nose-cap; the former also has a projecting box magazine, and both have sling swivels under the butt and the barrel band[7]. All three have straight-tapered barrels—rather than the stepped Karabiner 98k type—and tangent-leaf back sights. German guns are often found with short tubular front sight guards, while Hungarian issues are not.

7. 43.M rifles often have German-style butt and band sling fittings as well.

DATA

Calibre: nominally 8mm, actually 7.92 ± 0.02mm.
Rifling: concentric, 4 grooves 0.15mm deep and 4.4-4.5mm wide; 1 turn in 240mm approximately, right hand (pitch of 5° 54').
Magazine: internal staggered-column box, 5 rounds capacity.
Loading system: charger, or single rounds.
Length overall: 1,095-1,100mm.
Barrel length: 600mm.
Weight: 4,080gm without sling.
Sights: (front) protected barleycorn; (back) a tangent-leaf sight graduated from 100 to 2,000 metres in 100m increments.
Performance: see cartridge data (Appendix 2).

Accessories

BAYONET

The standard German S 84/98 (TGB, pp. 88-92) was usually issued with the Gewehr 98/40.

OTHERS

A sling, a cleaning rod, a muzzle protector and the Reinigungsgerät 34. No rifle has yet been examined with a mount for a telescope sight.

The German Rifle

Part three

Appendices

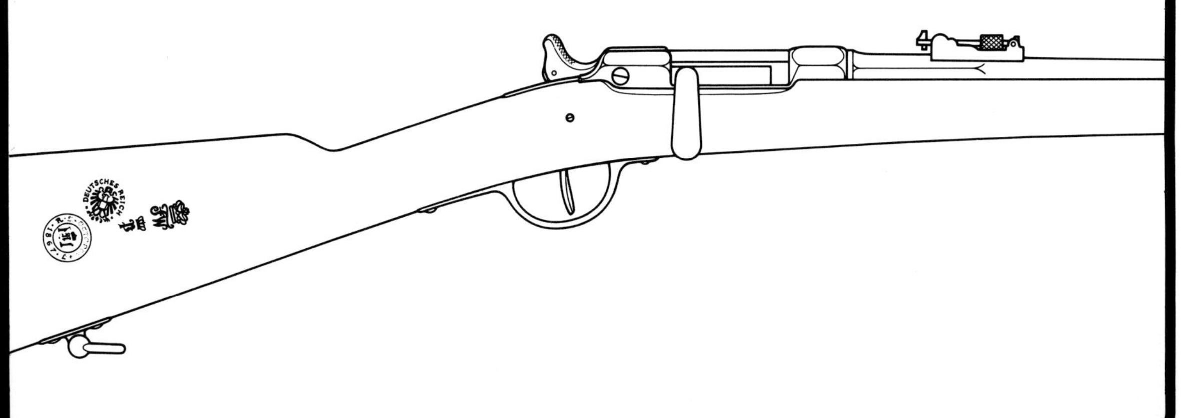

One the Mle 1866 Chassepot needle rifle

Events in Prussian ordnance circles were usually logged with great interest by the French, since the two countries had long traditions of enmity: the 'Freedom Wars' of 1813-15 still rankled with the French. The Dreyse needle-rifles were introduced in Prussia in December 1840. They saw action in 1849, and underwent extensive testing abroad in the 1850s. One example was surrendered to the French authorities in 1850, by a Prussian deserter, and was tested at the Ecole Militaire de Vincennes later in the same year. Its mechanism was not considered to be sufficiently gas-tight or robust, and the ballistics of the cartridge were rightly found to be inferior to the 'à Tige' and Minié patterns being issued in the French Army. The examiners concluded that there were few advantages in the bolt mechanism and, therefore, failed to appreciate the value of a breech- (rather than muzzle-) loading firearm.

By the mid-1860s—spurred on by inventors such as Manceaux and others—the French finally realized that the days of the Minié-pattern muzzle-loaders were numbered. Experiments began in earnest, although they had been proceeding fairly leisurely since the late 1850s, and continued until the submissions were reduced to a handful. The eventual winner was a needle-rifle designed by Antoine Alphonse Chassepot[1], whose first design had been patented in November 1857. Although promising trials with a Manceaux-Vieillard rifle had been undertaken in 1862, the Chassepot was preferred by 1864. Finally, after alterations had been made to the bolt

1. Chassepot was born in Mutzig in 1833 and died in Paris in 1905; although Martin in *Armes à Feu de l'Armee Française, 1860-1940*, p. 142, gives the date of his demise as 1886. An armourer at Saint-Etienne when he began work on his rifles, he rose to become the Contrôleur Principal d'Armes and was awarded the Légion d'Honneur.

Right: the actions of the original French (top) and converted German (bottom) Chassepots.

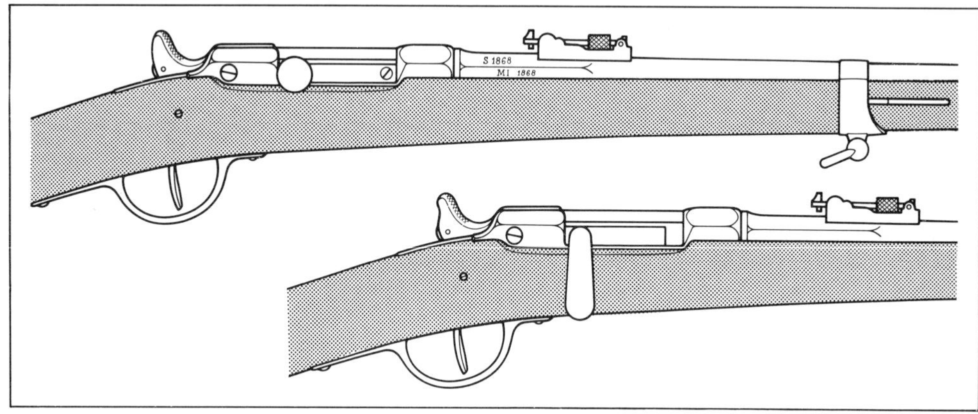

mechanism, the trigger system and the stock fittings, the experimental 'Fusil Chassepot des essais du camp de Châlons'[2] became the 'Fusil d'Infanterie Modèle 1866' on 3 August 1866. Cavalry and gendarmerie carbines and a 'Mousqueton d'Artillerie' were introduced in 1870-71—during and after the Franco-Prussian War—but production capacity was initially concentrated on the infantry weapons. The Chassepots saw service in campaigns in northern Italy in 1867-68, when their excellent performance did not escape the trained eyes of Prussian military observers[3] who were forced to report that development of the Dreyse had stagnated, and that French technology had overtaken them.

Even the King of Prussia, Wilhelm I, was moved to complain that, ". . . our rifle is less than perfection; we seek a modification which will give us higher initial velocity and, if it permits, a quicker loading . . .".[4] The result was the so-called Beck Transformation, adopted in 1870 but very few of which were manufactured before the Franco-Prussian War[5].

First issues of the French Mle 1866 were made in September 1866 to the Bataillon des Chasseurs à Pied de la Garde; the last, to the remaining infantrymen, in April 1868. By July 1870—when the opposing forces massed for war—the French had on hand 315,667 smoothbore muskets and carbines, 1,673,734 rifled muskets and carbines, 342,115 Fusils

2. This weapon which greatly resembled the Mle 66 but took a different bayonet, is pictured by Martin, in *Armes à Feu de l'Armee Française, 1860-1940*, p. 165.

3. Thanks to the rash report of de Failly, the French commander in Italy.

4. Martin, *Armes à Feu de l'Armée Française 1860-1940*, p. 128, quoting the despatches of Colonel Baron Stoffel, the French military attaché in Berlin.

5. Some French sources have maintained that no 'Beck' guns were used in 1870-71, among them Martin's *Armes à Feu de l'Armée Française 1860 à 1940*. However, three infantry units were carrying them.

à Tabatière[6] and 1,037,555 Chassepot needle-rifles. About thirty thousand of the needle-rifles had been issued to the navy, which left about a million in the army's hands. As the Prussians had about 1.15 million Dreyse needle-rifles (of all types), the two armies were fairly evenly matched. All the French guns were infantry rifles: the Carabine de Cavallerie was not introduced until shortly after hostilities had commenced; the Mousqueton d'Artillerie, which was actually shorter than the cavalry carbine, appeared towards the end of the war; and the Carabine de Gendarmerie after the war had ended. Thus the French cavalrymen were often to be found with full-length infantry rifles in mid-1870 and the artillerymen had the old Mousqueton Mle 1829T bis.

The French government arsenals in Châtellerault, Mutzig, Saint-Etienne and Tulle were delivering about 30,000 rifles per month at the outbreak of war. However, the French forces contrived to lose vast quantities of rifles, which were either captured or unserviceable: they are said to have lost 665,327 Mle 1866 rifles and cavalry carbines in addition to about half a million others[7]. Martin[8] records that the Germans captured about 540,000 of the needle-guns, while Götz[9] puts the figure at 600,000—44,000 of which were in Bavarian hands.

These vast quantities of captured guns, which were undeniably superior to the Dreyse in most respects, came as an unexpected bonus to the German authorities. One immediate result was the issue of some completely unaltered French rifles—with their

6. Converted muzzle-loading rifle muskets with a hinged sideways breech block rather like the Snider.

7. By the end of the war, the French Army and Défense Nationale units had issued about 1 million firearms acquired from many sources, and in 89 different models.

8. Martin, *Armes à Feu de l'Armée Française 1860 à 1940*, p. 170.

9. Hans-Dieter Götz, *Die deutschen Militärgewehre und Maschinenpistolen 1871-1945*, p. 52.

Below: the action of the French Mle 1866 'Chassepot' rifle (fig. 3), from Schott's *Grundriss der Waffenlehre*.

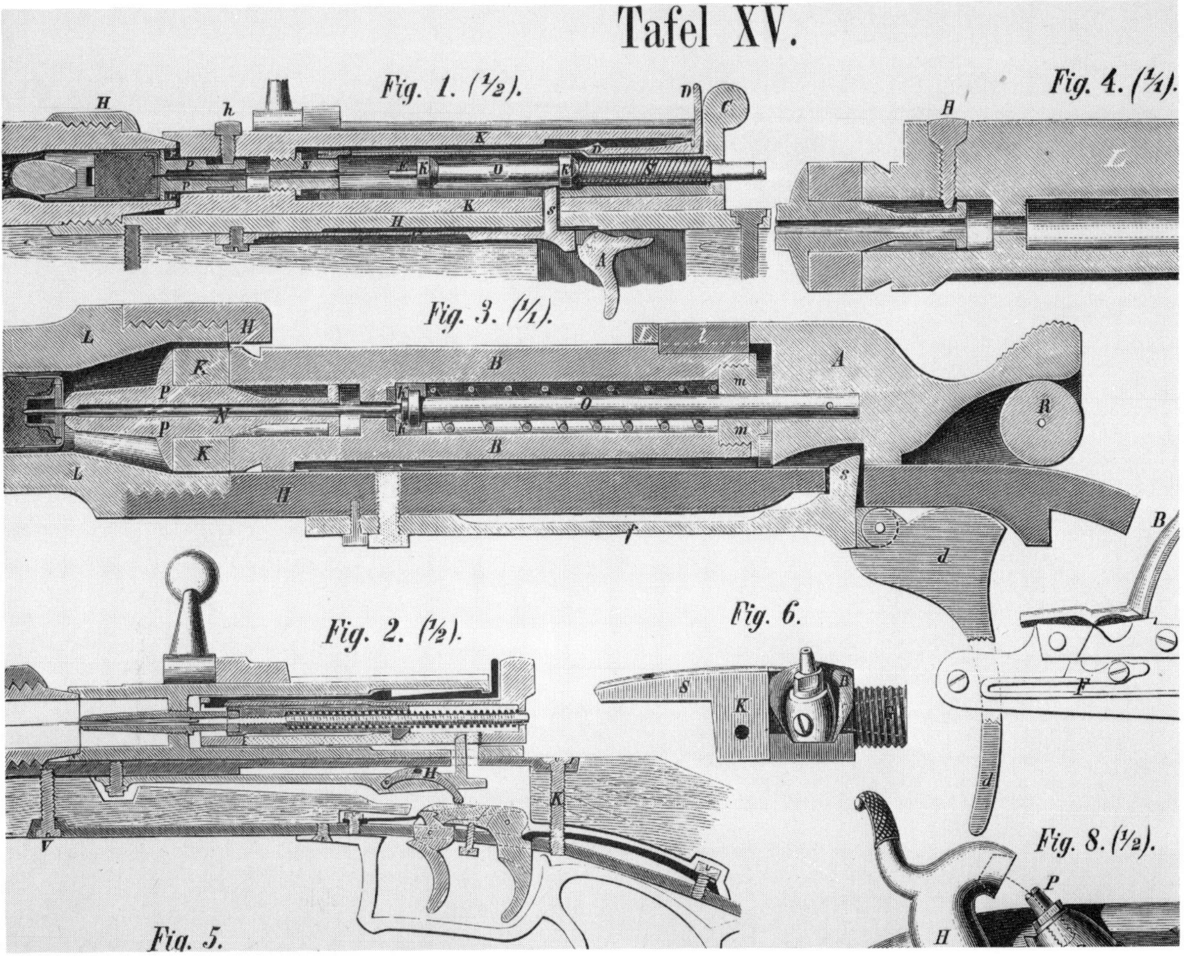

original combustible ammunition—to Prussian cavalrymen, though others had their muzzles shortened while retaining their original cartridges. After the war had been concluded, attempts to convert the Chassepots for metallic cartridges began in Bavaria, Prussia and Saxony. Most were intended as cavalry weapons, since, with the government arsenals concentrating on making new infantry rifles, it was realized that the introduction of a new cavalry carbine would be delayed for some years[10].

10. The Mauser cavalry carbine was adopted in August 1876.

The Bavarians seem to have made the first attempts to alter the Chassepot, for the 11mm M/69 (Werder) cartridge in the early part of 1871, while the Prussians and Saxons followed shortly afterwards. Most of these guns are described later (see Mechanical description and variations).

Production history

The French needle-rifles were manufactured by several contractors, but principally by the government arsenals in Châtellerault (which used the serial prefix letters A-C), Mutzig (D, E), Saint-Etienne (F-Q omitting I and O) and Tulle (R-T). The letters U and V were reserved for a private entrepreneur named Cahen-Lyon, who imported guns made abroad in Birmingham[11], Brescia, Liège, Vienna and Planencia (Spain). The contracts were placed because the French government wanted more guns than its arsenals could provide in a limited period.

11. These were the work of the National Arms & Ammunition Co., and bear NA&ACo marks.

Production of the needle-rifles began in mid-1866, and more than a million had been delivered by July 1870: 1,037,555 were then on the inventory. The arsenals were delivering about 30,000 per month at the outbreak of war and about 122,000 were made between 17 September 1870 and 22 February 1871. But during the war, the French are said to have lost about 665,327 needle-guns: 540,000 to the Germans and the remainder, presumably, to accidents, damage and attrition. Production continued after the war until the Mle 1874 ('Gras') rifle, the first examples of which were converted from Chassepot needle-guns, was introduced. The government factories (renamed 'Manufactures d'Armes' in 1871) were making 45,000 per annum by 1872, when a total of about a million remained serviceable.

The letter suffixes to the serial numbers betray the manufacturer, valuable in cases (notably the M 1873 Saxon metallic cartridge conversions) where the receiver marks have been erased. So far as the Mle 1866 was concerned[14], the code was:

A, B, C—Châtellerault.
D, E—Mutzig.
F, G, H, J, K, L, M, N, P, Q—Saint-Etienne.
R, S, T—Tulle.
U, V—Cahen-Lyon (private contractor).
X—'Commission d'Armement de 1870/71'.
Z—reserved for isolated purchases of sabre bayonets.

The original French rifles had a circular stamp on the right side of the butt, defaced on most rifles converted and/or issued in Germany. The original marks contained several pieces of information, thus:

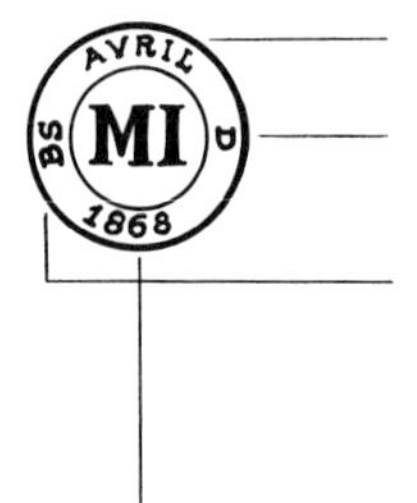

Markings

The French rifles bear an interesting selection of marks-manufacturers', governmental and otherwise. The inscription 'MANUFACTURE IMPERIALE'[12] appears above the name of the arsenal, St. Etienne for example, on the left side of the receiver in front of the designation 'MLE. 1866'. An 'MI' mark ('MA' after late 1870) appears on the right side of the barrel alongside the breech, together with the initial of the factory and the date ('S 1868': Saint-Etienne, 1868). The left side of the barrel displays the serial number G49693 underneath and to the rear of the back sight base; while the initials of the steel supplier, the Directeur de la Manufacture and the Contrôleur Principal[13]—AF, B and D on the gun examined—lie on the upper left-side flat of the barrel octagon behind the sight. The proof mark, the month-number and an inspector's mark appear under the barrel.

12. This was changed to 'Manufacture d'Armes' after the fall of the Second Empire in 1870.

13. The factory director and the chief inspector.

The serial number is repeated in whole or in part on most of the pieces, together with inspectors' marks taking the form of small raised letters in squares, circles or diamonds.

The Prussian guns are usually found with standard inspectors' marks—small crowned letters—notably on the left side of the receiver at the breech, and usually the monarch's cypher (a crown over 'FW' or later simply 'W') on the left side of the barrel at the breech. Most of the French marks were erased or defaced, while additional markings were stamped into the right side of the butt. These usually included a large crowned script *FW* cypher and one or two inspectors' marks. Many guns have been reported with an additional butt-marking comprising a stylised displayed or spread eagle and the legend 'DEUTSCHES REICH'.

Mechanical description and variations

The Chassepot is a needle-rifle of similar conception to the Dreyse, relying on a long spring-loaded needle running through a hole bored longitudinally in the bolt head. The removable bolt head is retained by a screw through the forward reinforcing extension of the bolt handle. The needle fits onto a larger diameter

Right: the components of the Mle 1866 bolt head.

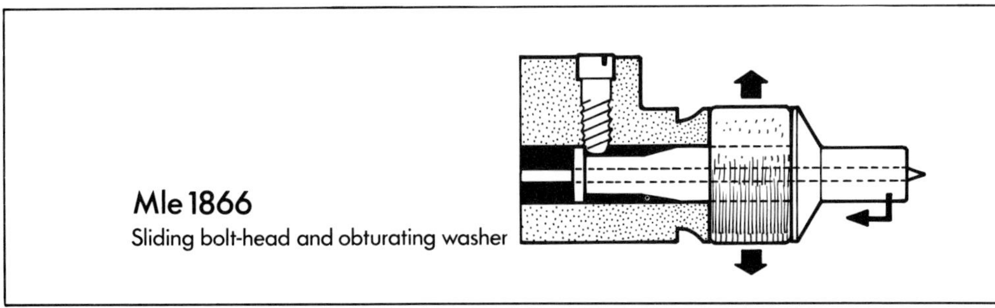

14. Other rifles had different codes, since different makers were often recruited.

15. The bolt handles of the carbines and the Mousqueton d'Artillerie were bent downwards, however.

16. Ludwig Baer, *Die leichten Waffen der deutschen Armeen, 1841-1945*, pp. 32-33.

supporting 'pillar', which provides a guide for the coil-type mainspring; in its turn, the needle-guiding pillar attaches to the cocking piece, which has a unique guide roller—acting as a support while minimizing friction—secured by a lateral pin. Unlike the Dreyse bolt, which locks at a distinctive upward diagonal angle, the French type locks with its handle horizontal[15]. The greatest claim to fame (or notoriety, depending on viewpoint) concerns the specially treated india-rubber washer placed behind the removable bolt head, which was allowed a very limited amount of longitudinal movement. When the rifle was fired, the pressure of the propellant gas forced the bolt head very slightly backwards and squeezed the india-rubber washer, or 'obturator', outwards against the chamber walls. This, or so Chassepot claimed, minimized the escape of propellant gas from the breech. However efficient this may have been in theory, the system as put into practice suffered one important weakness; after a few rounds had been fired, the heat of combustion destroyed the resilience of the india-rubber washer (by no means an ideal choice of material in the circumstances) until it finally disintegrated. And being a needle-rifle, there were the inevitable drawbacks of chamber and bolt-head erosion, and chamber fouling. The Chassepot cartridge had its priming compound in its base, unlike the Dreyse, and the French needle did not have to pass through the entire length of the combustible cartridge body where it would be exposed to excessive heat. Even this improvement—although it was, undeniably, a step forward—had an attendant drawback, since the cartridge was considerably longer and thinner than Dreyse's and, consequently, much more susceptible to damage in transit. It was also much more prone to premature ignition from knocks or blows during handling.

The Mle 1866 bolt head has a small-diameter forward extension which, in pushing the cartridge fully into the chamber, ensured that a 'combustion chamber' lay behind the cartridge base. This feature was shared with the Dreyse and was thought to be essential to the proper combustion of the black powder propellant.

The Mle 1866, like the Dreyse series, had to be cocked by pulling back the cocking piece before the bolt could be opened and retracted for loading; unlike the Dreyse, a rudimentary safety device was provided by half-raising the bolt handle while retracting the cocking piece at the same time. This permitted a small blade-like insert ('pièce d'arrêt') in the forward extension of the cocking piece to mesh in a small guide-way in the rear of the bolt body, preventing the needle reaching the cartridge base and stopping further rotation of the bolt. The cocking piece had then to be fully retracted before the bolt could be opened, and the gun could not possibly fire.

The Chassepot has a one-piece receiver of a split-bridge pattern, which is similar in design to that of the Dreyse, but it has a much cleaner and a much more modern-looking pattern. (See Appearance and distinctive features, below.)

GERMAN VARIATIONS

There were several German variations, although many unaltered French rifles were issued—with original French combustible ammunition—as a temporary measure pending the development of metallic cartridge conversions. The Bavarian pioneer battalions, for example, are said to have been given ex-French rifles, the muzzles of which had been shortened, though no other alterations were made. In some instances, rifles were modified locally by unit armourers, probably on a strictly unofficial basis.

Baer[16] pictures an Mle 66 rifle with a shortened muzzle and a special nose-cap through which the barrel protrudes. The bolt handle has been turned down, the overall length reduced to about 1,180mm and the weight to about 4kg. He claims this gun to have been the work of '23.Dragonerregiment', which suggests that it was developed in Hessen since the full title of the unit was 'Grossherzoglich Hessisches Garde Dragoner-Regiment Nr. 23'.

Several conversions of the Mle 66 were attempted, among the more successful being the M 1871 Prussian and M 1873 Saxon alterations for the 11mm Reichspatrone 71; both of these were officially adopted and, consequently, are covered elsewhere in this book (see pages 58 and 61). The Bavarians considered adapting the Chassepot for the then standard 11mm M/69 ('Werder') metal-cased cartridge in the early 1870s, but little became of the experiment.

Appearance, distinctive features and data

The French rifles of the cartridge era, notwithstanding their often important design deficiences, were invariably elegant; the clean lines of the Chassepot and its sabre bayonet were no exceptions. The bolt mechanism of the Mle 66 is much neater than that of the M 1871 Mauser, despite being six years the older, and the machining and finish are generally of better quality. The French infantry rifles have a one-piece walnut stock with two barrel fixtures: a barrel band carrying a sling swivel, and the nose-cap. The second sling swivel lies on the under-edge of the butt.

The head of a cleaning rod protrudes below the muzzle, which has a typically French bayonet attachment consisting of a standard T-lug on the right side of the muzzle, with a long lead-in bar, and a small tenon on the left side of the muzzle crown. The leaf-pattern back sight lies on the barrel across the juncture of the cylindrical and short octagonal portions. Unusually, the sight leaf is pivoted at the front of the sight bed.

DATA

Calibre: nominally 11mm.
Rifling: concentric, 4 grooves 0.3mm deep and 4.5mm wide; 1 turn in 550mm, right hand (pitch of 3° 36').
Magazine: none—single-shot only.
Loading system: manual insertion of cartridge in chamber.
Length overall: 1,300mm.
Barrel length: 825mm.
Weight: 4,050-4,150gm without sling.
Sights: (front) open blade; (back) a leaf sight graduated from 200 to 1,200 metres in 100m increments.
Performance: see cartridge data (Appendix 2).

Accessories

BAYONET

The French Sabre-Baïonnette Mle 66 (TGB, pp. 41-44).

OTHERS

A sling, a cleaning rod and a pouch containing two spare needles, plus, presumably, some spare india-rubber washers as well.

Two ammunition

The following pages contain brief details of the construction and performance of the principal German service cartridges used in the period 1847-1945. But it cannot hope to be much more than a guide. To do justice to the subject, which, like the story of the rifles themselves, is very complicated, would require tens of thousands of words.

There were many variations of the Patrone 88, for example; they included the Patr. 88★, Patr. 88•★•., Patr. 88 n/A, Patr. 88 n/A•, Patr. 88 n/A• mit Pulver 436 and the Patr. 88/E, in addition to blank and drill rounds. The cartridges for the Gewehr 98 show even greater variety, since they were developed into countless special-purpose items: tracers, explosive bullets, armour-piercing bullets and incendiary bullets among them . Experiments were also undertaken to reclaim the valuable raw materials in the bullet jackets, particularly, and led to a series of iron and sintered-iron bullet cores, steel and aluminium cases and revised primers. The interested reader is directed to Daniel W. Kent's *German 7.9mm Ammunition* (published privately by the author in 1973), which remains the only source of data. Regrettably, it is not completely accurate. Parts of Hans-Dieter Götz's book *Die deutschen Militärgewehre und Maschinenpistolen, 1871-1945* (Motor-Buch Verlag, Stuttgart, 1974) are also very useful.

1. Many of these were for use in machine-guns rather than infantry rifles, however.

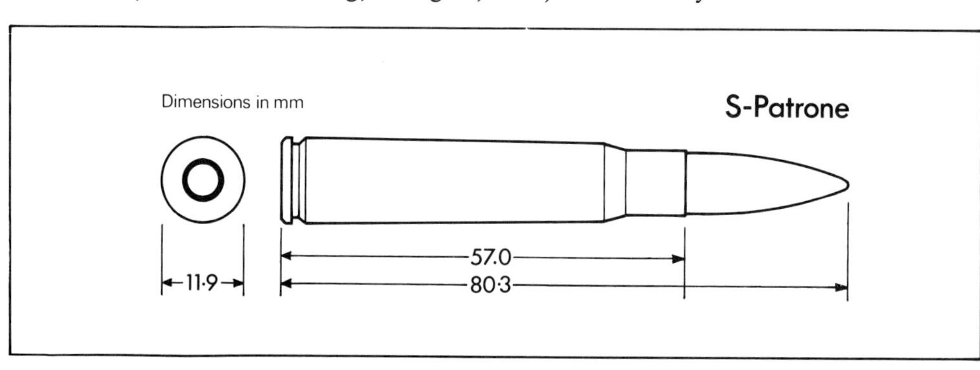

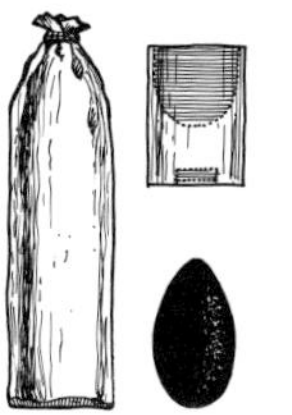

Dreyse cartridges		M 1847	M 1855	Karabiner-Patrone	Beck-Patrone
CARTRIDGE	Length (mm):	60	60	60	58
	Weight (gm):	40	40	38.5	30.7
CASE	Length (mm):	60	60	60	58
	Material:	Paper, enclosing the bullet and the papier-mache sabot in which the latter is seated.			
BULLET	Weight (gm):	31	31	31	21
	Length (mm):	27-28	27-28	27-28	26
	Diameter (mm):	13.6	13.6	13.6	12
	Type:	Lead, oviform, with its point forwards (M 1847 only) or backwards (M 1855, Karabiner-Patrone, Beck-Patrone).			
PROPELLANT	Type:	black powder throughout			
	Charge weight (gm):	4.8-4.9	4.8-4.9	3.6-3.7	4.85
	V_0 (m/sec):	295	295	225	340
	Barrel length (cm):	91	91	38	84
PRIMER	Type:	Pellet of mercuric fulminate seated in the base of the sabot, immediately behind the bullet.			

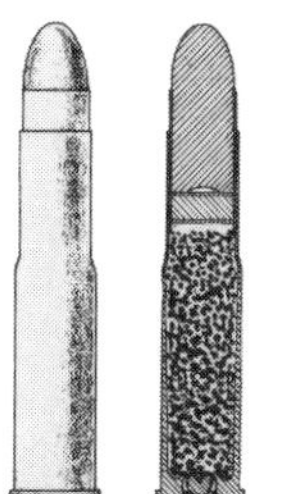

Early metal-case cartridges		M 1869 (Bavaria)	M 1871	M 71/84
CARTRIDGE	Length (mm):	65	78	76.5
	Weight (gm):	36.0	43.4	43.4
CASE	Length (mm):	50.2	59.5-60	59.5-60
	Type:	rimmed, bottleneck	rimmed, bottleneck	rimmed, bottleneck
	Material:	brass	brass	brass

BULLET	*Weight (gm):*	22	25	25
	Length (mm):	24.3	27.7	26.2
	Diameter (mm):	11.5	11	11
	Type:	lead, hollow based, 3 cannelures; round-nosed.	lead, paper patched; round-nosed.	lead, paper patched; round-nosed with a flat tip.
PROPELLANT	*Type:*	Bayr. Gew. Plvr. n/A*	Gew. Plvr. 71*	N.Gew. Plvr. 71 ('Gew. Plvr. 71 n/A')*
	Charge weight (gm):	4.3	5.0	5.0
	V_o (m/sec):	435	430	430
	Barrel length (cm):	89	85	85
PRIMER	*Type:*	Berdan	Zdh.71, Berdan	Zdh.71/84, Berdan

*All three were types of black powder propellant.

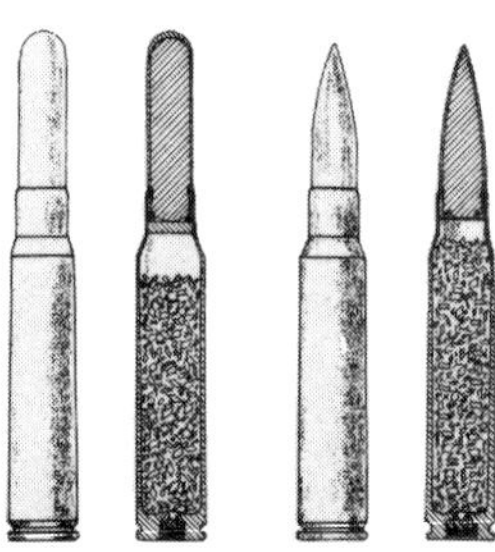

Later metal-case cartridges

		Patr.88	*S-Patr.*	*sS-Patr., brass case*	*sS-Patr., steel case*
CARTRIDGE	*Length (mm):*	82.5	80.3	80.5	80.5
	Weight (gm):	27.3	23.8	26.2	26.7
CASE	*Length (mm):*	57	57	57	57
	Type:	All four were rimless bottleneck patterns, with a straight-sided or cylindrical body.			
	Material:	brass	brass	brass	steel*
BULLET	*Weight (gm):*	14.7	9.8	12.8	12.8
	Length (mm):	30.7	28.0	35.3	35.3
	Diameter (mm):	8.10	8.22	8.22	8.22
	Type:	All four cartridges were loaded with steel jacketed lead-cored bullets, the jackets being plated with tombak or cupro-nickel. The Patr. 88 was usually loaded with a round-nosed bullet, the S-Patr. with an ogival flat-based type, and the 'sS' with a streamlined ogival 'boat-tail' pattern.			
PROPELLANT	*Type:*	Gew. Bl. Plvr. 88	Spand. Plvr. 682b	Nz.Gew.Bl. Plvr.	Nz.Gew.Bl. Plvr.
	Charge weight (gm):	2.75*	3.2	2.85	2.75
	V_o (m/sec):	630	870	785	755
	Barrel length (cm):	74	74	74	60
PRIMER	*Type:*	Zdh.88	Zdh.88	Zdh.88, Zdh.30	Zdh.30, Zdh.30/40

*Often found with a thin copper wash and/or a coat of lacquer.

*Reduced to 2.67gm in the mid 1890s, with a consequent reduction in muzzle velocity to 615m/sec.

Three issue of firearms in August 1914

The following pages give details of the units comprising the German armies at the outbreak of the First World War, based on material extracted from B. Friedag's *Führer durch Heer und Flotte* (1914, since reprinted by J. Olmes, Krefeld, 1975) and amendments supplied by Hans-Rudolf von Stein and others.

Each rifle and carbine-carrying rank is listed with the officially issued bayonet, according to the abbreviations noted below. An idea of the unit marks applied to the weapons can be obtained from the introduction to each section. Unlisted ranks were issued with Parabellum pistols or the older commission-designed revolvers, and no attempt has been made to list the cavalrymen's swords and sabres.

Although the material is as accurate as it can be, so far as August 1914 is concerned, the widespread substitution of older German and captured foreign firearms, and the appearance of the all-metal Ersatz bayonets, quickly blurred the precise issue. Even by 1915, line infantry regiments were not necessarily armed with the Gewehre 98: some had the older Gewehre 88, others, the captured Russian Mosin-Nagants.

ABBREVIATIONS
G 98: Gewehr 98.
K 98 AZ: Karabiner 98, 1908 version.
KS 98: Kurze Seitengewehr 98 (TGB, pp. 56-58).
RG 98: Radfahrer-Gewehr 98.
SG 71/84: Seitengewehr 71/84 (TGB, pp. 44-46).
SG 84/98: Seitengewehr 84/98 (TGB, pp. 60-63).
SG 98: Seitengewehr 98 (TGB, pp. 51-60).
SG 98/05: Seitengewehr 98/05 (TGB, pp. 63-71).
SG 98/05 m.S.: as above, saw-backed version.

INFANTRY

PRUSSIA

Garde-Regiment zu Fuss. Armed as infantry. Typical mark: '1.G.10.25.'—1.Garde-Regiment zu Fuss, 10th company, weapon number 25. Regiments concerned: 1 to 5.

Garde-Grenadier-Regiment. Armed as infantry. Typical mark: '1.G.G.10.25.'—Kaiser Alexander Garde-Grenadier-Regiment Nr. 1, 10th company, weapon number 25. Regiments concerned: 1 to 5.

Grenadier-Regiment. Armed as infantry. Typical mark: '6.R.10.25.'—Grenadier-Regiment Graf Kleist von Nollendorf (1.Westpreussisches) Nr. 6, 10th company, weapon number 25. Regiments concerned: 1 to 12, 89 (Mecklenburg), and 109 and 110 (Baden), numbered in the same sequence as the line infantry units.

Infanterie-Regiment. Armed as noted. Typical mark: '27.R.10.25.'—Infanterie-Regiment Prinz Louis Ferdinand von Preussen (2.Magdeburgisches) Nr. 27, 10th company, weapon number 25. Regiments concerned: 13 to 32, 41 to 72, 74 to 79, 81 to 85, 87 and 88, 91 to 99, 111 to 132, 135 to 138, and 140 to 176.
Fähnriche: G 98 and SG 98
Sergeanten: G 98 and SG 98
Unteroffiziere: G 98 and SG 98
Kapitulanten: G 98 and SG 98
Gefreite: G 98 and SG 98
Gemeine: G 98 and SG 98
Radfahrer: K 98 AZ and SG 84/98
(Notes: the Radfahrer had the RG 98 prior to the adoption of the K 98 AZ. Non-commissioned officers and men of the infantry machine-gun companies, who normally carried pistols or revolvers, were required to complete marksmanship training with the

BAVARIA

Leib-Infanterie-Regiment. Armed as infantry. Typical mark: 'L.5.45.', or sometimes 'B.L.5.45.'—5th company, weapon number 45.

Infanterie-Regiment. Armed as Prussian infantry (qv). Typical mark: 'B.16.R.5.45.'—16.Bayerisches Infanterie-Regiment Grossherzog Ferdinand von Toskana, 5th company, weapon number 45. Regiments concerned: 1 to 23.

SAXONY

The Saxon infantrymen carried the same weapons as the Prussians so far as firearms and bayonets were concerned. Typical mark: as Prussia. Units concerned: 1. (Leib-) Grenadier-Regiment Nr. 100, 2. Grenadier-Regiment Nr. 101, Schützen (Füsilier)-Regiment Nr. 108, Infanterie-Regimenter Nr. 102 to 107, 133 and 134, 139, 177 to 179, 181 and 182.

WÜRTTEMBERG

As Prussia. Regiments concerned: Infanterie-Regimenter Nr. 119 to 127, and 180.

G 98. The infantry units raised in Mecklenburg, —numbers 89 and 90—and 115-18 and 168, raised in Hessen, were armed in the same manner as the Prussians.)

Garde-Füsilier-Regiment. Armed as infantry. Typical mark: 'G.F.10.25.'—10th company, weapon number 25.

Füsilier-Regiment. Armed as infantry. Typical mark: '36.R.10.25.'—Füsilier-Regiment Generalfeldmarschall Graf Blumenthal (Magdeburgisches) Nr. 36, 10th company, weapon number 25. Regiments concerned: 33 to 40, 73, 80, 86, and 90 (Mecklenburg), in the same sequence as the infantry units.

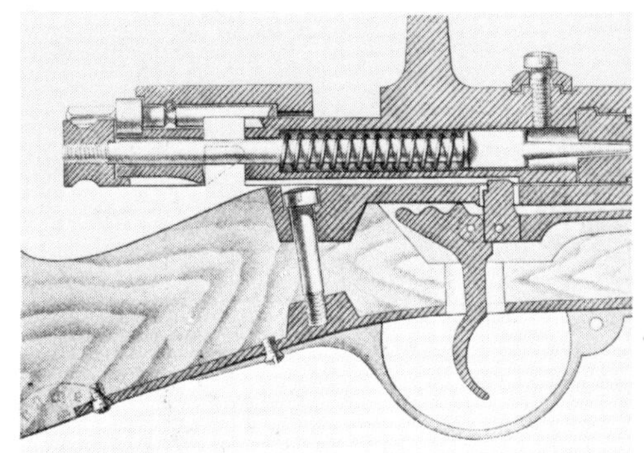

RIFLEMEN

PRUSSIA

Garde-Jäger-Bataillon and Garde-Schützen-Bataillon. Armed as Jäger. Typical marks: 'G.J.3.25.', 'G.S.3.25.'—Garde-Jäger-Bataillon and Garde-Schützen-Bataillon, 3rd company, weapon number 25.

Jäger-Bataillon. Armed as noted. Typical mark: '2.J.3.25.'—Jäger-Bataillon Graf Yorck von Wartenberg (Ostpreussisches) Nr. 2, 3rd company, weapon number 25. Units concerned: 1 to 11, 14 (Mecklenburg).
Fähnriche: G 98 and SG 98
Sergeanten: G 98 and SG 98
Oberjäger: G 98 and SG 98
Kapitulanten: G 98 and SG 98
Gefreite: G 98 and SG 98
Jäger: G 98 and SG 98
Radfahrer: K 98 AZ and SG 84/98

BAVARIA

The two Bavarian Jäger-Bataillone, numbers 1 and 2, carried the same weapons as the Prussians. Typical mark: 'B.1.J.3.25.'—1.Bayerisches Jäger-Bataillon Prinz Ludwig, 3rd company, weapon number 25. This unit was renamed 'Jäger-Bataillon König' when Ludwig became king in 1913.

SAXONY

The two Saxon Jäger-Bataillone were numbered 12 and 13 in the regular Prussian sequence, and carried the same weapons. Typical mark: as Prussia.

WÜRTTEMBERG

No Jäger units.

INDEPENDENT MACHINE-GUN DETACHMENTS

PRUSSIA

Garde-Maschinengewehr-Abteilung. Armed as regular units. Typical mark: 'G.M.G.A.1.25.'—Garde-Maschinengewehr-Abteilung Nr. 1, weapon number 25. Units concerned: 1 and 2.

Maschinengewehr-Abteilung. Armed as noted. Typical mark: '3.M.G.A.15.' or 'M.G.A.3.15.'—Maschinengewehr-Abteilung Nr. 3, weapon number 25. Units concerned: 1 to 7.
Maschinengewehr-Schutzen: K 98 AZ and KS 98

BAVARIA

The single Bavarian independent machine-gun unit, 1.Bayerisches Maschinengewehr-Abteilung, was armed as the Prussians.

SAXONY

The state army had three independent machine-gun units by August 1914-18, 12 and 19 in the Prussian sequence—and carried the same weapons as the Prussians.

WÜRTTEMBERG

No machine-gun units.

PIONEERS

PRUSSIA

Garde-Pionier-Bataillon. Armed as regular pioneer battalions. Typical mark: 'G.P.1.55.'—1st company, weapon number 55.

BAVARIA

The four Bavarian pioneer battalions carried the same guns and bayonets as the Prussians. Typical mark: 'B.2.P.5.35.'—2.Bayerisches Pionier-Bataillon, 5th company, weapon number 35.

Pionier-Bataillon. Armed as noted. Typical mark: '3.P.2.25'—Pionier-Bataillon von Rauch (Brandenburgisches) Nr. 3, 2nd company, weapon number 25. Units concerned: 1 to 11, 14 to 21, 23 to 30.
Fähnriche: G 98 and SG 98/05
Sergeanten: G 98 and SG 98/05
Unteroffiziere: G 98 and SG 98/05
Kapitulanten: G 98 and SG 98/05
Gefreite: G 98 and SG 98/05
Pioniere: G 98 and SG 98/05
Radfahrer: K 98 AZ and SG 98/05
Scheinwerferzüge (searchlight units)
All ranks, except Fahnenschmiede and Fahrer: K 98 AZ and KS 98

SAXONY

The two Saxon pioneer battalions, 12 and 22, carried the same firearms and bayonets as the Prussian units. Typical mark: as Prussia.

WÜRTTEMBERG

Pionier-Bataillon Nr. 13 (Württembergisches) carried the same weapons as its Prussian equivalents, and was numbered in the same sequence. Typical mark: as Prussia.

CAVALRY

PRUSSIA

Regiment der Gardes du Corps. No ranks carried firearms before the First World War began.

Garde-Dragoner-Regiment. Armed as dragoons. Typical mark: '1.G.D.3.35.'—1.Garde-Dragoner-Regiment Konigin Viktoria von Grossbritannien und Irland, 3rd squadron, weapon number 35. Regiments concerned: 1 and 2.

Dragoner-Regiment. Armed as noted. Typical mark: '3.D.3.25.'—Grenadier-Regiment zu Pferde Freiherr von Derfflinger (Neumärkisches) Nr. 3, 3rd squadron, weapon number 25. Despite its title, this was a dragoon unit. Regiments concerned: 1 to 24.
Kapitulanten: K 98 AZ
Gefreite: K 98 AZ
Gemeine: K 98 AZ
Radfahrer: K 98 AZ
(Note: no bayonets were carried until after 9th November 1914, when the SG 84/98 was authorized.)

Leib-Garde-Husaren-Regiment. Armed as dragoons. Typical mark: 'G.H.3.25.'—3rd squadron, weapon number 25.

Husaren-Regiment. Armed as dragoons. Typical mark: '5.H.3.25.'—Husaren-Regiment Fürst Blücher von Wahlstatt (Pommersches) Nr. 5, 3rd squadron, weapon number 25. Regiments concerned: 1 to 17.

Garde-Ulanen-Regiment. Armed as dragoons. Typical mark: '2.G.U.2.20.'—2.Garde-Ulanen-Regiment, 2nd squadron, weapon number 20. Regiments concerned: 1 to 3.

Ulanen-Regiment. Armed as dragoons. Typical mark: '11.U.5.20.'—Ulanen-Regiment Graf Haeseler (2.Brandenburgisches) Nr. 11, 5th squadron, weapon number 20. Regiments concerned: 1 to 16.

Jäger zu Pferde. Armed as dragoons. Typical mark: '1.J.P.3.25.'—Regiment Königs-Jäger zu Pferde Nr. 1, 3rd squadron, weapon number 25. Regiments concerned: 1 to 13.

BAVARIA

Schwere-Reiter-Regiment. Armed as Prussian dragoons, as far as firearms were concerned. Typical mark: '1.s.*R*.2.25.'—1.Schweres-Reiter-Regiment Prinz Karl von Bayern, 2nd squadron, weapon number 25. Regiments concerned: 1 and 2.

Ulanen-Regiment. Armed as Schwere Reiter. Typical mark: 'B.1.U.3.25.'—1.Bayerisches Ulanen-Regiment Kaiser Wilhelm II, König von Preussen, 3rd squadron, weapon number 25. Regiments concerned: 1 and 2.

Chevaulegers-Regiment. Armed as Schwere Reiter. Typical mark: '3.Ch.3.25.' or 'B.3.Ch.3.25.'—3. Bayerisches Chevaulegers-Regiment Herzog Karl Theodor, 3rd squadron, weapon number 25. Regiments concerned: 1 to 8.

SAXONY

Garde-Reiter-Regiment. Armed as Prussian dragoons, so far as firearms were concerned. Typical mark: 'G.R.R.2.35.'—2nd squadron, weapon number 35.

Karabiner-Regiment. Armed as Garde-Reiter-Regiment. Typical mark: 'K.2.25.'—2nd squadron, weapon number 25.

Husaren-Regiment. Armed as Garde-Reiter. Typical mark: '18.H.2.35.'—Königlich Sächsisches 1.Husaren-Regiment König Albert Nr. 18, 2nd squadron, weapon number 35. Regiments concerned: 18 to 20, continuing the Prussian sequence.

Ulanen-Regiment. Armed as Garde-Reiter. Typical mark: '21.U.2.35.'—Königlich Sächsisches 3.Ulanen-Regiment Nr. 21, Kaiser Wilhelm II, König von Preussen, 2nd squadron, weapon number 35. Regiments concerned: 17, 18 and 21 in the Prussian sequence.

Garde-Kürassier-Regiment. Armed as dragoons. Typical mark: 'G.K.3.35.'—3rd squadron, weapon number 35.

Kürassier-Regiment. Armed as dragoons. Typical mark: '5.K.3.35.'—Kürassier-Regiment Herzog Friedrich Eugen von Württemberg (Westpreussisches) Nr. 5, 3rd squadron, weapon number 35. Regiments concerned: 1 (Leib), 2 to 8.

(Note: 'Prussian' units raised in Hessen and Mecklenburg carried distinctive swords, but their firearms and bayonets were the same as those of the regular issue.)

WÜRTTEMBERG

Dragoner-Regiment. Armed as Prussian dragoons. Typical mark: '25.D.2.45.'—Dragoner-Regiment Königin Olga (1.Württembergisches) Nr. 25, 2nd squadron, weapon number 45. Regiments concerned: 25 and 26 in the Prussian sequence.

Ulanen-Regiment. Armed as dragoons. Typical mark: '20.U.3.15.'—Ulanen-Regiment König Wilhelm I (2.Württembergisches) Nr. 20, 3rd squadron, weapon number 15. Regiments concerned: 19 and 20 in the Prussian sequence.

FIELD ARTILLERY

No field artillerymen were issued with rifles or carbines prior to the First World War, since all carried either pistols or revolvers.

FOOT ARTILLERY

PRUSSIA

Garde-Fussartillerie-Regiment. Armed as regular foot artillerymen. Typical mark: 'G.A.F.2.65.'—2nd battery, weapon number 65.

Fussartillerie-Regiment. Armed as noted. Typical mark: '6.A.F.4.65.'—Fussartillerie-Regiment von Dieskau (Schlesisches) Nr. 6, 4th battery, weapon number 65. Regiments concerned: 1 to 11, 13 to 18, 20, and the Lehr-Regiment der Fussartillerie-Schiess-Schule.
Fähnriche: K 98 AZ and SG 98/05 m.S.
Sergeanten: K 98 AZ and SG 98/05 m.S.
Unteroffiziere: K 98 AZ and SG 98/05 m.S.
Kapitulanten: K 98 AZ and SG 98/05 m.S.
Oberfreite: K 98 AZ and SG 98/05 m.S.
Gefreite: K 98 AZ and SG 98/05 m.S.
Gemeine: K 98 AZ and SG 98/05 m.s.
Radfahrer: K 98 AZ and SG 98/05 m.S.
Note: many minor units were attached to the foot artillery, particularly munitions columns ('Munitionskolonne'). Among the marks that can be found are: '3.A.F.II.1.H.55.', light munitions column, howitzer unit, II.Bataillon, Fussartillerie-Regiment General-Feldzugmeister (Brandenburgisches) Nr. 3, weapon number 55; and '4.A.F.III.1.M.55.', as the previous example, but a mortar ammunition column attached to III.Bataillon, Fussartillerie-Regiment von Encke (Magdeburgisches) Nr. 4.

BAVARIA

The state army had three foot artillery regiments in 1914, numbered from 1 to 3, and their weapons were the same as the Prussians—so far as the combination of carbines and bayonets was concerned.

SAXONY

The Saxon foot artillery regiments, numbers 12 and 19 in the Prussian sequence, carried the same weapons as the Prussians. Typical mark: as Prussia.

WÜRTTEMBERG

No foot artillerymen.

TRAIN

PRUSSIA

Prior to an order of 19 March 1914, the Train-Abteilungen were known as Train-Bataillone, and the squadrons were referred to as 'companies'.

Garde-Train-Abteilung. Armed as regular train units. Typical mark: 'G.T.2.25.'—2nd squadron, weapon number 25.

BAVARIA

Train-Abteilung. Armed as Prussians, so far as firearms were concerned. Typical mark: 'B.2.T.2.20.'—2.Bayerische Train-Abteilung, 2nd squadron, weapon number. 20. Units concerned: 1 to 3.

SAXONY

The two Saxon Train-Abteilungen, 12 and 19 in the

Train-Abteilung. Armed as noted. Typical mark: '9.T.3.25.'—Schleswig-Holstein'sches Train-Abteilung Nr. 9, 3rd Squadron, weapon number 25. Units concerned: 1 to 11, 14 to 18.
Wachtmeister: K 98 AZ
Vizewachtmeister: K 98 AZ
Fähnriche: K 98 AZ
Sergeanten: K 98 AZ
Unteroffiziere: K 98 AZ
Trompeter: K 98 AZ
Hilfstrompeter: K 98 AZ
Kapitulanten: K 98 AZ
Gefreite: K 98 AZ
Gemeine: K 98 AZ
Radfahrer: K 98 AZ
No bayonets were issued prior to the First World War, during which, however, the train carried all sorts of obsolete firearms. There were many minor train units and all kinds of unusual markings. These included '9.T.B.2.25.', Feld-Bäckerei-Kolonne Nr. 2 (field bakery column), attached to Train-Abteilung Nr. 9, weapon number 25; '9.T.F.3.25.', Fuhrpark-Kolonne Nr. 3 (transport or park column), otherwise as before; '9.T.L.3.25.', Feldlazarett Nr. 3 (field hospital), otherwise as before; '9.T.P.3.25.', Proviant-Kolonne Nr. 3 (supply column), otherwise as before; '9.T.P.D.1.25.', Pferde-Depot Nr. 1 (horse depot), otherwise as before; and '9.T.S.3.25.', 3.Sanitäts-Kompagnie, Train-Abteilung Nr. 9, weapon number 25. Units raised in Hessen and Mecklenburg carried the same firearms as the Prussians.

Prussian sequence, carried the same weapons as the Prussians. Typical mark: as Prussia.

WÜRTTEMBERG

Württembergisches Train-Abteilung Nr. 13 was armed in the same manner as the Prussian units, so far as its firearms were concerned. Typical mark: as Prussia.

Right: typical pages of the 1909 marking regulations, *Vorschrift über das Stempeln der Handwaffen*. Courtesy of Anthony Carter.

— 20 —

7. Schwerer Rheinbrückentrain nebst Pionier-Begleitkommando, desgl. .... B. T. 25.

Zu Nr. 3 bis 7. Die Waffen der Divisions-Brückentrainreserven werden wie die Waffen der Brückentrains gestempelt; die Nummer der Brückentrainreserve wird dem B. T. vorgesetzt.

Die Waffen des Begleitkommandos eines Brückentrains werden als zu dessen Waffen gehörig betrachtet und dementsprechend gestempelt.

8. Pionier-Abteilung einer Kavallerie-Division, z. B. der Garde- oder der 3. Kavallerie-Division, Waffe Nr. 1 .... P. G. K. D. 1.
P. 3. K. D. 1.

VII. Telegraphenformationen.

1. Korps-Telegraphen-Abteilung des Gardekorps, Waffe Nr. 50 .... T. A. G. 50.
2. Armee-Telegraphen-Abteilung Nr. 6, Waffe Nr. 2 .... A. T. A. 6. 2.
3. Funkentelegraphen-Abteilung Nr. 1, Waffe Nr. 10 .... F. T. A. 1. 10.
4. Fernsprech-Abteilung des Gardekorps, desgl. F. A. G. 10.
5. Desgleichen des IV. Armeekorps, desgl. .. F. A. IV. 10.

VIII. Luftschifferformationen.

1. Feld-Luftschiffer-Abteilung Nr. 1, Waffe Nr. 3 .... L. A. 1. 3.
2. Gaskolonne der Feldluftschiffer-Abteilung Nr. 1.

Zu Nr. 2. Die Waffen der Gaskolonnen erhalten dieselbe Bezeichnung wie die der Abteilungen. Die laufenden Nummern der Waffen der Gaskolonnen schließen sich den Nummern der Waffen für die Abteilungen an.

Deckbl. 25. Feldtrupp für Lenkluftschiffe Nr. 1, Waffe Nr. 5 L. L. 1. 5.

IX. Train.

1. Schlesisches Train-Bataillon Nr. 6, Proviantkolonne Nr. 3, VI. Armeekorps, Waffe Nr. 4 6. T. P. 3. 4.
2. Desgleichen, Fuhrparkkolonne Nr. 4, VI. Armeekorps, Waffe Nr. 12.......... 6. T. F. 4. 12.
3. Desgleichen, Pferdedepot Nr. 1, VI. Armeekorps, Waffe Nr. 10 .... 6. T. P. D. 1. 10.

— 21 —

4. Desgleichen, 2. Sanitätskompagnie, VI. Armeekorps, Waffe Nr. 150 .... 6. T. S. 2. 150.
5. Desgleichen, Feldlazarett Nr. 10 des VI. Armeekorps, Waffe Nr. 4.......... 6. T. L. 10. 4.
6. Desgleichen, Feld-Bäckereikolonne Nr. 2, VI. Armeekorps, Waffe Nr. 90 .... 6. T. B. 2. 90.

Anmerkung: Stempelung der Waffen der Bataillonsstäbe siehe I. Allgemeine Bestimmungen unter 5, Seite 4.

D. Reservetruppen.

I. Stäbe.

1. Generalkommando nebst Feldverwaltungsbehörden, z. B. des III. Armeekorps, Waffe Nr. 10 .... R. III. 10.
2. Kommando einer Reserve-Division nebst Feldverwaltungsbehörden und Verstärkung, z. B. der 1. Garde- oder der 3. Reserve-Division, Waffe Nr. 5 .... 1. G. R. D. 5.
3. R. D. 5.
3. Kommando einer Reserve-Infanterie-Brigade, z. B. der 1. Garde- oder der 5. Reserve-Infanterie-Brigade, Waffe Nr. 3 ... 1. G. R. İ. B. 3.
5. R. İ. B. 3.
4. Kommando einer Reserve-Feldartillerie-Brigade, z. B. Garde-Reserve-Feldartillerie-Brigade, Waffe Nr. 5 .... G. R. A. B. 5.

Zu I. Die Waffen der vorgenannten Stäbe erhalten nur die hier angegebene Bezeichnung durch Buchstaben und außerdem bei jedem Stabe jede Waffenart für sich eine fortlaufende Nummer.

II. Infanterie.

1. 1. Garde-Reserve-Regiment, 5. Kompagnie, Waffe Nr. 50 .... 1. G. R. 5. 50.
2. 3. Garde-Grenadier-Reserve-Regiment, desgl. 3. G. G. R. 5. 50.
3. Garde-Füsilier-Reserve-Regiment, desgl. ... G. F. R. 5. 50.
4. Reserve-Infanterie-Regiment Nr. 6, desgl. 6. R. 5. 50.

Zu Nr. 1 bis 4. Stempelung der Waffen eines Regimentsstabes siehe I. Allgemeine Bestimmungen, unter 5, Seite 4.

VERKEHRS TRUPPEN

Eisenbahntruppen (railway troops). Armed as noted. Typical marks included 'E.2.85.', Eisenbahn-Baukompagnie (railway construction company) Nr. 2, weapon number 85; 'E.A.2.85.', Eisenbahn-Arbeiter-Kompagnie (railway work company) Nr. 2, weapon number 85; 'E.B.2.85.', Eisenbahn-Betriebskompagnie (railway operating company) Nr. 2, weapon number 85; and 'E.D.1.25.', Militär-Eisenbahn-Direktion (military railway control) Nr. 1, weapon number 25. Units concerned: Eisenbahn-Regimenter Nr. 1 to 3, Eisenbahn-Bataillon Nr. 4, Bayerisches Eisenbahn-Bataillon.
Fähnriche: G 98 and SG 98/05 m.S.
Sergeanten: G 98 and SG 98/05 m.s.
Unteroffiziere: G 98 and SG 98/05 m.S.
Kapitulanten: G 98 and SG 98/05 m.S.
Gefreite: G 98 and SG 98/05 m.S.
Pioniere: G 98 and SG 98/05 m.S.

Note: all kinds of obsolete and captured rifles were issued during the First World War, to free Gewehre 98 for front line units.

Telegraphentruppen (telegraph and field telephone units). Armed as noted. Typical marks included 'A.𝒯.A.2.25.', Armee-Telegraphen-Abteilung Nr. 2, weapon number 25; 'ℱ.A.III.25.', Fernsprech-Abteilung (field telephone unit) des III.Armeekorps, weapon number 25; 'ℱ.A.G.25.', Fernsprech-Abteilung des Gardekorps, weapon number 25; and '𝒯.A.G.25.', Telegraphen-Abteilung des Gardekorps, weapon number 25. The script 'T' was written as '𝒯' in Prussia, Saxony and Württemberg, but as '𝔗' in Bavaria. Units concerned: Telegraphen-Bataillone Nr. 1 to 6 and Nr. 8 (Prussia), Nr. 7 (Saxon), 1. and 2.Bayerisches Telegraphen-Bataillone, Festungs-Fernsprech-Kompagnien Nr. 1 to 6 and Nr. 8 (Prussian), Nr. 7 (Saxon).
Kapitulanten: K 98 AZ and KS 98
Gefreite: K 98 AZ and KS 98
Gemeine: K 98 AZ and KS 98
Radfahrer: K 98 AZ and KS 98

Luftschiffertruppen (airship units). Armed as noted. Typical markings included 'L.A.1.15.', Feld-Luftschiffer-Abteilung Nr. 1, weapon number 15; and 'L.L.1.15.', Feldtrupp für Lenkluftschiffe Nr. 1, weapon number 15. Units concerned: Luftschiffer-Bataillone Nr. 1 to 5, and the Bayerisches Luft- und Kraftfahr-Bataillon.
Sergeanten: K 98 AZ and KS 98
Unteroffiziere: K 98 AZ and KS 98
Kapitulanten: K 98 AZ and KS 98
Gefreite: K 98 AZ and KS 98
Pioniere: K 98 AZ and KS 98

Kraftfahrtruppen und Versuchs-Kompagnie (motor transport troops and the trials detachment).
Sergeanten: K 98 AZ and SG 84/98
Unteroffiziere: K 98 AZ and SG 84/98
Kapitulanten: K 98 AZ and SG 84/98
Gefreite: K 98 AZ and SG 84/98
Pioniere: K 98 AZ and SG 84/98
Radfahrer: K 98 AZ and SG 84/98